Koxx

5/96

25.00

PUBLIC PROSECUTORS AND DISCRETION

Public Prosecutors and Discretion

A Comparative Study

JULIA FIONDA

CLARENDON PRESS · OXFORD
1995

Oxford University Press, Walton Street, Oxford OX2 6DP
Oxford New York
Athens Auckland Bangkok Bombay
Calcutta Cape Town Dar es Salaam Delhi
Florence Hong Kong Istanbul Karachi
Kuala Lumpur Madras Madrid Melbourne
Mexico City Nairobi Paris Singapore
Taipei Tokyo Toronto
and associated companies in
Berlin Ibadan

Oxford is a trade mark of Oxford University Press

Published in the United States
by Oxford University Press Inc., New York

British Library Cataloguing in Publication Data
Data available

Library of Congress Cataloging in Publication Data
Fionda, Julie.
Public prosecutors and discretion : a comparative study / Julie
Fionda.
p. cm.—(Oxford monographs on criminal law and criminal
justice)
Includes bibliographical references and index.
1. Sentences (Criminal procedure)—Great Britain. 2. Public
prosecutors—Great Britain. 3. Sentences (Criminal procedure)—
Netherlands. 4. Public prosecutors—Netherlands. 5. Sentences
(Criminal procedures)—Germany. 6. Public prosecutors—Germany.
I. Title. II. Series.
KJC8304.F56 1995
364.6'0941—dc20 94–48658
ISBN 0–19–825915–8

1 3 5 7 9 10 8 6 4 2

Typeset by Graphicraft Typesetters Ltd., Hong Kong

Printed in Great Britain
on acid-free paper by
Bookcraft Ltd., Midsomer Norton, Avon

For my mother, my father,
Martin, and Jacqueline

General Editor's Introduction

THE Crown Prosecution Service has now been part of the criminal justice system of England and Wales for around ten years, but its powers are still more restricted than those of public prosecutors in most other European jurisdictions, including Scotland. In England, for example, official pronouncements have long been coy about the influence of prosecutors over sentence. Julia Fionda's study uses the fruits of comparative research into the prosecution systems of Scotland, the Netherlands and Germany as a basis for reconsidering the proper scope of prosecutorial decision-making in this country. Should the Crown Prosecution Service be given the power to deal with cases by means of prosecutor fines or other forms of diversion from court? What objectives should determine the answer of this question —restorative principles, considerations of operational efficiency, or the preservation of the credibility of the criminal justice system? Questions of this kind are likely to be of growing importance in the coming years, and this study provides a well-researched and carefully argued foundation for the debate.

Andrew Ashworth

Preface

THIS book is about a branch of the criminal justice process often neglected in academic research, especially in England and Wales. Some excellent work has been published on the role of public prosecutors, but it is generally the judge, the police officer, and the prison service who have stolen the limelight in criminological debate in recent years. To be fair, in this country this is partly due to the fact that the Crown Prosecutor has only been in existence since 1986. Nevertheless, it is hoped that this study might bridge a small section of that gap. A discussion on any branch of the criminal process could consider a wide variety of practical, procedural, or theoretical issues, all worthy of detailed study. To discuss them all would be impossible in one small volume. So, the scope of this book is restricted to one specific aspect of the prosecutor's role. For those who find this narrowness a point of criticism, apologies.

The selection of the 'sentencing' aspects of the prosecutor's role was not random. While it is a controversial and, to some, an alarming topic for study, the main thesis of the book grew from an increasing realization that in the last decade, in some European jurisdictions, the prosecutor has been a significant figure behind some remarkable penal trends. This influence of the prosecutor has often been referred to by commentators rationalizing such trends in various countries, but has not formed the basis of a discrete and specific inquiry. Furthermore, in England and Wales the development of any facet of the prosecutor's role is a topical issue, as the Crown Prosecution Service has been regularly subjected to the curiosity and critical gaze of government committees, keeping a maternal check on this 'fledgling' branch of the criminal process. The analysis of the influence of the public prosecutor over the sentencing process, and of the increasingly active role of prosecutors in other jurisdictions in administering criminal sanctions, may at least give some food for thought to those faced with steering the Crown Prosecutor in a consistent direction in forthcoming years. Written in the midst of a media panic in England and Wales (and, to some extent, elsewhere) over crime and public order, developments in criminal justice are fast-moving, dynamic, and constantly changing. As far as possible, the factual information in this book is correct up to 1 August 1994.

This study would simply not have been possible without the support and generous assistance of a great many people. In each jurisdiction that I visited, many extremely over-worked practitioners and academics kindly gave their time to talk to me about their work, their ideas, and their opinions. I am indebted to a long list of 'victims' for their sincere interest and their valuable response to my questioning. As a matter of policy, I have avoided mentioning the names of such 'victims' who are currently in practice in the criminal justice systems studied, in case they made admissions and statements which they later regretted! However, their omission from the following list of names does not, in any way, detract from the depth of gratitude owed. In Scotland, Dr Jacqueline Tombs from the Scottish Office Central Research Unit, John Waterhouse from the Social Work Services Group in Edinburgh, and William Chalmers, retired Crown Agent, gave extremely helpful interviews. So too, in the Netherlands, did Professor Corstens and Dr Peter Tak from the Katholeike Universiteit Nijmegen, Professor de Doelder and John Blad from Erasmus University, Rotterdam, and Jan van Dijk and Dato Steenhuis from the Ministry of Justice. In Germany, Thomas Weigend from Köln University was also generous with his time. I am particularly grateful to Christian Pfeiffer for his remarkable support and assistance during my visit to Germany and to Professor Johannes Feest for his friendly advice and enthusiasm for this project. In England, David Connor, Ken Ashken, and Roger Daw from the CPS Headquarters kindly offered their views of prosecutorial developments in this country.

My thanks also to other people who generally gave me advice and information on the research of this project and who offered helpful comments on the many previous drafts of parts of this book: Willem de Haan, Professor David Downes, Dr Penny Green, Dr Sue Warner, and Professor Andrew Ashworth. My deepest gratitude is owed to Professor Andrew Rutherford, whose guidance has always been constructive and inspiring and whose unceasing patience with each draft of this book was greatly appreciated. He was a constant source of support during my six years as a student at Southampton University and has continued to offer intellectual guidance as a colleague. My affectionate thanks are also due to David Cowan for his frank comments on this book, his expert tutoring in the 'black-letter' aspects of the project and for his remarkable tolerance, patience, and loving support while I 'suffered for my work'! My father, Michael Fionda, provided much-needed technical back-up to a computer-illiterate academic and, together with the rest of my family, are thanked for their incredible support, loving encouragement and for constantly reassuring me that I could do it!

JULIA FIONDA

London, August 1994

Contents

TABLE OF CASES   xv
TABLE OF STATUTES   xvii

Chapter 1: The Discretion of the Prosecutor: An Introduction   1

Chapter 2: The Crown Prosecution Service: The Potential
Sentencers   14

1. Introduction   14
2. Background   16
3. Public Interest   22
4. The Police   30
5. The English Prosecutor's Involvement in Sentencing   35
   a. Lack of Alternative Sanctions   35
   b. Prosecutor Fines   37
   c. Cautioning   38
   d. Recommending Sentence   41
6. 'Unduly Lenient' Appeals   46
7. Indirect Influences on Sentencing   51
   a. Mode of Trial   51
   b. Charging   54
   c. Remand   57
8. The Role of the Crown Prosecutor in the English Criminal
   Justice Process   57
   a. The Neutrality of the Prosecutor   57
   b. Independence   58
9. Accountability   60
10. Conclusion   62

Chapter 3: The Scottish Procurator Fiscal Service: The Reluctant
Sentencers   65

1. Introduction   65
2. The Stewart Committee   67
3. 'Reluctant Sentencers'   70
4. The Issue at Hand   71
5. Procurator Fiscal Fines   73
6. Procurator Fiscal Warnings   78
7. Diversion   80

8. Recommending Sentence   87
9. Accountability   89
10. Policy Making   91
11. Conclusion   92

**Chapter 4: The Dutch Openbaar Ministerie: The Kingpin
Sentencers**   96

1. Introduction   96
2. Prosecutorial Powers   97
    a. Technical Waivers   97
    b. Policy Waivers   98
    c. Transactions   100
    d. Warnings   102
3. Prosecutorial Influence over Judicial Sentencing   103
    a. Recommending Sentence   103
    b. Charges and Mode of Trial   106
4. Victims   107
5. Features of the New Policy   109
    a. The 1985 Policy Plan   109
    b. 1985–90   110
    c. Planning Ahead   110
    d. In Practice   113
6. The Direction of Change   116
7. Rationales for Change   119
8. Accountability and Constitutional Issues   124
9. Conclusion   128
Appendix 4.1: Crime Prevention in the Netherlands   131

**Chapter 5: The German Prosecution System: The Developing
Sentencers**   133

1. Introduction   133
2. Options for Dismissal   135
    a. Unconditional Dismissals   135
    b. Conditional Dismissals   136
    c. Combining Offences   137
    d. Juveniles   139
    e. Guidelines   140
3. Penal Orders   141
4. At Trial   146
    a. Choice of Charge   146
    b. Mode of Trial   147
    c. Recommending Sentence   148

5. Appeals   149
   a. The Victim   149
   b. The Accused   150
   c. The Prosecutor   151
6. Reparation   151
7. Current Trends   154
   a. Remand   154
   b. The Prison Population   157
   c. Prison Capacity   158
8. Judicial Independence   159
9. Safeguards and Accountability   160
10. Policy Making   162
11. Working Philosophies in German Criminal Justice   164
    a. Restorative Justice   164
    b. Cultures of Penality   165
    c. The Erosion of the Legality Principle   167
12. Conclusion   169

Chapter 6: Models of Prosecutorial Sentencing   172

1. Introduction   172
2. Models of Prosecution Decision-Making   173
3. The Operational Efficiency Model   176
4. The Restorative Model   180
5. The Credibility Model   188

Chapter 7: Using the Models in Practice   194

1. Introduction   194
2. Issues of Constitutionality   196
3. Accountability   207
4. 'Net-Widening'   215
5. Natural Justice and Access to the Courts   219
   a. The European Perspective   220
   b. Natural Justice in England and Wales   223
6. Public Interest   227
7. Policy-Making   231
8. Conclusion   234

**Chapter 8: Recognition and Reform of the Prosecutor's
Sentencing Role**   237

BIBLIOGRAPHY   247

INDEX   263

Table of Cases

Associated Provincial Picture Houses Limited *v.* Wednesbury
Corporation [1948] 1 KB 223 213
Attorney-General's Reference No. 2 of 1989 (1989) 11 Cr. App.
R. (S) 481 48
Attorney-General's Reference No. 3 of 1989 (1989) 11 Cr. App.
R. (S) 486 48
Attorney-General's Reference No. 4 of 1989 [1989] 3 All ER
571 48–9
Attorney-General's Reference No. 5 of 1989 (1989) 11 Cr. App.
R. (S) 486 48–9
Attorney-General's Reference No. 1 of 1990 [1992] 3 All ER
169 61
Cooper *v.* Wilson [1937] 2 KB 309 224
Council of Civil Servants' Union *v.* Minister for the Civil Service
[1984] 3 All ER 935 213
Glynn *v.* Keele University [1971] 2 All ER 89 224
Her Majesty's Advocate *v.* McKenzie (Unreported, 19 Oct
1989) 94
Manley-Casimir *v.* Attorney-General for Jersey [1965] Crim. LR
243 45
Oyler *v.* Boles (1962) 82 Sup. Crt. 501 214
People *v.* Navarroli (1989) 121 Ill. 2d 516 204
Pugach *v.* Klein (1961) 193 F. Supp. 630 229
R. *v.* Atkinson [1978] 2 All ER 460 42
R. *v.* Civil Service Appeal Board, ex parte Cunningham [1991] 4
All ER 310 212
R. *v.* Commission for Racial Equality, ex parte Cottrell and Rothon
[1980] 1 WLR 1580 224
R. *v.* Croydon Justices, ex parte Dean [1993] 3 All ER 129 . . . .
                                                    34–5, 59–61
R. *v.* General Council of the Bar, ex parte Percival [1990] 3 All ER
137 61
R. *v.* Harrow Crown Court, ex parte Dave [1994] Crim. LR
346 212
R. *v.* Hartrey [1993] Crim. LR 230 42–4
R. *v.* Higher Education Funding Council, ex parte Institute of Dental
Surgery [1994] 1 WLR 242 212

R. *v*. Inland Revenue Commissioners, ex parte Mead [1993] 1 All ER
772 61
R. *v*. Leighton, Lattimore and Salih (1975) 62 Cr. App. R. 53 . . 17
R. *v*. Paris, Abdullahi and Miller (1993) 97 Cr. App. R. 99 8
R. *v*. Secretary of State for the Home Department, ex parte Doody
[1993] 3 WLR 154 212
R. *v*. Skinner (1993) 14 Cr. App. R. (S) 759. . . . . 90, 212
R. *v*. Tait and Bartley (1979) 2 ALR 473 44
R. *v*. Thames' Magistrates Court, ex parte Polemis [1974] 1 WLR
1371. 225
Santobello *v*. New York (1971) 404 US 257. 205
Scott *v*. Scott [1913] AC 417 224
Smith *v*. Her Majesty's Advocate [1952] JC 66 91

Table of Statutes

Children and Young Persons Act 1969 24
Code of Criminal Procedure (Germany) 141, 143, 147, 150,
                                                      151, 168
    s. 152(II). 135
    s. 153 . . . . . . 136–37, 140, 148, 150, 157, 159, 162, 167, 169
    s. 153(a) 136–37, 139, 140, 150, 151,
                                                 153, 157, 159, 162, 167, 169, 239
    s. 154 137
    s. 160(II) 133
    s. 374 150
    s. 376–377 150
    s. 395 150
Code of Criminal Procedure (Netherlands)
    Art. 12 127
    Art. 167. 99
Code of Judicial Organisation (Netherlands)
    Art. 5 126
Criminal Justice Act 1982 152
Criminal Justice Act 1988
    s. 36 . . . . 43, 44, 46–50, 63, 64, 172, 242
Criminal Justice Act 1991 123
    s. 1(2)(a) 49
    s. 2(2)(a) 49
    s. 2(2)(b) 49
    s. 25. . . . . 52, 63
    s. 53. 52
    s. 53(4) 52
Criminal Justice (Scotland) Act 1987
    s. 56(2) 73
    s. 56(3)(ii). 73
    s. 56(3)(c). 76
Criminal Law Act 1967
    s. 4(1) 34
Juvenile Court Act (Germany)
    s. 45. 139–40
Magistrates' Courts Act 1980
    s. 38. 52

Petty Infractions Code (Germany)
s. 47 135
Police Act 1964
s. 49 14
Police and Criminal Evidence Act 1984 19
Police (Scotland) Act 1967
s. 17 66
Prison System Act 1995 (Netherlands) 115
Property Sanctions Act 1983 (*Wet Vemogenssancties*, Netherlands)
. . . . 100, 110, 125, 238
Prosecution of Offences Act 1879 14
Prosecution of Offences Act 1985 19
s. 1(7) 14, 52
s. 10 19
Road Traffic Offenders Act 1988
ss. 75–77 76
Sheriff Courts (Scotland) Act 1876 65
Transport Act 1982 76

1

The Discretion of the Prosecutor: An Introduction

WITHIN any given criminal justice system, the prosecutor holds a number of multifarious and varied duties ranging from reviewing police files, and making dispositional decisions in respect of each case, through to conducting the case for the Crown or the State at trial. How each duty is carried out at any one time may reflect current criminal justice policy, or, indeed, determine it. Such is the unique, central, and pivotal position of the prosecutor in the structure of the criminal justice process that practice at that stage can have wide-reaching, reverberating effects on the decision-making practice of all other agencies throughout the process, both at the initial stages (that is, the police) and at the 'back door' of the system (that is, the courts, the probation service, and the prison service). Paul Rock has expressed these influences thus: 'Independent interdependence is the weak force that binds the criminal justice system together',[1] and indeed, it is this interdependence which has elevated the central player in most (though not all) systems, the prosecutor, to such a position of importance in setting the boundaries of a coherent criminal justice policy, while upholding and respecting the hallowed independence of each agency.

This book aims to explore the limits of the discretionary role of the prosecutor in the field of 'sentencing'. 'Sentencing' is a wide-ranging word which generally evokes a common misconception of a solely judicial function—in the English sense meaning a function performed solely by a judge under the veils of independence and impartiality. The word 'sentencing', however, can be used more widely in the sense of allotting a penalty to an offender in response to his or her criminal behaviour—which definition exceeds the limited jurisdiction of the judge and falls, to some extent, within the remit of other officials within the criminal justice system.

Thus the role of the prosecutor as a sentencer has an indirect influence on the judicial process of sentencing by means of deciding charges on the indictment, mode of trial, and so on. However, this role can also be a positive and active 'sentencing' procedure in which the prosecutor makes an adjudication of guilt and then issues a penalty which, depending on the

---

[1] P. Rock, *Helping Victims of Crime* (Oxford, 1990), 39.

circumstances of the case, may be punitive or rehabilitative. The following chapters will illustrate the extent to which the prosecution systems of Scotland, the Netherlands, and Germany have developed this sentencing role of the prosecutor, as well as indicating further potential for reform, in this respect, of the prosecutor's jurisdiction in England and Wales.

However, it must be decided how far this role can be allowed to progress within the limits of constitutionality and the proper administration of justice. Of van de Bunt's[2] three perceived 'hats' of a prosecutor—namely as a government employee, a manager, and a magistrate—the last may, and in some jurisdictions has, become the most important role and accounts for the greatest part of the prosecutor's energy and interest. Nevertheless, it is clear that it should not take over the other two; the prosecutor is not a judge and never should be. He or she remains a public servant with a close public accountability which is crucial and maintains a healthy independence from the Bench, which is equally important. The dividing line between the judge and the prosecutor may become less clearly delineated, but it should never become totally indistinct.

Consideration should also be given to the repercussive effect of an extension of the sentencing role of the prosecutor on the role of the trial judge. As a prosecutor begins to handle a greater proportion of offenders within his own sentencing jurisdiction, the remit of the judge must also change. With prosecution in court becoming increasingly a last resort, the nature of the cases appearing before a judge may become less varied. The judge may be dealing with only the most problematic, complicated, controversial, or grievous offences and it is possible that his sentencing policy might change in response to this. If these extreme forms of criminality are dealt with by the judge without any regard to their peculiarities, sentencing policy may easily lose touch with reality. Furthermore, a judge's view that he deals only with the hard core of criminality could also have far-reaching effects on sentencing levels. It is in this area that the public prosecutor's indirect and direct influences over sentencing merge; his direct sentencing powers may only apply in theory to 'minor' offences, but his own definition of 'minor' in this context, as developed through his policy-making role as a government employee, will have an important effect on the types of offences dealt with by a judge and, thus, on general sentencing levels. Ultimately, the prosecutor's office may become a 'lower court of justice' in itself and each established court of justice would then take a step up the hierarchical court structure as a form of appeal court which deals increasingly with a narrower, more selective list of cases.

The principal questions which this study seeks to investigate are summarized thus:

[2] H. van de Bunt, *Officieren van Justitie—verslag van een participerend observatieonderzoek* (Zwolle, 1985) (summary in English).

1. How far will 'the constitution' allow the prosecutor's positive sentencing role to extend before the independence between him and the judge is deemed to diminish below reasonable bounds?

2. How far can we allow a prosecutor to have a positive sentencing role without requiring him to make decisions in an open forum with the high level of accountability required of a judge?

3. Does the positive sentencing role of the prosecutor conflict with his other roles of administrator and government employee—for example will his search, as a manager, for maximum efficiency in the criminal justice process influence his sentencing policy?

4. How far will the positive sentencing role of the prosecutor affect the input and output of the other branches of the criminal justice process such as the judiciary or the prison system?

Three jurisdictions in Northern Europe have been explored in depth; namely, Scotland, the Netherlands, and Germany. These three countries serve as useful comparative models when considering the role of the Crown Prosecution Service (CPS) in England and Wales, and also compare interestingly with each other, having developed the role of the prosecutor at different paces, at different times, and in widely differing socio-political contexts. Scotland was chosen as a comparator principally because of the extension of the sentencing role of the prosecutor there in recent years, and because that jurisdiction provides an example of the development of this role in a country with a legal, social, and historical heritage similar to that of England and Wales. (Scotland's justice system is still theoretically adversarial, although it now reflects the inquisitorial systems of Europe more substantially.)

By contrast, the role of the prosecutor in Germany in the last five years has developed in the context of significant political upheaval and the inevitable repercussions of these marked changes in German society on the workings of the criminal justice system have made the study of that jurisdiction all the more interesting and relevant. Germany was originally chosen as a comparator in the light of a notable reduction in the size of its prison population during the late 1980s, which has been attributed to the diversionary practice of prosecutors. However, in recent years, since the reunification with the Eastern States, an increasing crime problem has presented itself as a new challenge to the criminal justice system, and prosecutors have had to adjust their decision-making accordingly.

Finally, the Netherlands were chosen for this study in view of the central position of the prosecutor there in implementing fundamental changes in criminal justice policy over the last ten years. The prosecutor has been recognized for many years as a key influential character in the criminal justice system and recent U-turns in criminal policy formulated by the Ministry of Justice have served to heighten and increase his importance.

4 *Public Prosecutors and Discretion*

The study is based primarily on empirical data gathered from interviews with practitioners, academics, and researchers in those countries. However, it was never intended to embark upon a detailed statistical study of dispositional decision-making in each country. Rather, the interviews were designed to elicit from prosecutors their own views about their role in the criminal justice process, and about how they put that role into practice. In some jurisdictions the data required for a full statistical study were simply not available in published form and such a study would require a detailed analysis of the cases passing through an individual, isolated prosecutor's office to be of any value. However, this study, conducted on a much broader base throughout Scotland, the Netherlands, and Germany, merely aims to add to the current literature on the role of the public prosecutor, based on the personal views of the professionals themselves. The interview technique lended itself particularly well to this project since prosecutors were able to give reflective and thoughtful explanations of their own experiences in the system as well as their opinions and views about current criminal policy in general.

In Scotland the interviews were principally based in Glasgow and Edinburgh, the two major cities in that country. Edinburgh houses the centre of the administration of the fiscal service in the Crown Office as well as being a hard-working, inner city fiscal's office. Glasgow was also included in the study and emerged as evidently the busiest office in the service; Glasgow District Court is said to be the busiest criminal court in Europe[3] and the pressures of workloads, staff shortages, and inadequate resources are especially apparent there. Further, given that the office serves a city containing some of the most socially deprived areas in Britain, crime rates are inevitably high and perhaps require rather different consideration from crime problems in the rural areas of Scotland. Indeed, figures quoted in the report of the National Audit Office on the fiscal service[4] show that not only does the fiscal office in Glasgow receive more reports of cases than any other in Scotland (78,989 in 1987), but it receives over one and a half times as many as the Edinburgh office which comes second in the 'league table' (42,707 in the same year). Further information about Scotland was compiled from written evidence to the Stewart Committee (see Chapter 3). However, permission was granted for access to this information only on condition that individual witnesses were not named or identified with particular viewpoints. Thus, ideas and opinions from this material have been used in Chapter 3 in a general manner and the writer is unable to give a source for any of the material quoted.

[3] Interview with Procurator Fiscal for Glasgow (1990).
[4] National Audit Office—Report by the Comptroller and Auditor General—*Prosecution of Crime in Scotland: Review of the Procurator Fiscal Service*, HC 187 (Edinburgh, 1989). See table 2a, 12.

Prosecutors interviewed in the Netherlands and Germany were from a wider range of offices throughout those jurisdictions. Information and viewpoints were gathered from large inner city offices in cities such as The Hague, Amsterdam, Hamburg, Hanover, and Bremen as well as from smaller offices such as Nijmegen and Haarlem in the Netherlands and Braunschweig in Germany, each office currently dealing with crime problems of varying types and proportions.

Whilst several Crown Prosecutors were interviewed in England, the study of the English prosecution system was less empirically based. The purpose of the English study was principally to provide an historical background feature, against which to compare the operation of systems in Europe. The writer did not set out to conduct a detailed exposition of prosecutors' reflections of their role in England and Wales. The overall project was to study European prosecution systems, with a view to considering directions of change for the comparatively new and blossoming system in England. Further, a full empirical study of the English system would be inappropriate in a project which addresses the sentencing role of the public prosecutor, because that aspect of the Crown Prosecutor's functions is much less fully developed in England and Wales. The European jurisdictions were selected for the study on the basis of their development of this role and therefore, while it was interesting to draw conclusions from the European experience which might have some relevance to reform in this country, the approach in England and Wales was rather different.

The position of the prosecutor in England and Wales is more complicated and is considered separately, in view of the curious nature of the shared responsibility for prosecution decision-making with the police. Although the CPS was set up as an independent body in 1986 with primary responsibility for decisions about prosecution, the police maintain a significant role in the process. First, the police have retained the initial discretion to charge an offender and to institute a prosecution. This means that the Crown Prosecutor has only a secondary decision-making power to continue proceedings, change the charge, or drop the case. Secondly, the cautioning procedure still rests with the police and did not, in this country, become part of the prosecutor's jurisdiction upon the establishment of the CPS (although Crown Prosecutors are entitled to refer cases back to the police with a request for a caution if it is felt that prosecution would not be in the public interest). This situation contrasts sharply with the system of warnings being administered as a prosecutorial disposal in the comparative European jurisdictions.

Finally, some police forces informally operate a 'cautioning plus' system, where a formal caution is combined with some further sanction such as payment of a sum of compensation to the victim. Hence, in England and Wales, the limited possibilities for constructive diversion and pre-trial sanctioning rest primarily with the police rather than the prosecutor. The tensions which have arisen out of this overlap between the roles of the police and the prosecutor as 'sentencer' will be discussed fully in Chapter 2, but since this study focuses on the prosecutor rather than the police as 'sentencers', this shared discretionary role in England and Wales is a further reason why the empirical study was essentially confined to the European jurisdictions. The English Crown Prosecutor's decision-making powers are, at present, inappropriate as an example of a widening 'sentencing' jurisdiction at the pre-trial stage. Ironically, the police may have provided a more suitable role-model in England and Wales.

Interesting comparisons can be made between the three European jurisdictions which have a number of corresponding similarities. However, the contextual features, whether legal, social, political, or historical, should be taken into account in any attempt to draw conclusions about the operation of a prosecution system in those countries, and more particularly when trying to apply those conclusions to suggestions of change in England and Wales. First, there are fundamental differences between the legal systems of each country. In addition to different individual criminal laws, criminal procedures, and legislative procedures, the Netherlands and Germany operate within an inquisitorial system of criminal justice, which has great bearing on the extent to which the role and duties of the prosecutor can be appropriately developed. The legal systems of Scotland and of England and Wales, by contrast, operate under the adversarial system of justice and the fundamental difference in the foundations of the respective systems of criminal procedure have to be borne in mind when considering how aspects of the European prosecution systems studied might work in England and Wales. For many historical reasons the relationships between the public prosecutors and other key characters in the criminal justice system, such as the judge or the police, will vary from country to country and will be subject to different causes of antagonism and friction depending on the underlying philosophy of the legal system. In adversarial systems, for example, where the trial resembles a contest between two opposing teams, the relationship between the prosecutor and the judge is distant and hierarchically separated with the judge as a neutral but passive 'referee' in a trial.[5] On the other hand, in inquisitorial systems the judge is more active in examining witnesses at trial and the prosecutor plays a genuinely neutral, objective role in providing all relevant information to the court. Impassioned petitions to the sympathy of the jury do not feature in the trial processes of Germany and the Netherlands where, as the term 'inquisitorial'

---

[5] Although the Crown Prosecutor has adopted the role of neutral arbiter of fact, more akin to his European counterparts in inquisitorial systems. Indeed, the Crown Prosecution Service stated as much in their evidence to the Royal Commission on Criminal Justice (1991), para. 7.2.2.

would suggest, the aim is to uncover the true facts of the case and to sentence or dispose of the case accordingly. Thus the relationship between prosecutors and judges in the Netherlands and Germany is much closer, and the mutual respect between the two professions enables the judge more easily to accept the enhanced sentencing role of the prosecutor. Also, in the Netherlands and Germany judges and prosecutors usually train together on the same postgraduate training course, with some law graduates opting to enter the judicial branch of the legal profession and others the prosecution and defence branches.

Diametrically distinct purposes thus lie behind the trial process and affect the atmosphere of the courtroom and the functions of the participants. The prosecutor's role, both inside and outside the court, has to be examined in this context, bearing in mind that procedures which are perfectly acceptable in one system may be wholly inappropriate in another. Recently, calls have been made by the Law Society[6] and by the Liberal Democrat Party[7] for reform of the adversarial system in England and Wales. In their evidence to the Royal Commission on Criminal Justice in 1991, the Law Society called for various changes to the present system, particularly the appeal system, to prevent further miscarriages of justice. These changes were to include the creation of an 'independent review body' to assess whether leave should be given to defendants to appeal against convictions where a miscarriage of justice is alleged,[8] taking this decision out of the hands of the Home Secretary. A more enhanced diversionary role for the CPS was also proposed. However, the Law Society were too cautious actually to recommend changing to a European-style inquisitorial system and their criticisms were similar to those made of such systems by Torquil Dick-Erikson. These criticisms focus on the enormous powers of the judge (usually a career judge) who holds the responsibility for both accusing and interrogating a suspect:

the essential characteristic of the inquisitorial system is the blurring of the distinction between investigator and accuser; these roles are combined in the inquisitor who is always a judge . . . It is the inquisitor, appointed by a central authority, who arrests; commits the suspect to trial; prosecutes; hands down the verdict and determines the sentence, if required.[9]

However, such a view severely undermines the importance of the prosecutor who deals with a large majority of cases outside the courtroom and who plays a significant and objective role inside the court, not least in

---

[6] A. Sage, 'Law Society calls for reform in criminal courts', *Independent*, 19 Nov. 1991.
[7] T. Dick-Erikson, 'Europe needs British justice', ibid., 21 Sept. 1990.
[8] The essence of this suggestion was ultimately taken up by the Royal Commission when they recommended in their Report (1993) that a new 'Authority' be set up to consider allegations of miscarriages of justice and refer them where necessary to the Court of Appeal.
[9] Dick-Erikson, (1991) op. cit.

presenting all relevant evidence and in recommending a sentence to the judge. Dick-Erikson also appears to have overlooked the role of the defence lawyer who acts on behalf of the defendant and sees that his rights and liberties are protected. Further, it is clear that a professional, objective 'inquisitor' is unlikely to have any motive to fabricate or obtain evidence by duress in the way that police officers in England and Wales are alleged to have done in the recent infamous cases of miscarriages of justice such as the Guildford Four, the Birmingham Six, and the Maguire Seven.[10] Furthermore, the establishment of the CPS within the adversary structure as a safety check on such evidence reaching the court has not always been effective, as the 1991 case of *R. v. Paris, Abdullahi and Miller* has shown. This case involved the conviction of five defendants for the murder of a Cardiff prostitute, on the basis of false confessions and despite contradictory forensic evidence and the existence of alibis for some of them. They have now been released from prison and their appeals against their convictions to the Court of Appeal were successful.[11]

Nevertheless, the adversarial nature of the English system is not necessarily a fatal stumbling block to reform along European lines; indeed, Chapter 3 on the Scottish procurator fiscal and the American materials referred to in Chapter 6 illustrate how wide a prosecutor's discretion can be within an adversarial system. As noted above, Scotland's criminal justice system operates under the adversary label, although recently it has developed into a quasi-inquisitorial system, reflecting its mainland European neighbours. However, the USA provides a clear example of the development of a wide diversionary discretion for prosecutors within a highly adversarial setting.

Legal principles governing the decision-making process in criminal cases are another contextual feature affecting the extent to which a prosecutor's role can reach into the realms of sentencing. Particular models of criminal justice may be strongly evident in a system and this may have limiting effects on the discretion of the prosecutor. For example, Packer's 'due process model' will severely restrict the level of discretion at the pre-trial stage, in order to safeguard the civil liberties of the accused. On the other hand, the aims of Packer's 'crime control model' would be achieved with a high degree of dispositional discretion at this early stage.[12] In the context of prosecution systems, the two legal principles of most importance are the 'expediency principle' and the 'legality principle'.

---

[10] Prosecutions were brought against the police involved in some of these cases, although none of the allegations of fabrication of evidence and obtaining confessions by duress have resulted in criminal convictions of the police officers concerned.

[11] (1993) 97 Cr. App. R. 99.

[12] See H. Packer, *The Limits of the Criminal Sanction* (Stanford, 1968), ch. 8. These models are also analysed in Chapter 6 of this book.

These two principles are concerned with the degree of discretion permitted or expected from all branches of the criminal justice process, particularly at the prosecution stage. The expediency principle, also known as the 'opportunity principle', describes a model of justice where a high level of discretion is permitted, and is often delegated to decision-makers at the very early stages of the criminal process. Thus, the mere commission of an offence and probable guilt of a named offender do not necessarily trigger the formal legal procedure of prosecution and trial; in many cases the accused will not be formally dealt with by the courts despite the existence of sufficient evidence to secure conviction. The expediency principle may, however, be expressed in a positive or negative sense, depending on the emphasis given to the public interest reasons for non-prosecution; that is, whether they become reasons *to* prosecute or reasons for *not* prosecuting. So, strict adherence to the expediency principle will place great emphasis on diversionary discretion in the hands of the prosecutor, who will not be obliged to prosecute any case simply because it can be prosecuted, and indeed, where the principle is interpreted positively, may be discouraged from so doing.

The legality principle, on the other hand, excludes all discretion from the early stages of the criminal process. Under this principle, prosecution of all offences where sufficient evidence exists of the guilt of the defendant is compulsory, and public interest criteria are irrelevant in the prosecutor's decision-making. Thus, discretion is minimized and the prosecutor is precluded from taking a pro-active diversionary role. The Rule of Law dictates that all cases must be adjudicated in the open forum of a courtroom, with independent, objective judges who are free from the influences of the public or the executive. This study would simply not apply to a jurisdiction where the legality principle is practised in its strictest sense.

The extent to which either principle is practised in any particular criminal justice system will vary considerably. Very few countries operate a system based purely on one principle or the other—Italy is perhaps an exception, with its strict adherence to the legality principle. The Netherlands was perhaps the closest example of the operation of pure expediency, although even here this principle is being diluted in the penal policy of that jurisdiction (see Chapter 4). Most systems are mixed, with the characteristics of the combination of principles often being determined by practical necessity, constitutional rules, or political demands. For example, to avoid a backlog of cases being delayed by the formal procedure of the criminal justice system, as often experienced in Italy, countries such as Germany have developed exceptions to the rule of compulsory prosecution (see Chapter 5); the rule will, in effect, only apply to serious forms of criminality. On the other hand, constitutional principles, such as natural justice, may preclude the widespread use of the expediency principle and checks may have to be made on the extent of discretion at the early, 'closed', stages of the criminal process.

A system which operates either model to the exclusion of the other will inevitably be accompanied by difficulties. Systems based purely on the legality principle will be expensive, and will engender delays and backlogs in the court and prison system, which may in turn jeopardize the overall aim of protecting the rights and interests of the accused. In an ideal world, where resources were unlimited, the legality model would be more attractive than the expediency model. However, to ignore the limitations of reality is naïve. On the other hand, a system based purely on the expediency principle will be criticized for riding rough-shod over civil liberties and fundamental constitutional principles. A more useful application of the models is to operate elements from both principles in one system, varying the emphasis according to the seriousness of the offence. Definitions of 'seriousness' vary, but where a serious charge (however defined) is levelled against an accused, the expediency model will generally be inappropriate because of the greater risk to the defendant's liberty, which must be protected, whatever the material cost to the system. Imprisonment must be used sparingly, and this must be reflected in the criminal justice procedure. Conversely, where the charge is unlikely to attract a custodial sentence, strict adherence to the legality principle may be an exaggerated response, which might backfire if the stigma of court proceedings outweighs the punishment ultimately imposed. It is arguably unjustifiable in the context of a system which operates with limited resources. Which model is preferable will therefore depend on the seriousness of the offence and on what is at stake for the accused. A system based exclusively on either model will result in extremism which will itself result it unfairness.

Other major contextual features to be considered include the political, social, and historical background of a particular jurisdiction which affect or even determine policy statements in criminal justice. The criminal process must be considered in the light of the political structure of the state within which it operates. For example, is that state federal or unified? Such political factors will be crucially relevant when comparing the organization and policy-making process of each prosecution system. Within that political structure, the political agenda of the governing Party may also play a large (if indirect) part in determining the direction of policy reform and the degree to which a prosecutor's discretion can be used in a diversionary way. For example, in England and Wales, the Conservative Party's political emphasis on law and order, and its emphasis on the heavier end of criminal sanctions, may limit the degree of diversion which is acceptable to the legislature and policy-makers. Indeed, the changing nuances of the political make-up of the three jurisdictions considered here provided an interesting backdrop to the study and helped to explain the important policy changes that were being made. Both the Netherlands and Germany have recently experienced shifts to the right of the political spectrum and this has had varying effects on criminal policy. In the Netherlands, the expediency principle has changed in nature and become rather more punitive, although just as diversionary. In Germany, a similar pattern is evident: the prosecutor's use of diversion has increased, but the severity of the sanctions which complement that diversion has also increased.

An understanding of the social context in which a prosecution system operates is also essential in the process of comparison, both within jurisdictions and between them. The extent and type of criminality in any society very much determines the reaction of its criminal justice practitioners. Hence, sociological factors such as the economic climate, unemployment figures, and rates of homelessness, may have a varying impact in rural and urban areas of the same jurisdiction on crime rates. The rate and the type of offences may also be affected by varying sociological factors which are likely to produce a similarly varying impact on the way that a practitioner's discretion is used to deal with such problems.

Finally, the historical make-up of both the legal system of a jurisdiction and the political philosophy of a country is also highly relevant. In Germany, for example, where the horrors of the dictatorial Nazi regime are still very recent history to politicians and policy-makers, cautious limits are laid down on the extension of the discretion of any criminal justice agency, to prevent executive interference in the process of justice and abuse of discretionary powers. In the Netherlands, the traditional spirit of leniency and tolerance in criminal justice policy may be attributed to historical features and the fact that Dutch society has traditionally been a haven for refugees from all over the world since as early as the settlement of the French Huguenots in the seventeenth century.[13]

Therefore, the jurisdictions studied here cannot be compared without a deep understanding of the context in which the criminal justice system operates. Furthermore, any consideration of the operation of the English prosecution system, compared with the European experience, must be carefully considered in the light of these contextual differences. Hugh Collins has explored the problems involved in comparing foreign legal systems in the area of contract law, which are equally applicable in the field of criminal justice:

Direct transplants from foreign legal systems have often been criticised on two distinct grounds. In the first place, a transplant of a legal rule may prove inappropriate because of the different social and economic structures of the two

---

[13] The sociological and historical process which have produced the phenomenon of leniency in the Netherlands are discussed in depth by Downes in *Contrasts in Tolerance* (Oxford, 1988) but hotly disputed by Herman Franke in his review of Downes's work—'Dutch Tolerance: Facts and Fables' (1990) *British Journal of Criminology*, 30: 81–93.

societies . . . A second objection to transplants of legal rules insists that legal concepts fit into clusters of concepts which together comprise a coherent and consistent set of rules and principles for the regulation of some aspect of social life. One cannot transplant a single foreign concept into domestic law without undermining the coherence of its conceptual scheme, which ultimately causes confusion and inconsistency.[14]

However, the object of comparing prosecution systems in this book is not necessarily to find a suitable alternative system in Europe to 'transplant' into the criminal justice system in England and Wales. The aim of the following chapters is principally to illustrate how the prosecutor's role has been perceived as more important and wider, and how the prosecutor is viewed as a more fully rounded professional in certain states in Europe. Whilst it may be possible, after analysis of these systems, to find various concrete suggestions for the extension of the English Crown Prosecutor's duties and discretion, the overall objective of the study is much broader. The aim is to find a combined model from these European systems for the direction in which the Crown Prosecution Service should be developed in the years ahead.

Comparative studies of European prosecution systems have been made in the past to highlight particularly successful or innovative practices in foreign criminal justice systems. Leigh and Hall Williams's study of the prosecution systems in Sweden, Denmark, and the Netherlands,[15] Moody and Tombs's study of the Scottish Procurator Fiscal,[16] and Graham's recent research on the German criminal justice system[17] are examples of comparative work in this area. However, these studies have not directly addressed the sentencing aspect of the public prosecutors' functions. Graham's study, for example, considers the impact of the prosecutor (amongst others) on the reduction of the prison population in Germany in the late 1980s and Leigh and Hall Williams's study is a much wider analysis of the organization of prosecution systems in Europe and the relationship between prosecutors and the police in the three jurisdictions studied as well as the public prosecutor's duties and decision-making powers. This book differs somewhat from those previous works in that it concentrates on the quasi-judicial role of the public prosecutor and his impact on the sentencing process, and introduces a discussion on the very recent developments in prosecution and general criminal justice policy in the jurisdictions chosen for analysis.

[14] H. Collins, 'Methods and Aims of Comparative Contract Law', *Oxford Journal of Legal Studies* (1991), 11: 396–406.
[15] L. H. Leigh, and J. E. Hall Williams, *The Management of the Prosecution Process in Denmark Sweden and the Netherlands* (Leamington Spa, 1981).
[16] S. R. Moody, and J. Tombs, *Prosecution in the Public Interest* (Edinburgh, 1982).
[17] J. Graham, 'Decarceration in the Federal Republic of Germany: How Practitioners are succeeding where Policy-makers have failed', *British Journal of Criminology* (1990), 30: 150–170.

The following chapters will, therefore, systematically explore the field of prosecutorial influence over sentencing in Europe and analyse the implications for reform in this country. Chapter 2 provides a legal and historical explanation of the prosecution system in England and Wales, including an exposition of the problems involved in the combined investigation and prosecution roles of the police, which the establishment of the CPS aimed to overcome.

Chapters 3, 4, and 5 detail the operation of the prosecution systems in Scotland, the Netherlands, and Germany respectively, and include comments on the exercise of discretion by public prosecutors in those countries and on the influence of recent policy developments on the prosecutor's sentencing jurisdiction. Chapter 6 takes a collective view of the concept of the prosecutor as a sentencer in Europe. Three models of prosecutorial justice, that is the Operational Efficiency model, the Credibility model, and the Restorative model, emerged from the data included in Chapters 3, 4, and 5 and are fully expounded in Chapter 6. These models illustrate how the extension of the sentencing role of the prosecutor has been justified and accounted for. In Chapter 7 the models have been used to show how the constitutional and civil liberties issues which inherently arise in the extension of an administrative form of justice have been addressed in the three jurisdictions.

Finally, Chapter 8 draws conclusions from the European experience and analyses the implications of this experience for the consideration of reform of the Crown Prosecution Service in England and Wales.

2

The Crown Prosecution Service: The Potential Sentencers

1. Introduction

THE prosecution system of England and Wales has been the subject of possibly the most significant, fundamental reform programme in British criminal justice this century. The creation of a new, independent public prosecution service in 1986 heralded a constitutional breakthrough in removing the responsibility for the prosecution of criminal offences away from the police and investing it in a new, publicly accountable agency, thereby ending a tradition of over 150 years. The police were designated the first public prosecutors in 1829, rather more circumstantially than deliberately, due to the absence of a suitable alternative public agency. They have finally now been returned to their primarily investigative role. Fifty years later the post of Director of Public Prosecutions (DPP) was established by the Prosecution of Offences Act 1879 to: 'institute, undertake or carry on such proceedings and to give such advice or assistance to chief officers of police, clerks to the justices and other persons, as may be for the time being prescribed by Regulations under this Act or may be directed in a special case by the Attorney-General.' The nature and number of cases in which the DPP is entitled to intervene, however, is relatively small and includes a number of serious offences such as homicide cases, large-scale fraud cases (under the Prosecution of Offences Regulations 1978), complaints of alleged criminal behaviour committed by a police officer (under s. 49 of the Police Act 1964), and a number of sensitive areas of criminality where the DPP's consent is required before a public prosecution can proceed.[1] Under the Prosecution of Offences Act 1985, s. 1(7), any Crown Prosecutor can now act on behalf of the DPP in consenting to such prosecutions.

Hence, while the DPP has retained an unfettered discretion to apply the standards for public interest to a number of important cases, his/her role, even since 1986, has remained somewhat limited in terms of the range and

---

[1] G. Mansfield, and J. Peay, *The Director of Public Prosecutions: Principles and Practices for the Crown Prosecutor* (London, 1987). See 8–9 for an explanation of the application of this regulation.

proportion of offences referred to him/her. Indeed, Mansfield and Peay estimate that the DPP takes a decisive role in only 3 per cent of all indictable cases and offers advice to the police in only 5 per cent of cases.[2]

Whilst the emphasis of recent reforms has been on the public sector of prosecutions, the right of private prosecution has been consistently maintained, although used comparatively rarely by private individuals. The Royal Commission on Criminal Procedure re-emphasized the importance of this right in their report as 'the ultimate safeguard for the citizen against inaction on the part of the authorities'.[3] Also, they conducted a research study on the exercise by local authorities, independent bodies such as the RSPCA, the Post Office, and government departments, of the right to prosecute cases themselves[4] with the aim of discovering the extent to which that right is employed.

Rather ironically, the 'prosecution policy' of certain bodies who conduct their own criminal proceedings against offenders provides a model example, in some cases similar to that of the European systems discussed in the following chapters, of the successful use of prosecutorial alternatives to avoid recourse to the courts. For example, it is a long-standing policy of the Inland Revenue to use out-of-court financial settlements (similar, for instance, to the Dutch prosecutor's transactions—see Chapter 4) to deal with tax defaulters wherever possible.

In Hawkins's study[5] on the enforcement of the laws relating to the regulation of pollution, it is shown that here also, prosecution is used *in extremis*, as a last resort where negotiations and out-of-court settlements are unsuitable or have failed. Indeed, the study shows that water authorities and other pollution control agencies have found such alternative forms of action more effective in achieving the original aims of the pollution laws than prosecutions: 'pollution control staff must display patience and tolerance, rather than legal authority, for their goal is not to punish but to secure change.'[6] To this extent, so-called 'technical' or 'scientific' breaches of the regulations with no criminal intent are more suitably dealt with by a negotiated settlement. In the same way, morally colourless criminal offences in which there is little or no public interest in prosecution could be dealt with by some form of prosecutorial sanction or settlement, rather than with the 'blunt instrument' of the law. Hence, in addition to seeking

---

[2] Ibid., 8.

[3] Royal Commission on Criminal Procedure, *Report* Cmnd 8092 (HMSO, 1981) para. 7.47.

[4] K. W. Lidstone, R. Hogg, and F. Sutcliffe, *Prosecutions by Private Individuals and Non-Police Agencies*, Royal Commission on Criminal Procedure Research Study No. 10 (HMSO, 1980).

[5] K. Hawkins, *Environment and Enforcement: Regulation and the Social Definition of Pollution* (Oxford, 1984).

[6] Ibid., 197.

ideas for reform from other European systems, examples of a more 'civilized' system of prosecutorial decision-making can be found within the existing English criminal justice system.

The history of the development of prosecution procedure in England and Wales, including its gradual transition from the private to the public domain, is recounted in more detail by Sir Thomas Hetherington.[7] In this chapter, emphasis will be placed on recent developments concerning the newly created Crown Prosecution Service (the CPS) and the problems with which the service has had to contend. The role of the Crown Prosecutor in England and Wales is rather less developed than its European counterparts, but the potential for reform to remedy this situation, following to a certain extent the role-models to be found in Northern Europe, will also be explained.

2. BACKGROUND

Given the rather haphazard way in which the public prosecution system of England and Wales grew up,[8] it comes as little surprise that problems of inconsistency of approach and unequal application of the law soon became the subjects of complaint. One of the first principal bodies of criticism came in the form of a report by the Committee of JUSTICE (the British section of the International Commission of Jurists)[9] in 1970 which set out to explore three fundamental problems with the existing structure of prosecution procedure. These mainly concerned whether the police should continue to be responsible for, or even involved in, the prosecution of criminal offences. The resulting report of their inquiry was fiercely critical of the lack of objectivity in prosecution decision-making by a body too heavily involved in the investigative process, which, according to the report, resulted in 'disquieting anomalies and variations which have, from time to time, resulted in errors and miscarriages of justice, sometimes of a very serious nature'.[10] In addition to setting out their own model for a new, independent prosecuting agency (modelled along the lines of the Scottish Procurator Fiscal Service described in Chapter 3) the Committee of JUSTICE recommended a 'fundamental reappraisal' of the entire pre-trial criminal justice system.

Some seven years later the government responded by setting up a Royal Commission on Criminal Procedure on 23 June 1977, chaired by Sir Cecil Henry Philips. Their broadly based terms of reference included a root and

---

[7] T. Hetherington, *Prosecution and the Public Interest* (London, 1989).
[8] Ibid., ch. 1.
[9] JUSTICE, *The Prosecution Process in England and Wales* (London, 1970).
[10] Ibid., 1.

branch review of the powers and duties of the police in the investigative stages, the system of prosecution of criminal offences, and many other aspects of criminal procedure and evidence relating to those matters.[11] In those intervening seven years, another matter gave further impetus for setting up the Royal Commission. In 1972, three youths (one of whom was mentally retarded) were convicted for the murder of Maxwell Confait on the basis of false confessions, in the case of *R. v. Leighton, Lattimore and Salih*.[12] Their successful appeal against conviction in the Court of Appeal, after a long campaign by various groups convinced of their innocence, prompted the setting up of an inquiry, led by Sir Henry Fisher, into police procedures relating to the interrogation of suspects. The inquiry report, published in 1977[13], made recommendations for major changes in the system of investigation of homicide cases, including the adoption of powers for a prosecutor to investigate all cases of sudden death, rather like the French and Scottish prosecution systems. The recommendations of this report, as well as the growing public concern at the time about rising crime figures, played a key part in prompting Parliament to set up the Royal Commission in 1977.

The Commission reported four years later after a formidable programme of research which included visits to Scotland, the Netherlands, the USA, and Australia amongst other jurisdictions, and the gathering of written and oral evidence from no less than 443 witnesses. Having set out a detailed analysis of the existing law and procedure of the investigation and prosecution of crime,[14] the report set out a rather more in-depth critique of the prosecution system.[15] In view of the alarming number of directed acquittals in Crown Courts across the country[16] caused by insufficiency of evidence in prosecuted cases and by the potential partiality of police decisions on prosecution,[17] similarly suggested by the JUSTICE report and more recently by Sanders,[18] the Philips Report made proposals to separate the investigative and the prosecution functions of the police. It also proposed three alternative new prosecution systems,[19] involving different

[11] Royal Commission on Criminal Procedure (1981)—Terms of Reference, 3.
[12] (1975) 62 Crim. App. R. 53.
[13] House of Commons, *Report of an Inquiry by the Hon. Sir Henry Fisher into the circumstances leading to the trial of three persons on charges arising out of the death of Maxwell Confait and the fire at 27, Doggett Road, London SE6* (HMSO, 1977).
[14] Royal Commission on Criminal Procedure, *The Investigation and Prosecution of Criminal Offences in England and Wales: The Law and Procedure* Cmnd 8092–1 (HMSO, 1981).
[15] Royal Commission on Criminal Procedure (1981), *Report*, op. cit.
[16] Based on Baldwin and McConville's study of Birmingham and Manchester Crown Courts—Royal Commission on Criminal Procedure, *Report*, op. cit., ch. 6, 130–1, particularly para. 6.20.
[17] Ibid., ch. 6, 132, para. 6.24.
[18] A. Sanders, (1985) 'Prosecution Decisions and the Attorney-General's Guidelines' [1985] *Crim. LR* 4–19, at 10–14.
[19] Royal Commission on Criminal Procedure (1981) *Report*, op. cit., ch. 7.

systems of organization and management for the prosecution service. The first was a totally centralized, national service funded by central government and under the direct control of a Minister of State, rather like the Dutch Openbaar Ministerie. The second option used the existing police force areas as a framework for forty-three small, local prosecution offices controlled by a local authority supervisory body, more akin to the fragmented German system of prosecution. The Royal Commission's final suggestion was a hybrid of the other two options, with larger, regional prosecution offices, centrally accountable to and funded by a central government department.

After careful consideration, the majority of the Royal Commission concluded that the second option was most advantageous. The national centralized system, whilst more likely to produce consistent, national prosecution policies and figures, would be costly and fraught with organizational difficulties. Further, the highly localized system provided the fewest practical problems in its establishment. However, the inherent weaknesses and proven problems of the existing local police authorities were not discussed by the Royal Commission as a disadvantage to this system of organization, and it is perhaps for this reason, together with the findings of the Home Office Working Party's Report (1982),[20] that the legislation of 1985 finally opted for the hybrid system which has an agreeable combination of both a local and a national service without many of the hazardous disadvantages.[21]

The government's response to the Philips Report was to set up an Inter-Departmental Working Party on Prosecution Arrangements in 1982, to decide on which of the three options to base the new prosecution system. The Working Party, chaired by W. J. Bohan of the Home Office, proposed a system similar to the hybrid system proposed by the Royal Commission.[22] A year later a White Paper was published setting out legislation to create a national prosecution service, headed by the DPP and under the supervision of the Attorney-General, with regional offices financed from central government funds.[23] The new service would be independent from the police forces of England and Wales and would have local prosecutors taking full responsibility for the conduct of criminal proceedings, after the initial investigative and charging processes still performed by the police.

[20] Home Office, *Report of the Working Party on Prosecution Arrangements*. Published as an annexe to White Paper *An Independent Prosecution Service for England and Wales*, Cmnd 9074, (HMSO, 1982).

[21] The thirty-one CPS areas originally created under the 1985 Act have recently been decreased to 13, so that greater administrative focus will be at the individual Branch level.

[22] Home Office, (1982) *Report of the Working Party on Prosecution Arrangements*, op. cit.

[23] Home Office White Paper, *An Independent Prosecution Service for England and Wales*, Cmnd 9074 (HMSO, 1983).

The resulting Prosecution of Offences Act 1985, which, as well as seeking to achieve fairer, more objective, and nationally consistent decision-making, also sought to counterbalance the strengthening of police powers under the Police and Criminal Evidence Act 1984, the other significant piece of legislation emanating from the Philips Report.

The CPS was set up finally in 1986. A number of articles published in various legal journals at the time set out the hopes and aims of the new service, including various prognoses on the functions and powers of Crown Prosecutors and the proper interpretations of the two criteria to be assessed in deciding whether to prosecute: the 'evidential sufficiency' criteria and the new 'public interest' criteria laid down in the Code for Crown Prosecutors, drawn up and published pursuant to s. 10 of the Prosecution of Offences Act 1985.[24] With hindsight, however, issues such as the role of the prosecutor, his relationship with the other branches of the criminal justice process, and the overall administration of the service have been addressed in some depth in more recent years, both in official government circles and in the media.[25] Most of the media attention has centred around the quarrelsome exchange of criticisms given in evidence to the Home Affairs Committee, which conducted a review of the operation of the CPS in 1990.[26] Scathing attacks on the 'failure' of the CPS to fulfil its objective of improving the national standard of criminal justice were launched by various bodies representing all branches of the criminal justice process, including the Association of Chief Police Officers, the Police Federation, the General Council of the Bar and the Magistrates' Association. The staff shortages, the incompetence of CPS staff and outside agents contracted to conduct prosecutions,[27] poor administration, and the 'civil service mentality' of the service were also highlighted.

The government's review of the CPS, if a little more sympathetic, centred on the same issues. Problems regarding lack of resources, staff shortages,

[24] See F. Bennion, 'The Crown Prosecution Service' [1986] *Crim. LR* 3–15; A. Sanders, 'An Independent Crown Prosecution Service?' [1986] *Crim. LR* 16–27; and J. Timmons, 'The Crown Prosecution Service in Practice' [1986] *Crim. LR* 28–32.

[25] Joshua Rozenberg sets this media criticism out in some depth in *The Case for the Crown: The Inside Story of the Director of Public Prosecutions* (Wellingborough, 1987), at 106–1.

[26] See Home Affairs Committee, *Crown Prosecution Service: Memoranda of Evidence*, HC 118–i (HMSO, 1990).

[27] It is hoped that, in time, the Crown Prosecution Service will employ a sufficient number of advocates to be able to do all of its advocacy 'in house'. Under present arrangements, Crown Prosecutors consider that they, having fully reviewed a file in order to decide whether to prosecute, can present cases in court with better knowledge of the file than outside agents might have. In written evidence submitted to the Home Affairs Committee in 1994, the CPS present figures which do in fact show quite a substantial reduction in the use of private practitioners in magistrates' courts since 1991—Home Affairs Committee, *Minutes of Evidence*, HC 193–i, 26 January 1994. (They clearly have no option but to use private agents in the Crown Court; see below.)

and administrative inefficiencies were addressed in two reports, one by the National Audit Office in 1989[28] and the other by the Committee of Public Accounts in 1990.[29] The National Audit Office concluded that given the onerous task of setting up the service and the inevitable problems caused in the administration of all branches of the criminal justice system, the CPS had, in fact, done the best they could in the circumstances and that many of the staff and financial problems were, to a certain degree, unavoidable. Despite these problems, the report showed that the proportion of direct acquittals had fallen since 1986 and that the filtering role of the prosecutor in screening out weak cases had been reasonably effective. The Public Accounts Committee were critical of the fact that the CPS had cost the government almost twice as much as previous prosecution arrangements,[30] due in part to the uncertainty of initial estimations of cost, but also to the levels of understaffing and the heavy reliance on expensive and 'less than satisfactory' legal agents from outside the service.

Whilst these practical and administrative problems remain for the politicians and law officers to sort out, the need for greater resources to attract high calibre lawyers to the service is an essential part of the reforms proposed in this chapter. The expansion of the prosecutor's discretion and the recognition of his central role in the criminal justice system is substantially dependent on well-informed lawyers' support for and acceptance of such a wide-ranging role, as the experience in Scotland has shown (see Chapter 3). In particular, a proposal by the Lord Chancellor's Green Paper on the *Work and Organisation of the Legal Profession*[31] to allow Crown Prosecutors a right of audience in the Crown Court should be addressed. At present, the anomalous situation exists where barristers employed by the CPS are not allowed to address the Crown Court and this is hardly an incentive for high-quality advocates to join the Service. Indeed, Barbara Mills QC, the current DPP, argued in evidence to the All-Party Home Affairs Select Committee in November 1992, that she had been 'affronted' by the loss of her rights of audience in the Crown Court on joining the CPS, and claimed that the right of audience 'would encourage a beneficial movement in and out of the public sector in the legal profession'.[32] Problems with the recruitment of high-calibre staff have been further exacerbated recently by low morale amongst lawyers in the CPS, caused mainly by the bombardment of criticism directed at the Service and by the DPP's

[28] National Audit Office, *Review of the Crown Prosecution Service: Report by the Comptroller and Auditor General*, HC 345 (HMSO, 1989).
[29] Committee of Public Accounts, *Second Report: Review of the Crown Prosecution Service*, HC 164 (HMSO, 1990).
[30] Ibid., para. 3(ii), v.
[31] Cm 570, 1988.
[32] See J. MacLeod, 'CPS pushes for new trial powers', *Law Society Gazette*, No. 40, 4 Nov. 1992, 5.

extensive reorganization of the Service into thirteen larger areas which, they claim, has decreased their chances of promotion.[33]

In support of its bid to create Crown Court rights of audience for CPS lawyers, the CPS have drawn up a list of criteria for choosing advocates which it hopes will be approved by the Lord Chancellor.[34] This is despite the staunch opposition to this move by the Chairman of the Bar, Lord Williams of Mostyn QC, who intends to: 'stand firm and hold the line. Those who want to follow the foolish bogey of CPS audience rights can be defeated with argument',[35] although Lord Williams did not expand upon quite what line that 'argument' would take, and it may be tied up with the self-interest of members of the Bar who currently undertake advocacy for the CPS. In 1993 the Lord Chancellor's Department announced that solicitors in private practice were to be given Crown Court audience rights, but this did not extend to employed solicitors, such as Crown Prosecutors. This matter is still under review, and the Bar are still vehemently opposed to the idea, fearing a substantial loss of work for junior barristers. Furthermore, the Lord Chancellor's Advisory Committee on Legal Education and Conduct has recently argued that barristers or solicitors employed by the CPS, conducting prosecutions in the Crown Court, would lack the objective independence of private agents and that the CPS should not have a monopoly over state prosecutions,[36] a suggestion which Barbara Mills dismissed as 'nonsense'.[37] Indeed, the CPS was established in the first place to take over the *full* responsibility for the conduct of prosecutions in this country and one might reasonably assume this to include acting as trial advocate to the logical end of a prosecution.

Finally, a recent attempt to outline the future direction of the prosecution system was made by the Home Affairs Committee in 1990.[38] The Committee limited its inquiry to the rather insular boundaries of the English criminal justice system, and failed to take the opportunity of a full review of prosecution arrangements in other European states, and its report was somewhat ambiguous in its statement of future reform policy. The diversion of offenders away from the courts, and thus also from the overburdened prison system, certainly featured as an important aspect of the prosecutor's role. However, the limited sentencing function of Crown Prosecutors (most notably: the discretion to request the police to caution) was,

---

[33] See S. Webster, 'Change is a matter of trial and error', *Independent*, 15 Oct. 1993.

[34] E. Gilvarry, 'CPS advocacy rights bid', *Law Society Gazette*, No. 40, 4 Nov. 1992, 4.

[35] 'Williams: "no" CPS audience rights' *Law Society Gazette*, No. 40, 4 Nov. 1992, 6.

[36] P. Goldsmith, 'Rights of Audience', *Counsel*, July 1993, p. 13.

[37] See her oral evidence to the Home Affairs Committee, HC 193–i, 26 Jan. 1994, at 41.

[38] Home Affairs Committee, *Fourth Report: Crown Prosecution Service*, HC 118–I (HMSO, 1990).

by contrast to their Dutch and German counterparts, not extended. Both the report and the Government's response to it[39] welcomed the extension of the cautioning system to include 'cautioning plus', a form of pre-trial sentencing in all but name. It was felt by the rather tentative Home Affairs Committee that development along European lines into the realm of prosecutorial alternative sanctions was too radical an advance to be contemplated at that time, although no reasons for this were given. Consequently, little became of the recommendations of the Home Affairs Committee, which have quietly fallen by the wayside. The Royal Commission on Criminal Justice (RCCJ), reporting in 1993, did consider various aspects of the prosecutor's role in the criminal justice process, but more as a by-product of their extensive review of pre-trial and court procedures in the light of the infamous miscarriages of justice. Hence, their recommendations tended to be piecemeal, and they did not address the wider issue of the right and proper, general role of the public prosecutor.

3. PUBLIC INTEREST

One of the important features of the independence of the new CPS from the investigative stage is that it has allowed the notion of public interest to be included in prosecution decision-making. Whilst sufficiency of evidence is necessarily the initial consideration in deciding whether to prosecute, the Code for Crown Prosecutors now instructs the prosecutor to consider a number of policy considerations, set out in some detail in paragraph 6 of the new Code,[40] to satisfy himself that the public interest requires a prosecution. Such policy considerations were only included to a limited extent in the discretion of a prosecuting body heavily involved in the investigation process and politically unaccountable, such as the police, although a Home Office Circular (26/1983—*Prosecution Policy*) issued by the Attorney-General to Chief Constables in England and Wales, listed a set of public interest criteria, almost identical to that listed in the Code for Crown Prosecutors, which were to be considered by prosecuting solicitors as a secondary set of considerations after the evidential sufficiency criterion.

Hence, the public interest criteria used by the CPS today were applied to prosecution decision-making by the police before 1985. Indeed, the matter of policy considerations was a point of controversy in the discussions of the Philips Commission. A number of witnesses to the Commission were wholly opposed to giving the Crown Prosecutor such a wide,

[39] Home Office, *Crown Prosecution Service: The Government Reply to the Fourth Report from the Home Affairs Committee*, Cm 1145 (HMSO, 1990).
[40] The Code was originally published in 1986. Since then there have been two re-drafts, the latest being published in July 1994.

independent discretion, preferring that discretion to be confined to legal issues such as the sufficiency of evidence, particularly since the independent public prosecutor has no personal contact with the accused or with the victim. The Commission itself proposed that the Crown Prosecutor should have a wider discretion which involved considering the public interest criteria. However, Elliman[41] has argued that the two types of criteria are difficult to distinguish because the evidential sufficiency criterion relies on an estimation of the likely prospect of conviction, which, in turn, involves public interest considerations such as the opinion of the jury. Nevertheless, the Home Office, in giving evidence to the Commission, were in agreement with the Commission's views, and even went as far as to say that such broad, public interest considerations should be left in the hands of the police in their initial decision to begin prosecution proceedings: 'The task of weighing the public interest in relation to individual prosecutions and prosecution policy in general, demands a comprehensive understanding of the problems of law enforcement in the area and is the Chief Constable's responsibility.'[42] Nevertheless, in the Code for Crown Prosecutors, a set of guidelines for prosecution decision-making, the public interest criteria were laid out in a most explicit and clear-cut list of considerations[43] including matters such as the staleness of the offence, the old age or youth of the accused, and any mental illness or stress suffered by him.

However, the weight to be given to these considerations by the prosecutor is unclear. Certainly they are secondary to the assessment of the sufficiency of evidence. But whether they indicate a presumption for or against prosecution in any case was ambiguously stated in the first two drafts of the Code. Whereas in the Netherlands, for example, it is clear that the existence of public interest criteria have a positive emphasis, in that they sway a decision towards prosecution and away from the accepted presumption not to prosecute (see Chapter 4), the situation in England and Wales appears rather different. Ashworth's analysis of the criteria[44] gave a literal interpretation of the Code. In Ashworth's view the second element to prosecution decision-making described as 'whether the public interest *requires* a prosecution' would suggest a presumption against prosecution, unless the circumstances of the individual case indicate otherwise. Mansfield and Peay reiterate this view, claiming that the public interest criteria set out reasons for not prosecuting, or reasons for offering a caution instead of prosecution.[45]

[41] S. Elliman, 'Inadequate Guidance', *NLJ* 140: 14–16 at 14.
[42] Home Office Evidence to the Royal Commission on Criminal Procedure, Memorandum No. VIII, *The Prosecution Process* (HMSO, 1978).
[43] Code for Crown Prosecutors (CPS, 1986). See para. 8.
[44] A. Ashworth, 'The "Public Interest" Element in Prosecutions' [1987] *Crim LR* 595–607.
[45] Mansfield and Peay (1987) op. cit., at 34.

On the other hand, the actual wording of the criteria listed in paragraph 8 of the 1985 and 1992 Codes, is rather more negative. It would seem to indicate a presumption in favour of prosecution *unless* the likely penalty in a case would be purely nominal or the suspect were old or infirm, for example. The new Code, published in 1994, seems to have settled this matter. Paragraph 6 (which now contains the public interest factors) and the accompanying explanatory notes[46] both indicate that prosecution in most cases, especially those of any seriousness, will 'usually' take place. Some of the public interest factors may influence a reversal of this presumption, but the general rule is evidently that prosecution is the normal course of action. In the Netherlands, a reversal of the emphasis given to the public interest criteria in the late 1970s produced a substantial difference in the degree to which cases were diverted away from court. Ultimately, however, the criteria applied in England and Wales would seem to reduce diversion less than the amount of paperwork involved in a non-prosecution. Webster quoted one senior Crown Prosecutor who believed that the level of bureaucracy involved in exercising this discretion outweighed the benefits of avoiding a trial: 'I feel people are reluctant to take hard decisions and discontinue cases because they must fill in a dozen forms to do this.'[47] No doubt some of his colleagues would argue, though, that the paperwork involved in sending a case to trial is even more burdensome.

In practice it would seem that the Crown Prosecutors operate their own informal presumption against prosecution in relatively minor cases, where the defendant has no previous record.[48] In fact, the Home Affairs Committee endorsed this presumption, particularly in relation to juveniles,[49] although they were rather more cautious about endorsing the same procedure in the adult field.[50] The presumption against prosecution of juveniles has a longer history. The diversion of juveniles from the criminal justice process at as early a stage as possible has been a key element in police cautioning policy for some time. In 1969 the Children and Young Persons Act laid a statutory foundation for diversion of juveniles by providing for consultation between the police and social workers, teachers and the like in making decisions regarding the way that the criminal process would deal with juvenile offenders. Although this provision has never been implemented and has now been repealed, it is clear from statistics quoted by Morris and Giller,[51] showing a marked increase in the use of cautioning

---

[46] CPS, *Explanatory Memorandum: An Explanatory Memorandum for use in connection with the Code for Crown Prosecutors* (London, 1994).

[47] Senior Crown Prosecutor quoted in Webster (1993) op. cit.

[48] Cf. M. McConville, A. Sanders, and R. Leng (1991), *The Case for the Prosecution: Police Suspects and the Construction of Criminality* (London, 1991), 126–31.

[49] Home Affairs Committee (1990) *Fourth Report*, op. cit., para. 51.

[50] Ibid., para. 53.

[51] A. Morris, and H. Giller, *Understanding Juvenile Justice* (London, 1987), see table 5.1, 142.

for juveniles between 1975 and 1985, that the underlying intentions and aims of this provision were achieved in practice. In 1978, a Home Office Circular on police cautioning (70/1978) further endorsed this practice by re-emphasizing a presumption against prosecution in cases involving juveniles. In this respect, the recent policy and practice of the CPS reflected a long-standing legacy of police decision-making regarding the prosecution of juveniles.

Further, Baroness Faithfull, during the House of Lords debate on the Prosecution of Offences Bill 1985,[52] moved an amendment requiring specially trained prosecutors to use prosecution in juvenile cases as a last resort, with a heavy presumption in favour of cautioning in suitable cases, thereby carrying the ethos of police practice into the policy of the new prosecution service. Lord Elton, in his reply to this amendment,[53] indicated that this 'ethos' would be clearly reflected in the guidelines for Crown Prosecutors which were due to be drawn up by the Attorney-General. However, this presumption is increasingly likely in future to apply only to a first-time offender, since a new Home Office Circular (18/1994—*The Cautioning of Offenders*) has discouraged the use of repeat cautioning except where the subsequent offence is particularly trivial or occurred a substantial time after the first offence: 'Multiple cautioning brings this disposal into disrepute.'[54] The expected result of this Circular, if it is implemented, is that less diversion will be practised in youth justice, and many more young offenders will be prosecuted in the Youth Court.[55]

The new Code has taken the ethos of this Circular on board. The 'youth of the offender' is no longer a part of the public interest criteria *per se*. A new, much shorter, paragraph entitled 'Youth Offenders'[56] essentially paraphrases the larger section of the old Code devoted to young offenders. It tentatively suggests that prosecution can be harmful to young people and they should therefore 'sometimes' be dealt with out of court, but goes on to say that the youth of an offender in itself should not be a reason for not prosecuting. Where a young offender had committed a serious offence (that is, too serious for a caution) his/her youth was never a bar to prosecution under the previous guidelines. However, paragraph 6.8 provides a weak statement of policy for Crown Prosecutors dealing with this category. As well as being self-contradictory and inconsistent in terms of policy, the paragraph has lost, along with much of its detail, the firm commitment to the cautioning practice as an effective way of dealing with

---

[52] Baroness Faithfull, House of Lords Debates 1984–5, 17 January 1985, vol. 458, col. 1112.

[53] Ibid., col. 1114, *per* Lord Elton.

[54] Home Office Circular, 18/1994, *The Cautioning of Offenders*, at para. 8.

[55] See further, R. Evans, 'Cautioning: Counting the Cost of Retrenchment' [1994] *Crim. LR* 566–75.

[56] Code for Crown Prosecutors (1994) para. 6.8.

many young offenders, including those who reoffend. The statement of policy on cautioning in paragraph 6.9 does not mention young offenders specifically, but merely contains a vacuous statement relating to all offenders, which reminds prosecutors to refer cases back to the police and request a caution where this is 'suitable'.

In relation to adults, the Home Affairs Committee in 1990 did recommend a presumption against prosecution in cases where the offender was suffering from mental illness or stress.[57] This was in response to a suggestion from the Howard League in their evidence to the Committee that 'the sections [of the Code] on young adults and on mentally disordered persons [should] be strengthened so as to further enhance the presumption against prosecution'[58] and the Code was, in 1992, redrafted to this effect.[59] A formal proposal by the Committee to extend this presumption to all first-time adult offenders would certainly have assisted the diversion of 'some of the trivia which the courts deal with routinely day-by-day'.[60] However, much of the detailed guidance to prosecutors under the 1992 Code has been deleted from the new draft, and mental disorder or stress now forms only a part of the public interest factors, including old age and physical ill health, which weigh against a decision to prosecute.

The public interest element in the Code has greatly enhanced the discretion of the public prosecutor in England and Wales, and the Code itself may be seen as the greatest attempt yet by Parliament (or at least the key policy-makers at the Headquarters of the CPS who formulated the Code and the unpublished Policy Manuals issued to all Crown Prosecutors) to set out clear guidelines on decision-making in criminal justice. However, the criteria set out in the Netherlands, where the inexhaustive list of criteria numbers 52 (see Chapter 4), or in Germany where they are unwritten (see Chapter 5) render the prosecutor's discretion much wider. The number of public interest factors have increased in the newly redrafted Code, which, for the first time, explicitly states that the list of criteria is not exhaustive. The public interest criteria are now listed in two separate paragraphs, the first giving factors which should weigh in favour of a prosecution and the second listing those favouring a non-prosecution decision.

Some new factors have been added, particularly in favour of prosecution. For example: a discriminatory motive, the use of a weapon, the fact that the offence was committed in breach of a court order, or that there are grounds for believing that the offence might recur. All these factors will now weigh for continuance of a prosecution decision. This has balanced the public interest criteria, to some extent; under the old Code most of the

---

[57] Home Affairs Committee (1990) *Fourth Report*, op. cit., para. 52.
[58] Home Affairs Committee (1990) *Memoranda of Evidence*, op. cit., 93.
[59] Code for Crown Prosecutors (1992), para. 8(v).
[60] Home Affairs Committee (1990) *Fourth Report*, op. cit., p. xvii, para. 53.

criteria listed set out reasons for not prosecuting. So the increase in the number of factors listed does not necessarily indicate any policy swing towards increased expediency, but rather gives a fuller picture of the factors to be taken into account when considering the circumstances of an offence. Crown Prosecutors are specifically directed not to carry out a balancing exercise themselves; the purpose of listing factors for and against prosecution is not to encourage them to add up plus and minus points mathematically. Rather they must look for factors in the list which carry significant weight one way or another.

The Home Affairs Committee sought to confine the new discretion somewhat further by recommending that the Crown Prosecutor 'should adhere rigidly to its Code' in making decisions under his public interest hat.[61] The government was critical of this in its response to the Committee's report, regarding the rigid application of the Code as 'inappropriate'.[62] This recommendation, and a proposed duty on the prosecutor to give reasons to the police for dropping a case, as well as the recommended presumption in favour of prosecution, may be seen as unduly fettering an already limited discretion. Indeed, even in 1950 the Attorney-General of the day, Sir Hartley Shawcross, was quoted in the House of Commons as stating the need for a completely independent discretion in this area:

The truth is, of course, that the exercise of discretion in a quasi-judicial way as to whether or when I must step in to enforce the criminal law is exactly one of the duties of the Attorney-General, as it is of the Office of Director of Public Prosecutions. It has never been the rule in this country—I hope it never will be—that suspected criminal offences must automatically be the subject of prosecution . . . public interest is the dominant consideration. So under the tradition of our criminal law the position is that the Attorney-General and the DPP only intervene when they consider it in the public interest so to do.[63]

The new Code is intended to make the public interest criteria clearer, more comprehensive and more 'user-friendly'.[64] The result is certainly a clearer, more concise document, but the side-effects of this quest for plainer English are rather more disturbing. Much of the detail that has been deleted from the new Code has presumably been swept into the Policy Manuals which are unpublished. Thus much of the information and guidance on the discretion of the Crown Prosecutor, which may have provided some form of accountability, has now been removed from the public eye.

---

[61] Ibid., para. 32.
[62] Home Office (1990) *Government Reply to Fourth Report of Home Affairs Committee*, op. cit., 2.
[63] Sir Hartley Shawcross, House of Commons Debates, vol. 483, col. 681, 29 Jan. 1951.
[64] This was the purpose for re-drafting, as expressed by both the Attorney-General in announcing to the House of Commons that a review of the Code was under way in December 1993, and by the DPP in her evidence to the 1994 Home Affairs Committee, op. cit.

In particular, paragraphs which gave guidance on how prosecutors should deal with certain offences have been dropped from the published Code altogether. Unfortunately these offences, such as conspiracy to defraud and sexual offences, are precisely those which often attract widespread public attention when controversial decisions are made about prosecution. Such public attention and comment will, in future, be made without the benefit of knowing the policy of the CPS on such matters.[65]

The discretion to divert cases from the overburdened court system in England and Wales is restricted by the absence from the Code of various criteria which are widely used in Europe. The concepts of 'trivia' and of 'minor guilt' are only very loosely included in the Code under the 'likely penalty' criteria (paragraphs 6.5*a* and 6.5*c*) which direct a prosecutor to weigh the degree of damage caused and the moral guilt of the offender against the penalty likely to be imposed by a court. The consideration of the cost of proceedings, which used to form part of this balancing exercise, has now been dropped from the Code altogether, perhaps in response to criticisms in the media of the use of expediency by the CPS based on such material considerations. The CPS has recently been criticized by the Police Federation for dropping charges 'to save time'.[66]

The European prosecutor's discretion to waive prosecutions on public interest grounds is founded on this notion of saving resources and easing the workload of the court, and is justified by the fact that public interest is served as much by such savings as it is by the full enforcement of the criminal law. The rationale for developing the prosecutor's sentencing role and giving him quasi-judicial functions is, after all, primarily to ease the burdens of such functions on the judiciary themselves. It is interesting to note, however, that one particular Dutch academic has expressed anxieties about the rather liberal use of the expediency principle in the Netherlands. These concerns are echoed in the opinions expressed by some of the groups who gave evidence to the Home Affairs Committee in 1990. Professor 'tHart of the University of Utrecht traces the history of the gradual adoption of the expediency principle as a positive feature of criminal law policy in the Netherlands, rendering prosecution an absolute last resort where all other options involving prosecutors' out-of-court settlements and alternatives run by the social services have been exhausted or are simply not suitable.[67]

[65] See further, A. Ashworth, and J. Fionda, 'Prosecution, Accountability and the Public Interest: The New CPS Code' [1994] *Crim. LR* 894–903.

[66] J. Weeks, 'Prosecutors drop charges "to save time"', *Daily Telegraph* 19 May 1989. Barbara Mills in fact countered this by arguing that most cases dropped at the prosecution stage had to be discontinued because the police were failing in their duty to provide sufficient evidence for a prosecution. See Home Affairs Committee (1994) *Minutes of Evidence*, op. cit., at page 34.

[67] A. C. 'tHart, (1988) 'Criminal Law Policy in the Netherlands' in J. J. M. van Dijk, *et al.* (eds.), *Criminal Law in Action: An Overview of Current Issues in Western Societies* (Arnhem, 1988).

Chapter 4 will also indicate how the use of the principle of expediency and the figures of non-prosecution rose to an all-time high in the early 1980s as a result of this policy.

'tHart, however, points out the problems that this policy actually caused, which ironically enhanced the problems that the policy was intended to solve. By the mid-1980s, he argued, it became apparent that the prosecution policy of finding community solutions to community crime problems was not only placing an intolerable burden on the resources of the welfare state, but was also producing an unsatisfactorily low level of law enforcement. The new criminal policy in the Netherlands, first expounded in a government white paper in 1985, apparently attempts to redress the failure of such 'lenient' prosecution policy, and is reflective of the problems caused by it.

'tHart views Dutch criminal policy in the last decade with less optimism about the opportunity principle in Europe than many of the other academics who have reminisced fondly about the mild penal climate in the Netherlands, and warns against proceeding too far down the road of expediency. No doubt 'tHart's article will be useful ammunition to fuel the arguments against any large-scale extension of the public interest discretion of prosecutors in this country. The new Code certainly provides no indication that such an extension is on the policy agenda. Indeed, the reverse appears to be true. Having re-emphasized the importance of the evidential sufficiency criteria as the primary consideration of Crown Prosecutors, the public interest has taken more of a back seat. As a statement of expediency, the public interest criteria have been weakened by the inclusion of many factors which tend towards prosecution rather than against it.

A reluctance to use the public interest as a mechanism for discretionary decision-making certainly exists. Public interest reasons account for about 31 per cent of all cases discontinued,[68] yet there is a distinct reluctance to extend this figure. Indeed, in giving evidence to the Home Affairs Committee in 1994, the DPP tried to play down the extent to which the public interest is used to dismiss cases, stressing the fact that the majority of cases discontinued were due to a lack of evidence supplied by the police. This was admittedly in the face of questioning which expressed a certain anxiety that any cases should be discontinued at all.[69] One member of the Committee in fact asked: 'These are serious offences and yet a decision is being taken by the Crown Prosecution Service not to proceed because you take the decision that a nominal penalty will be imposed. Is that really the appropriate role for the CPS to be playing?'[70] Such reluctance to

[68] See M. Clarke, 'They Don't Understand', *Police Review*, 4 Feb. 1994, 24.
[69] Home Affairs Committee (1994) op. cit., at 34–7.
[70] See Mr Byers, Home Affairs Committee (1994) op. cit., 37. See also J. Rozenberg, (1987) op. cit., 156, who shares this anxiety about the public interest criteria.

acknowledge the public interest criteria as a proper part of the prosecutor's discretion is peculiarly English; European prosecutors are far more proud of their capacity to exercise this discretion and, whether as a consequence of this or not, tend to use it more frequently. To try to sweep it under the carpet almost assumes that it is somehow inappropriate or illegal to use the public interest as a relevant consideration in decision-making. This is clearly not so. The Code openly acknowledges the role of the public prosecutor as guardian of the public interest and so, therefore, should prosecutors and policy-makers also.

4. THE POLICE

Since the inception of the CPS, relationships between the new service and the police, whose prosecuting functions they assumed, has been fraught with antagonism and hostility. The removal of a substantial body of police work has apparently caused friction between the two agencies, with the police suffering a case of 'sour grapes'. This enmity fuelled the quarrelsome exchange of criticism between the DPP of the time, Sir Allan Green, and bodies such as the Police Federation in giving evidence to the Home Affairs Committee in 1990.

On the one hand, Green claimed, in his oral evidence, that 'the introduction of the Service was a bitter pill for some police officers to swallow'[71] and accused senior police officers of refusing to co-operate with and even obstructing the work of the CPS, although he denied that there was an ongoing feud between them. On the other hand, the Police Federation told the Committee that the criminal justice system was at 'crisis point' because of the incompetence, underfunding, and poor performance of the CPS, and accused them of ignoring victims in their use of expediency in decision-making to save time and money. The police have always fervently denied any lack of co-operation and, indeed, several senior officers have publicly welcomed the separation of the investigation and prosecution processes. Mike Bennett, Chairman of the Metropolitan Police Federation, claimed in a letter to the editor of the *Independent*: 'I have never heard of resentment by police officers over the loss of the prosecuting powers. Quite the contrary, as far as we are concerned we do not want the responsibility to prosecute given back to us.'[72]

It seems that, with the passage of time, wounds are healing and the

---

[71] Sir Allan Green quoted in J. Pienaar, 'DPP accuses police of obstructing CPS', *Independent*, 1 Feb. 1990.
[72] Mike Bennett in a letter to editor of *Independent*, 2 Feb. 1990. See also comments of David Owen, Chief Constable of North Wales, quoted in J. Pienaar, 'Criminal justice system at crisis point, senior police tell MPs', *Independent*, 8 Feb. 1990.

relationship is gradually improving as police officers and Crown Prosecutors are fully trained in mutual co-operation. In an effort to improve the situation, the 1990 Home Affairs Committee recommended the implementation of a fuller programme of training for both the CPS and the police 'so that each is familiarised with the other's work and responsibilities'.[73] Indeed, the CPS Annual Report for the year 1988–9 reported that CPS lawyers had begun, in some regions, to give lectures as part of police training courses and had set up groups for 'multi-lateral discussions' on the work of the CPS.[74] In recent years, co-operation has extended further. An initiative called Pre-trial Issues (PTI) has been set up whereby a number of agencies in the criminal justice process, including the CPS, wrote a Manual of Guidance for the police setting out minimum standards for the preparation and submission of case files. Furthermore, a Joint Performance Management Machinery Group (JPMM) has been established at the policy level, to bring together representatives from all branches of the process to work alongside the local area committees of the Criminal Justice Consultative Council to improve communication and liaison between the CPS and the police. The Royal Commission on Criminal Justice (RCCJ) reiterated the need for close liaison and co-operation at this crucial stage and recommended that this be done locally on an informal basis, the police seeking the advice of the CPS wherever necessary in accordance with guidelines to be drawn up.[75]

The importance of co-operation between Crown Prosecutors and the police is essential for optimum efficiency in the preparation and conduct of prosecutorial decision-making. The CPS, in considering both prosecution criteria, need well-presented police reports with clear, concise, but fully detailed information and, moreover, the information needs to be available at the earliest possible stage. The evidence submitted by the CPS to the RCCJ explains the need for a relationship 'based on mutual respect for the professionalism, integrity and competence of the officers in both organisations'.[76] A number of academic commentators have recognised this.[77]

A question that still needs to be addressed in England and Wales, however, is the constitutional position of the police in relation to the CPS, and

---

[73] Home Affairs Committee (1990) *Fourth Report*, op. cit., para. 29.

[74] Crown Prosecution Service, *Annual Report 1988/89* (London, 1989), at 28, para. 2.1.10.

[75] Royal Commission on Criminal Justice, (1993) *Report*, op. cit., Recommendation 93.

[76] Crown Prosecution Service (1991) Unpublished Evidence to the Royal Commission on Criminal Justice, para. 5.2.2.

[77] See Mansfield and Peay, (1987) op. cit., 47. Also, J. Wood, 'Relations with the police and the public, and with overseas police and judicial authorities' and R. Tarling, 'Interdependence and the Crown Prosecution Service' both in J. E. Hall Williams, ed., *The Role of the Prosecutor* (Aldershot, 1988).

whether the latter should be involved in the investigative stage. In Scotland, where the office of Procurator Fiscal pre-dates that of the police officer, the police hold a position subordinate in law to the prosecutor. Recommending the implementation, in England and Wales, of this aspect of the Scottish criminal justice process, Robb has argued that:

The true independence of the prosecutor from the police is not to be found in the total separation of the investigative and prosecutorial functions, but rather in the prosecutor's authority over the police in relation to the evidential side of criminal investigation . . . and in the total freedom of the police from any responsibility for prosecution.[78]

In England and Wales, given the resentment which arose upon the creation of the office of Crown Prosecutor, it may be futile, even foolish, to suggest such a change. Indeed, the RCCJ declined to do so,[79] arguing that the CPS would have insufficient training in investigation techniques, and that this would blur the investigation and prosecution roles too far. However, the evidence of the CPS to the Royal Commission was that they have been given the 'responsibility for the conduct of prosecution without the power to require that it is properly investigated and prepared'[80] and feel heavily dependent upon the police for sufficient information and evidence to conduct a case.[81] Nevertheless, again in fear of blurring the prosecution and investigation processes only recently separated, they did not appeal for a supervisory role over the police: 'The CPS should no more have the right to manage the police than the police to manage the CPS.'[82] The experience of Scotland, though, and that of Germany and the Netherlands (see Chapters 3, 4, and 5 below) has shown that a power invested in the public prosecutor to give instructions and advice on the investigation of particularly serious or complex cases does not produce any undue difficulties in the independent decision-making of prosecutors; in fact, if anything, the reverse is true. Allowing a prosecutor to be involved in a supervisory capacity in the investigation of a crime simply enables him to ensure that all the precise evidence and information he requires to prosecute or divert a case is produced. One would hope that a system of professional advice on investigation could be kept clearly separate from the consideration of the public interest reasons for not prosecuting. This has been achieved in Germany, where the Federal Ministry of Justice is especially careful about clearly delineating the roles of each branch of the criminal justice process

---

[78] L. Robb, 'Note: A Scottish Contribution' in Hall Williams, ed., (1988) op. cit., at 28.

[79] Royal Commission on Criminal Justice, (1993) *Report*, op. cit., ch. 2, para. 67.

[80] CPS Evidence to the Royal Commission on Criminal Justice, op. cit., para. 5.5.1.

[81] Hence the DPP's criticism of the police, whom she sees as 'culpable' for the majority of discontinued cases (see above).

[82] CPS Evidence to Royal commission on Criminal Justice, op. cit., para. 5.5.4.

(see Chapter 5). Leigh and Zedner recommended to the Royal Commission that the German example be followed in England and Wales, but to no avail.[83]

There is a further argument in favour of a prosecutorial review of all cases reported to the police as in Germany where the legality principle still governs police activities. At present the police act as the gatekeepers to the criminal justice system, and this filtering role may taint the discretion of the prosecutor. All cases currently received by the prosecutor have already been initiated as prosecuted offences and the prosecutor's decision is whether to *continue* that prosecution or not. In this sense, the presumption in favour of prosecution is already present in the rules of procedure and may gather momentum through the public interest criteria as argued above. Indeed, police reports are also likely to contain heavy presumptions towards prosecution and, according to Giller and Gelsthorpe, it is unlikely that the police will 'actively seek information that could establish innocence.'[84]

Moreover, McConville, Sanders, and Leng allege that the CPS may continue with prosecutions in weak cases where the police have brought policy prosecutions against members of 'undesirable' groups.[85] The CPS may not operate with the same values, or within the same culture, as the police and may not therefore adopt such an ethically doubtful policy. However, their unwitting acquiescence may at times be inevitable because their decisions as to whether to continue prosecutions are made on the basis of the police reports provided to them. If those reports are heavily loaded with the cultural values of the officers compiling them, then the influence to decide in favour of continued prosecution may overcome other considerations. For example, McConville, Sanders, and Leng argue that a police report which ascribes to a suspect a value-laden label, such as 'football hooligan', or which uses emotive terms to describe an offence, such as 'vicious', may weight the argument in favour of prosecution, even if the evidential sufficiency or public interest criteria are not met. This is a result, not of inefficiency or lack of professionalism on the part of the CPS, but of the wider system in which they operate and which has denied them sufficient independence properly to screen out such cases. (A discussion of the independence of the Crown Prosecutor appears below.)

Giving to prosecutors the initial filtering role as well as complete independence in prosecution decision-making would enable them to review

[83] L. Leigh, and L. Zedner, *A Report on the Administration of Criminal Justice in the Pre-Trial phase in France and Germany*, Royal Commission on Criminal Justice Research Study No. 1 (HMSO, 1992).

[84] H. Giller, and L. Gelsthorpe, 'Prosecuting Juveniles—CPS and the Decision-Making Process', *AJJUST*, Feb. 1990, pp. 11–14, at p. 12. Sanders also makes this point in 'Incorporating the "public interest" in the decision to prosecute' in J. E. Hall Williams (ed.), (1988) op. cit., at p. 36.

[85] McConville, Sanders, and Leng, op. cit., 126.

cases much more objectively. Again, the RCCJ considered this as a possible reform, having received suggestions to this effect, but declined to recommend such a change on the basis that it would be an inefficient waste of manpower resources in the CPS.[86]

It was made clear in both the 1990 Home Affairs Committee's report and the government's reply that the police should not have any powers to override the decisions of the CPS. In evidence to the Committee, the Association of Chief Police Officers (ACPO) made the radical suggestion that the police should have a secondary discretion to prosecute cases dropped by the CPS 'as a safety valve and a means of protection to the Service generally'.[87] The suggestion was rejected outright, by the DPP who considered it 'utterly unacceptable', by the Committee who claimed that 'giving the police the power to second-guess the CPS would be wholly inconsistent with the principles upon which the CPS has been set up'[88] and by the government in its reply.[89] To give the police such a power would be to revert to pre-CPS days and would negate all the beneficial reasons for the creation of an independent prosecution body. The fact remains, however, that the relationship between the police and the prosecutor in England and Wales is somewhat anomalous in that the filtering role at the early stages of the criminal justice process is shared; the blurred division of responsibility for the prosecution function may have contributed towards the antagonism mentioned above.

The lack of clearly defined boundaries between the involvement of each agency in the decision to prosecute, and the confusion this can cause, was emphasized by the recent High Court decision in the case of *R. v. Croydon Justices, ex parte Dean*.[90] In this case a prosecution initiated by the CPS, after the police made a representation to the defendant that he would not be prosecuted, was ruled capable of being an abuse of process. This judicial review case involved a 17-year-old defendant committed to the Crown Court on a charge of doing acts with intent to impede the apprehension of another, contrary to s. 4(1) Criminal Law Act 1967. (He had, in fact, assisted in the destruction of a car used by some of his associates to carry out a murder and had received a representation from the police that he would not be prosecuted in connection with the murder but would instead be called as a prosecution witness in the trial of his associates.) The High Court laid down a clear precedent that 'the prosecution of a person who had received a promise, undertaking or representation from the police that

---

[86] Royal Commission on Criminal Justice (1993) *Report*, op. cit., ch. 5, para. 21.
[87] Home Affairs Committee (1990) *Memoranda of Evidence*, op. cit., at 68, para. 4.11.
[88] Home Affairs Committee (1990) *Fourth Report*, op. cit., at para. 33.
[89] Home Office (1990) *Government Reply to Home Affairs Committee Fourth Report*, op. cit., para. (ix).
[90] [1993] 3 All ER 129.

he would not be prosecuted was capable of being an abuse of process'.[91] This decision clearly shows that the police still have some influence over the prosection decision and have therefore not been relegated to the non-discretionary position of, for example, the Scottish police.

The CPS in fact protested in this case that it was their exclusive right to decide whether to prosecute, but while the High Court accepted this submission, they went on to decide that the decision to prosecute was capable of being an abuse of process. Their only advice was: 'If the CPS found that its powers were being usurped by the police, the remedy must be a greater degree of liaison at an early stage.'[92] Although it is difficult to envisage how a Crown Prosecutor, without any powers to supervise the investigation stage, could prevent the police making such undertakings, this case does clearly emphasize the great importance of co-operation and smooth interaction between these two branches of the criminal justice system. At least with a constructive system of consultation, misunderstandings as to these undertakings could be avoided. Nevertheless, such sound advice would be of little comfort to the CPS as a body fervently trying to protect their independence and establish the clarity of the boundaries between their functions and those of the police.[93]

5. The English Prosecutor's Involvement in Sentencing

It is stressed at this point that the author does not advocate pre-trial punishment of all suspects. The following pages address the degree to which the Crown Prosecutor should be empowered to issue penalties to an offender who has admitted guilt, but who is not convicted by a court. The important civil liberties implications are dealt with below. However, the first of these is that it should be a prerequisite of any prosecutorial sentencing that an admission of guilt has been made.

(a) Lack of Alternative Sanctions

The potential sphere of influence of the English Crown Prosecutor over the later stages of the criminal justice system, including the workload of the courts and the overall imprisonment rates, is limited by the lack of options alternative to prosecution. Beyond his or her decision on whether to prosecute or not, the Crown Prosecutor is almost powerless to deal with minor cases in any other way. The problems caused by this are highlighted by three particularly frustrating inadequacies of the present system.

[91] Ibid. *per* Lord Justice Slaughton.   [92] Ibid.
[93] For further comment on this case, see J. Fionda, 'The Crown Prosecution Service and the Police: A Loveless Marriage?' (1994) *LQR* 110: 376–9.

The first relates to so-called 'problem' cases. It was common practice, under the old system, for police officers to opt for prosecution in cases which did not merit court action, whether for policy or evidential reasons, simply in order to bring a 'problem' offender to the attention of the social services at court. The police would also sometimes prosecute cases of an offence particularly prevalent in their area as a PR exercise. Although the Home Office guidelines on prosecution policy[94] provided for prosecution in the public interest where the offence is prevalent, the police sometimes (according to one Crown Prosecutor interviewed) prosecuted despite insufficient evidence in order to avoid criticism that they were being too lenient in respect of that offence, or that they were failing in their investigative responsibilities. The police were thereby using the blunt instrument of the law, a rather disproportionate response, in order to provide an offender with counselling or social help to attempt to curb his offending. The CPS, under the guidelines laid out in the Code, are unable and unwilling to follow the same practice. Even where the evidence is sufficient to prosecute, the duty to consider the public interest elements in the case will often prevent a decision to prosecute. In this way, defendants who require a rehabilitative response are inadequately dealt with by the criminal justice system. In other systems, defendants with problems such as alcoholism, drug addiction, mental disorder, or domestic problems which are directly connected with their offending can be referred at the pre-trial stage to various schemes of counselling or help as a condition of non-prosecution, so that even without recourse to the court, those offenders can be dealt with in a positive way.

The second inadequacy of the present system concerns the victim. Where a prosecution is discontinued, the opportunities for the victim to retrieve compensation for the criminal behaviour of the offender are severely narrowed. Without a court order for such compensation, the victim's only possibility is to pursue a civil action against the offender, which may be costly and is frequently unsuccessful. This could be avoided if the prosecutor were able to forego prosecution on condition that the offender pay compensation to the victim, or arrange some other form of reparation and/or mediation between the two parties. Given the recent criticism made of the CPS in ignoring the interests of the victim, and particularly in 'making decisions based on expediency or cost rather than on the victim's feelings',[95] the availability of alternative courses of action which address the compensatory rights of the victim would be welcome. In principle, whilst recognizing that the CPS is not a 'Victim's Prosecution Service', the DPP has pledged firm support to the interests and needs of the victim.[96]

---

[94] Home Office Circular No. 26 of 1983—*Prosecution Policy.*
[95] T. Kirby, 'Police say CPS ignores victims', *Independent*, 19 May 1989.
[96] Crown Prosecution Service, *Statement on the Treatment of victims and witnesses by the*

However, this goes little further than a requirement to bear the victim's interest in mind when making decisions, which are primarily based on the offence and the offender. There is no positive commitment to develop powers which would actually compensate victims of criminal behaviour.

Finally, the matter of the proportionality of the response to very minor forms of offending should be addressed. Where a minor offence is committed by a defendant with one or more previous convictions, and there is sufficient evidence to prosecute, the odds weigh heavily in favour of court action, particularly in view of the inherent presumption towards prosecution mentioned above. Despite this, in trivial cases with a minor degree of guilt, for example criminal damage costing less than £50 to repair, and certain morally 'colourless' offences, for example driving a car without a valid MOT certificate, the use of the prosecution procedure may be an unwieldy and disproportionate response. As Ashworth points out: 'In many . . . cases which are not of a serious nature, it is appropriate for society to show a sense of proportion by punishing offenders without resort to court proceedings.'[97] If prosecutors were given a quasi-judicial sentencing function, and were able to issue penalties such as a small fine or short periods of community service, this would restore that proportionality, as well as ease the burden on the courts.

(b) Prosecutor Fines

The Crown Prosecutor in England and Wales has, at present, no power to offer an offender the option of a fine as a condition of non-prosecution. Although the police operate a fixed penalty system for very minor traffic offences, which to some extent resembles the procurator fiscal fine system in Scotland, it has always been felt inappropriate to give the prosecutor in this country any power to issue such a sanction, outside of the courtroom. The Philips Commission certainly did not approach the idea. If the fiscal fine system had then been introduced in Scotland they may have addressed the issue, since their comparison of the Scottish system played an important part in formulating their proposals for a new national prosecution system. However, more surprisingly, the Home Affairs Committee in 1990 also failed to consider the possibility of increasing the prosecutor's sentencing role to include such a power. Their recommendation to introduce

Crown Prosecution Service (HMSO, 1993). Also see Crown Prosecution Service, *Statement of Purpose and Values* (HMSO, 1993) pp. 8 and 10 and the Code for Crown Prosecutors (1994) para. 6.7.

[97] Ashworth, 'Prosecution, Police and the Public—A Guide to Good Gatekeeping?', *Howard Journal*, 23: 65–87 at 77. See also Sanders, 'Incorporating the "public interest" in the decision to prosecute' in Hall Williams, ed. (1988) op. cit., at 38, where he agrees that the judicial role of the prosecutor could usefully be expanded.

a system of 'caution plus' with additional penalties being annexed to the existing cautioning procedure may have incorporated some form of fining. Eventually they decided to leave the function of cautioning in the hands of the police who operate with little accountability. This would necessarily limit the degree of open discretion allowed in such decision-making to avoid the process of 'net-widening' or abuse of the offender's rights of due process.

The RCCJ was the first body to consider seriously the establishment of a system of prosecutor fines. They considered, in two very brief paragraphs, the operation of prosecutor fines in other jurisdictions, most notably Scotland. Ultimately, their conclusion was that such a system, modelled partially on the Scottish system, should be introduced in England and Wales, principally because 'there would be a small cost to the magistrates' courts' fine collection machinery but this should be considerably outweighed by the savings in magistrates' court trials'.[98] The system of fines that they recommended, however, differed from the Scottish system to the extent that the level of fine should be discretionary rather than fixed by statute (see Chapter 3). Despite the financial savings that this suggested system would incur, it has yet to be seriously considered by policy-makers and has not been included in the Criminal Justice and Public Order Bill 1994, currently working its way through the legislative process.

The advantages of such a system, as stated by the Royal Commission above, mainly concern the saving of valuable resources, and the ability to give a proportionate response to a minor offence without recourse to the already overworked court system. The CPS evidence to the Royal Commission points out a number of disadvantages of expanding the cautioning system and allowing penalties to be imposed pre-trial.[99] However, the following chapters will show that, in practice, fears about net-widening and abuses of power are often settled by built-in safeguards, such as the voluntary nature of the offer of such penalties, which ensures that the offender can refuse a fine and go to trial if he chooses. Further, whilst the CPS saw the power to add a fine to a caution as a procedure which 'usurps the function of the court', their European counterparts take a more positive view; that is, they view the quasi-judicial power as a means of assistance to the judiciary in easing a heavy workload and allowing valuable court time to be spent on more serious and complex cases, a function which the judiciaries of those countries condone.

(c) *Cautioning*

As stated above, the only alternatives to prosecution in a minor case are discontinuance or the cautioning process. At present, a prosecutor must

---

[98] Royal Commission on Criminal Justice (1993) *Report*, op. cit., at ch. 5, para. 63.
[99] Crown Prosecution Service (1991) Evidence to Royal Commission, op. cit., at 98.

refer a case back to the police and request a caution where he believes that this is the appropriate sanction. Cases originally cautioned by the police are never seen or reviewed in any way by the independent prosecutor. The power has, however, been used increasingly in recent years, especially in the juvenile field, where the CPS has some trained juvenile specialists to handle such cases. Whereas most adult offenders committing their first minor offence are likely to be cautioned, juveniles committing their second, third or subsequent offences may be repeatedly referred to the cautioning system before the prosecutor finally resorts to a prosecution (although, as stated, this practice is to be discouraged by Home Office Circular 18/1994 and the new Code for Crown Prosecutors).

The proposal for a 'caution plus' system, whereby additional penalties are given in connection with a warning, has been aired in both the 1990 Home Affairs Committee report and in the evidence of the CPS to the RCCJ. It seems likely that the development of a diversion system in this country will be through an extension of the cautioning system, rather than the introduction of prosecutorial alternatives. The possible penalties to be annexed to the caution, as listed in the CPS evidence to the RCCJ[100] might include a small fine, an order for compensation, community service, attendance at a drug or alcohol rehabilitation centre, or probation counselling; the same forms of diversion available to the Scottish procurator fiscal, but administered in the cautioning context. As it seems unlikely from the tone of the 1990 Home Affairs Committee report, and the government's reply to it, that there will be any legislative effort to create a statutory sentencing role for the prosecutor, the 'cautioning plus' system may be the next best thing for the time being. If nothing else, legislation to this effect would, at long last, give the entire cautioning system a firm legal foundation, after over a century of practising the process under the informal authority of the Home Office guidelines, and this statutory footing has been recommended by the CPS,[101] the RCCJ,[102] and was even advocated by the Philips Commission as long ago as 1981.[103] Evidently, the CPS are keen to place any cautioning procedure on a statutory basis before their sentencing role is developed to any extent, principally because of the security that a statutory footing would give them. Members of the Policy Group at the CPS Headquarters pointed out that it would be unnerving to progress too far with 'caution plus' unless it had legislative foundations because at any time the House of Lords could put a stop to the practice,

[100] Ibid., 96.   [101] Ibid., 94, para. 6.7.1.
[102] Royal Commission on Criminal Justice (1993) *Report*, op. cit., at ch. 5, para. 57. They recommended a legislative basis for cautioning under which national guidelines could be drawn up by the CPS and the police to promote nationwide consistency.
[103] Royal Commission on Criminal Procedure (1981) *Report*, op. cit., para. 7.59, 164, states 'We believe that the time has come for the use of the formal caution to be sanctioned in legislation and put on a more consistent basis...'

declaring it unlawful.[104] However, this is another recommendation by the RCCJ which appears to have been sacrificed in the legislative agenda, in favour of more pressing concerns.

However, in the shadow of such proposals for reform, the advantages of passing the responsibility for 'cautioning plus' sanctions up to the Crown Prosecutor should be considered. There are a number of reasons why this extended form of cautioning should be removed from the remit of the police. First, the level of accountability of the independent prosecution service is much higher than that of the police, and decision-making, which is reviewable by the DPP and the Attorney-General (who is accountable to Parliament) as well as the courts, is much more open and objective and therefore less prone to abuse. The fears expressed by NACRO and others (in their evidence to the Home Affairs Committee in 1990) about net-widening and other dangers of 'hidden decision-making' may be allayed if a more accountable body administered the caution.

Secondly, the types of penalty envisaged in the 'caution plus' system are those which, in all the other jurisdictions considered in the next chapters, are administered by the public prosecuting agency. Indeed, in giving evidence to the 1990 Home Affairs Committee, one of Her Majesty's Inspectors of Constabulary declared that he did 'not believe it should be a function of the police to administer this sort of caution'.[105] The assessment of cases requiring diversion to counselling and rehabilitation schemes is thought, in Scotland, to be better performed at the objective prosecution stage, away from the investigation, where the public prosecutor can ask for reports from, for example, psychiatrists and social workers who can assess the offender's suitability for such schemes. Despite this, the 1990 Home Affairs Committee were of the reverse opinion, recommending that the cautioning function, even in its extended form, should remain with the police, believing that this would have more effect on the offender than a caution administered by the CPS. There is certainly something to be said for the deterrent effect of a caution given by a uniformed, high-ranking police officer in the aura of a police station.

The final argument for re-allocating the cautioning responsibility to the Crown Prosecutor is that the caution could then become a condition of non-prosecution, thereby safeguarding the rights of due process of the accused. As long as the right to caution and the final prosecution decision remain in the separate hands of the police and the prosecutor, the two sanctions cannot be combined. There is no question of the police being empowered to make such conditions. Further, although the 'caution plus' as a condition of non-prosecution is to be used only in cases where the offender's consent has been obtained, similarly to a straight caution the

---

[105] Home Affairs Committee (1990) *Fourth Report*, op. cit., para. 56.

accused could be assured of his right to proceed to court by refusing to accept the penalty. This would probably result in the reversion to a simple caution, against which the offender has no appeal.

The CPS would prefer to take on the 'caution plus' decision-making role rather than leave it in the hands of the police, despite their reluctance, not least on the part of the current DPP, to enter into the realm of sentencing. This reluctance has prompted the CPS to support a non-discretionary, strictly circumscribed approach to cautioning. This would involve Parliament laying down statutory limits on the amount of fines to attached to a caution and on the types of offences and offenders to which a 'caution plus' should apply. Further, the CPS would be reluctant to take on the role of enforcing any different diversionary conditions attached to a caution, for example community penalties. Their hope is that the existing court fines office would take on responsibility for the collection of financial penalties. They presumably, therefore, would have been content with the recommendation of the RCCJ to expand the existing informal 'caution plus' system nationwide, but to leave the administration of such a system to the probation service and the police. It was felt that the police were the appropriate body to issue cautions, but where decisions were to be made as to the suitability of any rehabilitative scheme to a particular offender, the probation service was the body best qualified to make such decisions. They may well be right, although in other jurisdictions an all-round compromise has been made by giving the prosecutor the overall authority to divert an offender to a rehabilitation scheme, subject to detailed advice and reports from the probation services. The prosecutor is regarded as more accountable than the police at the pre-trial stage, and, after all, if we can trust judges to make appropriate decisions on these matters with the help of pre-sentence reports from the probation service, then there seems little reason why we cannot trust the independent and neutral prosecutor to do the same.

(d) Recommending Sentence

This form of direct influence on judicial sentencing, whereby the prosecutor has a legal duty to recommend an appropriate sentence in the course of conducting a prosecution, does not currently exist in English law. Indeed, several commentators have resolutely denied the constitutionality of such an influence. For example, the Code of Conduct of the Bar of England and Wales states: 'prosecuting counsel should not attempt by advocacy to influence the court in regard to sentence. If, however, an accused person is unrepresented, it is proper for prosecuting counsel to inform the court of any mitigating circumstances as to which he is instructed.' Further, Lord Scarman, in 1978, commented:

in some systems of law . . . the prosecution are entitled to make submissions as to the character or length of the sentence. In such systems of law it is possible for a bargain to be driven between the defence and the prosecution, but never, so far as my researches have gone, with the court itself. In our law the prosecution is not heard on sentence. This is a matter for the court, after considering whatever has to be said on behalf of an accused man.[106]

That the English prosecutor has no interest in sentencing, however, is simply not the case, as the later sections of this chapter will show. Ashworth has bluntly stated his rebuttal of this view: 'that generalisation is so plainly wrong that it does not deserve serious attention . . . It is contended here that, just as the defence plea in mitigation may urge the court to adopt or not to adopt certain sentences, so the prosecutor should draw the court's attention to any relevant principles of sentencing.'[107] Zellick has further argued for a reform of English prosecution procedure to this effect, so that the public interest element, as well as the defendant's interest, is represented at the sentencing stage.[108]

A recent Court of Appeal judgment has shown that the barriers described in these academic commentaries which emphatically restrict the role of prosecuting counsel in the sentencing process appear to be fading. In the case of *R. v. Hartrey*,[109] Mr Justice Wright in the Court of Appeal stated: 'It is the duty of both prosecuting counsel and defence counsel to inform themselves of the court's sentencing powers in any case in which they are instructed, to know what sentencing options are open to the trial judge and to correct him if he should make a mistake.'

It is clear from this judgment that the prosecutor is required to bear the issue of sentencing in mind during trial proceedings and to correct a judge who errs from his proper jurisdiction. In *Hartrey*, the trial judge exceeded his sentencing powers when issuing twenty-one concurrent 9-month sentences of imprisonment for breach of probation orders to the appellant. Prosecuting counsel were criticized in the Court of Appeal for not pointing this error out to the judge, which error was considered: 'unfortunately only too easy to [make] in the morass of legislation which governed the subject.' In this statement, Mr Justice Wright appears to be setting a duty for prosecuting counsel (and defence counsel) to guide the judge in the matter of sentencing (albeit negatively to avoid a mistake, and a costly appeal) where established judicial and legislative guidelines are confusing or contradictory.[110]

[106] *per* Lord Scarman in *R. v. Atkinson* [1978] 2 All ER 460.
[107] Ashworth, 'Prosecution and Procedure in Criminal Justice' [1979] *Crim. LR* 480–92 at 486.
[108] G. Zellick, 'The Role of Prosecuting Counsel in Sentencing' [1979] *Crim. LR* 493–503.
[109] [1993] *Crim. LR* 230.
[110] For further analysis of this case see Fionda, 'Prosecuting Counsel and the Sentencing Process: A Changing Debate', *Criminal Lawyer*, March/April 1993, 1–2.

The judicial comments in this case contradict those of Lord Scarman and others about the influence of prosecuting counsel in sentencing. Furthermore, the introduction of a more positive duty to recommend a sentence at trial is a very short step away from current procedure. Anthony Thompson QC has recently supported a more positive role for prosecuting counsel at trial, although also stopping short of supporting a prosecutor's duty to recommend a particular sentence:

In reality prosecutors have always had a lively interest in a trial's outcome.... Rather than leave the judges to try to get it right unaided, might it not now be appropriate for prosecuting counsel to tell the judge the sentencing bracket within which they contend the case falls, as commonly happens in other jurisdictions? ... Judges are independent enough not to be intimidated by suggestions from prosecutors. Such advice might help to eliminate some of the anomalies in sentencing, as well as help judges in getting the new sentencing provisions right.[111]

The arguments in favour of such a duty for the prosecutor in the Scottish context are put forward in detail in Chapter 3. In England, moreover, the argument is stronger, in that the duty to recommend a sentence may, to some extent, balance and make more sense of the power to appeal against sentence recently given to the prosecution service in s. 36 Criminal Justice Act 1988. It seems more logical (although not necessary) to be able to appeal against a sentence after having made a recommendation of sentence which has not been followed. Indeed, Lord Lane tentatively suggested the same during the House of Lords debates on the passage of the Criminal Justice Bill in 1987:

I respectfully suggest that the argument that the Crown should have no part in sentencing is not sustainable ... The Crown has a part to play—and it is a part which it plays increasingly now—in assisting the judge to determine, against the mass of sentencing options that are now on the statute book, what his powers are and to draw his attention to the guidelines, if there are any referrable to the particular case ... Indeed, the more the prosecution can play a part in the sentencing process—without, it hardly needs saying, demanding X years as the minimum —the less likely it is that the need will arise for the Crown to appeal against an over-lenient sentence.[112]

In mainland European jurisdictions, judges do not seem to have found recommendations of sentence to be an undue fetter on their independence; on the contrary they find such recommendations helpful given the sometimes complex, sometimes vague and unhelpful sentencing guidance they are given. The trial judge in *Hartrey* might certainly have benefited from this arrangement. It should be possible to implement a system of neutral advice and guidance for judges without interfering with their independent discretion.

[111] A. Thompson, 'A Say in Sentencing', *The Times*, 23 Feb. 1993.
[112] Lord Lane, House of Lords Debates, 26 Oct. 1987, vol. 490, col. 326.

There have been calls for an extension of the prosecutor's role in the similarly adversarial criminal justice system of Australia. This has met with vehement opposition in some states (particularly Queensland and the eastern states), where the very idea of the prosecutor being involved in the process of sentencing is regarded with a degree of distaste which matches the sentiments of judges and others in England. Nevertheless, some academic support the view that increasing the prosecutor's influence to include recommending a sentence at trial is a natural and positive step.[113] At present, the Australian Crown Prosecutor's role at trial is neutral, including the presentation of all relevant evidence, and extends only as far as the role of prosecuting counsel envisaged in *Hartrey*; that is guiding judges on the applicability of complicated sentencing legislation and assisting with selecting (though never recommending) an appropriate penalty. This principle was given judicial approval in Australia in *R. v. Tait and Bartley* in 1979:

> It would be unjust to a defendant to expose him to double jeopardy because of an error affecting his sentence, if the Crown's presentation of the case either contributed to the error or led the defendant to refrain from dealing with some aspect of the case which might have rebutted the suggested error. The Crown has been said not to be concerned with sentence . . . but when a statutory right of appeal is conferred upon the Crown, the Crown is under a duty to assist the Court to avoid appealable error.[114]

By way of explanation, Australian Crown Prosecutors have a right of appeal against sentence, similar to s. 36 Criminal Justice Act 1988, but the right includes not only unduly lenient but also unduly severe sentences.

One Australian commentator has noted that an increased sentencing role of the prosecutor, including recommending a sentence at trial, could have positive due process benefits in an adversarial criminal justice system in terms of balancing the 'sentencing' role of the prosecutor at the pre-trial stage with more open powers at trial:

> There is explicit recognition that the system of justice we employ necessitates adversarial debate in the sentencing as well as in the adjudicative stages of the criminal trial. The visibility of the adversarial debate on sentencing which . . . most recent Australian authorities call for, is in contrast with the concomitant low-visibility of the increased power in pre-trial negotiations. This has yet to be addressed in the cases calling for greater activism on sentence by Crown Prosecutors.[115]

These calls for a greater sentencing role for prosecutors in Australia support the view that such a role is not inconsistent with the independence of

---

[113] See, for example, I. Temby, 'The Role of the Prosecutor in the Sentencing Process' (1986) *Criminal Law Journal*, 10: 199–215.

[114] (1979) 2 ALR 473, at 476.

[115] I. G. Campbell, 'The Role of the Crown Prosecutor on Sentence' (1985) *Criminal Law Journal*, 9: 202, at 231.

the judge in an adversarial system. The public prosecutor, acting on behalf of the public interest in this adversarial debate, is not out of place in the sentencing arena; indeed, representations on behalf of the public interest at this stage can have positive benefits.

A little nearer to England and Wales, it is interesting to note that the prosecuting Attorney-General of Jersey is able to recommend a sentence at trial in the Royal Court of Jersey. In the Royal Court the prosecutor always concludes the summary of facts by recommending the imposition of a particular penalty in respect of the offence in question. The penalties requested are referred to as the 'conclusion' of the prosecutor, and the suggestion of those penalties is referred to as 'moving conclusions'. In 1965, the legal basis of this practice was challenged in the case of *Manley-Casimir* v. *Attorney-General for Jersey*[116] where the defendant claimed that the process of moving conclusions was a fundamental breach of criminal procedure. However, the Privy Council upheld the legality of the practice under the law of Jersey and further held that the English common law and practice had no application to Jersey. This remains today an anomaly in the British Isles, confined to Jersey, which perhaps English policy-makers should seriously consider in a more widespread application.

A common argument raised against increasing the prosecutor's influence over sentencing is that such a move would breach the principle of judicial independence; prosecutors would be treading on the judges' toes. It is accepted that judicial independence is an important constitutional principle which should not be compromised. However, other instances where prosecutors, defence lawyers or the executive have an involvement in the sentencing issue do not seem to excite such vehement disapproval. The arguments are not consistent. If the prosecutor can request sums of compensation, if the Home Secretary (and the Parole Board) can decide the upper limits of a life sentence,[117] why should *recommending* (not demanding or deciding upon) a sentence be so abhorrent?

This constitutional principle is generally stated in terms of avoiding 'undue influence' over judicial decisions and enabling judges to remain 'autonomous in their field'.[118] These concerns are clearly relevant to activities such as offering bribes to judges or persuading them to make judgments based on extra-legal criteria, and to political considerations and executive interference in the hiring and firing of judges. The question which needs to be considered in the context of this book, however, is

---

[116] [1965] *Crim. LR* 243.

[117] To be fair, it is acknowledged that many have criticised this executive involvement in the determination of the length of a sentence. See, for example, Committee on the Penalty for Homicide (1993) *Report of an independent inquiry into the mandatory life sentence for murder* (London: Prison Reform Trust).

[118] R. Brazier, *Constitutional Reform: Re-Shaping the British Political System* (Oxford, 1991).

whether the offering of expert advice as a means of guidance through complicated legislative provisions and precedent, often aimed at achieving greater consistency and fairness, should be included in this list of 'undue influences'. It is argued that it should not. Such expert advice does not exert *undue*, or the wrong sort of, influence on judges any more than the offering of pre-sentence reports by the probation service. Pre-sentence reports contain a recommendation of a sentence, amongst other information, made by a probation officer, and offered to the judge for his assistance in sentencing a particular case. To argue that such a recommendation by a prosecutor constitutes an executive interference with sentencing brings into question the constitutional position of the CPS. Are they part of the executive? In Europe, prosecutors are firmly situated in the judicial branch of government. In England, to suggest that prosecutors are part of the executive would mean questioning their rightful power to decide whom to prosecute, with what and where. This suggestion cannot, therefore, be right, because as part of the executive they would not be sufficiently objective or independent to carry out a quasi-judicial function. Therefore, by default, the CPS must fit into the judicial branch, like their European counterparts, since they are clearly also not of the parliamentary branch. Although their constitutional role has never been specified, there seems no other explanation but this. Influence on the level of punishment applicable to any particular case, offered by the prosecutor as a non-mandatory piece of advice, should be positively viewed as a form of assistance, rather than negatively as a form of corruption.

6. 'UNDULY LENIENT' APPEALS

A new power given to prosecutors under the Criminal Justice Act 1988, s. 36, has given them a direct influence over the sentence given by a court. Section 36 allows the prosecution to appeal against an 'unduly lenient sentence'. Under this power, the Attorney-General may refer cases of indictable offences to the Court of Appeal for review of a sentence he thinks is too low.

The possibility of this new power had been discussed for some time. In 1965 the Donovan Committee, an Interdepartmental Committee on the Court of Criminal Appeal, discussed the idea, but rejected it, most notably because the proposal would be 'a complete departure from our tradition that the prosecutor takes no part, or the minimum part, in the sentencing process'.[119] During the Parliamentary debates on this section of the Criminal Justice Bill 1988, the Lord Chancellor, Lord Mackay, echoed this

---

[119] Donovan Committee, *Report of Interdepartmental Committee on the Court of Criminal Appeal*, Cmnd 2755 (HMSO, 1965) at para. 196.

view. His arguments were similar to those of others who have objected to prosecutorial influence on other areas of sentencing, such as recommending a sentence: 'Prosecuting Counsel is not an avenging angel; he is an instrument of justice. It is not his business now, it will not, I hope, ever be his business in the future, whatever the result of this proposal . . . to ask the court to impose a particular sentence. Particularly, it is not his business to ask a court to impose a particular sentence in a direction of severity.'[120] More recently, the general pros and cons of a prosecution appeal procedure were fully expanded by Spencer in 1987.[121] In 1986 a government White Paper had considered the question of an appeal procedure against unduly lenient sentences, prior to the drawing up of the Criminal Justice Act 1988. The White Paper took up the government's concern that the public interest element in the sentencing of offenders should be given adequate airing in the courts and 'not left to the subject of uninformed public debate' in highly controversial cases.[122]

The White Paper suggested two ways in which sentences generally felt to be unduly lenient could be adequately reviewed or increased. First, they proposed a system, originally included in the Prosecution of Offences Bill 1985 but subsequently dropped at the Committee stage, whereby the Attorney-General would have the power to refer such cases to the Court of Appeal for review. The Court of Appeal would be given the authority to increase sentences in these cases. Secondly, they suggested that the sentencing guidelines of the Judicial Studies Board should be published under a statutory authority to regulate the sentencing decisions at the Crown Court level. Of these two options, the government gave their preference to the latter and proposed legislation to that effect.

It is interesting that, in the name of judicial independence, the government objected to the Attorney-General having a power to refer cases to the Court of Appeal, on the premise that this would involve the prosecution in sentencing to such an extent that the fetter on independent judicial discretion would be unconstitutional. However, their preferred proposal would provide little more than the existing system of judicial guidelines, although in a published form, and if the intention was to give any more force to such guidelines than under the previous system, that would have been just as much of a fetter on independent judicial discretion as the Attorney-General's power. Their objections to the latter would appear to reflect the 'blind' rejection of the prosecutor's involvement in the sentencing stage, whether in an advisory or appellate capacity, that is found in comments such as that of the Lord Chancellor quoted above.

---

[120] Lord Mackay, House of Lords Debates, 1987–8, vol. 490.
[121] J. R. Spencer, 'Do we need a prosecution appeal against sentence?' [1987] *Crim. LR* 724–36.
[122] Home Office White Paper, *Criminal Justice: Plans for Legislation*, Cmnd 9658 (HMSO, 1986) at para. 7, 6.

Nevertheless, section 36 of the Criminal Justice Act 1988 is evidently founded upon the first option in the White Paper, so that a significant new prosecution power to appeal against sentence, vastly enhancing the Crown Prosecutor's sentencing function, has arrived on the statute books rather more by accident than by carefully considered and planned policy. Whether the Attorney-General's power was included as a compromise during the Parliamentary debates on the Bill or as part of a change of heart by the government, it was certainly an unexpected and perhaps unintentional change in the law.

It was never anticipated by the legislators that the new appeal procedure would produce a flood of references; they envisaged only about 15 such cases per annum. However, in the first four years following implementation of s. 36, 98 referrals had been made, in most of which the sentences have been increased by the Court of Appeal. In fact, 57 of those cases involved an increase in the sentence; in 7 cases the sentence was unchanged, and in 1 case the sentence was reduced. In 3 cases leave to appeal was refused by the Court of Appeal, 13 cases were withdrawn, and 17 cases were outstanding.[123] By 5 February 1991, an 80 per cent success rate was reported in *The Times*, and most of the reported cases, involving offences such as incest,[124] robbery,[125] and causing death by dangerous driving,[126] provided an opportunity for the Court of Appeal to lay down guidelines on the sentencing of these offenders and to raise the 'tariff' in respect of the same. Indeed, in the *Attorney-General's Reference (No. 4 of 1989)* the Court of Appeal even laid down guidelines for assessing whether a sentence is unduly lenient for the purposes of a section 36 appeal, emphasizing that leniency should be assessed by reference to previous precedents, guideline cases, and all the circumstances of the case and should not be judged subjectively by the Court of Appeal, that is: the Court of Appeal should not increase a sentence simply because it is unduly lenient by their own standards. Furthermore, there should be a general presumption against increasing a sentence:

However, it must always be remembered that sentencing is an art rather than a science; that the trial judge is particularly well placed to assess the weight to be given to various competing considerations; and that leniency is not in itself a vice. That mercy should season justice is a proposition as soundly based in law as it is in literature.[127]

---

[123] Figures supplied by the CPS Headquarters, London, Feb. 1993. Stephen Shute quotes more recent figures in 'Prosecution Appeals Against Sentence: The First Five Years' (1994) *Modern Law Review* 745–72 and Table 1.

[124] *Attorney-General's Reference No. 4 of 1989* [1989] 3 All ER 571.

[125] *Attorney-General's Reference No. 2 of 1989* (1989) 11 Cr. App. R. (S) 481.

[126] *Attorney-General's Reference No. 3 of 1989*, and *Attorney-General's Reference No. 5 of 1989* (1989) 11 Cr. App. R. (S) 486.

[127] *Attorney-General's Reference No. 4 of 1989* [1989] 3 All ER 571, *per* Lord Chief Justice Lane at 46.

A slightly different test was laid down by the Court of Appeal in *Attorney-General's Reference No. 5 of 1989*[128] which states that the judge must, rather than imposing an 'unreasonable' sentence, have made an error or imposed a sentence which, if allowed to stand, would diminish the confidence of the public in the criminal justice system. Although public opinion may sway the Attorney-General's decision to refer the case to the Court of Appeal for review, it is interesting that it also becomes relevant in this test and affects the sentencing decision. Public opinion is not deemed a relevant criterion in the first-instance decision on penalty, and neither is it relevant in the prosecutor's decision to proceed with a case (public *interest*, it is argued above and in Chapter 7, is very different from public *opinion*). If a prosecution were brought on the basis that public opinion, rather than public interest, required it, then inclusion of that criterion in the ultimate sentencing decision would make sense. In England, however, this is not the case, except to the extent that the prevalence of an offences may weigh in favour of a prosecution. Furthermore, sentencing principles in the Criminal Justice Act 1991 specifically deters judges from sentencing according to wider public concerns.[129] The credibility of the criminal justice system, and the response to (often ill-informed) public opinion, are considerations for policy-makers rather than practitioners.[130]

In this way, the prosecution power to appeal against an unduly lenient sentence can have both a direct influence on the sentence in question and a more indirect influence on other similar cases where an appeal results in an increase of the tariff.[131] The prosecution power to appeal against unduly *severe* sentences, as held by German and Dutch prosecutors, may have an even more beneficial indirect influence in lowering the tariff for certain offences. However, under the existing procedure in England and Wales, a case is referred to the Court of Appeal for complete review and the Court is at liberty to decrease the sentence as well as increase it, even though the appeal was brought on the 'unduly lenient' grounds.

The procedure of reviewing cases for appeal is not exactly clear, and only a thorough analysis of all the s. 36 appeals conducted since 1988 will show whether the CPS select particular types of cases with a view to making a policy statement on sentencing levels for individual offences. However, a number of basic principles of procedure can be elicited from the statutory provisions of the Criminal Justice Act 1988 and from recent practice. First, the power relates exclusively to indictable only offences, at the most serious end of the scale of criminality, although arguments have

---

[128] S. Shute, (1994) op. cit. 755.

[129] Sections 1(2)(a), 2(2)(a), and 2(2)(b).

[130] C.f. the concerns for credibility among European prosecutors and judges, discussed in Chapters 6 and 7 below.

[131] For a full analysis of the case law emanating from the s. 36 appeal procedure, see R. Henham, 'Attorney-General's references and Sentencing Policy' [1994] *Crim. LR* 499.

been put forward suggesting the extension of the power to cover cases which are triable either way.[132] Secondly, potential appeal cases are usually selected by Crown Prosecutors who will seek the advice of prosecuting counsel before referring the case to the CPS Headquarters. From there the case will be brought to the attention of the Attorney-General who will consider referring it to the Court of Appeal. There appear to be no published criteria relating to the degree of undue leniency required of a sentence before it is considered for appeal, although sentencing guidelines, judgments, and other precedents are referred to. Evidently, the discretion of the Attorney-General is central to the selection of suitable cases. Finally, the s. 36 appeals may be selected by the Attorney-General in response to a complaint from the media, a Member of Parliament, a member of the public, or the police[133] that the sentence in a particular case was too low. However, as yet the only piece of in-depth research which has been conducted into the operation of the power to appeal against unduly lenient sentences and its effectiveness in terms of influencing the sentencing process has found that the procedure has been unable to meet its potential as a sentencing reform because so few cases are referred and the procedure is so limited.[134]

Since this power is the first direct form of influence given to Crown Prosecutors over judicial sentencing, the question of whether it will lead to a widening of the prosecutor's direct powers of influence in England and Wales should be raised. It has already been mentioned that the role of prosecuting counsel at trial has been accepted as including a duty to assist the judge in finding his way through the 'morass' of sentencing legislation. However, Allan Green QC, commenting on the introduction of the s. 36 appeal procedure, has suggested that a more enhanced sentencing role for prosecutors might eventually follow on from this first, tentative step:

I do not think it is appropriate to confine the prosecutor's role in our sentencing process at trial within its existing limits and I do not believe that a change to a more active role at first instance must inevitably flow from the recent legislation. But at a time of rapid and profound change in our legal institutions, no one could confidently rule out radical developments in the prosecutor's role in sentencing at the trial itself.[135]

---

[132] D. A. Thomas, 'The Criminal Justice Act 1988—(4) The Sentencing Provisions' [1989] *Crim. LR* 43–55 at 53.

[133] In a recently reported example, the police are planning to put pressure on the CPS to review the sentence given to a 15-year-old boy after his conviction for rape. A £500 compensation order that the boy was ordered to pay to his victim so that she could 'have a good holiday' was considered by the police to be 'inadequate'. See I. MacKinnon, 'Police to seek review of boy's rape sentence', *Independent*, 8 Feb. 1993.

[134] R. Henham, 'Attorney-General's references and Sentencing Policy' (1994), op. cit.

[135] A. Green, 'Asking for more? References of Unduly Lenient Sentences' in (1990) *Current Law Problems*, 50: 55–75.

These views of a former DPP are an encouraging development in the debate over the legitimate sentencing role of the prosecutor, although it remains to be seen whether the new DPP will take the CPS any further down the 'sentencing road' in the next few years. Arguments about fettering the independence of the judiciary appear to be a major stumbling block to further reforms such as allowing the prosecutor to recommend a sentence after conviction. However, these could be seen as a convenient disguise for reasons based purely on conservatism. Could it not equally be said that the power to appeal against unduly lenient sentences constitutes such a fetter? Does this not involve the prosecutor interfering in the issue of sentencing at the trial or post-trial stage? Whatever fears judges or policy-makers might have had about this fetter on judicial independence were kept under wraps and were evidently overcome when this provision passed through Parliament.

7. INDIRECT INFLUENCES ON SENTENCING

(a) Mode of Trial

In cases of triable either way offences, the court can ask the Crown Prosecutor during committal proceedings for his opinion on mode of trial: summary or Crown Court. The magistrates will already have formed their own opinion on this matter and they will then also ask the defendant whether he wishes to elect for Crown Court trial or summary trial. The defendant's preference for a particular mode of trial will usually be upheld, unless both the prosecutor and the magistrates themselves agree to differ with the defendant, in which case the defendant's wishes can be over-ridden. Since the mode of trial pre-determines the maximum sentencing powers of the court hearing the case the Crown Prosecutor has an indirect influence over sentence here. Research conducted by Moxon and Hedderman in a number of Crown Courts in England has shown that mode of trial does affect the eventual sentence. Although in many cases the Crown Court will issue a penalty that a magistrate could have imposed, in a significant number of cases the Crown Court was more severe than magistrates in their sentencing of similar cases.[136] However, the prosecutor's opinion is merely used in a consultative way, and if it does sway the mode of trial decision, the *extent* to which this affects the sentence may be limited.

However, a recent Home Office consultation paper on committal proceedings[137] has proposed changes to the present system of deciding on

---

[136] D. Moxon, and C. Hedderman, 'Mode of Trial Decisions and Sentencing Differences between Courts' (1994) *Howard Journal*, 33: 97–108.

[137] Home Office, *Consultation Paper on the Future of Committal Proceedings* (HMSO, 1989).

mode of trial, which will have the effect of giving the prosecutor a more dominant role in the matter. Option 2 proposed by the Home Office recommends that in giving notice to the defence of their intention to proceed to trial, the Crown Prosecutor should, in triable either way cases, also state whether the trial would take place in the magistrates' court or the Crown Court. Whilst the defendant would retain his right to elect Crown Court trial within a specific notice period, this proposal effectively shifts the responsibility for the mode of trial decision away from the magistrates' court and to the CPS who, the consultation paper claims, are 'better qualified to take these decisions . . . such decisions no longer require the attention of magistrates in a way that may have been necessary before the establishment of the Crown Prosecution Service'.[138] The government expressed interest in this option for reform but gave it little further consideration. If the proposal had been implemented, it would have put the Crown Prosecutor in a much stronger position to influence sentencing from this direction.

The Criminal Justice Act 1991 further restricts the role of the magistrate in this area of decision-making. Section 25, which deals with committals for sentence, re-drafts s. 38 of the Magistrates' Courts Act 1980, so that the decision to commit an offender for sentence in the Crown Court is more offence-based. Where the court considers that the offence in question was so serious that greater punishment should be imposed than the magistrates have power to inflict, or where a violent or sexual offence is committed by an adult offender over 21, the magistrates are entitled to pass the case to the Crown Court for the purpose of sentencing. As a result, the prosecutor's role in deciding which charges to bring against a particular suspect at the outset may have a significant impact on the ultimate sentence passed, where the choice of charge is now also a determining factor itself in the 'mode of trial' decision.

Also, s. 53 of the Criminal Justice Act 1991 allows the DPP to transfer certain cases involving child witnesses or victims to the Crown Court without a prior 'mode of trial' decision by the magistrates, where it is in the interests of the welfare of the child to do so (for example, where there is an urgency to get cases before the Crown Court, but *not* merely where the Crown Prosecutor seeks to avoid a child giving evidence in committal proceedings). However, 'the DPP' has been interpreted as meaning any Crown Prosecutor acting under the authority of the DPP (Section 1(7), Prosecution of Offences Act 1985), so the prosecutor will have a greater impact in those exceptional cases in respect of the mode of trial decision. Further, this decision to transfer cases is not subject to appeal (s. 53(4)) although it may be challenged by judicial review.

---

[138] Ibid., 61.

The present DPP, Barbara Mills QC, has taken the debate over the role of the prosecutor in the mode of trial decision a step further. In giving evidence to the All-Party Home Affairs Select Committee recently, she argued that the decision should rest entirely with the Crown Prosecutor in view of the large proportion of defendants (70 per cent) who plead guilty to charges having previously elected Crown Court trial. This, she argued, 'was not helpful to anyone' and 'time and money might be saved . . . by allowing the CPS itself to pick the trial court'.[139]

The RCCJ also made recommendations on mode of trial, which, if implemented,[140] would enhance the prosecutor's influence in this area and minimize the role of the magistrate. Essentially, the Commission recommended that the defendant should lose his *right* to elect a Crown Court trial. Instead, the defence could still make submissions about the mode of trial decision, but the Crown Prosecutor's proposal would carry more weight. Where the defendant elects a jury trial and the prosecutor agrees that this would be appropriate, the case would be heard in the Crown Court. Similarly, where the prosecutor and the defence agree that a trial in the magistrates' court would be appropriate, that is where the case will be heard. However, the magistrates would only become involved as an arbiter where the defendant disagrees with the prosecutor's proposal; in these cases the defendant will no longer be able to insist on a jury trial.[141]

This reasoning behind this recommendation again involves savings of time and money. The idea is to reduce the use made of magistrates' time in mode of trial proceedings; the prosecutor is effectively being charged with more responsibility here to ease the burden on the magistrates' court. However, in the process of enhancing the prosecutor's responsibility here, 'admirably' justified on economic grounds, the RCCJ have swept away an important safeguard of the defendant's rights of natural justice. This aspect of the recommendation did not overly concern the Commission, devoting only two short paragraphs to the strong objections which they had received in evidence.[142] This was one of the few aspects of their report which, not surprisingly, generated an enormous amount of criticism and media attention. Lord Taylor LCJ, for example, has spoken widely on the demerits of this recommendation, arguing that the Commission have

[139] J. McLeod, 'CPS pushes for new trial powers', *Law Society Gazette*, No. 40, 4 Nov. 1992, 5. See also F. Gibb, 'DPP says defendant's right to jury trial should be scrapped' (1993) *The Times*, 21 April 1993, where the DPP again campaigns for an increased role for Crown Prosecutors in the mode of trial decision, in order to reduce the number of cases where defendants (in her view) unnecessarily make too much use of scarce resources by electing Crown Court trial in inappropriate cases.

[140] They have thus far been ignored and are not in the Criminal Justice and Public Order Bill 1994.

[141] Royal Commission on Criminal Justice (1993) *Report*, op. cit., recommendation No. 114.

[142] Ibid., 88, paras. 17 and 18.

unjustifiably removed a 'fundamental right' of the defendant to be tried before his peers.[143] Ashworth, on the other hand, argues that the defendant's existing right to insist on Crown Court trial is not an inalienable 'fundamental right' and further argues that the advantages of a jury trial are often exaggerated.[144] This is not the place for such discussions, but the recommendation does provide an example of policy-makers' over-enthusiasm for increasing efficiency and productivity at the expense of the civil liberties (fundamental or otherwise) of the accused. Very often the prosecutor becomes enmeshed in these policy debates, because they are perceived as concerning means by which judges or magistrates can be relieved of much work which would ultimately increase the responsibility of the prosecutor. Expanding the role of the latter must, therefore, be carefully considered in this respect, rather than being blindly accepted as a progressive, and therefore a positive step. There are negative implications, and these will be discussed further in Chapter 7.

(b) Charging

A further indirect influence over the sentencing decision of the court is the prosecutor's ability to reduce or increase the charges brought by the police, and to accept guilty pleas in return for reducing a set of charges. Michael Shea's research found that the charge presented to magistrates often affected their sentencing practice, although this phenomenon was more pronounced with certain offences. This also appeared to be true where magistrates were aware that an alternative charge could have been brought, and even where they felt that that alternative charge may have been more appropriate.[145] This practice of 'charge selection' is particularly relevant to offences such as theft and deception, assaults, public order, and indecency where the range of alternative charges which could apply to the circumstances of the case is wide. The 1992 Code for Crown Prosecutors endorsed a practice which, although nothing like the widespread practice of American prosecutors, may be described as plea-bargaining. Section 12 of the old Code imposed a duty to keep the numbers of charges as low as possible and authorized the reduction of charges provided 'the charges laid . . . adequately reflect the gravity of the defendant's conduct'. In this respect, the public interest elements of saving court costs and time are

---

[143] Lord Chief Justice, Lord Taylor, in a speech to the 'Criminal Justice after the Royal Commission' Conference, London, Oct. 1993.

[144] Ashworth, 'The Royal Commission on Criminal Justice: (3) Plea, Venue and Discontinuance' [1993] *Crim. LR* 830–40, at 832.

[145] M. Shea, 'A Study of the Effect of the Prosecutor's Choice of Charge on Magistrates' Sentencing behaviour' (1974) *Brit. Jo. Criminology*, 14: 269–272.

weighed against the full enforcement of the criminal law.[146] However, the new Code has backed down in its approach to plea-bargaining and tends to discourage the practice. Prosecutors are now to choose charges which 'reflect the seriousness of the offending'; 'give the court adequate sentencing powers'; and 'enable the case to be presented in a clear and simple way'. Paragraph 7.2 specifically discourages charging practice which is based on the purpose of encouraging a guilty plea from the defendant by over-charging. This will not necessarily prevent the prosecutor from negotiating a plea with the defendant; it simply outlaws the practice of indirectly manipulating the defendant's plea without reference to him. However, the small amount of open guidance given on the subject of the extent of plea-bargaining which is allowed has disappeared from public view, possibly again to the more private Policy Manuals. This runs contrary to the general view of the RCCJ and the DPP that the practice should be more open and less clandestine, as discussed below.

Attention was given to this 'plea-bargaining' role in the evidence given to the 1990 Home Affairs Committee. Some witnesses, such as the Law Society, were content with the extent to which Crown Prosecutors were reducing charges to effect a guilty plea or to ensure a summary trial, whilst others, such as the Magistrates' Association and the Police Superintendents' Association were rather more alarmed at the practice: 'Plea-bargaining is a further cause for complaint . . . we suspect that the interests of justice are not being considered here, simply the questions of expense and convenience and a desire to avoid contested trials . . . it is plain that a "deal" has been done between the Crown and the defence.'[147] This statement was made notwithstanding that the Code, at that time, explicitly allowed for such 'deals' to be done in the interests of cost-effectiveness. Indeed, the Home Affairs Committee Report agreed with the principle that the expense and the capriciousness of outcome of trial by jury should be avoided where possible and recommended that the practice of charge reduction be increased.[148]

The RCCJ also considered the issue of plea-bargaining. This was the first time in English criminal justice history that the practice was considered openly by an official policy-making body (apart from the indirect reference to it in the 1992 Code for Crown Prosecutors). The Commission recommended that the Crown Prosecutor be involved in an open process of negotiation, initiated by the defence, in order to reduce charges where

---

[146] For an analysis of the application of sentencing principles by the Crown Prosecutor in choosing which charge to bring, see A. von Hirsch, and A. Ashworth, (eds.), *Principled Sentencing* (Edinburgh, 1992), 396–9.
[147] Home Affairs Committee (1990) *Memoranda of Evidence*, op. cit., 71.
[148] Home Affairs Committee (1990) *Fourth Report*, op. cit., para. 43.

this would encourage a guilty plea.[149] This was clearly aimed at reducing the number of full trials, and of 'cracked trials' where the defendant pleads guilty at the last moment before the trial begins. The process had clearly been operating behind closed doors in the past, but was a taboo subject for policy-makers until recently. Before the Commission reported, Barbara Mills had already recommended that the process become more open, simply to avoid the hypocrisy of denying the existence of a valuable process which 'occurs in the privacy of hallways, conference rooms, and judges' chambers'.[150]

On the other hand, McConville and Mirsky have argued that to 'open the closet' on the plea-bargaining process may be hasty, and may additionally reveal its hidden dangers such as the pressure it places on offenders to plead guilty where they might otherwise prefer a trial which assumes their innocence.[151] The 1994 Home Affairs Committee also addressed this when they took oral evidence from the DPP. They were particularly concerned with allegations that the CPS had been known to reduce charges 'on the grounds of economy',[152] despite the fact that this is exactly what the RCCJ had recommended. Mrs Mills was keen to deny this and argued that the principal reason for reducing charges in any case was merely that there had been a change in the evidential circumstances and that the new charge was the most appropriate in the light of this change. This reflects the general distaste in this country for 'grounds of economy' to justify any form of decision making, which is curious given the heavy influence that these economies had on the recommendations of the RCCJ generally.

The public debate over the legality of plea-bargaining has centred around these two opposing views: safeguards of the offender's rights to a fair hearing, a presumption of innocence, and a fair trial must be weighed against the perceived need to economize the resources of the criminal justice system. As with the mode of trial decision, the power of prosecutors to influence the trial and sentencing process must be carefully balanced with sufficient safeguards of the rights mentioned above. An obsession with economizing can render policy-makers blind to the consequences of their reforms on the civil liberties of the defendant and could render the new powers given to prosecutors unconscionable. A compromise needs to be found between such unconscionable powers and a system which allows the prosecutor to assist with the realistic aim of safeguarding precious resources.

[149] Royal Commission on Criminal Justice (1993) *Report*, op. cit., recommendations 156–63.
[150] Barbara Mills QC, DPP, quoted in M. McConville, and C. Mirsky, 'The Skeleton of Plea-Bargaining' (1992) *NLJ* 142: 1373–81.
[151] Ibid., See also J. Baldwin, and M. McConville *Negotiated Justice: Pressures to Plead Guilty* (Oxford, 1977).
[152] Home Affairs Committee (1994), *Minutes of Evidence*, op. cit., at 42.

(c) Remand

The prosecutor's decision to oppose bail, or to seek bail upon conditions, may also have an indirect effect upon sentence where the sentencing judge has regard to the remand in custody or bail ordered at the pre-trial stage. In this decision-making area the prosecutor's impact, not only on the sentencing process but, further, on the level of imprisonment, is not insignificant, as the experience in Germany in the latter half of the 1980s has shown (see Chapter 5).

In order to assist the Crown Prosecutor with his decision, and to provide sufficient information to reassure him that bail is appropriate, a pilot Bail Information Scheme was set up in the Inner London area by the VERA Institute of Justice in 1988, whereby a prosecutor was provided with a probation service report of the defendant's suitability for bail in cases where the police had opposed bail in their report.[153] The scheme was reported a success, both by prosecutors who found the information, often not forthcoming from the police, invaluable in their decision-making, and by the report of the Scheme which noted an increase in the use of bail by magistrates without any undue increase in the bailees' failure to appear at court. VERA also suggested that those concerned with the costs of such schemes could rest easy; the savings made in the provision of remand accommodation more than covered the cost of this scheme. The 1990 Home Affairs Committee Report and the RCCJ Report even recommended an expansion of such schemes throughout the country.[154]

8. The Role of the Crown Prosecutor in the English Criminal Justice Process

(a) The Neutrality of the Prosecutor

The neutral position of the Crown Prosecutor, both in general decision-making and in the trial process itself, was emphasized at the creation of the CPS. The separation of the investigation and prosecution processes meant that the CPS, as an independent body, would objectively assess the evidence gathered by the police, would consider both the legal position and the policy considerations in the case, and weigh up the reasons for or against prosecution. Hence, the legal position is that the prosecutor is not

---

[153] See C. Stone, (1988) *Public Interest Case Assessment. Volume 2 of the Final Report on the Probation Initiative "Diversion from Custody and Prosecution"*. See also Sanders, 'From Suspect to Trial' in M. Maguire, R. Morgan, and R. Reiner, *The Oxford Handbook of Criminology* (Oxford, 1994) who analyses the PICA Scheme on 804.

[154] Home Affairs Committee (1990) *Fourth Report*, op. cit., at para. 124. See also Royal Commission on Criminal Justice (1993) *Report*, op. cit., recommendation No. 112.

interested in securing a conviction at all costs, but rather, as Ashworth suggests: 'the proper motivation of a prosecutor has often been likened to that of a Minister of Justice . . . the aim of the prosecutor is to secure the result to which, on his view, the evidence fairly leads.'[155] This is a role intentionally opposite to the perception of the 'over-zealous' police officer who set out to secure a conviction on the strength of his own investigation, regardless of the sufficiency of evidence or any considerations of public interest.

The extent to which this neutral role fits into the adversarial nature of the English criminal justice process where the 'trial is essentially a contest between the prosecution and the defence',[156] is debatable. The CPS are charged with the duty to ensure that the court is furnished with all the relevant evidence which might be probative in proving innocence or guilt. To this extent, the English prosecutor's role is becoming more akin to the neutral one performed by their European counterparts in inquisitorial justice systems. As the CPS themselves have stated: 'The notion . . . that opposing parties generally look after their own interests is an over-simplification of the present system and one which necessarily creates a false impression because it ignores the prosecution's duty of disclosure and their role in presenting the facts.'[157] The CPS, for the moment, have declined to call for a major change to the inquisitorial system for various reasons, principally concerning the increasingly active role of the judge in the gathering of evidence. Indeed, the neutrality of the prosecutor is an aspect of the European inquisitorial systems which may beneficially be incorporated into the English accusatorial system without any major upheaval. This question will be further discussed in Chapter 7 below.

(b) Independence

The independence of the CPS from the police was a central feature of the new system and has been welcomed by all branches of the criminal justice process, including the Law Society, pressure groups such as NACRO and the Howard League, the Criminal Bar Association, and the judiciary.[158] However, it was this independence which, as mentioned above, caused a good deal of resentment and hostility on the part of the police.

It is submitted here, however, that the CPS, being still reliant on the police to make the initial decision to prosecute, is not as independent as

[155] Ashworth, 'Prosecution and Procedure in Criminal Justice' [1979] *Crim. LR* 81–492 at 482.
[156] Crown Prosecution Service (1991) *Evidence to Royal Commission*, op. cit., para. 7.2.2, p. 102.
[157] Ibid., para. 7.2.7, 104.
[158] Home Affairs Committee (1990) *Memoranda of Evidence*, op. cit.

it could usefully be. The 1990 Home Affairs Committee have recommended that the Crown Prosecutor's independence should be further fettered by a duty to explain in all cases, in written as well as oral form, why a particular charge has been dropped or reduced.[159] A degree of consultation on this point will enhance a harmonious relationship between the CPS and the police and will greatly assist the police in setting informal rules of practice in making decisions, but, as the government have agreed, to impose this duty on the Crown Prosecutor in respect of all cases referred would be unduly burdensome on the service as a whole.[160]

Some have argued that the independence of the CPS has meant very little at all since the Service was established. Sanders, for example, suggested that in practice Crown Prosecutors would be faced, when deciding whether to drop proceedings already initiated by the police, with a choice between the Devil and the deep blue sea. That choice, according to Sanders, is either to continue with dubious charges in order to preserve a harmonious relationship with the police or to 'drop them in it' by effectively reversing their decisions.[161] It has subsequently been found that prosecutors often fail to discontinue cases for other reasons directly stemming from their limited independence.

The procedure whereby the Crown Prosecutor only receives the files of cases which have already been screened by the police and where the prosecution system has already been instigated means that the momentum for prosecution already exists, and the prosecutor has only a secondary discretion, to drop the case or not. This was discussed above, and Gelsthorpe and Giller have found evidence that the reports received by prosecutors from the police are likely to be heavily weighted in favour of prosecution. In a system where the prosecutor becomes involved in a case at a stage when the odds are already stacked in favour of prosecution, the objective and independent review of files which is expected of them is a difficult duty to carry out. Full independence of the CPS requires that (*a*) they are enabled to review all but the most trivial unsolved criminal cases; (*b*) that they are furnished with as much material evidence and information about a case as possible; which in turn requires (*c*) that their relationship with the police is harmonious enough to encourage full co-operation in the collation of files; and (*d*) that the CPS are free from fetters on their discretion by the police. The distinction of their respective roles has been further blurred by the recent High Court decision in *R. v. Croydon Justices,* ex parte *Dean*.[162] It could be argued that these necessary conditions

---

[159] Home Affairs Committee (1990) *Fourth Report* op. cit., para. 32.
[160] Home Office, (1990) *Government Reply to Fourth Report of Home Affairs Committee,* op. cit., p. 2.
[161] Sanders, 'An Independent Crown Prosecution Service?' [1986] *Crim. LR* 16–27, at 24.
[162] [1993] 3 All E.R. 129.

for the operation of a truly independent CPS have never existed; in any event the *Dean* decision has placed a large question mark over whether they operate with any meaningful independence now, if the courts are willing to allow police decisions to override those of the CPS and to bind Crown Prosecutors in their decision-making.

9. ACCOUNTABILITY

The CPS as a whole is accountable, through the Attorney-General, to Parliament; the Attorney-General is answerable to the House for the general conduct of prosecution policy. However, the extent of an individual Crown Prosecutor's discretion must also be balanced against an acceptable level of public accountability; an important, if difficult, exercise. The introduction of the public interest criteria in the Code for Crown Prosecutors has significantly widened the prosecutor's discretion. In an effort to balance this increased power, the 1990 Home Affairs Committee called for an external monitor to review CPS decisions in individual cases. This was not a new idea, indeed the Philips Commission had previously suggested that 'the [Home Secretary] should also establish a prosecutions inspectorate within his department. This would inspect and report to the [Home Office] and to the police and prosecutions authority on the organization and policies of, and the discharge of their functions, by individual Crown Prosecutors' departments, and advise Crown Prosecutors.'[163] Shortly after the publication of the Home Affairs Committee report in 1990, the government reacted by announcing plans for a national inspectorate to monitor the decisions of Crown Prosecutors.[164] The CPS Field Director (Operations) will monitor the use of the prosecutor's discretion to maintain regional consistency of decision-making and to prevent abuses of power.

It is interesting to note that no such a national inspectorate has been created in the Dutch and German prosecution systems where the prosecutor has an almost unlimited discretion to dispose of cases in a wide variety of ways. With such an external monitor already in existence in England and Wales, the CPS will be in a prime position to consider the further expansion of prosecutorial discretion and the implementation of further alternatives to prosecution, without the anxieties which arise in the Netherlands and Germany over the accountability of the public prosecutor.

As well as the national inspectorate, the Crown Prosecutor has been subject to another form of accountability. Recent years have seen Crown

[163] Royal Commission on Criminal Procedure (1981) *Report*, op. cit., para. 7.61.
[164] See Pienaar, 'National Inspectorate to Monitor CPS Decisions', *Independent*, 18 July 1990 and, Home Office (1990) *Government Reply to Home Affairs Committee Fourth Report*, op. cit., 13.

Prosecutors' decisions increasingly brought before the courts for judicial review. There is no formal appeal procedure, via the courts, for an offender or victim who is aggrieved with a decision made by the CPS, as there is in the Netherlands and Germany, for example. Furthermore, the CPS is not, in theory, accountable to the courts, in the sense that the courts are not in a position to direct a Crown Prosecutor as to how to exercise his discretion (although they may be entitled to criticize him when an unfair decision has been made).[165] However, the use of judicial review seems to be changing this position. The *Dean* case discussed above, is one such case where the courts have reviewed a CPS decision, albeit in that case on the basis that the committal to the Crown Court, following a Crown Prosecutor's decision to prosecute, was an abuse of process. Prosecutions can indeed be stayed for various reasons, including undue delay, as an abuse of process, following guideline decisions such as *Attorney-General's Reference No. 1 of 1990*.[166] The courts have, though, directly reviewed decisions of Crown Prosecutors to prosecute[167] as well as decisions not to prosecute.[168]

More recently, the High Court has scrutinized a Crown Prosecutor's consideration of public interest in judicial review proceedings. In an unreported case heard on 18 February 1994, the High Court held that a decision not to prosecute a police officer for unlawful sexual acts committed on his wife should be overturned on the basis that the public interest had not been properly considered, and the DPP was ordered to reconsider the public interest considerations in the case.[169] As stated above, no formal appeal procedure has been developed to deal specifically with the decisions of the Crown Prosecutor which are deemed unjust, unlawful, or inappropriate by an interested party. Neither do the CPS have a formal internal appeals process whereby a grievance can be reported to a senior prosecutor (although the DPP has been keen to publicize the fact that she is willing to investigate any cases which cause controversy or grievances).[170] However, the existing common law procedures of judicial review, whereby the decisions of any public body can be judged for fairness and reasonableness, may well provide the necessary framework of a system of accountability necessary for the expansion of the prosecutor's role.

It will be shown in the next chapters how a powerful and influential role

---

[165] See Mansfield, and Peay (1987) op. cit., at 31.

[166] [1992] 3 All ER 169. See further A. Choo, *Abuse of Process and Judicial Stays of Criminal Proceedings* (Oxford, 1993).

[167] *R. v. Inland Revenue Commissioners, ex parte Mead* [1993] 1 All ER 772.

[168] *R. v. General Council of the Bar, ex parte Percival* [1990] 3 All ER 137. See further, C. Hilson 'Discretion to Prosecute and Judicial Review' [1993] *Crim. LR* 739.

[169] Case reported in Campbell, 'DPP "wrong" to reject sex assault case', *Guardian*, 19 Feb. 1994.

[170] See CPS (1993) *Statement of Purpose and Values*, at 11.

for the prosecutor must be counterbalanced with a sufficient system of accountability. A wide and general accountability to Parliament is not enough to ensure that individual decisions are made fairly and equitably. However, if the English Crown Prosecutor were to be given enhanced sentencing powers, there are some mechanisms in place which enable judges to judge the quasi-judges.

10. CONCLUSION

The rather insular attitudes of English policy-makers and practitioners towards reform of the prosecution system has been a major fetter on progress. For example, John Timmons, a Prosecuting Solicitor under the old prosecution system, commented: 'Principle should come before expediency. No sensible person ignores waste or extravagance, but surely the true worth of a system of criminal law is to be found by posing the question—"does it do right between men?" not—"does it satisfy the performance indicators within the parameters which have been delineated at a one-to-one interface with the Treasury?"'[171] This is indicative of a reluctance to face up to the necessary characteristics and priorities of a modern criminal justice system. Saving costs and time are now recognized as facts of life in the English system, which is overburdened, under-funded and allegedly at 'crisis point'. The report of the RCCJ is littered with references to the need to make economies, and it has been pointed out throughout this chapter that many of their recommendations aim to do this by increasing the influence of the Crown Prosecutor. The other reforms of the prosecutor's role suggested in this chapter are aimed at using the prosecutor's central position in the criminal justice machinery to achieve such cost-effectiveness, particularly in view of the improbability that radical, modernizing reforms will take place within the judiciary or the police in this country.

All this, however, must be carefully balanced with the need to protect the fundamental civil liberties of the defendant. The RCCJ appeared to be so concerned with efficiency that they tended to ride roughshod over some of those civil liberties. This is not advocated here; rather a rational programme of reform needs to be carefully considered so that the full potential of the prosecutor to assist in creating a fair, efficient, and consistent criminal justice process is achieved.

Admittedly, the enhanced sentencing role of the prosecutor which has been discussed here is not easy to achieve within the confines of the present,

---

[171] J. Timmons, 'The Crown Prosecution Service in Practice' [1986] *Crim. LR* 28–32, at 28.

often rather retrogressive system without a major overhaul of current attitudes and practices. For example, the proposal that prosecutors might serve some useful purpose in recommending sentences at trial could never be effectively implemented in this country unless the views and professional respect of the judiciary towards Crown Prosecutors were radically changed. In reality this would be virtually impossible without a substantial retirement and re-recruitment programme, or unless a career judiciary were considered for this country, which is even more unlikely.

Nevertheless, the prosecutor's potential for reform to achieve the aims and objectives of a modern, efficient, and fair justice system should not be denied by ill-justified objections to the principle of quasi-judicial sentencing powers for the prosecutor. In this respect, the policy-making efforts in England and Wales compare unfavourably with those of our European counterparts. The haphazard history of the public prosecutor in this country, and the piecemeal and *ad hoc* reform of his or her role lies in stark contrast to the organized and coherent criminal law policy of the systems discussed in the next three chapters. The introduction of section 36 of the Criminal Justice Act 1988, giving the Attorney-General the power to appeal in the Court of Appeal against unduly lenient sentences, is a clear example of the 'accidental' and fragmented progress of the development of the Crown Prosecutor's sentencing function. Similarly, much of that sentencing function is indirect and arose as a consequence of other criminal law procedures, for example the increased importance of the prosecutor's changing role under section 25 of the Criminal Justice Act 1991. Throughout a period of tremendous upheaval and significant change in the prosecution system of England and Wales in the last ten years, no consistent and deliberate course of policy has emerged which recognizes the value of a prosecutor who plays an active part in the sentencing of offenders. Instead the picture is very much a negative one—with commentators, judges and policy-makers alike persistently denying the constitutionality of such a function and a number of isolated, independent reforms of the law which contradict such statements.

The European prosecutor has achieved a powerful and authoritative status, which the English prosecutor struggles to approach. Policy in the Netherlands, for example, is strikingly organized and determinate, consistently implementing a carefully considered and coherent working philosophy. 'tHart's article quoted earlier describes the meticulous way in which criminal law policy in the Netherlands is pre-determined, clearly set out in published documents, and systematically implemented. The policy plans of 1985 and 1990, discussed in Chapter 4, are excellent examples of this. Further, in Scotland, while policy during the 1980s was not so explicitly set forth, it was clear that the major reforms of the procurator fiscal system throughout the last decade stemmed from a central source of inspiration in the form of William Chalmers, who set out to model the fiscal service on the European systems of prosecution he had witnessed in other states (see Chapter 3).

The CPS has been slow to develop a coherent working philosophy and has maintained its bureaucratic culture. However, the DPP has drafted a *Statement of Purpose and Values* for the Service. Individual members of CPS staff were consulted on the contents of this policy statement, which covers subjects such as the neutrality of Crown Prosecutors and the 'openness and integrity' of the Service, in an aim to increase public awareness of it. However, the Statement is merely a list of bland promises, not unlike a Crown Prosecutors' Charter, and does not indicate the views of the DPP on the development of the prosecutor's role in the next few years. Most of the recent policy initiatives, such as the re-drafting of the Code for Crown Prosecutors and the recommendations of the RCCJ and the 1990 Home Affairs Committee, have responded pragmatically to the bombardment of criticism directed at the Service from many different directions. The CPS is very much on the defensive and the haphazard movement for reform reflects this. Even the 1994 Home Affairs Committee, which took evidence from the CPS and the DPP, appears to concentrate on micro-issues and responses to further criticisms, and a wide-scale re-appraisal of the prosecutor's role is unlikely to emerge from their deliberations. All these reviews of the operation of the Service have failed to produce an agenda for reform on the macro scale—a fundamental change in emphasis of the prosecutor's role.

It is surprising, under these circumstances, that the Crown Prosecutor has managed to emerge from reforms such as s. 36 Criminal Justice Act 1988 as a central player in the criminal justice process. However, until English policy-makers realize the full potential of the prosecution role in regulating the smooth running of the criminal justice system, reform will continue to be piecemeal and undirected.

3

The Scottish Procurator Fiscal Service: The Reluctant Sentencers

1. INTRODUCTION

THE Scottish criminal justice system has enjoyed the advantages of a public prosecution system, with independent prosecutors working in the public interest, for a good deal longer than England and Wales. The term 'procurator fiscal' dates back to early feudal courts where it referred to the representative of the local Lord, in a court presiding over civil matters. In criminal matters, the Sheriff originally acted as prosecutor and judge, but some time later his role was separated and the term 'procurator fiscal' was used to describe the prosecutorial part of the role.[1] It was the Sheriff Courts (Scotland) Act 1876 which gave prosecutors the full responsibility in law for the prosecution of all criminal offences, but Moody and Tombs (1982) suggest that, in practice, these functions were delegated to fiscals, by the Sheriffs, considerably earlier than this.[2] Hence the office of public prosecutor has been developing gradually in Scotland over the last century, and the fiscal service which exists today presents a very different picture to that of the Crown Prosecution Service of England and Wales, set up comparatively recently in 1986.

The fiscal service is run under the overall supervision and responsibility of the Scottish Law Officers, the Lord Advocate and the Solicitor-General, working from the Crown Office in Edinburgh. The Lord Advocate also, from time to time, issues directions and circulars on particular types of criminal offences, or general guidelines. Below these two political appointees there is the Crown Agent, a senior civil servant also working from the Crown Office, who is the permanent civil service head of the fiscal service.[3]

The six sheriffdoms of Scotland are headed for administrative purposes

---

[1] For a fuller explanation of the history of the role of the procurator fiscal, see R. Shiels, 'Focus on the Fiscals', *CPS Journal* May/June 1991.

[2] See S. R. Moody and J. Tombs, *Prosecution in the Public Interest* (Edinburgh, 1982), 18–22, for a historical account of the development of the office of procurator fiscal.

[3] See table 1 'Organisation of the Procurator Fiscal Service' in the Crown Office's publication: *The Prosecution of Crime in Scotland*.

by a Regional Procurator Fiscal, but the procurators fiscal are the Lord Advocate's 'local agents', responsible for the prosecution and investigation of crime at the local level. The police, or other law-enforcement agencies such as the SSPCA, the Office of Fair Trading, or the Health and Safety Executive, produce a report in each alleged case of law-breaking for the fiscal, who will decide whether or not to institute criminal proceedings, by what procedure (summary or solemn[4]), and on what charges—a process known as 'marking'.

One principal difference is the hierarchical position of a procurator fiscal in relation to the police. Since the office of fiscal was created early in the nineteenth century before permanent police forces were set up, the police remain in law subordinate to the prosecutor in the investigation of crime, a position now embedded in statute: 'It shall be the duty of the constables of a police force where an offence has been committed to take all such lawful measures and make such reports to the appropriate prosecutor . . . and in relation to the investigation of offences the Chief Constable should comply with such lawful instructions as he may receive from the appropriate prosecutor.' (s. 17 Police (Scotland) Act 1967).

This independence from and supervisory role over the police produces a more 'truly' independent role for the prosecutor, more akin to that of prosecutors in Continental inquisitorial systems than to the adversarial role of English Crown Prosecutors who are not involved in the investigation of crime. The procurator fiscal does have an investigation role. In everyday cases this takes the form of supervision and advice rather than 'hands on' involvement, although the fiscal does, like his counterpart in France, have a duty personally to investigate the scene of any sudden or suspicious death.

Indeed, Scottish fiscals see their role in the courtroom very much in terms of presenting all relevant evidence, whether favourable or unfavourable to the prosecution case. It is for the court to decide the outcome; prosecutors simply aim for a reasonable sentence in any case and act in the public interest. The traditional two-sided adversarial fight seen in English trials is less evident in a Scottish trial, and elements of the inquisitorial systems of Northern Europe are stronger. This is not surprising given that, historically, Scottish criminal procedure owes much of its heritage to various traditions from Europe.

The European influence is particularly strong in the new powers for the disposal of cases. Recent reforms have increased the number of options available to fiscals in dealing with offenders. Now, when marking a case,

---

[4] 'Summary procedure' is a trial by a judge sitting alone, and may take place in either the Sheriff Summary Court or District Court. 'Solemn procedure' is trial by a judge sitting with a jury, in either the Sheriff's Court, or, in very grave cases, in the High Court of Justiciary. It should be noted that a defendant in Scottish criminal proceedings has no right to elect trial by jury, as he does in England or Wales.

instead of merely deciding whether or not to prosecute, they must also consider a number of alternative disposals, so that prosecution becomes a last resort, only to be instituted if the public interest requires it. In this way also, the role of the fiscal is becoming increasingly similar to that of prosecutors in other Northern European countries such as Holland and Germany.

More importantly, these alternatives illustrate the increased role of fiscals in the sentencing process, both in terms of influencing the court decision on sentencing, and in dispensing penalties themselves which divert cases away from the courtroom altogether. The role of the prosecutor as a sentencer seems to have been much more widely, if implicitly, recognized and developed by policy-makers in Scotland in recent years, but, as will be made clear, they have been less successful in convincing the fiscals themselves of this aspect of their job.

2. THE STEWART COMMITTEE

The main thrust of the recent reforms came from the second report of the Committee on Alternatives to Prosecution (the Stewart Committee), which was published in 1983.[5] The Stewart Committee was set up by the Rt. Hon. Bruce Millan, Secretary of State for Scotland, in 1977. This was another incidence of other European systems having a substantial influence on the development of the fiscal service; the Committee looked in considerable detail at foreign systems, namely those of Sweden, the Netherlands, France, and Norway. The remit of the Committee was as follows:

To consider the effect on criminal courts and the prosecution system of the volume of minor offences at present dealt with by summary prosecution and whether some other process might be devised to deal with such offences while maintaining essential safeguards for accused persons.[6]

This remit instructed the investigation of alternatives to prosecution for minor offences in the light of the volume of such cases coming before the courts at the time. Consequently, the Committee issued a questionnaire with thirty-five headings, covering a wide variety of issues, to a number of associations and groups representing interests in the legal profession, courts, police, social work, and the news media, and the replies reflected a broad cross-section of concerns and attitudes.[7]

[5] Stewart Committee, 2nd report—*Keeping Offenders out of Court: Further Alternatives to Prosecution*, Cmnd 8958 (Edinburgh, 1983).
[6] Ibid., 9.
[7] Individual witnesses to the Stewart Committee cannot be named or associated with any viewpoint represented here as a condition of permission for access to their replies to the questionnaire—see explanation in Chapter 1.

But why was the Committee set up? The remit suggests that the increasing workload of the courts needed easing; indeed, Chapter 2 of the report gives a great deal of attention to this matter. On the other hand, the title of the second report, *Keeping Offenders out of Court: Further Alternatives to Prosecution* rather suggests concern over the plight of the defendants themselves and a need for more constructive ways of dealing with them.

Opinion amongst those interviewed was divided on this. John Waterhouse, a member of the Committee, was inclined to believe, as the remit suggested, that the immediate problem was undue pressure on the court system which needed to be eased, and that the exercise was essentially one of cost-saving. Others were concerned at the number of custodial sentences being imposed in courts, and believed that the exercise also aimed to find a more appropriate way of dealing with offenders. William Chalmers, as the Crown Agent of the day, was the prime mover in the setting up of the Committee. Whilst it is encouraging to see the impetus for reform coming from within the service rather than from above, Chalmers admitted he was acting in his capacity as the administrator of the fiscal service and thus his prime concerns were to reduce the number of cases requiring detailed preparation by prosecutors for trial in the courts, and to develop a means of dealing with the increasing number of cases with the modest resources allocated to the system. Nevertheless, he clearly also recognized other benefits of diversion, most notably: finding a positive and useful means of dealing with behavioural problems of the accused. It is perhaps ironic that, although certain diversion schemes have produced constructive and appropriate alternatives, significant saving of time or money have not resulted in the criminal justice process as a whole. Some forms of therapy and assistance offered on those schemes take a lot longer to deal with and are costly in terms of the time and resources of the procurator fiscal, although possibly less costly than imprisonment.

The ideas that the Committee discussed were comparatively advanced for their time. The reforms they considered included prosecutorial fines, procurator fiscal warnings, diversion to social work, psychiatric assistance, reparation and the like. Part of the inspiration for these ideas must have come from the countries mentioned above, where many of them were already in practice. Indeed, the Committee took evidence from European experts such as Professor Hulsman of Erasmus University in Rotterdam, and from members of the Oslo Police Department. Members of the Committee visited other legal systems to see the ideas working in practice (an opportunity that the House of Commons Home Affairs Committee failed to take up in 1990 when considering the future of the CPS in England and Wales).

However, much of the impetus for change came from various personalities on the Stewart Committee itself. The members were drawn from a wide range of professions, including a Sheriff, a Chief Constable, academics, prosecutors, and John Waterhouse from the Social Work Department in Edinburgh. Hence, they were able to draw on very different kinds of experience and brought to the Committee different concerns about the criminal justice process. The major influence, however, cited by *everyone* interviewed in this study, was the Crown Agent of the time, William Chalmers. Chalmers was known to be a very outward-looking Crown Agent with particular interest in developing the fiscal service into a body working towards a specific, coherent philosophy. Indeed, it was Chalmers who first advocated investigating the workings of foreign prosecution systems. After meeting several Swedish prosecutors at a conference in Geneva, he was particularly impressed with their system of prosecutors' fines. He accepted that the Scottish prosecution system lacked a tradition of allowing prosecutors a 'quasi-judicial' role, well established in the Swedish system, but he felt that if the Stewart Committee did not provide the momentum to start such a tradition in Scotland then the system would never progress at all. Such a forward-thinking, progressive leader of a prosecution service appears to be lacking in England, and Scotland's logical and systematic search for models of reform provides a stark contrast to the attempts of the House of Commons Home Affairs Committee in 1990 to find a basis for solving the 'teething' problems of the CPS.[8] It would have been difficult to level the criticisms concerning anti-theoretical attitudes and excessive concern over bureaucratic issues which have been fired at the CPS recently[9] at the Scottish fiscal service, with a personality such as this at its head.

Thus, the inspired gathering of personalities on the Committee, and their willingness to look far and wide for possibilities for change, gave the report much potential to achieve far-reaching reforms. Their recommendations did justice to this. Generally their suggestions, if implemented, would have shifted much of the decision-making in the criminal justice process further towards the 'front' of the system (that is, towards the pre-court stages), and thus to keep as many offenders away from court as possible.[10] The recurring theme was to ensure that prosecution really was the last resort: 'Procurators Fiscal should give prime consideration to the alternatives to prosecution we propose before opting for prosecution.'[11] However, in addition, the methods of diversion suggested, such as reparation, medical and psychiatric treatment, referral to social work departments and the like, aimed to ensure that offenders were 'dealt with' in the true sense; that

[8] See Fourth Report of the Home Affairs Committee: *Crown Prosecution Service*, HC 118–1 (London, 1990).
[9] For example, see John Pienaar, *Independent*, 12 Feb. 1990, Mark Linton, *Guardian*, 1 Feb. 1990, John Weeks, *Daily Telegraph*, 19 May 1989 and Colin Brown, *Independent*, 12 May 1989.
[10] Stewart Committee, 2nd Report, op. cit. 77–80.
[11] Ibid., 77, para. 2.

is that they were given constructive help in cases where it was appropriate. The prosecutor would have yielded immense influence over the sentencing process under these recommendations. The recommendation to allow prosecutors to warn or to fine offenders as well as divert them to the above-mentioned schemes, would have given them numerous options for penalizing offenders without reference to the court, thereby vastly enhancing their role as sentencers.

3. 'RELUCTANT SENTENCERS'

However, William Chalmers' spirit of progression has been somewhat dampened in recent years by the reluctance of prosecutors to accept their new powers. Such reluctance was very apparent from responses to the interviews in both Edinburgh and Glasgow. Ironically, when asked why they should be 'reluctant sentencers', all the prosecutors interviewed mentioned the word 'tradition', although in a more retrospective sense than Chalmers' use of the word in Section 2 above. While the Crown Agent was trying to establish a new tradition for the fiscal service, prosecutors themselves continue to cling to the traditions of the past where fiscals had no part to play in the sentencing of offenders. This tradition stems perhaps from the separation of the judicial and prosecutorial roles of the Sheriffs, which deliberately created the fiscal service as a separate and independent entity from the judiciary. There is apparently no more sinister reason for this reluctance than that. One Senior Assistant Procurator Fiscal in Glasgow admitted to being something of a traditionalist himself and expressed concern that the Crown's position in court would be eroded if it became involved in sentencing; to move in that direction 'would not enhance the dignity and respect in which prosecutors are held'.[12] Prosecutors generally expressed the view that it has historically been the judge's job to sentence, the defence counsel's job to mitigate and the prosecutor's job to furnish the court with objective and relevant facts to assist both, and that this is how people expect the system to work—clearly a case of 'better the devil you know'. Certainly Lord Stewart, Chairman of the Stewart Committee, was originally opposed to some of Chalmers' ideas because they did not fall within the traditional role of a fiscal.

However, whilst Chalmers was hopeful that this reluctance was voiced in the main by the older fiscals, approaching the end of their career in the service, or by the group of 'stick-in-the-muds' that exist in any large organization, the interviews conducted in Scotland failed to find any prosecutor, young or old, who has unequivocally welcomed the existing new

---

[12] procurator fiscal, Glasgow, July 1990.

powers or the suggestions for further ones. Even Duncan Lowe, Procurator Fiscal for Edinburgh at the time of interview and now currently Crown Agent, had his doubts about taking the sentencing role any further.

The set of questions issued by the Stewart Committee's inquiry which asked witnesses directly about further developing the role of the prosecutor as sentencer, not surprisingly, provoked the most excited response. When prosecutorial fines were introduced into the Criminal Justice (Scotland) Bill 1987 (new Clause 16) at a rather late stage in the legislative proceedings, there was no opposition whatsoever from Members of Parliament in the House of Commons or on the Scottish Grand Committee. It seems likely, therefore, that a large part of the wide-ranging resistance to the idea must have been voiced in response to these questions. Indeed, one witness, in response to the question relating to increasing the discretion of prosecutors not to prosecute minor offences, simply remarked: 'The assumption on which this group of questions is based is one which I never expected to see in any serious document.' With this evidence of reluctance to accept a quasi-sentencing role for the procurator fiscal, the extensive development of the quasi-judicial functions of the fiscal in recent years is all the more remarkable, given that strong, progressive reforms have been made in the face of vehement opposition.

4. THE ISSUE AT HAND

The issue before the Committee may have been interpreted in a number of ways and the Government may have had a number of ideas in mind. They may have intended to remove offences from the statute book which there seemed no further need to discourage by law. Alternatively, they may have intended to decriminalize certain offences which are better dealt with by a civil process (for example the non-observance of a technical, statutory requirement), or to retain some offences but to find alternative methods to prosecution. A perusal of the questions contained in the questionnaire would indicate, however, that the Committee adopted the third analysis and set about looking for methods by which minor offences, while remaining ultimately competent of prosecution in a criminal court, could be dealt with in a more appropriate and satisfactory way without recourse to judicial procedure. At the time in Scotland, the fiscal already had a limited discretion to mark a case for non-prosecution if it was not in the public interest to proceed. However, the balance of proof was different to that suggested by the Stewart Committee; the assumption prior to the Committee's recommendations was that prosecution was always in the public interest unless there were significant contra-indications. The suggested change in balance of proof was met with varying degrees of enthusiasm.

The witnesses whose evidence was available unanimously agreed that there was scope for the removal of certain minor statutory offences from the summary prosecution process. These, it was felt, could be dealt with by some alternative process. However, opinion was greatly divided as to whether the same should be the case for minor common law offences. Those who believed that common law offences were appropriate for disposal outside the prosecution process, however, stressed the importance of prosecutors retaining the right to prosecute in any case, so that diversion to an alternative process remained an option rather than an obligation.

Amongst those who positively welcomed the idea of an alternative process, the interpretation of what constitutes a minor offence (whether common law or statutory) again differed widely. For some, the definition of a minor offence depended on the procedure introduced to deal with it (although this could be circular argument. The question of whether an offence were classified as minor or not would depend on whether a procedure other than prosecution were appropriate, while the question of whether an alternative procedure were appropriate would be determined by whether the offence were perceived as minor.) For example, it was suggested that the fixed penalty system administered by the police was more suitable to types of petty offences where the offender is easily traceable (such as vehicle offences or use of television sets without licences), whereas prosecutor fines may be more suitable for offences where more care is needed in proving both the commission of the offence (such as minor assaults or theft cases) and the identity of the offender, and where mitigating or aggravating circumstances may need special consideration. Others preferred the 'criteria model', whereby the extent to which offences are considered 'minor' depends on criteria such as the extent of damage (to persons or property), individual offender characteristics, any mitigating or aggravating circumstances of the offence, the extent of public concern, possibilities of reparation and the like. Certainly, this definition seems more rational as it gets behind the stereotypes commonly attached to some offenders and overrides the labelling process associated with the criminal justice system and introduces a form of 'individualized' justice, with sentencing criteria similar to those used by judges. This is perhaps particularly appropriate in relation to diversion schemes where the individual circumstances of the offence and its perpetrator are of the utmost importance and where any form of stereotyping or labelling can be extremely detrimental and counterproductive. To simplify matters, however, one could opt for the rather more straightforward and technical definitions suggested, such as defining minor offences in terms of the maximum penalty permitted by law or, even wider, in terms of any offence not currently punishable by imprisonment or disqualification from driving.

5. PROCURATOR FISCAL FINES

Since the publication of its report in 1983, many of the Stewart Committee's recommendations have been followed and implemented by legislation. Perhaps the most notable reform has been the introduction of a power for prosecutors to fine petty offenders—procurator fiscal fines.

The Criminal Justice (Scotland) Act 1987 gave prosecutors the option in certain cases to offer an alleged offender a fixed penalty. If the case falls within the category of 'relevant offences' under s. 56(2),[13] the prosecutor can send the offender a notice of a conditional offer of a fine, which is currently fixed at £25. Following a note of dissent in the report,[14] prompted by a concern that it was unfair to give a fixed fine without giving an offender reasonable time to pay, this can be paid in instalments (s. 56(3)(ii)).

In the evidence received by the Stewart Committee those who welcomed an extension of the procurator fiscal's discretion were most in favour of administrative fines. Since references frequently linked them to fixed penalties, they were perhaps associated with that similar existing system and therefore not considered too radical a reform. On the other hand, many disagreed with the introduction of such fines, preferring this function to be left in the hands of judges after the full 'pageantry' of a criminal trial. As one witness remarked: 'Cheap justice is bad justice and no amount of juggling with procedure will get away from these facts.' Besides the concern for judicial independence, witnesses also expressed concern for the protection of essential safeguards for the accused, which they feared would be eroded if administrative fines were introduced. Prosecutors, it was claimed, would not have the independent and objective quality of the judiciary to assess guilt. It was further claimed that the offer of an administrative fine may be used in the process of plea-bargaining so as to encourage early pleas of guilty where the accused feared a greater penalty in court, and that the issue of innocence might be forgotten. This argument does not take account of the requirement for sufficient evidence in any case, before it can be disposed of in any way at all, whether by a judge in the courtroom or by the prosecutor in some form of diversionary alternative (although this may be rather easy to say with hindsight, having seen the full recommendations and views of the Committee in their second report and, more recently, the system working in practice). Furthermore, the accused can refuse to accept a fiscal fine, and may find access to the courts in this way. Nevertheless, there is no standard appeal procedure for an alleged offender who accepts one of these fines. This is particularly worrying given that Duff's research revealed that many prosecutors

---

[13] Relevant offences for the purpose of s. 56 means any offence in respect of which an alleged offender could competently be tried before a District Court.
[14] Stewart Committee, 2nd Report, op. cit. 82.

deliberately use fiscal fines in cases where they would not otherwise have prosecuted (albeit for reasons of triviality), preferring to use the fine as a form of 'half-way house' between a warning and a full prosecution.[15] The issue of net-widening will be expanded upon below.

A further criticism was that the introduction of administrative fines would not reduce the burden of the courts' work sufficiently to justify the risk of erosion of the accused's civil liberties. Indeed, given that the prosecutor would have to give full consideration to all the evidence in a case in order to make an adjudication of guilt, it was alleged that the new system would simply pose a greater burden of work on the prosecutor. This argument was not an accurate prophecy, though, in relation to the numbers of persons diverted by means of prosecutorial fines. The figures quoted below show that fines make up a significant proportion of the total number of cases diverted and that latter figure represented a majority of all cases reported. Besides, one would hope that diverting petty offenders away from the stigmatization associated with the courtroom, in cases which would not attract a large fine or a sentence of imprisonment, would have greater benefits than simply saving time or money.

The fines were nevertheless recommended by the majority of the Committee, but this issue caused one of the main points of contention in the discussions. William Chalmers took the view that prosecutors already have a quasi-judicial role and are, indirectly, involved in penalty, since they decide which court will hear any particular case and since the jurisdiction of the court limits the sentence which is eventually given . He therefore felt it was logical that the fiscal should have a more positive sentencing influence, that the fine system duly reflected that role, and that issuing fines was a good way of relieving pressure on the lower courts. Although Scottish prosecutors have acquired fining powers they have never really taken on a full 'punishment' role, which in this instance requires that they should decide not only whether to award a fine but also at what sum to pitch it. Interestingly, other prosecuting bodies, such as the Inland Revenue and Customs and Excise, are able to impose fines and to exercise a discretion in their extent, yet the prosecution system appears to have rooted itself in the fixed penalty mode of thinking.

This is particularly curious given that the basis of a prosecutor's job is to exercise discretion—it is an essential element of the prosecution system which is exercised every day in every decision made. Indeed, it would be seen as inappropriate for prosecutors merely to 'rubber-stamp' the views and decisions that the police and other agencies report to them. To allow prosecutors a discretion to fine any amount below a statutory maximum

[15] P. Duff, 'The Prosecutor Fine and Social Control' (1993) *British Journal of Criminology*, 33: 481–503.

would certainly allow for a more flexible system which could divert a wider range of cases from the courts and still award an appropriate and realistic penalty.

The judicial lobby of the Committee, like many who gave evidence to it, however, were not so keen, and were, predictably, concerned about prosecutors encroaching upon their independence as arbiters and sentencers. The majority recommendation was very much a compromise. The judicial element agreed to the introduction of the fines but only on the condition that the penalty was fixed in Parliament by statute. Their real objection, therefore, was apparently to prosecutors having any *discretion* in sentencing, rather than to their having sentencing powers at all. Chalmers affirmed that Lord Stewart himself opposed the discretionary fine and, being a respected judge, his opinion carried a lot of weight. However, Chalmers also felt that such opposition was probably not wholly based on a feeling amongst the judges on the Committee that their independence was being threatened and that prosecutors would be usurping part of their remit. Although some would have thought that, Lord Stewart merely felt that the fixed fine system was easier to administer and, perhaps more importantly, easier to sell to the public. The more flexible system of fines would certainly be very useful in Glasgow, however, where the District Court is in constant danger of overloading. Presumably, avoiding that danger would be equally appealing to the public.

On publication of the Stewart Committee's report, however, the resistance to the idea of fines grew stronger. There was the inevitable hostility from the judiciary, reflecting the attitudes of the judges on the Committee, but some of the strongest opposition came from within the fiscal service itself. Procurators fiscal evidently did not share the forward-looking views of their Crown Agent, and were reluctant to take on a power which, they felt, usurped a judicial function. As far as they were concerned sentencing was not within the remit of a prosecutor—as the writer was told in one interview: 'sentencing should be up to judges—that's what they're paid for.'[16]

Trying to push this piece of legislation through Parliament was not expected to be an easy task. However, as mentioned in Section 3, there was no debate at all recorded in Hansard, hostile or otherwise, on the inclusion of the new Clause 16 to the Criminal Justice (Scotland) Bill 1987. The opposition was evidently overcome, probably due to the ever-increasing momentum to remove offenders from court to reduce costs and time. As Jacqueline Tombs suggested, the reason for pushing prosecutors' fines through the legislative process had much less to do with principle than with cost-effectiveness and the management of the workload within

[16] Procurator fiscal, Edinburgh, Mar. 1990.

the criminal legal process. Perhaps what also swung the argument was the fact that the police were already able to issue fixed penalty tickets for stationary (though not moving) traffic offences,[17] and, since the implementation of the Transport Act 1982 and ss. 75–7 of the Road Traffic Offenders Act 1988, procurators fiscal have been able to make conditional offers of fixed penalties for both moving and stationary road traffic offences.

Response to the introduction of procurator fiscal fines in Glasgow and Edinburgh appears to have been very mixed. The objections raised, however, tended to be technical and detailed objections to the way in which the fine system actually operated, rather than a disapproval of the principle of a prosecutor being able to issue a penalty. One prosecutor admitted never having considered the matter from such a theoretical point of view, but had only thought about the practical difficulties. Others contradicted their previous emphatic stand that prosecutors should not play an active part in sentencing offenders and agreed that the idea was sound but needed one or two amendments in practice.

A restriction on the application of the fiscal fine system, referred to by a procurator fiscal in Glasgow, is the sum at which the fine is currently fixed. According to him, the fixed sum of £25 was far too low for the system to be at all useful. He made very little use of fines because he would very rarely have expected a fine as low as £25 to be imposed in the District Court, and besides, a fine as low as £25 without an accompanying visit to court would, in his view, have very little deterrent impact on the accused.

A further problem in the technical operation of fines stems from John Waterhouse's efforts to ensure that the £25 may be paid in instalments. The rule is contained in s. 56(3)(c) Criminal Justice (Scotland) Act 1987. After the first instalment of a fiscal fine is paid, any liability for conviction of the offence is discharged, and this results in many offenders paying only the first instalment and no more. The prosecutor has relinquished his right to prosecute for the offence in question by accepting the first instalment and is thus powerless to penalize the accused in any other way when the fiscal fine system fails. This has certainly deterred the service as a whole from using such fines; prosecutors and their deputes are evidently tired of issuing the penalties and seeing only a proportion of them being paid and the accused generally 'getting away with it'.

It is interesting to note that the only prosecutor interviewed who supported and welcomed the new power did so for administrative reasons rather than reasons of principle. He was thankful to have another option available to relieve the pressure, because with trials becoming longer and the number of cases growing, there is simply not enough time to prosecute

---

[17] This was the principal outcome of the first report of the Stewart Committee, *The Motorist and Fixed Penalties* (Edinburgh, 1980), Cmnd 8027.

all cases. The fact that fiscal fines have been comparatively widely used since their introduction perhaps indicates similar attitudes amongst other prosecutors. Between January and November 1989, 1,241 fiscal fines were issued in the Lothian and Borders region, which amounted to around 3.5 per cent of the total number of cases reported.[18] This figure was higher than the number of fiscal warnings issued in the same period, which was 1,184. Furthermore, Duff and Meechan report that across Scotland, fiscal fines accounted for the disposal of 4.6 per cent of all cases reported to the procurator fiscal in 1990. This figure had increased from 2.8 per cent in 1988.[19] Whilst they argue that the use of fiscal fines has probably reached its ceiling they are used more than fiscal warnings, and in 1992 the rate at which fiscal fines were used increased further to 4.9 per cent of all cases reported to the fiscal in Scotland (compared with warnings which accounted for 3.9 per cent of disposals).[20]

These figures are encouraging in that they indicate a reduction in the number of prosecutions, which will have beneficial effects on both the offender and the criminal justice system. However, there is a darker side. Duff has shown that since the introduction of the fiscal fine, a process of 'net-widening' has occurred. Fiscal fines are often being used to reduce the number of complete waivers (or 'no-pro's'), and are being used in situations where a prosecution would not have been brought because the case was felt to be too trivial. In other words, rather than being an alternative to prosecution, the fines have become an alternative to a warning or to no further action at all. Whilst this process may fulfil the aims of the Stewart Committee in terms of increasing efficiency (a fiscal fine may involve more work than a 'no-pro' but is much more efficient than a prosecution) it does so at the expense of the more welfare-based aims of diversion. In making his own analysis of this process, Duff concurs with the scepticism of Cohen[21] and McMahon[22] that net-widening, if it can be conclusively proved, should not detract from the other benefits of diverting offenders away from the full rigours of the criminal process. This debate over the pros and cons of net-widening in the prosecutorial diversion process will be continued in Chapter 7. In the Scottish context, whether it is seen as a pro or a con will ultimately depend on one's view of the purpose of fiscal fines. If they were introduced as a means of saving the resources of the court (as the Stewart Committee suggested) or if they were introduced as a form of penalty applicable to a precise set of cases where a warning

---

[18] Figures supplied by Procurator Fiscal's Office, Edinburgh.
[19] P. Duff, and K. Meechan, 'The Prosecutor Fine' [1992] *Crim. LR* 22–9.
[20] See *Annual Report of the Crown Office and Procurator Fiscal Service 1992/93* (Edinburgh, 1993), 16.
[21] S. Cohen, *Visions of Social Control* (Cambridge, 1985).
[22] M. McMahon, 'Net-widening: Vagaries in the Use of a Concept' (1990) *British Journal of Criminology*, 30: 121–49.

would be insufficient but a prosecution too severe (Sheehan's 'half-way house')[23] then net-widening would merely be viewed as an inevitable, perhaps deliberate but not necessarily unfortunate, result. The concerns about over-intervention by the state in the name of welfare might, in this case, be better directed at the powers of the fiscal to divert offenders to rehabilitative measures (see below—Section 7).

6. PROCURATOR FISCAL WARNINGS

Another option for diversion considered by the Stewart Committee was that of procurator fiscal warnings. This was not a new idea; fiscals already had such a power, but the Committee recommended that greater use be made of it.[24] It was also suggested that police officers have the power to issue formal written warnings under the guidance of the procurators fiscal, but the system remains different to that of England and Wales and only fiscals may issue warnings. This form of prosecutorial diversion was far more popular amongst witnesses to the Stewart Committee than administrative fines. Many who had disputed the extension of a fiscal's powers to the issuing of fines were in favour of them giving formal (and in most cases, written) warnings. Such warnings were regarded as appropriate to minor offences, again as defined is Section 4 above.

Warnings are usually written, although very rarely a fiscal will give an offender an oral warning at his office. Generally speaking, the only criterion for a warning is that there should be sufficient evidence to merit a prosecution. There are no written guidelines to assist the decision and it is very much left to the discretion of the fiscal. This is generally accepted as a means of retaining flexibility in the system, so that geographical differences can be accounted for. For example, a varying degree of emphasis can be placed on the same offence in different areas where it may be more or less of a problem. In this way the prosecutor can respond to his or her community and his or her sentencing policy reflects, as far as possible, the interests of the local population.

Warnings are recorded locally in a fiscal office, but at present there is no national system of recording. Thus a previous warning will be used only by a local fiscal in a future case, rather like a previous conviction, in influencing the decision whether or not to prosecute. It should also have the purpose of deterring the offender from committing further crimes in the same area. If a national system of recording were introduced, this deterrence would be much more effective.

The requirement of sufficient evidence to prosecute is designed to prevent

---

[23] A. Sheehan, *Criminal Procedure* (Edinburgh, 1990).
[24] Stewart Committee, 2nd Report, op. cit. 78, para. 9.

the process of net-widening, whereby cases which would otherwise have been dropped for technical, evidential reasons are proceeded with using an alternative to prosecution. However, no admission of guilt is required from the offender, which raises the question of what happens when an individual disagrees with a prosecutor's decision to warn and proclaims his innocence? A wide loophole in the protection of the offender's civil liberties thus exists in relation to fiscal warnings.

In the evidence submitted to the Committee this was the only issue of controversy concerning the extension of this system of warnings. Whilst one witness felt that requiring a prosecutor to wait for an admission of guilt would negate the primary purpose of introducing the system (to dispose of cases with greater speed and efficiency) that witness, and most others, agreed that without such a condition the interests of the accused could be placed in jeopardy. Others felt that the warning would lose all cogency without an admission, but that there should also be a proviso that such an admission should not prejudice any further proceedings which might arise out of the matter, for example, if the offender subsequently failed to pay a fiscal fine. No admission of guilt is now required before a warning is given. This is a marked difference to the English cautioning system, and it is disturbing that in Scotland the procurator fiscal effectively adjudicates on guilt and offers a penalty even when the accused disputes that adjudication; this procedure has profound civil liberties implications.

Unlike other diversion options in which the emphasis is on the voluntary nature of the scheme, in the case of warnings there is no opportunity for the offender effectively to voice his disagreement. For example, if a defendant wishes to challenge a prosecutor's decision on the basis that he is innocent, he could refuse to pay a fiscal fine or to comply with a diversion scheme, in which event his case is likely to proceed to court where his innocence can be tested in an open forum. But if he receives a letter containing a formal warning he cannot refuse to accept it and take the matter to court—there is no appeal procedure. One of the downfalls of shifting decision-making to the pre-court stages and giving prosecutors 'sentencing' powers is that decisions are less easily challenged (the judicial review of prosecutors' decisions will be discussed later) and it becomes more difficult to regulate the criteria used for making them. Clearly in the case of fiscal warnings, the offender's right to due process—the right to have one's case heard in an open and objective courtroom—is ignored. Arguing against this, prosecutors interviewed claimed that the issue was not as serious as it appeared since the Scottish criminal justice system retains at all times the fundamental notion that one is innocent until proven guilty. However, an alleged offender who is given a fiscal warning has not been proven guilty but has been assumed to be guilty. If prosecutors are given powers to 'sentence' like judges, then their adjudication of guilt should be equally subject to public scrutiny; that is, it should be on the basis of standard criteria and subject to an appeal procedure. This feature of the warning system remains absent from the current system and the absence of an appeal procedure or other safeguard of the accused's right to due process produces its greatest criticism.

Prosecutors generally take account of a letter from an aggrieved defendant who disagrees with a warning decision in that they will make a note of it and, in a future case involving the same defendant, they may ignore the previous warning in view of the contention about its validity (although one procurator fiscal in Glasgow stated that he was unlikely to do this because he would not have issued the warning letter if he was not confident of its validity). In this way the effect of the warning on future cases can be neutralized but there is still no means of neutralizing the warning itself. The impression given is that offenders should be relieved to receive a warning in their case, which, under the evidential sufficiency rule, would have been competent for prosecution. In this way prosecutors are working on the fear that an accused would generally have of being prosecuted, almost a fear of the unknown, and certainly once the mystique of the court procedure has been removed, an offender may be less inhibited about getting into further trouble. A prosecution is their trump card and the alternative disposals available delay the necessity for the prosecutor to play it. Perhaps the system has that advantage, but it should not ignore what the Stewart Committee called the 'essential safeguard',[25] that is the right to have one's case heard in court. A wider discussion of the issue of balancing the benefits of diversion at the pre-trial stage with the defendant's·right of access to justice can be found in Chapter 7.

7. DIVERSION

Prior to the Stewart Committee's report, procurators fiscal diverted cases from prosecution on an informal basis depending on the local resources available to them and the individual circumstances of a particular case. Following the Committee's report, however, diversion in Scotland has become more formalized. As a result of the Committee's recommendations[26] there are now recognized procedures for diverting cases to psychiatric assistance, social work departments, or alcoholic and drug rehabilitation centres. With all alternative options the evidential sufficiency rule is still the central criterion, so that diversion is truly away from prosecution. However, within these schemes there are two possibilities: complete waiver of a case, where the fiscal's involvement in a case handed

---

[25] Ibid., 72, para. 5–23.   [26] Ibid., 78, paras. 15–16.

to one of the schemes is terminated, and deferred prosecution, where the waiver is conditional upon the scheme being satisfactorily completed after a reasonable time, until which time the possibility of proceeding with a prosecution is retained. (The latter option was favoured by the Stewart Committee.) The important factor in these schemes is that they are *voluntary*. Even if compliance with the scheme is a condition of waiver, a fiscal or any other agency involved cannot, under any circumstances, force the accused to take part. Their role is merely to advise the accused that such assistance will be more beneficial than prosecution.

In recent years, a great deal of attention has been given to referral of offenders to social work departments—there has been a considerable amount of research[27] and guidelines have been drawn up to help fiscals make decisions in this area. No formal training is given to fiscals to help them assess which of the cases reported to them are suitable to be referred to one of the schemes. As with most forms of prosecution decision-making in Scotland, much depends on the individual fiscal's discretion, based on experience with marking cases. Stedward and Millar's recent research found that: 'the introduction of diversion has not required any specialist training of marking staff. Rather procurators fiscal have tended to talk informally to their staff about the general principles of diversion and the scheme they had decided to operate, perhaps indicating categories of cases where diversion might be appropriate.'[28] This may be worrying given that in some circumstances, recognizing which offenders need psychiatric assistance, for example, they may be making quasi-medical decisions without medical qualifications. In England and Wales there was similar concern about police officers sifting out such problem cases for treatment in connection with juveniles. Many police officers were reluctant to take on a 'social work role', claiming that their training did not qualify them for the task.[29] There is also the possibility that the criteria upon which they base their assessment of any offender may become stereotyped or may even be founded on discriminatory assumptions.

In this respect, the information which the police forward to fiscals in their reports is crucial. Several persons interviewed stated that police reports are known to be stereotyped and often short of useful information, which tends to hinder well-informed decision-making at the prosecution stage. Recently, however, the police have been encouraged to produce better reports and to make fuller use of them in identifying problem

[27] See Scottish Office Central Research Unit paper entitled *Diversion to Social Work* by Gail Stedward and Ann Millar (1989). A similar report has been prepared by David Cooke on 'Diversion to Psychiatric Assistance'. See 'Psychological Treatment as an Alternative to Prosecution: A Form of Primary Diversion' (1991) *Howard Journal*, 30: 53–65.
[28] Ibid., 23.
[29] H. J. Giller, and C. Covington, (1985) 'Hampshire Constabulary Youth Help Scheme' (unpublished summary report of research findings).

offenders. Indeed, in some areas of Scotland there have been meetings between police officers, prosecutors, and other agencies to discuss the quality of information that each needs from the other. Generally, inter-agency co-operation here is high.[30] This is certainly one area where good relations between fiscals and the police is essential and where, if the lack of cooperation which exists in England and Wales were apparent, the system would not work so efficiently.

The Scottish system of diversion could perhaps benefit from useful techniques applied in English bail information schemes and the research being conducted in connection with the Inner London Probation Service. Under those schemes information is provided to the CPS, which directly addresses the Attorney-General's criteria for prosecution, to assist the Crown Prosecutor in identifying any public interest criteria when deciding whether to continue a prosecution.[31] It would be useful for the Scots to develop their diversion schemes on this model so that information provided by the police and the other agencies provides material relevant for the prosecution decision, even if the agencies are unable to provide any other form of assistance to the accused.

It should also be noted that fiscals only make these quasi-medical decisions at the very early sifting stage. Although at that stage they will not have any social enquiry report or equivalent pre-sentence report to help them, they will merely select cases which, on the surface, appear not to merit prosecution and in which the offender appears to need some kind of help. After this preliminary sifting, the fiscal will refer the case to the appropriate agency who will arrange an appointment with the accused and make their own assessment as to whether the person needs help, irrespective of the offence. The agency will report back stating whether they will accept the accused as a client and the fiscal can then make a decision about prosecution. It might be argued, however, that if the prosecutor is to take on a quasi-judicial role in diverting offenders to these schemes, they should be given assistance similar to that given to a judge in these circumstances. Some sort of per-diversion report, written by a probation officer, social worker, or other person acquainted with the offender's circumstances, provided to the procurator fiscal, would be beneficial. It is, nevertheless, conceded that the process of seeking these reports at an early stage of the process might prejudice some of the aims of prosecutorial diversion, namely the speed and efficiency in dealing with cases that the Stewart Committee were seeking to achieve through their recommendations. There is an in

---

[30] The Standing Advisory Committee in Glasgow is a good example of this—see Section 10 below.
[31] This scheme is more fully explained in the report from the Vera Institute of Justice— C. Stone, 'Public Interest Case Assessment'—vol. 2 of the *Final Report on the Probation Initiative 'Diversion from Custody and Prosecution'* (New York, 1989).

herent conflict here between justice and efficiency; this conflict is discussed in Chapter 6 below.

Further help for fiscals in this area has been forthcoming from the social work department itself, which has just drawn up draft guidelines—*National Guidelines on Diversion to Social Work Agencies*. These guidelines indicate what sort of information they will require from fiscals in order to make an assessment and recommend procedures for referral, assessment, and reporting—a good example of the high level of co-operation that exists in this system. However, this is another area where, although fiscals may benefit from guidelines and advice so as not to make stereotyped judgments of cases, it is impossible to make a central policy directive because account must be taken of local circumstances, attitudes, and prejudices.

Such local attitudes have been a strong determining factor in the decisions to divert cases of domestic violence to social work departments— particularly in the Strathclyde area. Women's groups in that area have lobbied to prevent diversion schemes being used for this category of offender, on the basis that the men in these cases ought to be prosecuted to reflect the public condemnation of their offence. They also based their concerns on research done by Dobash and Dobash,[32] who argued that the unwillingness of prosecuting authorities to take domestic violence cases to court meant that the offender was not really confronted with the consequences of his actions. The issue became a political one when a women's committee on the Lothian and Borders Regional Council refused to allow their local social work department to provide a service for the diversion schemes in domestic violence cases. As a result, various guidelines have been produced and projects set up. The social work department, in their draft guidelines, stated that they felt it was unwise for local authorities to determine prosecution policy and set out suggested procedures for social workers to provide information to fiscals, if only to inform them of the circumstances behind the case and assist in the decision to prosecute. Nevertheless, a local authority retains the option to refuse to provide a social work service for this purpose.

Projects have also been set up to give constructive assistance to domestic violence offenders after prosecution—that is, schemes to which the court may divert cases—thus allowing prosecution to go ahead to mark society's disapprobation, but allowing the offender to acknowledge his aggression and do something about it. Part of the impetus for setting up these projects was the Stedward and Millar report which gave special attention to domestic violence cases. Despite the focus of attention on diversion schemes, particularly to the social work department, it remains a relatively small part of the whole network of alternative options available to fiscals. It was

---

[32] R. E. Dobash, and R. P. Dobash, *Violence Against Wives* (New York, 1979).

never anticipated that these forms of diversion would have a large impact on saving time or money in the justice process. Rather, the concern was that cases in which it was not sensible to prosecute should not merely be waived, and that the persons involved might benefit from some assistance. In practice only a very small number of cases are dealt with in this way and it has had little impact on prosecution figures.[33] Nevertheless, the schemes have highlighted the progressive reforms to the prosecution process in Scotland in recent years.

In Glasgow, diversion from prosecution to other agencies generally takes one of three forms. The Reparation and Mediation Scheme organized by the Scottish Association for the Care and Resettlement of Offenders (SACRO) will be described in more detail below. In addition, arrests involving offenders with alcohol problems can immediately be referred to the Wayside Clinic which gives accommodation and counselling. However, the scheme, being specifically for alcoholics, has a rather limited application. Alternatively, the Douglas Inch Clinic will accept referrals of cases where there is a history of psychiatric problems, including offenders also having alcoholic problems. Both the Wayside Clinic and the Douglas Inch Clinic are considered to be 'complete diversion' because of the time involved in treating and counselling the accused. Certainly this type of treatment does tend to take longer than prosecution and any subsequent term of imprisonment. Once the referral has been made a period of 6 to 8 months may be allowed, after which the progress of the accused will be assessed. Even if this is unsatisfactory, the delay will often render the matter too stale for prosecution.

A three-year pilot Reparation and Mediation project was set up by SACRO in October 1987, with the aim of exploring the value of 'dispute resolution through mediated reparative agreements between victim and accused as a strategy for diversion'.[34] The scheme was based on the principle of deferred prosecution, and if either the victim or the accused does not agree to participate, or if the agreements reached are not fulfilled by either party, the prosecutor retains the right to prosecute for the original offence. The accused's involvement in the project is privileged information which may not be used as evidence of a confession in subsequent prosecution. The types of offences referred include theft, criminal damage, fraud, breach of the peace, and assault.

The procedure for referral is necessarily complicated since the full agreement of both parties to participate must be obtained. The full procedure

---

[33] In 1992, diverted cases accounted for just 0.3% of all cases reported to the procurator fiscal in Scotland—see *Annual Report for the Crown Office and Procurator Fiscal Service 1992/93* (Edinburgh, 1993) at 16.

[34] *Annual Report of the Reparation and Mediation Project 1989/90* (Edinburgh, 1990), see 3.

TABLE 3.1: SACRO Reparation and Mediation Project—Schema for Decision-Making Process

Stage	Action	Decision	Outcome
1. Referral	Case is proposed either by PF or mediator for discussion between Senior PF dep + mediator	Referral to project Y/N	N = pros Y⇒2
2. See victim	Assess victim's willingness to participate	Agree to participate Y/N	N⇒7 Y⇒3
3. See accused	Assess accused's willingness to participate	Agree to participate Y/N	N⇒7 Y⇒4
4. Mediation	Seek a negotiated agreement	Agreement made Y/N	N⇒7 Y⇒5
5. Endorsement	Agreement referred to PF for endorsement	Agreement endorsed Y/N	N⇒7 or <4 Y⇒6
6. Supervision	Is the agreement being kept? Mediator checks and reports to Procurator Fiscal	Agreement kept Y/N	N⇒7 or <4 Y⇒6
7. Ending	PF re-marks case	If 6 = Y, no prosecution; if 2–6 = N, need to prosecute is reviewed (exceptional circumstances may lead to no prosecution).	

is outlined in Table 3.1 and explained in more detail on page 4 of the Annual Report of the scheme for 1989/90.[35] Briefly, the procurator fiscal will make the initial decision to refer a case to the project and the project workers will then contact both the victim and the accused by letter and by a home visit to explain the scheme and ascertain whether they both consent. The accused will be presented with a negotiated reparation proposal which he will, if he agrees to it, endorse.

[35] Ibid., 4.

The initiative for the scheme came from personalities within SACRO and was set up without any form of Government funding. However, surprisingly, the scheme survived for three years on funding from Regional Councils, various charitable trusts, and some commercial sponsors including British Telecom, Marks and Spencer, and the Scottish and Newcastle Breweries, again secured by the work of SACRO staff. The figures published in the 1989/90 Annual Report indicated a good measure of success. In that year, of 460 victims approached, 367 (79.8%) took part and only 70 (15%) declined, (23 being untraceable).[36] Similarly, of 350 accused persons approached, 287 (82%) took part and only 34 (9.7%) declined.[37] Further, of all the cases where mediation took place, 94 per cent reached an agreement, a majority of which were successfully carried out.[38]

The scheme had many advantages, including that of wide application. As well as disputes between strangers, the cases dealt with have resolved neighbourhood and family disputes in cases where prosecution would have been more likely to increase the resentment between the parties than to solve the problem. The victim can be spared a court appearance which might be stressful or traumatic, and the scheme is particularly suited to cases where the victim desires to be reconciled with the accused or to give them another chance. Avoiding a court appearance would also be beneficial to the offender. As well as avoiding a criminal conviction, offenders are provided with a chance to express remorse and shame at their behaviour. Indeed, in some cases the accused insisted on paying a donation to a charity on behalf of the victim as well as paying compensation or making amends in some other way. Most settlements took the form of a cash payment to the victim or to a charity, but some involved apologies, non-harassment agreements and working to rectify any damage caused. The Project Manager for Glasgow, Phil Walker, summed up the surprising willingness of both parties to settle their cases in this way:

I was impressed both by the keenness of many victims to participate in the project and by the gratitude shown by both victims and accused at being given an opportunity to take a positive and active part in resolving their own experience of crime.[39]

The year 1990 was the final one of the experiment, and SACRO have been unable to continue running it due to lack of funding. However, it is to be hoped, given the success thus far of the scheme, that if funding were forthcoming from the Regional Councils it could be developed and expanded as a permanent feature of the range of diversion options available to prosecutors. The scheme has recently been the subject of a research

---

[36] Ibid., 17, fig. 2.   [37] Ibid., 17, fig. 3.   [38] Ibid., 18, fig. 4.   [39] Ibid., 7.

study by Stirling University, the results of which were published in October 1990.[40]

8. RECOMMENDING SENTENCE

As the Scottish fiscal service reflects European prosecution systems more and more closely, and fiscals take on an increasing sentencing role (whether they admit it or not), the writer suggested to those interviewed that perhaps it would not now be too radical a reform to allow fiscals to recommend a sentence to judges in court. The response was mixed. On the one hand, Jacqueline Tombs agreed with the idea. Concerned about the contradiction whereby prosecutors in Scotland evidently play a vital role in the sentencing process but are reluctant to admit to it, she feels that allowing fiscals to recommend sentences would bring their prosecution philosophy out into the open and make them more explicit about how prosecution decision-making is actually progressing. It is certainly impossible to imagine that fiscals make their decisions about prosecution without some idea as to what they think a reasonable sentence should be in any case. Therefore, allowing them to recommend that sentence in court would simply give formal recognition to a process which already occurs, covertly, in practice.

Others, however, were less happy about the idea and put forward further arguments about encroaching upon the judicial prerogative of sentencing. Prosecutors interviewed held to the notion that their function was to provide relevant evidence to the court, and the furthest they were prepared to go was in pointing out to a judge any aggravating or mitigating factors which might have a bearing on sentencing in a case, such as an early plea of guilty. At the point of conviction, it was felt that the prosecutor should stand aside and let the courts decide the penalty, without getting involved in the bartering between the judge and the defence.

William Chalmers' objection to the Continental idea of prosecutors recommending sentence was that sheriffs might not be impressed with those suggestions, and would not give much weight to them. However, perhaps this problem does not arise in other European countries where the status of judges and prosecutors is more equal. Judges and prosecutors in Scotland are not as hierarchically separated as their colleagues in England. The prospects of promotion from prosecutor to sheriff are positive and sometimes realized (although the reverse is most unlikely, unlike other

---

[40] See S. Warner, *Evaluation of the SACRO Reparation and Mediation Project—Final Report* (Edinburgh, 1990).

European jurisdictions). Indeed, William Chalmers knew of at least ten currently serving sheriffs who had previously been prosecutors. Nevertheless, in Scotland the two jobs are not regarded as having equal status and the transition from prosecutor to sheriff is undoubtedly seen as a promotion. Although fiscals may argue that they have a more active role and a greater workload than a sheriff who only need concern himself with the list of cases in front of him in any one day, sheriffs probably earn a higher salary, and have higher status. Hence, the opinion among prosecutors remained that they should continue to influence sentence merely by emphasizing mitigating or aggravating factors rather than by asking for a particular penalty.

This hesitancy in enlarging their existing role is surprising—in particular because, in one respect, prosecutors are already recommending sentences. In criminal cases involving damage or injury, it is for a fiscal to ask a judge to award compensation to the victim and to specify the level of compensation sought. This is, in effect, recommending part of the sentence, or at least part of the penalty given to the offender. If it is possible to recommend a specific penalty in the area of compensation, why should it be so contentious to introduce the idea in other areas? There is a converse argument that the case of recommending a sum of compensation to the judge is different because a compensation order is not a sentence *strictu sensu*. However, this is a pedantic means of distinguishing between a practice that is well established and a, not dissimilar, practice which is objected to.

The crux of the matter is the degree to which the prosecutor is stepping on the judge's toes in involving himself at the post-conviction stage. If the recommendation of a sum of compensation to the judge does not unduly fetter his independence then it is illogical to argue that recommending any other form of penalty does. It is interesting to note that studies of compensation orders in Scotland found that fiscals in the early days made a disappointingly low use of the orders. Part of the reason for this was found to be similar to the reason for opposition to the idea of recommending sentence; that is, fiscals were reluctant to use compensation orders because they felt it was not up to them to tell a judge how much compensation to award.

Despite the lack of progress of reform regarding recommendations of sentence by fiscals, another influence on judicial sentencing is under consideration. In 1992 the Scottish Conservative Party Manifesto promised that consideration would be given to the introduction of a right of appeal for the procurator fiscal against unduly lenient sentences. Following the general election in May 1992, Lord Macaulay of Bragar moved an amendment to the Prisoners and Criminal Proceedings Bill in the House of Lords to insert a clause giving the prosecutor the right to appeal against an unduly lenient sentence in solemn cases. In the event, the amendment was withdrawn, but the Lord Advocate has reiterated a commitment to considering the introduction of such a power of appeal in the near future.

9. ACCOUNTABILITY

The shifting of a large part of decision-making to the pre-court stages of the criminal process[41] may give rise to a concern about the lack of public scrutiny of those decisions and the protection of a defendant's civil liberties. As stated above, there is no appeal procedure against procurator fiscal warnings and although there are means of appeal in other diversion options, there is no case-by-case accountability of fiscals to the courts or any other independent body. There has, though, been surprisingly little public concern about the increase in hidden decision-making. The Scottish Council for Civil Liberties was not as vociferous as it might have been about the implications for civil liberties of the introduction of fiscal fines, and the only real public concern has been centred on isolated cases of miscarriages of justice. More outcry at present is being directed at judicial decision-making which appears to be inconsistent and chaotic.

It was suggested by some prosecutors that the fiscals have a general accountability to Parliament through the Lord Advocate and that this was sufficient. However, this would be no satisfaction to an individual aggrieved defendant. A solution would be to make judicial review available to alleged offenders in respect of disputed prosecutorial decisions. Indeed, Lord McCluskey, Solicitor General for Scotland, called for some sort of accountability of prosecutors to the courts:

when the system accords the public prosecutor a discretion it must also create machinery for guarding against its abuse, whether corruptly or misguidedly. Answerability to Parliament is not the only possibility; the courts or the Ombudsman could provide the check.[42]

Certainly this would counterbalance the current powerful position of prosecutors and judicial review is now being applied to a wider variety of decision-making. Most prosecutors interviewed felt that defendants are provided with sufficient protection by the ability to refuse a form of diversion and have their case heard in court, although they were unable to offer a satisfactory solution to the lack of this opportunity with warnings. There was certainly doubt as to whether formal judicial review was necessary and one prosecutor felt that a judicial review case involving, for example,

[41] Indeed, figures quoted for the Lothian and Borders region between January and November 1989 show that between 50% and 60% of all cases reported were diverted in one way or another. Nationally, the figure was about 45% in 1992. (*Annual Report of the Crown Office and Procurator Fiscal Service 1992/93*, op. cit.)
[42] Lord McCluskey, 'The Prosecutor's Discretion', *International Journal of Medical Law* (1980), 1: 5–9 at pp. 8–9.

a warning would probably be 'laughed out of court'—not least because, unlike other administrative decisions which could cause hardship to those affected (such as a planning decision), there would be no practical benefits from winning a judicial review case in relation to prosecution. In fact the defendant could end up much worse off if a decision to warn rather than to prosecute were reversed, and a conviction resulted in the inevitably harsher penalty of the court.

An alternative solution would be to impose a duty on prosecutors to provide reasons for their decisions in cases of doubt. This would open up a form of hidden administrative decision-making. Another effect may be to achieve more consistency in prosecution decisions, by making fiscals more aware of the reasons they are taking into consideration. Cases are often marked and proceeded with very quickly without serious consideration of the fiscal's reasoning. It would not take a great deal of extra time to note reasons on each file, which would be available if the decision was called into question. Fiscals would also be encouraged to consider and articulate the basis of their decision-making, which they do not do at present. In this process, any stereotyped or discriminatory criteria applied (perhaps subconsciously) by fiscals would come to light and could be eliminated. Indeed, Lord Chief Justice Taylor suggested these benefits of publicly giving reasons for a decision in the case of *R.* v. *Skinner* (1993), albeit in this context of judicial sentencing: 'If those who had to pass sentence specified reasons or explained the process by which they arrived at their sentence, then that would bring them to consider the likely effect and public reception of that sentence.'[43] The same can be said of prosecutors' decisions; a written statement of the reason for a decision would make the prosecutor consciously aware of how he arrived at his conclusion and of the general pattern, consistent or otherwise, of his decision-making.

Generally, however, the feeling among prosecutors was that to give reasons for a disputed decision would give the accused something to latch on to, and would prolong the correspondence in a case. They were also concerned at the diplomatic requirements of situations where the reasons for a decision may be unpalatable to the offender. One body which would benefit from understanding the basis of prosecutors' decisions is the police. Although relations between the police and the fiscal service are generally good, contention arises when police officers work hard on an investigation which results in a decision of 'no proceedings'. In those instances the police may be less aggrieved if they knew why the prosecutor made that decision. Where the consistent approach of the prosecutor is known to the police, fruitless investigation may also be avoided in cases where it becomes clear at an early stage that the prosecutor's criteria for prosecution will not be met.

[43] *R.* v. *Skinner* (1993) 14 Cr. App. R. (S) 759, *per* Lord Taylor, LCJ.

10. POLICY MAKING

Fiscals can also have an indirect influence on sentencing by contributing at grass roots level to the process of policy-making. In Scotland there are various avenues through which the views of individual fiscals on policy are heard and considered at the top level of the service. William Chalmers, as Crown Agent, made a point of visiting every single fiscal branch office at least once a year to discuss policy with fiscals. In turn Regional Procurators Fiscal have monthly meetings with the Crown Agent to discuss policy and they may well take to that meeting views expressed by prosecutors at district level meetings.

Most prosecutors evidently do concern themselves with policy matters—the Crown Office has always encouraged prosecutors to be liberal-minded and forward-thinking and it is to be hoped that those trained under Chalmers' influence will have carried on his progressive spirit. The fiscal service, though short of resources, is still able to recruit new members of staff and with a new generation of prosecutors gradually replacing the older, less forward-thinking ones, the service may develop even further towards the Continental-style systems. In addition, prosecutors are involved in policy meetings with the police. In Glasgow there is a Standing Advisory Committee, members of which consist of Chief Constables and procurators fiscal from that area. These meetings are like a more policy-oriented form of the 'gate-keeping meetings' in England and Wales between the police, the probation service, social workers, and others to discuss the disposal of individual cases in the youth justice system.[44] At their meetings they would typically discuss how each institution should treat particular types of offence. Prosecutors influence sentencing there by asking the police to report or not to report certain types of crime. These meetings are presumably also helpful in maintaining co-operation between the fiscal service and the police in relation to the quality and nature of police reports. This is often a problem with regard to diversion in various parts of Scotland where police reports may contain very little relevant or useful information, despite the requirement stressed by the Lord Justice-Clerk in *Smith* v. *HMA*,[45] to lay before a prosecutor all information known relating to a case, whether favouring the prosecution or the defence.[46] Thus, in the meetings of the Standing Advisory Committee the quality of police reports can be monitored and Chief Constables advised within a co-operative framework if members of their force fall below the required standard.

[44] See, for example, G. Davis, J. Boucherat, and D. Watson, 'Pre-Court Decision-making in Juvenile Justice' (1989) *British Journal of Criminology*, 29: 219–35.
[45] [1952] JC 66.
[46] See Section 7 above.

The criticisms of the National Audit Office in their report in 1989[47] regarding the geographical variations in policy of the fiscal service implicitly reflect the need for some sort of monitoring body, similar to the national inspectorate of the CPS, recommended in England in response to policy irregularities reported by the Home Affairs Committee.[48] Scottish prosecutors must submit monthly figures to the Crown Office relating to numbers of reports received, fines and warnings issued, files marked 'no proceedings' and the like, from which the Crown Office produces basic statistics. Marked regional variations in decision-making can then be investigated. However, these statistics deal only with overall figures and the Crown Office does not monitor decision-making in any individual cases, which will only be investigated by the Crown Office following a complaint by a member of the public. The Scottish Office publish annual statistics but the fiscal service itself has never published anything similar; it did not even publish an annual report until 1992. There had never been any Parliamentary pressure on the Lord Advocate to do so. However, another administrative section of the service is needed to collect the statistics and to write and publish the report, perhaps again like the prospective English national inspectorate. This would use up resources of money and manpower in the publication of the report which could otherwise be used in the prosecution or other means of dealing with crime.

Mr Chalmers' objection to a national inspectorate echoed the general criticisms of the National Audit Office's report—that it is naïve to expect the whole service to work to one overall, uniform policy. As mentioned in Chapter 1, Glasgow itself has specific crime problems in its inner city areas which require different considerations to the crime problems of the rural, highland areas of Scotland. Although some degree of uniformity of policy is obviously desirable so that prosecution decision-making in Scotland does not reflect their somewhat chaotic sentencing policy, it would be wrong to make robots of prosecutors. It is an essential and fundamental feature of their job that prosecutors use their discretion and apply their own minds and experience to each individual case, which, after all, will never be identical to any other.

11. CONCLUSION

Scotland's fiscal service, having grown up under the mixed influences of English common law and European systems, has become something of a hybrid system. Elements of the Scottish system, though, have eased the

---

[47] National Audit Office, *Review of the Procurator Fiscal Service*, op. cit., at para. 4.4, 13.
[48] J. Pienaar, 'National Inspectorate to monitor CPS decisions', *Independent*, 18 July 1990.

introduction and working of the recent reforms. Most notable is the relationship between the fiscals and the police. The co-operation here is critical in disseminating the information needed to make well-informed decisions. There are close links between senior fiscals and Chief Constables who have regular meetings to discuss policy. Hostilities rarely arise, and the tensions that exist in England and Wales are not present in Scotland. Clearly, the main reason for this is the fundamental supervisory structure which has grown up as an historical process. The competition between English prosecutors and police, perhaps born out of a feeling of sour grapes on the part of the police who have had part of their remit taken away, simply does not exist in Scotland where the subordinate role of police officers rules out much hostility.

Although retaining a position firmly beneath that of judges in the hierarchy of the criminal justice system, fiscals have been given many of the powers shared by their German and Dutch counterparts to make a positive and significant impact on sentencing policy—a far more progressive state of affairs than is reflected in the CPS in England and Wales. However, the attitude of prosecutors towards their own role is hindering the effectiveness of the recent reforms. Not all prosecutors are so 'anti-theoretical', especially those who have worked in Crown Office at some time, and who are willing to discuss policy and theory. But the majority still, like English prosecutors, see their job as an administrative, bureaucratic task. They simply will not accept a sentencing role, probably due to their lack of reflectiveness about the job they are doing. Their pragmatic approach means that they are less enthusiastic about any new ideas presented to them by researchers and academics. Their decision-making remains intuitive, very much learnt 'on the job' and efforts to make it more explicit and regulated are not well received. Making the process more explicit would make prosecutors more conscious of the kinds of decisions they are making and their ability to impose penalties is fundamental in that process.

Since their study in 1982 Moody and Tombs have remarked with surprise that the prosecutor's range of powers to dispose of cases at the pre-trial stage has increased dramatically over a comparatively short period of time.[49] So much so that they noted a reversal in the emphasis given by fiscals to the public interest criteria. A pro-prosecution policy, where the public interest criteria were used to justify prosecutions, has been replaced with a general presumption in favour of non-prosecution and the use of prosecutorial alternatives wherever possible. The net result is that prosecutions in 1991 accounted for the disposal of only about 50 per cent of all cases passed to the prosecutor:

[49] S. Moody, and J. Tombs, 'Alternatives to Prosecution: The Public Interest Redefined' [1993] *Crim. LR* 357–67.

A wider range of formal alternatives to prosecution is available to [fiscals] in making decisions and this appears to have had a decisive influence. . . . This shift in prosecution practices has undoubtedly paralleled a redefinition of what constitutes prosecution in the public interest.[50]

However, despite the myriad new powers given to prosecutors which increase their importance in the disposal of cases outside the courtroom, their continued reluctance to accept that they have a role as sentencers in the criminal process is very strong. This reluctance is fostered by the refusal of members of the judiciary to acknowledge this important aspect of a prosecutor's role. The Lord Justice General said in a recent case:

the Crown is the master of the instance at all times up to the moment when the prosecutor has moved the court to pronounce sentence. But at that stage the matter moves entirely from the Crown to the court and it is desirable for good reasons of public policy that the Crown should not be involved in the process of sentencing in any way whatever. It is known to all who practice in the criminal system of this country that the Crown has absolutely no goal or interest in this process.[51]

Indeed, the tenor of the replies from many of the judicial witnesses to the Stewart Committee suggested a resistance to the idea that prosecutors should have any more influence over the penalizing of offenders. This was certainly not the view of all; some academic witnesses were inclined to accept the suggestions for reform, and saw this enhanced role for prosecutors as the best way to ease the pressure on the court system. However, amongst others, comments such as those which follow expressed what they felt to be an unsuitable mode of reform:

I am opposed to any proposal which would enable the prosecutor . . . to dispose of the matter without legal proceedings. The questions of guilt and punishment in such a case must be questions for the Court alone and it is in the public interest that all should be resolved by the Court, in public, having regard to all relevant facts and circumstances.

It appears to me that the net result of acceptance of these proposals would be to create an *imperium in imperico* and an alternative criminal jurisdiction controlled by the Crown Office alone in a wide field of criminal conduct subject to no supervision or control by the constitutional courts of the realm.

I cannot emphasise sufficiently that the function of the prosecuting authorities is limited; it is not, and never should be, to prescribe and decide the appropriate penalty or curative treatment.

It is not particularly clear whether these statements stem from doubts as to the ability of prosecutors to make quasi-judicial decisions, or from doubts as to their independence and neutrality, or whether they are simply

---

[50] Ibid., 367. This reversal of a pro-prosecution policy mirrors a similar trend which occurred in the Netherlands in the 1970s—see Chapter 4.

[51] *HMA* v. *McKenzie*, unreported, 19 Oct. 1989.

resisting the removal of part of a judge's remit to another authority (rather like the resistance of the police in England and Wales to the CPS taking over criminal prosecutions in 1985). One might have thought that judges would be pleased to have some of the burden removed from their shoulders, and to relieve some of the pressure on the courts which prompted the establishment of the Stewart Committee.

The underlying operational philosophy of fiscals, therefore, has not changed, certainly since the publication of Moody and Tombs' study in 1982, even though the development of alternatives has greatly changed their working practices. Most fiscals will still not acknowledge the significance of their decision-making on sentencing options. They will admit that all the decisions they make have an indirect bearing, and some will admit, for example, deliberately choosing a mode of procedure to limit the sentence given, but they are very reticent to accept a positive role in sentencing. That is probably why there was so much opposition to the introduction of fiscal fines, because that legislation gave them power directly to impose a penalty, as opposed to pre-court disposals such as warnings which they felt were more acceptable.

During the interviews conducted, prosecutors were keen to point out their wide and varying decision-making options and expressed pride in their progressive system which allows them to dispose of cases in a more constructive way, but there was always a contradiction. At the same time, they emphatically denied any explicit interest in sentencing and the basic thesis of this project, the role of the prosecutor as a sentencer, was greeted with a measure of alarm. Their interest, they claimed, extended only to making decisions with an estimated sentence in mind and objectively presenting evidence in court to aim for a reasonable penalty in any case.

Those witnesses who disliked the policy reforms recommended by the Stewart Committee preferred reforms of a more 'administrative' nature; that is a preference for the expansion of the court system itself. Greater resources were called for to finance more staff and more court buildings to deal with the increasing workload. However, the bitter experience of the present government in trying to deal with the prison crisis in England and Wales shows that this means of coping with increasing pressure is often counterproductive, unpopular with the tax-payer, and results in the expensive exercise of reformers trying to 'swim against the tide'. Perhaps more beneficial would be a model for reform which gets to the nerve-centre of the problem and properly deals with the source of trouble, rather than merely applying cosmetic measures to numb its effect on the system.

4

The Dutch Openbaar Ministerie:
The Kingpin Sentencers

1. INTRODUCTION

PROSECUTORS in the Netherlands have always been recognized as important players in the field of criminal justice. Their influence is wide and their powers extensive in the determination of the penalty imposed upon an offender in any particular case; indeed, such is the effect of prosecution policy on other branches of the criminal justice system that Jan van Dijk was inspired to describe the prosecution service, Openbaar Ministerie, as the 'spider in the web' of the criminal process. Further, albeit within a smaller, more close-knit system than other European prosecution systems,[1] Dutch prosecutors can, and do, have a much more clearly defined and open influence on the sentencing policy of judges.

The wider variety of powers available to prosecutors in all aspects of their job are listed and described in some detail in Downes' study of the Dutch criminal justice system.[2] For the purposes of this chapter, however, attention will be focused specifically on those powers and duties which particularly illustrate the prosecutors' influence over sentencing policy, such as the waiving of prosecutions (conditionally or unconditionally) on policy grounds, recommending sentences in court, deciding which charges will be brought in any case, and issuing fines or 'transactions', out of court settlements. This list of powers may not at first appear extraordinary; indeed, apart from the duty to recommend a sentence during court proceedings, the list contains no powers that do not also exist, for example, in the Scottish procurator fiscal service. However, what is remarkable, particularly in contrast to the Scottish system, is the amount of discretion in the hands of the prosecutor within the perimeters of those powers and their vast application to all manner of cases. It is this wide discretion which has rendered the prosecutor so important in the Dutch criminal justice system

---

[1] There are only around 300 prosecutors in the Netherlands.

[2] See D. Downes, *Contrasts in Tolerance: Post-war penal policy in the Netherlands and England and Wales* (Oxford, 1988), 13–16. See also L. H. Leigh and J. E. Hall Williams, *The Management of the Prosecution Process in Denmark, Sweden and the Netherlands* (Leamington Spa, 1981), ch. 5, 53–64.

and which has given him a pivotal role in relation to the other criminal justice authorities.

Perhaps even more remarkable, however, is the extent to which the discretion of the prosecutor is being even further widened. New policy plans issued in 1990 envisaged an extension of the sentencing influence of the prosecutor further than ever before by focusing the flow of cases to be dealt with by the prosecutor without reference to the courts, as part of a wider policy shift towards severity. A question that needs to be considered, however, is how far this policy can extend before it exceeds the limits of constitutionality.

2. PROSECUTORIAL POWERS

There are many options open to the Dutch prosecutor in deciding how to exercise his discretion. Reports of all cases are passed from the police to the prosecutor and from that point the prosecutor can in theory, and certainly in the case of minor offences (*overtredingen*), take any decision he/she wants as to whether or not to bring the case to court.[3]

(a) Technical Waivers

As in the other jurisdictions considered here, the fundamental evidential sufficiency criterion applies in the Netherlands. Where a prosecutor considers that a judge would not allow a conviction because of insufficient evidence, or by reason of some other technical difficulty with the evidence, then he should not proceed with the case at all and waiver should be unconditional (*bevoegdheidssepot*). This is an important first consideration in any prosecution system with the obvious aim of preventing the process of net-widening. In Holland, the consideration of evidential sufficiency is perhaps even more important than in England and Wales, because in Dutch trials there is a much heavier reliance upon written evidence rather than the testimony of witnesses in person. In the Netherlands, for the purpose of speeding up a trial[4] most of the evidence will be presented to the judge in the form of written statements. Thus, any shortfall or inadequacy in the

---

[3] In theory he or she has a similar, unlimited discretion in respect of more serious offences (*misdrijven*) which carry maximum sentences of 6 years' imprisonment or less, but the prosecutor will be more restrained by public interest when considering alternative sanctions in cases such as armed robbery or rape.

[4] Dutch trials in general are considerably shorter than their English equivalents. Dato Steenhuis estimates that most trials are completed in approximately 10% of the duration an English trial. Generally speaking, for example, trials of drunken drivers take approximately 20 minutes, rape cases around one hour, and even the most complicated fraud cases are unlikely to exceed one day in duration.

compilation of statements by the police, or any discrepancy or technical error in their substance, would reduce the possibility of securing a conviction further than in an alternative system where such shortfalls could be made up in the oral testimony of witnesses, and this factor has to be borne in mind by the prosecutor when considering the evidential sufficiency criterion. Aside from these technical considerations, the options for alternative disposals of cases without reference to the court are numerous.

(b) Policy Waivers

A policy waiver (*beleidssepot*) allows a prosecutor to drop any case, despite sufficient evidence for its prosecution, where he or she considers that it is not in the public interest to prosecute the offender in court. This involves consideration of a number of extra-legal factors, both aggravating and mitigating, to assess whether the public interest requires that the case should be waived or indicates that a prosecution would not be prudent in the circumstances. In Holland, there is an unpublished list of such considerations which contains criteria similar to the CPS's list of public interest factors. However, whereas the Code for Crown Prosecutors in England and Wales lists twenty-two major public interest factors (fourteen in favour of prosecution and eight against), the Dutch list, produced by the Ministry of Justice and compiled by the five Procurators-General, contains no less than fifty-two such factors and is explicitly non-exhaustive. The reasons for dismissing cases are all vaguely stated and thus easily applied to a wide range of circumstances. Further, the list is merely for guidance and advice, to assist the prosecutor's decision-making and is in no way binding or complete. Therefore, this option gives the prosecutor practically unlimited freedom to stop the progress of a case to trial and to deal with it himself. It is little wonder that the prosecutor plays such a pivotal role in the Netherlands, when his process of filtering the cases proceeding towards the court is so effective. He is consequently in command of the extent of his own sentencing jurisdiction by limiting that of the judges at the next stage in the criminal justice process.

The reasons for non-prosecution are varied. Some, as mentioned above, are widely worded and generalized and seek to protect the general legal order of the state. Examples are waiving prosecution in order to preserve national security, or to prevent public disorder and unrest, also waiving prosecution in a case where there is a lack of national interest in its prosecution, where the offender is foreign or the crime was committed abroad. Other reasons, usually more closely concerned with the crime or the accused in particular, are more tangible and clearly stated and are common to many legal systems across Europe. Examples are the age and health of the accused, whether the accused has been convicted of and punished for subsequent offences, the triviality or the staleness of the offence, or where prosecution may be contrary to the interests of the victim. Many are simply reflective of common sense, for example not prosecuting where the damage has been repaired or compensated, or where the offender is untraceable.[5] For whichever reason the prosecutor decides to waive a case in the interests of the public, that reason must be briefly stated on the file. Since the listed, written reasons are coded, the prosecutor will often simply write the appropriate code number on the file; the important thing is that the reason is actually stated. The reasoning behind this procedure was not made clear by any of the persons interviewed, except perhaps the concern to clarify the reason for non-prosecution in case there is an appeal against the prosecutor's use of his discretion (see Section 8 below). However, neither each individual case, nor a random sample of cases, is routinely checked at any stage, so the practice is unlikely to have any effect in preventing either inconsisent decision-making or decision-making on the basis of irrelevant or improper reasons, although the practice may be a useful exercise to the individual prosecutor in subconsciously regulating and assimilating his non-prosecution policy.

The extent to which this diverting of cases away from the courts is utilized in the Netherlands has depended, over the years, on the basic legal principle governing prosecution policy as a whole—the legality principle (involving compulsory prosecution) or the expediency principle (see Chapter 1). In the Netherlands, where the discretion relating to public interest considerations is an integral part of prosecution decision-making, there is clear evidence that the expediency principle (*opportuniteitsbesingel*) is in operation and that principle has since 1926 been succinctly stated in the Code of Criminal Procedure: 'the public prosecutor decides to prosecute in the case where a prosecution seems to be necessary regarding the result of the investigations. Proceedings can be dropped for reasons of public interest.'[6] However, since the early 1970s, this principle has been reinterpreted in a more positive sense. During the 1970s, the number of waivers of prosecution rapidly and substantially increased, principally because the crime rate rose while the manpower and resources of the Openbaar Ministerie remained the same, so that the burden on each prosecutor became greater. As a matter of practical necessity, therefore, the waiver of prosecution became the starting point in prosecutorial decision-making and the emphasis on public interest was reversed. This major change in policy (stated in written form in the policy plan of the Ministry of Justice in the early 1970s) meant that public interest served as a reason *for* prosecuting, rather

---

[5] Peter Tak gives a more detailed list and analysis of the reasons for non-prosecution in *The Legal Scope of Non-prosecution in Europe* (Helsinki, 1986), 59–66.

[6] Code of Criminal Procedure, Article 167.

than a reason *against* prosecuting; the prosecutor proceeded to court only where the public interest specifically required him to do so. This policy continued throughout the 1970s until, by the early 1980s, policy waivers accounted for over 50 per cent of all cases being referred to the prosecutor by the police and was part of the political influence of the liberal and socialist ideologies then current in Dutch criminological thinking, which are now in danger of being swamped by the increasing influence of the new right-wing law and order lobby.[7]

(c) Transactions

In the early 1980s, policy makers and prosecutors alike began to realize that this was not a sound or sensible policy direction because the criminal justice authorities were perceived as turning a blind eye to, and not adequately dealing with, a majority of investigated criminality.[8] At that time, the possibility of the prosecutor acting in a quasi-judicial role of sentencer in issuing fines or transactions became much more widely used because it offered a suitable solution to the problem of adequately penalizing cases without referring them to the courts. Issuing a transaction or a fine was not a new power—indeed prosecutors interviewed in The Hague stated that the option was introduced over 30 years ago.[9] However, in order to facilitate its wider application, the 1983 Property Sanctions Act (*Wet Vemogenssancties*) allowed prosecutors in the Netherlands to offer a transaction for *misdrijven* (indictable offences carrying a maximum penalty of six years) as well as *overtredingen* (minor offences). So now a transaction can be arranged in respect of both minor offences and more serious felonies, although transactions arranged in response to the latter are not likely to include the most serious forms of violent crimes against the person, sexual offences, or serious drug offences. Nevertheless the scope is wide and in the Netherlands, where statutory maximum sentences are much lower than in England and Wales, this possibility of offering a transaction is applicable to most forms of criminality. The types of offences in that category of *misdrijven* which might attract a transaction would include shoplifting, minor drug offences involving soft drugs, drunken driving, minor assault, and the like.

In any of the above-mentioned types of cases, the prosecutor can offer the offender the option of making a transaction or a settlement out of court. The defendant is free to accept or refuse the terms of the transaction, which usually consist of an obligation on the part of the offender to pay

---

[7] See W. de Haan, *The Politics of Redress* (London, 1990), 70–3.

[8] The reasons for the rejection of this policy, connected with maintaining the credibility of the criminal justice system, will be outlined in more detail in Section 7 below.

[9] Hans Fangman and Rolf de Groot - interviewed at Stafbureau Openbaar Ministerie, the Hague, November 1990.

a fine to the prosecutor or a sum of compensation to the victim, but may also include an obligation on the offender to undertake community service, make reparation, or other conditions. If the offender refuses to accept the offer, the prosecutor must decide whether or not to proceed to court—he is not technically obliged to do so but, in the interests of maintaining the respect for and authority of the criminal justice system, prosecutors are generally encouraged to carry out their threats to prosecute in appropriate circumstances.

Unlike the Scottish system of procurator fiscal fines discussed in Chapter 3, the amount of sums to be paid under transactions is discretionary and limited only by the maximum and minimum penalty which could be imposed by a court for that particular offence. The prosecutor's discretion can range from a few guilders up to millions of guilders for large companies involved in serious environmental or fraud cases. Dato Steenhuis quoted an example of a famous case where an environmental pollution crime was committed by a tanker cleaning company in Rotterdam harbour. The company was offered a transaction amounting to 500,000 guilders which they were happy to pay to avoid the unfavourable publicity which might have been associated with a court case. Another prosecutor recalled offers of transactions involving millions of guilders, in one case 50 million guilders, where large companies had committed a number of offences for which transactions could be accumulated, or where a company had made a profit from their criminal activities which could be retrieved by the Openbaar Ministerie.

This system of discretionary fines imposed by an administrative body is not too far removed from the discretionary fine system operated by various independent prosecution agencies in England and Wales under the provisions for private prosecutions. Indeed, many forms of 'morally colourless' crime or white collar crime are dealt with by many different Government departments or independent bodies, such as the Post Office, the RSPCA, the Inland Revenue, the Department of the Environment, the Health and Safety Executive as well as many local authority departments such as Trading Standards, Environmental Health, and Building and Planning Departments. The right of private prosecution has been preserved throughout centuries of procedural change in England, although its use may be infrequent and, by now, restricted by statute.[10] In Europe, where these types of white collar crimes are also regularly dealt with out of court by administrative bodies, the fact that such substantial fines as those mentioned above in the Dutch context may be imposed in the form of a transaction at the pre-trial stage need not cause undue consternation.

A series of guidelines has been formulated by the fine Dutch Procurators General, in conjunction with the Minister of Justice, to give further assistance

---

[10] See Lidstone et al., (1980), op. cit., ch. 2, 111.

to prosecutors and to further structure the system to achieve greater consistency. There is now a large network of guidelines governing transactions, which recommend tariffs for transactions in respect of specific offences. For example, the recommended range of transactions for shoplifting and common theft is between 100 and 500 guilders, depending on the value of the stolen property. The recommended range of transactions is usually slightly lower than the equivalent recommendations of sentences in court, so that there is an incentive for the offender to accept a transaction and avoid a court appearance. For example, in the case of assault, the guideline suggests transactions between 250 and 500 guilders, whereas suggested recommendations of fines in court are between 300 and 600 guilders. Prosecutors retain the discretion to make transactions outside those guidelines without having to justify that departure, but generally speaking the guidelines are followed in straightforward cases.

In 1989 the power of the public prosecutor effectively to order a period of community service attached to a transaction as a condition of non-prosecution was removed. Community service now lies solely within the jurisdiction of the judge. As for diversion to various forms of counselling and rehabilitation programmes, there is a reluctance to include these options in the transaction procedure, although it is not forbidden and the procedure is flexible enough to allow for it. In practice, none of the prosecutors interviewed had either used the power themselves or known of other cases where they were used.

The prosecutor may also be involved in diversion to psychiatric counselling, supervision by a probation officer, attendance on a rehabilitation course for drunk drivers, or community service in another way. These options are not conditions of non-prosecution. The prosecutor can postpone prosecution until such conditions have been met and then present the case to the court with the defendant's fulfilment of the conditions acting as a strong mitigation of sentence. Therefore, whilst the prosecutor's powers here are somewhat restricted and remain within the context of a prosecution, the prosecutor nonetheless exercises a discretion and is directly involved in a diversionary form of welfare provision.

(d) Warnings

Dutch public prosecutors are empowered to give warnings in selected cases. As in the other continental jurisdictions considered here, the Dutch police do not have formal powers to issue warnings or any other equivalent to the English cautioning procedure, although they may issue informal warnings in the exercise of their limited discretion not to pass a case to a prosecutor. In the Netherlands, the warning procedure is not linked to the transaction system. The accused may refuse to accept the warning if guilt is disputed. Acceptance of a warning is not a condition of a transaction *per se*, but is a prerequisite for an unconditional waiver. In other words, it is a measure which falls between the conditional and unconditional types of waivers. Official statistics will record a warning as an unconditional waiver of a case with a reprimand, as opposed to a simple unconditional waiver. Thus, in the wider scheme of available prosecutorial penalties, the use of the warning has been encouraged by the Ministry of Justice as another means by which the prosecutor can dismiss cases with the dual, seemingly contradictory, aims of maintaining expediency whilst concomitantly increasing the severity of the response of the criminal process.

Warnings can be written or given orally by the prosecutor, and are technically available in respect of any offence, including felonies. Obviously a prosecutor will use discretion in deciding whether a warning is appropriate in very serious cases, weighing up the public interest factors which may require a prosecution and the specific circumstances of the case which may, exceptionally, render a warning suitable. As the least intrusive and punitive option of the public prosecutor, the warning tends to be used most often in relation to first-time offenders, and especially in relation to young offenders. For the latter group, the warning provides a more effective sanction than a simple unconditional waiver; it is presumed to be more cogent in terms of deterrence than taking no formal action at all. At the same time, the warning is not unduly stigmatizing, nor as inappropriately punitive as a financial transaction might be.

Practising prosecutors in the Netherlands have noted a trend away from the use of warnings in adult cases. Even where guilt is minor, or the offence trivial, a transaction is the preferred method of disposal. This coincides with the general policy trend towards an increase in the use of transactions, particularly in cases which might otherwise have been dismissed without formal punishment. This policy trend is analysed in depth below. However, for young offenders, the warning has been retained as a popular and oft-used disposal, not least because it is flexible, in that it is not rigidly governed by guidelines or legislative rules. Such flexibility is double-edged; lack of coherent guidance can produce inconsistency, net-widening, and discriminatory application, whilst at the same time the option is more widely applicable in an area where careful, considered, and restrained decision-making is called for.

3. PROSECUTORIAL INFLUENCE OVER JUDICIAL SENTENCING

(a) Recommending Sentence

Aside from the direct sentencing powers that the public prosecutor has in the Netherlands, there is also considerable potential for influence over sentencing carried out by judges. At court, the sentencing role of the prosecutor may be indirect but is no less powerful. The prosecutor's influence, especially in recommending a sentence to the trial judge, is such that sentencing is, at least in practice, a joint enterprise between prosecutors and judges. It is the duty of prosecutors to recommend a sentence in all cases of prosecution in court. The extent to which the judge actually takes the recommendation into account will vary according to the respect which the judge has for the individual prosecutor concerned. Although the judge is never bound by the prosecutor's recommendation, judges generally give serious consideration to the suggestions of prosecutors, and prosecutors therefore have an enormous impact on the sentencing policy of the judge.

Changes in sentencing policy, whether expansionist or reductionist, can therefore be indirectly effected or implemented by the public prosecutor in the Netherlands, and the impetus for such changes may well come from prosecutors rather than from the judges themselves. Van Duyne even argues that policy change is unlikely to happen unless the prosecutor has a change of attitude towards the use of a particular punishment: 'the wide powers wielded by the Dutch prosecutor . . . make(s) it clear that this institution is the only channel through which a criminal policy can be formulated and executed.'[11] Therefore, where policy-makers wish to achieve radical change, the body from which they most need support is the Openbaar Ministerie, without which support legislation or directives on sentencing policy cannot be implemented.

This phenomenon is recognized by Dutch policy-makers. In general a change in sentencing or in sentencing guidance tends to be effected through the issue to prosecutors of guidelines on the level of sentence to be recommended. It is felt that the influence of the prosecutor is sufficiently strong in most cases that demands for less or more sentences of imprisonment, for example, can be more effectively achieved through the prosecutors' recommendations than by issuing such guidance to judges. Van Duyne certainly appeared to have this assumption in mind when he conducted his research on the psychological process of sentencing in the Netherlands.[12] He considered ways in which sentencing as a problem-solving exercise could be analysed and then improved with appropriate guidance. In so doing, it is interesting to note that his fieldwork concentrated to a large extent (though not entirely) on the decision-making of the public prosecutor. Such a situation is inconceivable in England where judges view their sentencing as highly independent, specialized and peculiar to their own branch of the criminal justice process and change is dependent on an offensive launched directly at judges themselves.

[11] P. van Duyne, 'Simple Decision Making' in D. C. Pennington and S. Lloyd-Bostock, eds., *The Psychology of Sentencing* (Oxford, 1987), 145.
[12] Ibid.

The reasons why this form of partnership in sentencing is possible and acceptable in the Netherlands are not straightforward. At least two reasons can be identified. First, the proximity of the relationship between the judge and the prosecutor may make such a partnership more palatable to both parties. Most prosecutors and judges train together for six years and, on the whole, receive the same legal education, organized by the *Stichting Studiecentrum Rechtspleging*, funded, though not governed, by the Ministry of Justice. It is broadly equivalent to the Judicial Studies Board, run by the Lord Chancellor's Department in England and Wales, although the former trains both the sitting and standing judiciary (judges and prosecutors), whereas the latter trains only judges.[13] In the course of this training, trainees will spend time on secondment in the courts practising judicial skills, and in a prosecutor's office practising advocacy and prosecutorial skills. Therefore, a qualified public prosecutor has first-hand experience of the judge's function and vice versa, and therefore the prosecutor has some experience in making judicial decisions. This is not necessarily a justification for greatly enhancing prosecutors' sentencing discretion, since after all the prosecutor's and the judge's functions are discrete and independent. It may, however, make such an extension of the prosecutor's role, implemented on the basis of other justifications, more acceptable.

Another reason why policy-makers may prefer to implement sentencing reform in an indirect way through the prosecutor's function, is that the prosecution service is better suited to acting as a policy-making body. The mechanisms for policy-making are in place; its distinct hierarchy, with the five Procurators General at the head, is more geared up as a policy-making body. The Dutch judiciary do not have such distinct hierarchy or sufficient mechanisms for such a task. Holthuis has propounded the view thus: 'the judiciary is not regarded as the proper institution to set guidelines about levels of sentence.'[14] This may seem curious to international onlookers; in England and Wales the judiciary are very much the central branch in the criminal justice process and they wield the sole and independent power to set sentencing guidelines in the form of tariffs, guideline judgments and practice directions, in partnership with the legislature, not with the CPS.[15] Judges in England and Wales therefore, very much govern themselves. In the Netherlands, the fact that the sentencing practice of judges is controlled to such an extent by the prosecutor is indicative of the wide discretion and power of the Openbaar Ministerie which should not be under-estimated in

[13] See further, H. Holthuis, 'The Role of the Public Prosecutor in the Netherlands' in NACRO, *International Comparisons in Criminal Justice: The London Seminars* (London, 1993).

[14] Ibid., 18.

[15] See further Home Office White Paper, *Crime, Justice and Protecting the Public*, Cm 965, (London, 1990).

analysing the recent practice and policy changes in the use of imprisonment which will be discussed below. It is interesting to note that Ashworth's
proposal for a Sentencing Council in England, to assist with the development of sentencing reform through guidelines, will imitate the Dutch example to a degree. Public prosecutors would be involved in the development
of guidance through their membership of this Council, at least at the
higher echelons. Ashworth does not go so far as to propose a system
whereby sentencing guidelines are effectively prosecutorial guidelines, exercised in the process of recommending a sentence, but what he is suggesting is a procedure where the CPS bring their experience and different
viewpoint into the system of guidance for judges.[16]

(b) Charges and Mode of Trial

The prosecutor has some influence over judicial sentencing in this context,
although to a lesser extent. The judge carries a much more independent
and decisive role in respect of the charges which form the foundation of
a prosecution, although a limited initial discretion rests with the prosecutor. The latter will generally charge the defendant with the most serious
offence that he feels can be proven on the evidence supplied, but he also
gives a number of alternative charges. It is then for the judge to decide, as
part of his decision over guilt or innocence, which of the alternative charges
has been successfully proven. The initial choice of the range of charges is
within the discretion of the prosecutor and therefore his application of a
consistent policy at this stage may affect the eventual sentence. The prosecutor will also make a subjective assessment of the aggravating and
mitigating circumstances in a case, and the extent to which these factors
affect the choice of charge is a matter of discretion at the pre-trial stage.
However, where a charge which results in a conviction is flexible, the
choice of charge has less influence over sentencing.

Further, although the choice of mode of trial (or 'forum shopping') can
be carefully engineered so that the maximum statutory sentences can be
imposed, the prosecutor's influence is also limited here. In Holland there
are two types of court; first, the cantonal or police court (*Kantongerecht*)
with a single judge who can impose any sentence up to a maximum of six
months' imprisonment. In the district court (*Arrondissementsrechtbank*) a
bench of one to three judges can impose any penalty up to the statutory
maximum for a given offence.[17] In the Netherlands, where judges are per-
manently sitting in the same court and do not work on a circuit basis as
in England, it is easier to arrange for a particular judge to hear a case in

[16] See further, A. Ashworth, *Sentencing and Criminal Justice* (London, 1992), ch. 12.
[17] See *The Dutch Court System* (The Hague, 1987), for a general description of the court
structure in the Netherlands.

order to predetermine the severity of the outcome. Selecting a particular judge to hear a case may, in general terms, affect the severity of the eventual sentence given, but the prosecutor's discretion here is still limited by the inherently subjective and partially unpredictable nature of the discretionary decision-making by the judge.

4. Victims

The spirit of restorative justice is relatively new to penal policy in the Netherlands. Comparatively slow progress has been made in including consideration of the victim's interests and provision for them into dispositional decision-making. The emphasis has generally been centred on the offender and on crime control and/or prevention, the philosophy being that crime control and crime prevention in themselves cater for victims' interests by reducing the rate of victimization. This is, however, gradually changing and various provisions for victims show an acknowledgement that victim support is needed in the aftermath of a crime, in addition to the prevention of victimization at an earlier stage. The guidance given to prosecutors has, to some extent, always recognized the benefits of victim-offender reparation. One of the most oft-quoted public interest criteria, weighing against a prosecution, was whether the offender had volunteered to offer reparation or compensation for the damage caused by the criminal activity. However, it has only been in the past few years that the prosecutor has proactively sought to instigate such reparation.

Until recently, for example, the transaction was usually a financial settlement and the inclusion of reparative sanctions was comparatively rare. The transaction procedure allows prosecutors to impose restorative, rather than punitive, conditions in a transaction, including reparation, mediation, or compensation. The only limitation placed on this wide discretion is that the conditions should not violate the offender's political or civil rights. These conditions, which are increasingly being used, may include requiring the offender to apologize to the victim, or to offer to repair or make good any damage done. Such provision for victims is still dependent upon the enthusiasm and efforts of an individual prosecutor. There are few established schemes or mechanisms to arrange these reparative conditions on a formal basis; agreements for settlement of the case between the victim and the offender will usually be negotiated and organized on a case-by-case basis. Some cases which are referred to the probation service by the prosecutor before trial are, in fact, eventually settled by means of some form of reparation, this time arranged by the probation officer involved.

Evidently, where reparation is dependent on the efforts of an individual prosecutor, it is unlikely that the use of restorative conditions will greatly increase. Prosecutors are often too busy to devote such attention to any one case, unless the reparation is of a type which is easy to arrange, such as a meeting for an apology or an order to pay compensation. Lengthy negotiations between victim and offender, conducted by the prosecutor as arbiter, are likely to be out of the question. Therefore, a few structured reparation schemes, which effectively relieve the prosecutor of the burden of this role, are beginning to emerge in isolated locations around the Netherlands. One example of such a scheme is the *Schadebemiddelings-project* in Middelberg. Established in 1989, the project combines the roles of a victim support service, a mediation service which settles cases without reference to either a court or the prosecutor (neighbourhood disputes, or assaults between friends, for example), and a negotiator of reparation settlements in cases referred to them by the public prosecutor.[18] Research conducted into this project indicated that prosecutors were very willing to use it as a condition of non-prosecution, and where they did not do so the judge at trial heavily discounted the sentence of a defendant who had participated in some form of restorative effort towards a victim before trial. A change in the fundamental ideology of criminal law policy in the Netherlands (which will be explored below), has heightened policy-makers' awareness of the victim's interest and has incorporated this awareness more fully into practical initiatives. It is therefore to be expected that projects such as the Middelberg scheme will gradually burgeon on a national scale in the next decade.

On a higher policy level, a set of guidelines has been issued to all criminal justice practitioners, which sets out procedures and standards which should be followed in order to offer the victim a more satisfactory service from the criminal process. The guidelines evolved from the recommendations of the Committee Vaillant[19] and resembled a more concrete form of the *Victim's Charter* in England and Wales.[20] They require that the victim be given more information on the decisions made in respect of their case and the procedures through which it is being processed, and that both the police and the public prosecutor actively consider the possibility of compensation being paid or a settlement of the case which involves compensation or reparation, and that these should be suggested to the victim wherever appropriate. These guidelines indicate a strong policy stand in favour of the victim's interests in the criminal process, and also offer practitioners practical guidance on how best to implement the spirit of the guidelines to give maximum emphasis to such interests. As with all guidelines, their effectiveness will depend on the inclination of individuals to

[18] T. van Hecke and J. Wemmers, *Schadebemiddelingsproject Middelberg* (Arnhem, 1992).
[19] Committee Vaillant, *Eindrapport van de Werkgroep Justitieel beleid en slachtoffer*, (The Hague, 1985).
[20] See Chapter 2.

implement them, but clearly, at the policy level at least, the victim is shifting further towards centre-stage in the wider scale of criminal law policy in the Netherlands.

5. FEATURES OF THE NEW POLICY

(a) The 1985 Policy Plan

It was mentioned above that by the 1980s, politicians and others were dissatisfied with the prosecution policy at the time to waive large numbers of cases unconditionally and without any meaningful intervention by the criminal justice system. Hence, following the introduction in 1983 of a new power for prosecutors to intervene in a broader range of more serious offences, the policy plan produced in 1985 by the Ministry of Justice laid great emphasis on the full utilization of the new power.[21]

Having described in immense detail the problems that Dutch society faced in respect of rising crime figures,[22] both in the recent past and forecasted for the next few years, the plan set out an outline of policy to be adopted by all branches of the criminal process in the five years between 1985 and 1990 in order to combat the 'growing concern among the population over the increase in crime' and to 'improve the maintenance of law and order'.[23] A process of bifurcation (not unlike the developments in England and Wales in the late 1980s) began to differentiate between petty and severe forms of criminality. The former, over which the prosecutor most widely exercises his sentencing function, was to be dealt with by a combination of preventative and repressive measures, most notably a greater use of transactions; the latter was to be dealt with more severely in the courtroom. The expected effect of this on prosecution policy was a 50 per cent decrease in the number of cases unconditionally waived on policy grounds by prosecutors, thus officially and determinedly bringing an end to the unprecedented leniency of the 1970s. The 1985 policy plan may therefore be seen as the beginning of the end of what Dhondt has called the 'penal honeymoon' in the Netherlands.[24] Both Downes[25] and de Haan[26] predicted this end to the period of marked leniency in the late 1980s, and

---

[21] See *Samenleving en Criminaliteit: Een beleidsplan voor de kommende jaren*, (Society and Crime: A policy plan for the future) (The Hague, 1985). (Summary translated into English).

[22] Ibid., Section 2, 7–19.

[23] Ibid., 1.

[24] J. Dhondt, 'Holland—is the penal honeymoon over?' *Prison Report*, Issue 4, (London, 1988), 6–7.

[25] (1988) *Contrasts in Tolerance*, op. cit., 196 and 204, where he proposes that the 'limits of . . . tolerance' may have been reached by 1988.

[26] (1990) *The Politics of Redress*, op. cit., 70.

it can clearly be seen that the policy plan in 1985, together with changes in social and political outlooks on crime and criminal policy, brought about a relatively swift end to this liberal period in Dutch penal history.

(b) 1985–90

By 1990 the policy plan was fully implemented, and, from the Ministry of Justice's point of view, successfully so; unconditional policy waivers fell by 50 per cent. In 1989 a total of approximately 211,000 crimes (*misdrijven*) were reported to prosecution offices throughout Holland. Of those, 43 per cent were dealt with by a court, of which approximately one-fifth were dealt with in conjunction with other cases against the same offender, and 6 per cent were 'taken into consideration' at the sentencing stage. The remaining 51 per cent were disposed of by a prosecutor alone.[27] Hence, by the end of the 1980s, the prosecutor was already beginning to have a much more important role. Despite the large decrease in unconditional policy waivers, there was no marked increase in the number of cases being referred to court. The substantial number of cases which would otherwise have been dealt with by an unconditional policy waiver were dealt with, not by the courts, but rather by the prosecutor in a more repressive or severe manner than before, making full use of his powers to impose conditions or penalties on waiver. It appears, therefore, that the 1983 Property Sanctions Act (*Wet Vemogenssancties*) mentioned above had the desired effect of increasing the use made of the transaction procedure in serious cases. Indeed, in 1989 transactions arranged by the prosecutor in cases of *misdrijven* accounted for about 19 per cent of all cases reported to the Openbaar Ministerie.[28] These figures are concordant with the focus on repression in the 1985 policy plan, with the central character on the new stage being the prosecutor.

(c) *Planning Ahead*

Following the complete implementation of the 1985 policy plan, the current Minister of Justice issued another policy plan in 1990, entitled *Law in Motion*, setting out proposals for criminal justice policy generally over

---

[27] See Annual Report of the Openbaar Ministerie—*Jaarverslag Openbaar Ministerie 1989: Het OM en de Handhaving van de Milieuwetgeving*, (The Hague, 1989), 121, Table 2.3. For figures of prosecutorial disposals during the same period relating to young offenders in the Netherlands, aged between 16 and 20, see M. Kommer, (1990) 'The Role of the Prosecutor in Pre-Court Decision Making', paper presented at a conference on 'Young Adults in the Criminal Justice System', Nottingham Polytechnic, 5 Dec. 1990, Tables 2 and 3, 10.

[28] *Annual Report of the Openbaar Ministerie 1989*, ibid., Table 2.2. Graph 2.2 also indicates the marked degree to which the use of transactions has increased, at the expense of the use of unconditional policy and technical waivers. This increase is most marked after 1983 when the new legislation took effect.

the next five years.[29] The motivation for specifying future policy in 1990 is less clear than the evident concern about rising crime figures which prompted the policy plan of 1985. Crime rates are still increasing in Holland (albeit at a slower rate than prior to the 1985 policy plan) and anxiety has not been replaced by complacency; there is particular concern over organized crime and increasing armed robbery. The 1990 policy plan cites this increase in crime rates as a reason for reconsidering criminal policy and for building on the improvements made under the 1985 plan. In addition, the Ministry of Justice were concerned with the relatively high rate of victimization in the Netherlands compared with other countries (from evidence elicited from van Dijk *et al.*'s international victim survey)[30] and the pressures created by these crime problems on the system itself, resulting in delays and backlogs. Other problems that the policy plan aimed to solve were more social; for example discrimination, especially in police policies, in dealing with ethnic minorities and foreign offenders was in need of eradication.

However, one wonders whether the motivation for this new plan included political expediency, especially given the considerable credit given to the previous Minister for the initiative of the original plan in 1985 (the first for many years in the field of criminal justice). Whether or not this motive existed, there was a practical reason for producing a policy plan in 1990. The government had recently extended the budget of the Ministry and the policy plan was an ideal way to set out how the increased resources were to be applied.

The 1990 plan is different to the 1985 plan in that it has a much wider scope. It covers not only criminal law and criminal justice, but also areas such as immigration, the quality control of legislation and general policy—in short, it covers all the areas of responsibility of the Minister of Justice. The substance of the report is much broader and more generally worded than the previous plan and discusses policy in a wider sense than just the figures and targets related to criminal justice. Perhaps this is not surprising, given that the plan was drafted by a working party of representatives from all corners of the Ministry of Justice with very different concerns and viewpoints. To produce a coherent and homogenous report which covers all the issues raised, the document was inevitably generalized and broadly structured. The concerns and aims discussed in the document may be roughly summarized under three headings.

First, the plan emphasizes the importance of analysing the core functions of the Ministry of Justice (that is, broadly defining its aims and purposes) and of considering those purposes when formulating policy. Functions

---

[29] *Recht in Beweging: een beleidsplan voor Justitie in de kommende jaren*, (The Hague, 1990). (Law in Motion: a policy plan for justice in the future).
[30] *Experiences of Crime across the World*, (Deventer, 1990).

such as law enforcement, legislating, running a child care and protection system, and controlling the immigration of refugees are all fully defined in Chapter 3 of the plan.

Secondly, the Ministry emphasizes the need for each department to work in close co-operation with all others so that there is a system of networking between the various directorates within the Ministry as a whole. The plan in itself is a result of such networking, being itself a product of interdepartmental discussions and working groups. However, the principle of networking is to be extended and the plan advocates working in co-operation with public services, private companies, industry and the like— a reiteration of the principle that crime is a community problem and therefore the community as a whole has a duty and interest in its control. An excellent example of this is the work being done on crime prevention by the Directorate headed by Jan van Dijk, as described in Appendix 4.1.

The third key heading is modernization of the management and organization of the Ministry as a whole, including the criminal justice authorities, which involves increasing funding, introducing computerization, and increasing manpower. The aim of this part of the report was to instill an effective management strategy into the criminal justice process in order to improve efficiency and to cut down the delays arising from the increased activities of each branch of the system following the renewed crime control effort under the 1985 plan. This applied, not least, to the Openbaar Ministerie.

In terms of prosecution policy the policy plan starts where the 1985 plan left off. Following the successful 50 per cent reduction of unconditional policy waivers, the 1990 plan sets a fresh target of just 5 per cent of all reported cases as a maximum figure for such waivers. Again, however, these waivers are to be replaced by transactions rather than by prosecutions, so that the sentencing duties of prosecutors are increasing even further. This increased importance is illustrated by the fact that in 1990, just days after the publication of the Ministry of Justice plan, the Openbaar Ministerie produced their own policy plan, the first ever published by the prosecution service itself.[31] The plan concurs with that of the Ministry in terms of general policy direction, but by concentrating specifically on prosecution policy, it considers a more detailed set of issues. The core message of the prosecution plan was to increase the rate of prosecutorial intervention, that is: to increase the proportion of cases in which prosecutors issue a penalty in place of prosecution, rather than unconditionally waiving cases on policy grounds. As in the Ministry's plan, emphasis was placed on modernization involving computerization and an increase in manpower and financial resources.

---

[31] Openbaar Ministerie, *Strafrecht met beleid: Beleidsplan openbaar ministerie 1990–1995*. (The Hague, 1990).

(d) In Practice

It seems appropriate to talk of recent Dutch prosecution policy in terms of a harsher philosophy; indeed, persons interviewed often used the words 'repression' and 'severity' to describe that new philosophy. This spirit of repression and severity which seems to be evolving in the Netherlands, and which is clearly the foundation of the two recent policy plans, has also been evident in the day-to-day practice of prosecutors. The policy plan produced by the Openbaar Ministerie was a close reflection of the working philosophy of most prosecutors in the Netherlands. Most of the 200 prosecutors in the service were involved in some way in the process of drafting or contributing towards the plan. It is symptomatic of the important position of the prosecutor in the Dutch system that he can predetermine the direction of policy through his exercise of case-by-case decision-making.

The approach of prosecutors seems to have changed, and cases which would previously have been considered too trivial to warrant formal intervention are now being considered as serious. The operational definitions of, and the boundaries between, minor and serious offences appear to have shifted. Peter Tak mentioned a substantial widening of the category of *'kleine criminaliteit'* or petty criminality compared with twenty years ago. More cases are defined as minor offences and are dealt with more severely by the prosecutor, who has thus increased his own sentencing jurisdiction at the same time as restricting that of the judge.

The area of a prosecutor's influence over the sentencing process conducted by judges also appears to have been affected by the new severity of reaction. Generally, prosecutors interviewed felt that defendants proceeding to court were not being charged with more serious offences than before. The choice of charge by the prosecutor must ultimately influence the judge's choice of penalty, although the charging process is not a straightforward matter in the Netherlands (see above). Nevertheless, the choice of charge and the range of alternative charges can be carefully pitched so as to ensure that the offender receives as severe a penalty as possible.

Several prosecutors and academics interviewed also mentioned a trend of more severe sentences being recommended by prosecutors to judges. In general, the increased spirit of severity amongst prosecutors appears to have been passed on to the judges or 'sitting magistracy'.[32] Whereas there has been little change in the number of defendants being sent to court by the prosecutor in the last decade, there have been increases in both the rate of imprisonment and the average length of prison sentences. In 1990 the

---

[32] The term 'judiciary' in the Netherlands includes both judges and prosecutors. To differentiate between the two, prosecutors are referred to as the 'standing magistracy' because they stand up when they address the judge in court. The judges are collectively called the 'sitting magistracy' because they remain seated in court.

prison population was approximately 44 per 100,000 inhabitants, compared with 26 per 100,000 during the late 1970s.[33] The average length of prison sentences has increased in the last five years from 80 days to 140 days, and generally more longer sentences (9 months or over) are being imposed.[34]

The increased use of imprisonment in the Netherlands has produced some remarkable consequences in the penal policy of that country generally. The Dutch prison estate has undergone a large expansion in the last few years. The total capacity of the prison system in 1992 was just over 7,500; by 1996 it is anticipated that it will have increased to about 11,800, an expansion of over 57 per cent in the space of 4 years.[35] The increased capacity is to be achieved mostly through building extra places, either in existing sites or in new prisons. However, a proportion of the extra places will be found through emergency measures which the Minister of Justice has been forced to introduce as a result of a sudden increase of longer custodial sentences. The prison system (including remand detention) and the prison waiting list have both been subjected to enormous pressure from the courts who are sending more offenders their way. The situation reached a crisis when offenders with convictions for violent or serious offences had to be released to make room for other, more dangerous, prisoners without breaching the strict rule against overcrowding in the Dutch prison system. This sparked a media panic in the popular press, and calls were made for the Minister of Justice to resign. It should be noted that these calls for resignation were due to unease about the *release* of these prisoners, rather than a call for for a more lenient penal policy. In response, the Minister of Justice announced some unorthodox emergency measures[36] to prevent further releases being necessary. These measures included the creation of new temporary cells within existing prisons, to be constructed in recreation areas, and the temporary use of unoccupied cells reserved for illegal immigrants awaiting deportation. Most notably, however, for the first time in over fifty years, the rule forbidding the sharing of cells in Dutch prisons was to be breached on a temporary basis. This rule had been established by the Fick Commission in 1947 in order to preserve humanitarian conditions in the prison system and was often cited as one of the ways in which the Dutch have managed to keep their prison population so low compared with the rest of Europe. That this rule has

---

[33] Council of Europe, *Prison Information Bulletin*, (1990) No. 15.
[34] Between 1980 and 1990 they quadrupled. Figures supplied by Ministry of Justice, the Hague.
[35] Figures supplied by the Ministry of Justice, the Hague.
[36] Stalk, J. 'Dutch Prisons Overcrowded, Guests May Get Roommates', *International Herald Tribune*, 9 June 1993.

been breached is indicative of the firm commitment of policy-makers to the increased use of imprisonment for hard-core criminality, at the expense of principles regarding the importance of civilized restraint in penal policy.

Further evidence that the expansionist model is becoming ever more prominent in the Netherlands is provided by a recent document produced by the Ministry of Justice, outlining plans for new legislation on penal measures and prison regimes.[37] This document proposes, *inter alia*, to change the nature of prison regimes to enhance their effectiveness in terms of rehabilitation and reducing recidivism. This will involve increased security, the maintenance of decent standards, and improved facilities for work, recreation, and education. Furthermore, the Prison System Act, currently passing through the Dutch legislative machinery, will amend the parole procedure, so that parole will be reduced. A request for parole will be met with the response of 'no, unless . . .' instead of the previous 'yes, unless . . .'.[38] This means that while the front door of the prison system is opening wider, the back door is becoming more firmly shut, with a resulting increase of pressure on the system. The Ministry of Justice and Dutch politicians appear to have no desire to limit this expansionist programme in the near future. The proposed new legislation is likely to cause an expansion of the prison population from the already increased figure of 44 per 100,000 inhabitants to a figure of 78 per 100,000 by 1998.[39] If this estimate becomes a reality, the Netherlands will move from the bottom of the European 'League Table' of imprisonment rates, and will rapidly catch up with the traditionally more extreme rates of Germany, Spain, and Turkey. Indeed, they will not be far behind England and Wales who regularly feature at the top of this table. The 'politics of bad conscience', which de Haan argued had instilled some restraint upon policy-makers pursuing the expansionist track, have evidently given way to more pressing concerns about crime control.

How far the prosecutor may be responsible for these changes, by increasing the severity of their sentence recommendations, is unclear. There has been little conclusive evidence to connect the increase in court penalties with the new climate of severity amongst prosecutors. However, given the potential for influence over the sentencing policy of judges which is inherent in the duties and powers of a Dutch prosecutor (in particular the duty to recommend sentences at trial which, as discussed above, renders the prosecutor a near equal partner with the judge), it is unlikely that the two major shifts in policy are unrelated.

---

[37] *Effective Detention: Summary and implementation plan* (English translation of *Werkzame Detentie*), (The Hague, 1993).
[38] Ibid., 7.   [39] Ibid., 24.

6. THE DIRECTION OF CHANGE

The major changes taking place in prosecution policy (as opposed to the penal policy discussed above) in the Netherlands appear to be signalling a new era in the philosophy of the criminal justice system. As mentioned above, the words 'severity' and 'repression' cropped up frequently throughout all the interviews conducted, to describe the current trends in penal philosophy. They were not words that the writer expected to hear in a country which has in the recent past been heralded as a prime example of a rational and civilized justice system. Equally unexpected were the proposals of the Ministry of Justice to experiment with electronic tagging, as an alternative to short prison sentences, and to preserve resources for prison building by making the existing regimes 'more austere'.[40]

Numerous articles and publications during the 1980s described the generally lenient penal climate in the Netherlands at that time. Downes' study of post-war Dutch penal policy describes 'a long tradition of relative leniency towards, and acceptance of deviants, minority groups and religious dissent and which grants a respectable hearing to views which elsewhere would be dismissed as extreme or eccentric',[41] although Downes acknowledged the rather more repressive terms of the 1985 policy plan as perhaps signalling an end to this leniency. Dato Steenhuis et al. discussed the 'mild penal climate' of the Netherlands in 1983,[42] and with rather more cynicism in 1986 Steenhuis stated that 'Dutch criminal law has acquired a reputation throughout the world for its mild and humane nature, so much so that foreigners are sometimes inclined to talk with a certain affection of those simple-minded Dutchmen who still believe in the goodness of man.'[43] Franke, in response to Downes' work, argued that the tolerance of the Dutch had been over-exaggerated in the academic literature. Such 'tolerance' is rather more a liberal tradition amongst academics and some practitioners than a widespread, national characteristic.[44] Furthermore, reliance on such a 'fable' as a general tolerance at national level to explain penal policy over the decades is, in his view, misguided. De Haan is similarly cautious about over-emphasizing the influence of this sociological or cultural factor in Dutch penal policy without methodologically sound empirical data to

[40] Ministry of Justice, *Effective Detention.*, op. cit., 6 and 3 respectively.
[41] D. Downes, *Contrasts in Tolerance*, op cit., 69.
[42] D. W. Steenhuis, L. C. M. Tigges, J. J. A. Essers, 'The Penal Climate in the Netherlands: Sunny or Cloudy?', (1983) *British Journal of Criminology* 23: 1–16.
[43] D. W. Steenhuis, 'Coherence and Co-ordination in the Administration of Criminal Justice' in J. J. M. van Dijk et al., eds., *Criminal Law in Action: An Overview of Current Issues in Western Societies* (Arnhem, 1988), 229.
[44] H. Franke, 'Dutch Tolerance: Facts and Fables', (1990) *British Journal of Criminology*, 30: 81–93. Downes, however, disputed that he over-exaggerated this cultural phenomenon to the extent that his view of the more unsavoury aspects of Dutch penal history was blighted; see his 'Response to Herman Franke' *British Journal of Criminology* (1990), 30: 94–96.

support it.[45] Perhaps by the late 1980s, after so much comment and commendation, the concept of Dutch tolerance had been exalted to an almost mythologically exaggerated status, so that it is less of a surprise to Dutch commentators than to others to see the concept diminishing in favour of expansionism and severity. Whether this tolerance then existed is not a subject under close consideration here. However, the fact that leniency in Dutch penal policy has existed is difficult to dispute, as evidenced by statistics, practice, and influential academic commentary. That leniency is now threatened with extinction in the face of the new spirit of repression and severity.

The tradition of penal tolerance has not, however, completely disappeared; there is still a comparatively high tolerance in respect of petty criminality. Cases are still being unconditionally waived, and whilst the two policy plans have radically reduced the proportion of such cases, they have not sought to eradicate the possibility entirely. Even the high use of transactions shows some degree of clemency compared with systems which still prosecute a majority of similar offences. Indeed, the very nature of a transaction, as a voluntary out of court settlement or agreement between the prosecutor and the offender, allows for individual needs and circumstances to be taken into account, and transactions can incorporate reparation agreements and diversion to rehabilitative schemes. Further, the courts frequently use community service orders for offences punishable with up to six months' imprisonment, which, under Dutch statutory maximum sentences, includes some serious types of crime. In short, the idea of treating rather than punishing offenders whose criminality is symptomatic of an underlying problem is still a valid way of dealing with crime in the Netherlands. Expediency, therefore, has not disappeared altogether, but has acquired a new identity. The public prosecutor is more active and is expected to be more severe within the bounds of his sentencing powers.

Nevertheless, the degree of Dutch tolerance is certainly changing and the emphasis on severity has meant that leniency no longer extends to serious crime (this is part of the bifurcation process mentioned above). In fact, one prosecutor quoted a headline of a Dutch national newspaper reporting the publication of the 1990 Ministry of Justice policy plan thus: 'More More More Criminal Law!!!' This media prediction was borne out in practice a few years later when the prison system hit what, for the Dutch, was an overcrowding crisis (see Section 5(d) above).

The fact that change is occurring at a rapid pace in Holland is indisputable. However, the direction in which that change is pushing reform is rather less easily determined. The move towards greater severity and repression may be seen as a U-turn in policy, a reversion to the pre-1970s

[45] W. de Haan, (1990) *The Politics of Repression*, op. cit., 65–69.

situation, or to the situation in more conservative European countries which for years had seen the Netherlands as a model for progressive reform. Alternatively, the new philosophy behind this change (detailed below in Section 7) may be a step forward—a realization that the lenient approach of the 1970s was not the ideal route for progress in dealing with crime. The response to this dilemma from the persons interviewed was mixed. Professor de Doelder, a former prosecutor and now an academic and a part-time judge, was inclined to think that moves towards increased harshness were a step backwards from the more enlightened state of affairs over the last twenty years, perhaps a return to the 'neo-conservatism' discussed by de Haan[46] which recognizes: 'the necessity of deterrence and retribution for the credibility of criminal law enforcement and the maintenance of the social order.' This political shift to the right, which the Netherlands is not alone in experiencing in Europe in the 1990s, has shifted penal policy back to the approach of retributive justice and away from a more empathetic, welfare approach.

Others, however, stated that even if the trends were in any way backward-moving, they would not result in a complete U-turn of policy. The emphasis on non-prosecution and the presumption against prosecution (unless the public interest specifically requires it) are, according to Peter Tak, unlikely ever to be reversed, no matter how far the number of prosecutions increases as part of the repressive trend. The mere fact that a crime has been committed has not been since the early 1970s, and probably never will be again, a sufficient reason for prosecution. Further, there are practical limits on the extent to which the use of transactions can be increased. The transaction system relies on the willingness of offenders to agree to the terms and pay the fine. Not all offenders will be willing to agree to the terms in the first place, and not all offenders will pay the sum agreed, in which case prosecutions will necessarily result, limiting the maximum use of transactions.

David Downes analysed the 1985 policy plan (*Samenleving en Criminaliteit*), of which the 1990 plan is an extension, as a continuation of the reductionist aims of Dutch policy makers throughout the 1970s and 1980s.[47] The prison building programme, for example, he claimed, was 'the price to be paid for maintaining the principle of one to a cell, and the hope is maintained that the extra places will not be filled as long as drug problems "go out of fashion, or at least out of Holland."'[48] With hindsight, however, this statement has, ironically, been disproved. In the light

---

[46] W. de Haan, 'Abolitionism and the Politics of Bad Conscience', (1987) *Howard Journal* 26: 15–32.

[47] D. Downes, (1988) *Contrasts in Tolerance*, op. cit., 112.

[48] Ibid., 112. In the last part of this statement Downes quotes from an interview with Jan van Dijk.

of recent developments it is evident that Dutch penal policy is firmly adhering to the expansionist ideology. Indeed, John Blad of Erasmus University, Rotterdam, now uses the chapter on expansionism in Rutherford's *Prisons and the Process of Justice*[49] to illustrate the current state of penal policy in the Netherlands to his students, whereas previously he used the chapter on reductionism[50] which quoted the Dutch system as an example. England and Wales have witnessed an ineffectual expansionist penal policy over the last decade. Their academics and reformists previously looked to the Netherlands for both moral and empirical support for change. To them, the Dutch developments must appear retrogressive.

7. RATIONALES FOR CHANGE

While some may disagree over whether Dutch policy is progressing or regressing, it can confidently be said that it is moving. The 1990 policy plan (*Law in Motion*) prompted thoroughgoing reassessment of the aims and functions of the criminal authorities in dealing with crime. However, various reasons have been propounded for the increased emphasis on the punitive function of the prosecutor. The most widely advocated reason for the policy changes is concern about the credibility of the criminal justice system. The first expression of this concern in recent years was by Dato Steenhuis in the 1985 policy plan which emphasized the 'loss of confidence, on the part of the public, in government and its role as the protector of public and private interests and the fear of a further erosion in the citizen's conception of standards and in social control'.[51]

The credibility concept is based on what Steenhuis calls the 'intervention ratio' of criminal justice authorities. If too many offences, or 'infractions of the norm', go unnoticed or are ignored as trivial, the idea will circulate that it is not worth reporting an offence to the police because nothing will be done to follow it up. The same risk arises where the investigation of crimes is abandoned to save time or money. The effects of such public dissatisfaction (especially among victims) upon the credibility of and respect for the criminal justice system are largely immeasurable, but over a long period of time, they are probably substantial. The empirical research in this area is weak, but from research that has been conducted so far in the Ministry of Justice, Dato Steenhuis has identified a process which he describes as a 'blurring of norms'. When abnormal or anti-social behaviour

---

[49] A. Rutherford, *Prisons and the Process of Justice* (Oxford, 1986), see Part Two 'Choosing to Expand', 41–119.
[50] Ibid., Part Three 'Reductionism', 119–189.
[51] *Samenleving en Criminaliteit* (Society and Crime), op. cit., English translation of summary, 1.

which is technically defined as criminal is openly ignored or dismissed by the criminal justice authorities, the extent of its abnormality comes into question, and that behaviour becomes more widespread. An example is fare-dodging on the public transport system. People who failed to pay tram fares in Dutch cities went largely unnoticed after public transport companies withdrew inspectors, and because passengers need not pass or show a ticket to the driver around ten years ago. More and more people began fare-dodging in the knowledge that they were unlikely to be caught, and if they were, they were unlikely to be prosecuted. Until recently it was commonplace to see very few people, or none, buying a ticket when when boarding a tram. Fare-dodging, particularly in Amsterdam, had become a 'norm' in the sense that it was the common behaviour of the majority, even though it was still technically a criminal offence.

Concern about this 'blurring of norms' has dictated a change in the whole philosophy of criminal policy. The focus has shifted away from the perpetrator of an offence and towards the victim and the law-abiding citizen, the protection of whose safety and rights is now targeted. The philosophy is to ensure that *something* being seen to be done in most reported cases of crime, although what actually happens seems to be less important. The actual consequences of prosecution most concern the offender, whereas the rate of prosecutorial intervention is of more interest to the public, and has taken over a position of priority. The 1990 policy plan reflected Steenhuis's concerns about credibility in setting out its reasons for proposing change:

the law is in danger of gradually losing its capacity to create order and security. The intrinsic value of the law is diminishing. More and more legal rules are being introduced, but their average effectiveness is declining . . . Exasperation about all kinds of common offences is increasing among the population at large. More and more people are coming to appreciate how important it is for the quality of society that the legal order should function properly.[52]

This new climate, or change in philosophy, has wide-reaching effects on all branches of the criminal justice system, not least the prosecution service. The problem starts with police clear-up rates, the rate of arrests following reports of crime to the police, which are the initial determinant of the intervention ratio. In the Netherlands, the average clear-up rate is 22 per cent, so the role of the prosecutor in subsequently influencing the intervention rate is already severely limited. However, the prosecutor adds to the image of unreliability of the system by dismissing cases unconditionally for public interest reasons (which can simply mean a lack of time or resources to deal with the case). In individual cases, the public interest reasons for

[52] Ministry of Justice, *Law in Motion*, op. cit., 30–1.

dismissal may be cogent and convincing. However, if all cases of, for example, bicycle theft are dismissed to allow for resources to prosecute more burglaries, then the 'blurring of norms' process will begin in respect of bicycle thefts and victims of that offence will receive a poor service from the criminal justice system. Targeting specific offences is a politically hazardous business; policy-makers pursuing this line will inevitably please some sides in the criminal law debate, but never all. Hence the aim of the 1990 policy plan was to increase effective penalties for all offences. Within the framework of a bifurcated policy, the most serious cases were to be directed towards the judge for sentencing in court, and minor offences were to be handled by the prosecutor. The task of the Openbaar Ministerie was to reduce the number of unconditional policy waivers to 5 per cent of all cases reported to the prosecutor and to replace them with transactions and other conditional dismissals. Technical waivers can also be reduced by prosecutors, by exercising their supervisory authority over the police to improve the quality of reports and evidence. The policy plan of the Openbaar Ministerie also set a number of targets for improved police clear-up rates; the clear-up rate for burglary (13 per cent in 1990) is to be doubled by 1995. Prosecutors are also planning a cosmetic increase in the intervention ratio, by exercising their authority so that the police do not report to them certain types of cases which they do not wish to prosecute, thereby pre-empting further waivers.

The new philosophy does not appear to be the outcome of a new academic school of thought. Previous major changes in penal policy in the Netherlands and elsewhere have tended to follow a deep-rooted change in the ideology of practitioners and the philosophy of criminologists, and those policy changes produced fundamental and sustained reforms. In the Netherlands, the influence of the Utrecht School in the 1950s is legendary. To summarize,[53] it comprised three renowned academics, Pompe, a penologist, Kempe, a criminologist, and Baan, a psychiatrist. They combined their experience and expertise to develop a critique, based on humanitarian and treatment ideals, of the use of imprisonment. Theirs was not a new criminological theory as such, and neither was it essentially abolitionist. Rather, it was a deeply held and influential philosophy that offenders had rights to humane punishment and treatment within the criminal justice system. Their teaching (not least of future criminal justice practitioners) and practice, together with the highly regarded and influential book by Rijksen,[54] criticizing the use of long-term prison sentences as ineffectual, has left a legacy of restraint and temperance in Dutch penal

---

[53] For fuller accounts see D. Downes, *Contrasts in Tolerance*, op. cit., 87–100; W. de Haan, *The Politics of Redress*, op cit., 69–70, and P. Moedikdo, 'De Utrechtse school van Pompe, Baan en Kempe' in C. Kelk et al., eds., *Recht, Macht en Manipulatie* (Utrecht, 1976).
[54] R. Rijksen, *Meningen van Gedetineerden over de Strafrechts-pleging* (Assen, 1958).

policy.[55] This legacy is only just beginning to fade, over forty years after forming the *substratum* of judicial and prosecutorial practice.

In order to secure such deep-rooted reform in the criminal justice process, a fundamental change of heart is required amongst those who control the use of particular sanctions. In Germany, towards the end of the 1980s, the influence of one conference attended by academics and practitioners achieved a similar turnaround in the penal philosophy of those with the power to implement it. In short, many judges and prosecutors adopted a strong anti-imprisonment stance, which largely contributed to the decline in the use of remand and sentenced custody.[56] That philosophical turnaround may have been more short-lived than the radical reforms prompted by the Utrecht School, but its effect in the short term was comparable.

The influence behind the 1990 policy plan (and to some extent the 1985 plan before it) is somewhat different in nature. More inherently political, it is a reactive rather than a proactive philosophy—a political reaction to the real and apparent increase of crime witnessed or experienced by the public in general, and their inevitable feelings of insecurity. The reaction is intented to be stabilizing, aimed both at calming public anxieties and matching the rising crime rate with a rise in authoritative intervention and punishment. The philosophy emanated from within the Ministry of Justice and the Openbaar Ministerie itself and it has the full support of all the main political parties in the Netherlands. One wonders, however, how deep the conviction for greater severity goes; is it based on an objective political view that a harsher reaction is required to deal appropriately with the increased level of crime, and on a confident belief that the merits of the lenient policy of the 1970s and 1980s can now be discredited? Or, as the word 'credibility' suggests, is it an exercise on the part of the criminal justice authorities to react to the demands and criticisms of the public or media; that is ensuring that justice is at least seen to be done? It may be possible that the crime statistics published have been exaggerated to render a harsher reaction to crime more politically acceptable to the general public,[57] as de Haan described in his discussion of neo-conservative penal policy: 'the public fear of crime was used to pursue a penal policy based on the concepts of deterrence and retribution.'[58] It might therefore be surmised

[55] Moedikdo, however, is more cautious in analysing the long-term influence of the Utrecht School, arguing that it was merely one indirect factor contributing towards the mild penal policy of the Netherlands—op. cit., (Utrecht, 1976).

[56] See Chapter 5 below.

[57] Crime statistics are infamously unreliable as true indicators of the real level of crime. See recent article following the publication of crime statistics for 1990 in England and Wales: T. Kirby, 'Fight against crime obscured by statistics used out of context', *Independent*, 27 Mar. 1991. See also A. K. Bottomley and K. Pease, *Crime and Punishment: Interpreting the Data* (Milton Keynes, 1986), particularly Chapters 1 and 2.

[58] W. be Haan, 'Abolitionism and the Politics of Bad Conscience', op. cit., 22.

that the life of this political trend will be shorter than its predecessor since its empirical foundation appears to be weak and its implementation is dependent upon the commitment of practitioners to its ideology. Such commitment was not evident amongst practitioners interviewed and there was no consensus of opinion amongst academics regarding this new philosophy. Conflicts appear to be arising between the adherents of two schools of thought. The likes of van Dijk, perhaps the 'old school', retain an empathetic approach to crime, with understanding and prevention being the key targets. Further, de Doelder and John Blad object to the new direction in policy, partly because of its inherent severity and partly because of the way that it is changing the role of the prosecutor. The Openbaar Ministerie, they argue, are losing their autonomy as professional decision- and policy-makers. Just as the role by the probation service in England and Wales was changed by the implementation of the Criminal Justice Act 1991, prosecutors in the Netherlands are becoming the tools of the Ministry of Justice for carrying out political policies; they are losing their judicial, discretionary ability to set their own policy agenda:

professors from universities are now reproaching the public prosecutors for becoming more and more 'implementors' or executors of state policies instead of magistrates. I personally am in favour of them being magistrates to defend, to the greatest possible extent, the interests of the suspect . . . There is an implicit struggle here and there is also an implicit danger that the office of public prosecutor comes more and more in the hands of executive policies.[59]

On the other hand, there is a 'new school', represented by Steenhuis, whose approach concentrates on the management side of prosecution, with intervention ratios and scales of punishment being the main considerations in their almost corporate view of the criminal justice system. The management ideology, to which this new school subscribe, is neither inconsistent with the philosophy of the policy plan nor at odds with its proposals. The efficiency of the system and its mass-production of effective sanctions is another of the reasons underpinning the Ministry of Justice's decision to turn away from leniency. This would explain why, for example, the emphasis for increased intervention was focused on the prosecutor, using transactions rather than prosecutions, since this was a less expensive and less time-consuming means of implementing such a policy, whilst also conveniently paying lip service to leniency of a sort. Van Swaaningen et al. identify this corporate, bureaucratic ideology with the changing social and political outlook of the Dutch who, they argue, are less permissive in the 1990s than they were in the 1970s. This in turn has shifted criminological thinking away from moral and theoretical issues, towards administrative

[59] John Blad, Erasmus University, interview 1990.

concerns.[60] Where academics, practitioners and policy-makers concern themselves with such bureaucratic considerations, morality tends to take a back seat and the consequences of their expansionist reforms can be more easily justified.[61] Moreover, expansionist policies are more difficult to reverse than reductionist ones. Once extra resources have been ploughed into prison building, and the public have been convinced that their safety and well-being require such a harsh response to crime, there is less incentive halt the spiralling increase of imprisonment. This expansionist policy will in the long term leave the legacy of a large prison estate. Although political and philosophical trends may change, the fact remains that the cells will be available for judges to fill. It will require self-discipline and commitment to anti-custodial ideals on the part of the judiciary to resist the temptation to fill them.

8. Accountability and Constitutional Issues

The elevation of the prosecutor's importance in the Netherlands, achieved by effecting the majority of disposals at the prosecution stage, gives rise to a number of questions concerning the constitutionality of such heavy reliance upon administrative decision-making in the criminal justice system. For example, the substitution of transactions and conditional waivers in cases which would otherwise have been dropped unconditionally seems to be a process of 'net-widening', by drawing offenders into the penal system who would not otherwise have been punished.

In England and Wales, particularly in the context of juvenile justice, there has been much anxiety about the threat posed by net-widening to civil liberties, and about its tendency to criminalize youths. However, in the Netherlands net-widening is not perceived as a danger; the negative aspects of the process are not recognized. Indeed, the policy of the 1985 and 1990 plans is openly admitted to be a deliberate net-widening exercise. It is preferred in the Netherlands to consider the matter in terms of increasing reactions to crime by intensifying intervention, for the reasons stated above. However, objections were raised to this net-widening process by several academics favouring the earlier minimalist traditions, principally because of anxiety about the lack of openness and scrutiny of prosecutorial sentencing.

It is recognized that the prosecutor's power has increased to the extent that his authority is now almost wider than that of the judge, and this

---

[60] R. van Swaaningen, J. Blad, and R. van Loon, *A Decade of Criminological Research and Penal Policy in the Netherlands*, op. cit., ch. 1.

[61] See further: N. Christie, *Crime Control as Industry: Towards GULAGS Western Style?*, (London, 1993), and Chapter 7 below, for further discussion of this trend.

constitutional development has caused some concern. When the 1983 Property Sanctions Act came into force, giving the prosecutor the possibility of offering transactions in much more serious cases of crime, concern was expressed in some circles that the prosecutor may abuse that power. There has also been anxiety more recently at the aim to increase the use made of the power to issue transactions in the 1990 policy plan. Academics interviewed believed that criminal justice must be administered in a public forum; this should be the standard requirement, and while conceding that some prevalent, petty offences could be handled administratively, any cases involving complexities of law or fact should be dealt with in public to preserve natural justice. Abuses of power were also feared, such as prosecutors bargaining with defendants against whom evidence was weak or offering transactions as a condition of not prosecuting in cases which would never have been prosecuted in any event, another form of net-widening. Public concern may also be expressed when transaction settlements are made with companies who commit large-scale environmental crimes, because although the financial penalties are usually high, this policy allows offenders to buy their way out of a prosecution. While there is no political opposition to the policy, which was introduced as a result of political lobbying, some academics felt that this was the top of a slippery slope, leading to a position in which prosecution would become the exception rather than the rule; a rather dangerous route to take in their opinion.

The wide discretion of the prosecutor is structured by a system of guidelines. These in theory offer the possibility of democratic control of prosecutors' discretion, since the Minister of Justice is involved in the drafting of the guidelines, which are then published. However, to counter this it must be noted that the guidelines are only advisory. They have no mandatory force and a prosecutor can deviate from the guidelines without having to offer any justification. Thus, the discretion remains extremely wide despite the fact that in practice the guidelines are generally closely followed.

Although the Minister of Justice is present (or represented) when guidelines are discussed, it is generally the five Procurators General who formulate them during regular fortnightly meetings. They represent the practising prosecutor at the top level of the prosecution service, and so the guidelines reflect the experience of professionals. Policy, therefore, is practice-led, and every prosecutor in the Netherlands can influence the policy laid down in sentencing guidelines through the hierarchy of the Openbaar Ministerie. The theoretical role of the Ministry in the formulation process is in fact limited, a token gesture of accountability of the Openbaar Ministerie to Parliament.

The prosecutor's independence is perhaps too extensive given his or her almost unlimited discretion and multiple sentencing powers. Judges in the Netherlands are reluctant to develop their own network of sentencing guidelines, which they consider to be a matter for the prosecution service. They do not believe that their professional mandate extends to policy decisions about the appropriate sentence for any particular offence. A question which is currently being debated in Holland is whether the guidelines devised by the Openbaar Ministerie can actually be binding upon judges in any way; that is, whether the judge's independence and discretion can be fettered by prosecution policy. The matter is evidently a constitutional minefield. Judges are certainly beginning to give prosecution guidelines legal status. In some cases defendants are using a prosecutor's deviation from the guidelines as the basis for an appeal. Indeed, in 1990 the Supreme Court of the Netherlands stated that the propriety of deviation from the guidelines is a question of law, not fact. Further, the High Court ruled in June 1990 that these guidelines for prosecutors, if officially published or drawn up by an official body accountable to the public (such as the five Procurators General and the Ministry of Justice), have the status of law and that a judge must therefore examine the activities of the public prosecutor in each case for compatibility with those guidelines.[62] This check on the use of the prosecutor's discretion is aimed at preventing abuses of the defendant's due process rights and to ensure that the law is applied fairly and equally. If pursued further, it will also establish a fetter on the otherwise limitless independence of the prosecutor.

The rule was laid down during an appeal against a decision to prosecute a case of fiscal fraud involving a sum of less than 50,000 guilders, contrary to a prosecutorial guideline laid down by the Minister of Justice and the Procurators General in 1985, to the effect that all cases of fiscal fraud involving sums of less than 50,000 guilders would be handled by means of an administrative fine from the Treasury. Unfortunately, the High Court rejected the appeal on other grounds, but the fundamental statement of principle that prosecutorial guidelines have the binding and authoritative status of legal rules remains, although it will require further case law to determine the sanctions available to the court in cases where the prosecutor's violation of the guidelines is proved.

However, despite the growing status of the prosecutor, the Openbaar Ministerie is not constitutionally independent but remains under the control of the Minister of Justice. Under Article 5 of the Code of Judicial Organization, the Minister of Justice is entitled to give orders to all public prosecutors, including the five Procurators General. Obviously the extent to which this power is actually used in practice will depend very much on the circumstances and the personalities involved, but the fact that it exists

---

[62] Hoge Raad, 19 June 1990, published in Nederlandse Juriprudentie 1991, vol. 119.

is of fundamental constitutional importance, maintaining accountability to Parliament and a democratic element in the prosecution process. As the prosecutor's influence over justice increases, so equally does the importance of that democratic link, to ensure that the boundary between the independent judiciary and the prosecution is not blurred, even though it may have shifted. The 1985 and 1990 policy plans (the first for many years) may even be seen as a move by the Ministry of Justice to take a tighter grip of prosecution policy, and the 1990 policy plan issued by the Openbaar Ministerie (the first of its kind) could then be seen as its reaction, a re-assertion of independence. (However, the fact that the Ministry's plan was the product of co-operative discussions between the Ministry and the Openbaar Ministerie should not be overlooked.)

Thus, the Openbaar Ministerie is politically accountable on a general policy level to Parliament, through the Minister of Justice. On a case by basis, however, accountability is also imposed by the appeal procedure. Under Article 12 of the Code of Criminal Procedure, an 'interested party' may appeal to the Court of Appeal against the decision of a public prosecutor to institute a prosecution. This very rarely happens, however, and out of 50–60,000 non-prosecutions per year, only around 200 appeals are filed[63] and not all of those will be successful. Nevertheless, the existence of this procedure is of utmost importance in securing accountability and in restraining the abuse of power. In fact, the accountability is potentially widened by the definition of an 'interested party'—the first condition of an appeal. An 'interested party' must have a close connection with the offence committed, so that unconnected members of the public are excluded. However, as well as the victim, pressure groups or associations with a specific purpose which is laid down in their Articles of Association and closely connected with the offence (for example, an environmental protection group in cases of pollution, or a women's group in cases of rape and other sexual offences) qualify as 'interested parties'. The definition is not statutory, though, being a product of case law, so that status as an interested party may be difficult to prove. But the appeal procedure does extend beyond the victim, and is thus of wider application than in other justice systems.

A question which has not been fully addressed in the Netherlands, in the midst of rapid policy developments, is whether the provisions for prosecutorial accountability are sufficient to justify the expansion of their role and their increased independence from the judiciary. If criminal justice decision-making is to be pushed further away from both public and peer review, safeguards for suspects dealt with at this early stage must be established. More will be said on this in Chapter 7 below, but the

---

[63] Ministry of Justice, The Hague, 1990.

Netherlands provides a stark example of the need for stringent standards of accountability. Where the prosecutor is so powerful, and especially where the prosecution service is increasingly being used to effect the political aims and policy of the executive, these powers must be balanced by due process protections and checks. Such concerns should not be overlooked in the hurried implementation of new ideas, regardless of the how persuasive the reasons for those changes might seem.

9. CONCLUSION

In the turmoil of changes affecting the prosecution service in the Netherlands, it is difficult to predict the direction of future policy. Although its direction is clearly changing, there is no agreement on whether the change is expansionist or reductionist; cogent arguments have been put forward to support both views. Part of the reason for this ambiguous commentary on the new policy is that the policy is itself bifurcated. The philosophy of leniency and diversion away from prosecution has not disappeared altogether in respect of petty crime. However, that principle is now less firmly adhered to, and the diversion takes a more repressive form. On the other hand, diversion and leniency are disappearing in respect of serious crime. The expansionist nature of the new prosecution policy relates principally to hard-core criminality. The increased use of transactions by the prosecutor in minor cases does not conflict with a reductionist ideology in the sense that there is still a high degree of diversion away from the courts and therefore from the prison system. Nevertheless, the ideology behind this trend shows rather less compassion than might have existed in the 1970s. Bifurcated policies are inherently self-contradictory and will therefore produce conflict of opinion amongst those who comment on them.

Despite the debate over the direction of Dutch penal policy in the next decade, it is undeniable that policy is on the move. In a country where criminal justice issues feature as a high priority on the political agenda, this dynamic picture may be the normal state of affairs. Rapid change is no surprise in a system which has often taken a progressive lead in this field. The fact remains that the prosecutor in the Netherlands is becoming the most important figure in the criminal justice system, almost more important than the judge. Holthuis has noted the evolution of the prosecutor's role in recent years, up to the point where it has taken centre-stage in the criminal justice process:

From a body only dealing with cases reported to it by the police it has evolved into an important organ of criminal policy. It might even be the most important, because the public prosecutor is a the very centre of the criminal justice system and, at the same time, has (formal) authority over the police, is able to control the input intro the judiciary and is also responsible for the execution of sentences.[64]

The function which has elevated the prosecutor to such importance is that of a sentencer who issues penalties. The demand for fewer unconditional dismissals on the one hand, and the restraint on resources which prohibits an increase of cases proceeding to court on the other, has encouraged the prosecutor to deal in an active, quasi-judicial way with the large accumulation of cases in between.

The constitutionality of this development has already been called into question and doubts have been expressed about the adequacy of the prosecutor's public accountability in his wider jurisdiction. This concern has heightened with indications that the repressive policy may progress even further, with a greater number of cases being dealt with behind closed doors. If policy does continue to progress in this direction, it is likely that by the end of the 1990s prosecutors will be disposing of the majority of cases reported to them by the police. Further, an experiment is currently being conducted into allowing the police to offer transactions in more serious offences such as shoplifting (they have long had power to offer fixed penalties in minor offences, such as traffic offences) and in the current climate of penal policy it is likely that this scheme will be made law. The implications of this development are extremely serious. One of the justifications for allowing prosecutors such an extensive quasi-judicial role is that they are constitutionally part of the Dutch judiciary. Indeed, most (though not all) prosecutors have the same initial training as judges before electing to enter a different branch of the profession. As part of their six years' training prosecutors spend two years working with judges (often as court clerks, a more highly qualified, professional job than its English equivalent), and that valuable experience informs their quasi-judicial sentencing decisions. The police, however, have no such experience, and, unlike the older generations of English police, lack any experience as prosecutors. They operate under the supervision of the prosecution service and their public accountability is even more limited. Most academics interviewed were opposed to the sentencing role retreating this far behind closed doors.

The Dutch system appears to be advancing rapidly and purposefully. The direction of reform has been co-operatively discussed and arranged by top level policy-makers in the Ministry of Justice and seems to be generally concurrent with the practices and opinions of practising prosecutor. Policy matters in the Netherlands appear to progress in a confident and organized manner, and the change in policy direction has been planned

[64] H. Holthuis, *The Role of the Prosecutor in the Netherlands*, op. cit., 15.

well into the future. Unlike the Scottish experience, the development of the sentencing role of the prosecutor has not depended on the inspiration and charisma of individual personalities, but is deep-rooted in the political philosophy of policy-makers at the Ministry of Justice. Further, throughout the sweeping policy changes of both the 1980s and the 1990s, the prosecutor has consistently emerged as the 'winner', the key figure in the criminal process. During the 1980s when the policy of diversion was pushed to the fore, the prosecutor's powers of dismissal were relied upon to reach the waiver quotas set by the Ministry of Justice. The 1990 policy plan, while retracting from the widespread leniency practised during the previous decade, placed a still heavier responsibility upon the prosecutor to increase the number of interventions in cases of crime so that the use of transactions has become one of the most frequently used disposals in the criminal process.

Despite the contextual changes, the prosecutor retains his position in the Netherlands as a crucial element of the criminal justice system. Indeed, the last ten years have turned the prosecutor's sentencing role into the linchpin of current policy, controlling the input and output of the criminal justice process in accordance with those policy changes. It is possible that this central role of the prosecutor may stem from the personal views of Dato Steenhuis, one of the key policy co-ordinators in the Ministry over the last ten years, and a practising prosecutor heavily influential in drafting both policy plans. However, it is more probable that the importance of the prosecutor's sentencing role stems from the the generally held core philosophy of Dutch criminal justice practitioners.

Appendix 4.1
Crime Prevention in the Netherlands

PREVENTATIVE measures were an important secondary aspect of the criminal policy outlined by the Ministry of Justice in both the 1985 and 1990 policy plans. Following the report of the Roethof Committee,[65] the responsibility for and the organization of crime prevention was to have a strong base in the local community, and local authorities, businesses, private organizations, and individual citizens were to share largely in the combat against prevalent and petty crime. In 1985 a directorate was set up within the Ministry of Justice, under the control of Dr Jan van Dijk, to facilitate the execution of crime prevention policy. The full backing of the major political parties to these measures shows how crime prevention is a serious national concern.

The Government has provided a fund of 22 million ECU from which subsidies can be paid to encourage local authorities to develop social crime prevention policies. A local authority which receives a subsidy for a project must undertake to continue the project at its own expense if it should prove effective. Projects have been set up involving many different public institutions. In the public transport sector a permanent force of 1,200 surveillance officers has been employed in large cities. This began as a three year experimental scheme whereby the public transport systems in Amsterdam, the Hague and Rotterdam employed 1,200 young people as official inspectors on trams and on the metro system to curb incidents of fare-dodging, vandalism and violence. These officials were known as VIC's (*Veiligheid, Informatie, Controle*—Safety, Information and Control) and their impact on preventing petty criminal activity on the public transport system has been reported as successful. Van Andel[66] noted a fall in the number of cases of fare-dodging, violence, and vandalism in the first year of the experiment (1985), ascribed to the vigilance of the VIC's and to new boarding procedures on buses and trams.

In education, truancy is being curbed by a system of truancy registration,

---

[65] The Netherlands, *Eindrapport Commissee Kleine Criminaliteit*, Preliminary report of the Roethof Committee on Petty Crime, (The Hague, 1984).
[66] H. van Andel, 'Crime Prevention that Works: The Care of the Public Transport System in the Netherlands', (1989) *British Journal of Criminology*, 29: 47–56.

and schools are introducing measures against vandalism. Special youth projects have been set up to work with unemployed youngsters and other so-called 'high risk groups'. Planners and architects in the public housing sector are now working under new regulations concerning standards of security against crime in private and public buildings.

There have been a good number of applications by local authorities for subsidies for local crime prevention and about 200 projects have already been selected for support. The projects involve all departments and areas of responsibility of the burgomeister, including schools, neighbourhood watch projects (which in the Netherlands are government-sponsored), youth groups, street lighting, licensing, public transport, and shopping centres. The policy seems to have had some success. Since 1984, while there has been no fall in the overall number of crimes reported to the police, victim surveys have shown a reduction in the real level of crime.[67] The most successful projects have involved surveillance, for example on public transport, in shopping centres, and on housing estates where the obvious presence of surveillance officers has had a deterrent effect.

It is interesting to note that the Home Office in England and Wales has recently announced a similar policy of community involvement, and it has proposed a National Board for Crime Prevention. This will have amongst its members traders, industrialists, and local voluntary groups. They too hope that the prevention of crime in urban areas will be better achieved when the community are heavily involved. As the Home Office Minister, Michael Jack, stated when announcing the establishment of the Board: 'Fighting crime is a top priority which can only be successful with a partnership approach ... Our new strategy is designed to bring together all those concerned with tackling crime.'[68]

[67] The Netherlands, *Crime Control Policy in the Netherlands: Five Years of Policy Efforts,* (The Hague, 1990), a collection of three papers delivered at the Eighth United Nations Congress on the Prevention of Crime and the Treatment of Offenders, in Havana, Cuba, 1990.
[68] N. Crequer, 'Businesses urged to join city crime fight', *Independent,* 8 Jan. 1993.

5
The German Prosecution System: The Developing Sentencers

1. INTRODUCTION

THE office of public prosecutor in Germany is relatively new. The office of *Staatsanwaltschaft*, created around the middle of the nineteenth century, was essentially a compromise between the earlier situation in which an inquisitorial judge carried the responsibility for the investigation, prosecution, and adjudication processes, and a suggested alternative, in which the injured party should take over the prosecution role, with extensive rights of private prosecution. In the former situation, the prosecutor was found to be too closely connected with the investigative and adjudication processes to be sufficiently objective. The latter situation, with no public monopoly over prosecution, was thought to be equally undesirable. The result was a separation of the prosecution and the adjudication processes, and the creation of the office of public prosecutor. In order to prevent public prosecutors from merely adopting the findings of police investigations and over-zealously prosecuting as ciphers of the state's power, they were invested with neutrality and independence from the police and the judiciary (although, of course, they are subject to directions and instructions issued by the state). Thus the situation has arisen in Germany where the public prosecutor has an almost complete monopoly over the prosecution process,[1] but is required by the Code of Criminal Procedure to provide the court with 'not only inculpating but also exculpating evidence'.[2] The neutrality of the *Staatsanwaltschaft* was summed up by the nineteenth-century Prussian Minister of Justice, Savigny, when he described them as 'the watchmen of the law'.[3]

Aside from a few significant changes, the extent of the prosecutor's role and power has remained more or less the same over the last 150 years,

---

[1] Although the traditional rights of private prosecution have been maintained; see Section 5 below.

[2] Code of Criminal Procedure, s. 160(II).

[3] Savigny, quoted in J. Langbein, *Comparative Criminal Procedure: Germany*, (Minnesota, 1977).

despite fundamental historical changes, including the onslaught of the Nazi regime which took over Germany in the 1930s, and its aftermath during the Cold War years, followed by the recent reunification of the Communist Eastern states with West Germany. The emphasis on neutrality and independence from the judiciary has been firmly re-established in the latter part of the twentieth century in an effort to distance the modern system of criminal procedure from that practised during Hitler's dictatorship, when executive interference in matters of justice was rife. In this chapter the issues addressed arise from current trends and events in the criminal justice system which have had repercussions on, or which have significantly affected, prosecutors. In particular, the fall in the prison population over the last decade, followed by a resurgent rise in remand figures in the last two years, is addressed, and hypotheses are advanced as to the prosecutors' involvement in the causes of these changes. Also, the extension of prosecutors' discretion and their activities in formulating and executing diversion policies and the consequent erosion of the legality principle is addressed as a constitutional issue.

It should be emphasized that, unlike the other systems compared in this book (that is Scotland, England and Wales, and the Netherlands), the German criminal justice system is organized on a federal basis with the twelve German states each of which operates its own criminal justice system headed by a Ministry of Justice. Below the Minister of Justice, a Chief Prosecutor heads each of the 92 prosecution offices, each attached to a district court or *Landgericht* which in turn incorporates the jurisdiction of all magistrates' courts or *Amtsgerichte* in the district. These offices have a varying number of senior and ground level prosecutors.

As a result of the fragmentation of criminal policy and practice, local discrepancies are common and often pronounced, making any general analysis of national trends and statistics hazardous. Indeed, in the interviews conducted in Germany, Johannes Feest doubted that one could talk of general prosecution policy in Germany at all, since an individual prosecutor's discretion is so wide and state guidelines are so unspecific, so that individual office policies develop in each local court rather than on a state- or nationwide level.[4] Pfeiffer gave a statistical example of how different local offices may show an enormously different response to similar cases. In his example, the rate of use of prison sentences (suspended or not) for drunk-driving offenders with one previous conviction ranged from 0.9% to 67% across West Germany. Further, within the state of Hessen, three neighbouring offices showed varying imprisonment rates of 70%, 56%, and 28% for the same offence of burglary.[5]

---

[4] See Section 11 for a discussion of local 'court cultures' and policy traditions.
[5] All figures were provided by KFN, Hanover.

2. OPTIONS FOR DISMISSAL

All reports of crime must be passed from the police to the prosecutor after investigation, even if no suspect can be identified, and the prosecutor must then decide which of his powers to use in disposing of the case. The overriding principle governing the prosecution of all offences in Germany is the legality principle (*Legalitätsprinzip*). The 'compulsory prosecution rule', as it is otherwise known, is firmly rooted in statute. The Code of Criminal Procedure states that 'the public prosecutor is required to take action against all prosecutable offences, to the extent that there is a sufficient factual basis'.[6] Thus, evidential sufficiency is the governing criterion and in theory all infractions of the criminal code which can be proven and should be prosecuted in the courts. Therefore, the first option for the prosecutor to dismiss cases arises where the evidence is insufficient to secure a satisfactory conviction. However, in practice the prosecutor's further discretion to dismiss cases in which there is sufficient evidence to prosecute is much wider, and many different powers now exist which allow the prosecutor to dispose of cases with a variety of sanctions.

The second exception to the rule of compulsory prosecution does not involve the public prosecutor. A petty infractions code (*Gesetz über Ordnungswidrigkeiten*) allows for a number of minor offences, such as traffic offences, to be dealt with by the police or other administrative prosecuting agency by issuing a 'penance money decree' requiring the offender to pay a sum of money.[7] If no objection is lodged by the offender to the decree within one week, the decree becomes final and the sum falls due. The penance money decree is deliberately not described as a fine, to avoid criminal stigmatization, since the procedure is not a criminal procedure and, indeed, until recently decrees could not be enforced by means of imprisonment for default, by contrast with a fine. In March 1993 this rule was changed and default on a penance money decree can now result in imprisonment. A warning can also be a condition of the decree with or without an accompanying demand for payment of a penance.

(a) Unconditional Dismissals

The third major power for dismissing cases (which belongs to the prosecutor) applies where there is sufficient evidence to prosecute but where the level of the offence or the damage involved is minor so that the public interest does not require prosecution. In these minor cases, with the consent of the judge, the prosecutor may dismiss the case either conditionally

---

[6] Code of Criminal Procedure, s. 152(II).
[7] Petty Infractions Code, s. 47.

or unconditionally. The unconditional waiver of cases is authorized by s. 153 of the Code of Criminal Procedure, introduced in 1924, which provides for a prosecutor to refrain from prosecuting any minor offence (*Vergehen*) with the court's consent (which is in most cases a formality and is rarely withheld), an explicit expression of the *Opportunitätsprinzip* or opportunity principle in the German criminal justice system. The category of *Vergehen* includes all misdemeanours (offences punishable in court by a fine or imprisonment of up to one year) as well as the previously separate category of petty misdemeanours (offences punishable by imprisonment of up to six weeks or a fine of up to DM500) which was abolished in 1975. In March 1993, s. 153 of the Code was amended to enable prosecutors unconditionally to dismiss any case which involves an offence not carrying a mandatory minimum sentence (in fact, the vast majority of cases) without the consent of the court. This proposal was originally restricted to property offences, but was finally passed by Parliament as a wider provision applying to all types of offences. Therefore, this wide application of s. 153 gives the prosecutor discretion to dismiss cases of most types of criminality, except the most serious crimes, felonies or *Verbrechen* (offences punishable by imprisonment of one year or more). The discretion extends to important cases of large-scale economic crime as well as offences such as burglary which, under German sentencing practices, are not termed a felony.

(b) Conditional Dismissals

The Code of Criminal Procedure has, since 1975, also allowed a discretion for the prosecutor to attach conditions to the waiver of prosecution. Section 153a states that the prosecutor, in cases involving offences not carrying a mandatory minimum penalty, again without the consent of the court, may provisionally refrain from prosecuting on condition that the offender either provides some form of compensation for the damage caused by the offence or makes a payment to a charity or to the Treasury. The conditions are voluntary and an offender's acceptance of these terms of dismissal negates the public interest in prosecution. Most s. 153a orders involve the latter provision, payment to a charity or to the government in the form of a fine. However, within the realm of the former compensatory provision, conditional waivers can include some form of reparation or mediation between victim and offender. Most reparation cases are dependent on the willingness of the individual prosecutor to organize and administer the agreement, but, as will be discussed in Section 6 below, reparation schemes are beginning to be set up around Germany in an effort to replace a retributive system of justice with a restorative, victim-orientated one. In the adult field, however, the prosecutor is unable to arrange counselling or rehabilitation for the offender as part of a s. 153a dismissal, although after a conviction the case may be handed back to a prosecutor so that he can advise the offender to attend a drugs or alcoholic rehabilitation centre to avoid imprisonment. This, however, must be on the instigation of the judge.

As stated, most s. 153a orders no longer require the consent of the court and are a form of purely prosecutorial sentencing. Some, however, still require a judge's consent. In practice consent is rarely withheld, but two prosecutors currently working in Bremen gave varying reports on their experience here.[8] The more experienced the prosecutor, the more likely that consent will be granted without question. A less experienced prosecutor came across more denials of consent, which were apparently due only to his own standing, because when the same applications were submitted to the judge by the more experienced prosecutor they were granted. When consent is denied the case must be prosecuted in court.

(c) Combining Offences

A further, less significant, way in which a prosecutor can divert cases from the court is set out in the Code of Criminal Procedure under s. 154. That section provides that prosecution of a minor offence can be dropped where the offender has committed other more serious offences, or where the offender is already serving a sentence for a different offence which is sufficient punishment for the present offence also. This subsidiary sentencing or diversionary power of the prosecutor is used infrequently compared with s. 153 and s. 153a (as shown in Table 5.1). Lothar Spielhof, a prosecutor specializing in complex economic crimes in Bremen, described how he used his power under s. 154 in a form of bargaining with the judge in court. Where a judge appeared likely to sentence below the prosecutor's recommendation, Spielhof would threaten to reinstate minor cases into the accusatory papers, which had previously been dropped under s. 154, and to ask for a full trial of them all.

Table 5.1 shows the extent to which each of these options for dismissal of prosecutions of adults is used. The figures apply only to Lower Saxony because, as explained in the introduction, wide variation between districts renders unreliable any analysis of national figures. These statistics are compiled from all districts within the state of Lower Saxony. While they may not be typical of current practice in all parts of Germany, they are nevertheless an example of the German prosecutor's use of expediency. Cases which are passed to the prosecutor by the police, but in which there is insufficient evidence to prosecute, do not appear in this table. For example,

---

[8] Information is based on interviews with prosecutors, Bremen 1991.

Public Prosecutors and Discretion

TABLE 5.1: Prosecutorial Disposals in Lower Saxony 1985–1990

		1985	1986	1987	1988	1989	1990
Total cases with sufficient evidence to prosecute		137,378	133,316	133,095	138,343	140,491	146,876
Prosecutions, penal orders and S.212	No.	85,481	83,783	84,972	87,318	86,816	88,432
	%	62.2	62.8	63.8	63.1	61.8	60.2
Total cases dropped	No.	51,897	49,533	48,123	51,025	53,675	58,444
	%	37.8	37.2	36.2	36.9	38.2	39.8
Conditional dismissals S.153a	No.	19,205	19,483	21,013	22,300	23,109	25,515
	%	14.0	14.6	15.8	16.1	16.4	17.4
Unconditional dismissals S.153	No.	20,989	17,952	13,720	14,457	15,521	17,687
	%	15.3	13.5	10.3	10.5	11.0	12.0
S.154 dismissals	No.	11,703	12,098	13,390	14,268	15,045	15,242
	%	8.5	9.1	10.1	10.3	10.7	10.4

Ministry of Justice, Lower Saxony, Hanover, (1991)

in 1990 a total of 665,632 cases were recorded, of which 335,632 were reported to the prosecutor. Of these, only 146,876 had sufficient evidence to prosecute, leaving 188,756 or 56.2% of cases to be dismissed for lack of evidence. This indicates the importance of the existing duty on the part of the prosecutor to oversee police investigations and to ensure that enough evidence is gathered. Even further indication of the need for this duty is the number of cases in which the offender cannot be identified. In 1990 there were 330,000 such cases, around half of all recorded cases of crime.

(d) Juveniles

The sentencing options for German prosecutors in the juvenile field are substantially wider than those in the adult field. Under s. 45 of the Juvenile Court Act, the equivalent of s. 153a of the Code of Criminal Procedure, the prosecutor can: give a warning, order a period of community service, organize a reparative meeting between the victim and the offender, or refer the juvenile for rehabilitation or counselling as a condition of non-prosecution. The prosecutor here has a much wider scope to tailor a sentence to an individual case, subject to an overriding principle that the sentence must promote some aspect of education or reform. The tendency in Germany is to treat juveniles more harshly than adults. 'Educational' sentences are more severe. All dismissals under s. 45 are recorded state-wide, as are previous juvenile convictions, whereas they are only recorded locally in the adult field. Further, the application of the juvenile dismissal procedure under s. 45 extends to felonies as well as minor offences.

Christian Pfeiffer is endeavouring, through research, to change the working philosophy in the juvenile justice area, so that the central aim of education of offenders is achieved without a strong emphasis on punishment. However, the severity of prosecutorial sentencing in the juvenile field has deep historical roots. Several of those interviewed argued that prosecutors should not be empowered to divert adult cases to rehabilitation schemes, reparation schemes, social work, counselling, or the like because they are not supplied with sufficient background information to make a proper assessment of the social situation of the defendant, whom they will often not meet in person. The judge can order social enquiry reports and will see the defendant in court before making a judgment, and is therefore in a much better position to make such a decision. However, the prosecutor's sentencing responsibility in the juvenile field is as complex as that in the adult field.

The juvenile area was developed more fully and earlier than the adult alternatives. Reforms for juveniles reflected the movement in the USA which Tony Platt described as the 'child-savers' movement'[9] (although this

---

[9] A. M. Platt, *The Child Savers: The Invention of Delinquency*, (Chicago, 1969).

was a more patriarchal, reformatory movement than the sympathetic approach of workers in the juvenile justice system today). At the time reformers put most of their energy into the juvenile field because of their interest in that particular ideology. The legislation of the 1920s, during the very liberal government of Germany under the Weimar Republic, introduced many of the wider possibilities for young offenders which were intended to provide a model for the adult system as well. Feest[10] argues that the transformation of the adult system to include these diversionary options has simply been slow to materialize, and delayed by the interruption of the Nazi era in the 1930s and early 1940s. Reform in the adult field is concentrating on the extension of the diversionary side of justice and the concept of reparation and restoring the social imbalances caused by crime (see section 11(a) below).

(e) Guidelines

The German prosecutor's wide discretion is comparatively unfettered by guidelines. The few rules which have attempted to control the use of prosecutorial powers generally reflect the fragmentation of the system, being imposed at state or district level. Most offices will have their own set of informal rules (written or otherwise) for prosecutors. Such guidelines set out regulations concerning the use of s. 153 and s. 153a in the adult field and s. 45 of the Juvenile Court Act. Despite local variations, discrepancies have been reduced by agreements between states on common guidelines setting out criteria to be used in dismissing cases.

State-imposed rules and guidelines tend to be rather short, lacking in detail and couched in very general terms, so their effectiveness in harnessing the use of prosecutorial discretion is severely limited. There are certainly unlisted public interest criteria to guide a prosecutor as to the applicability of s. 153 and s. 153a. The concepts of 'lack of public interest' or 'minor guilt' are left wide open to interpretation. The only statutory attempt to define the concept of public interest simply serves as an example of the ambiguity of official guidance. The Uniform Rules of Criminal Procedure (*Richtlinien für das Strafverfahren und Bußgeldverfahren*) issued by the Ministries of Justice of all the German states attempt to define the two governing criteria for s. 153 and s. 153a dismissals. However, their advice on the assessment of minor guilt is simply to compare the case in hand with others relating to the same offence to see whether the conduct in question is more or less serious[11], which does not provide much elucidation for the prosecutor. Further, on the question of public interest,

---

[10] Interview Bremen, 1991.
[11] Uniform Rules of Criminal Procedure, Rule 83.

the rules deal only with frequently committed offences, for which the presumption should be in favour of prosecution to effect a general deterrence, or similarly a personal deterrence where the offender has previously been warned or punished for similar conduct.[12] However, the Rules do give statutory authority to the practice of what Lidstone et al. describe as 'buying off a prosecution',[13] whereby a prosecutor takes account of the conduct of the accused after the commission of the offence and uses mitigating factors such as returning stolen goods, donations to charity, or making good damage done as considerations which negate the public interest in a prosecution; a controversial form of bargaining.

Local regulatory guidelines formulated within each office and taught to probationary prosecutors can be used as a means of controlling the decision-making of branch prosecutors. Wolfgang Lesting, a prosecutor from Bremen, gave details of his experience of this. Many of his decisions were overturned by his senior colleagues when they reviewed the files on which he had worked. In this way senior prosecutors in the Bremen office used local guidelines to bring Lesting's rather liberal decision-making into line with local policy and to curb the use of his own political opinions in the exercise of discretion, so that to a certain extent the prosecutor is controlled by his own immediate hierarchical superiors practising their own notions of policy. It is interesting to note that German judges, unlike their English counterparts, are not subject to any form of sentencing guidelines at all. This is for historical reasons, state-imposed guidelines on judicial discretion being reminiscent of executive interference in sentencing during the dictatorship of the Third Reich.

3. PENAL ORDERS

A major proportion of cases with sufficient evidence to prosecute are dealt with out of court under the penal order system, which some view as an abbreviated form of prosecution and others as a form of prosecutorial sentencing. The penal order (*Strafbefehl*) is a document prepared by the prosecutor, setting out the details and facts of the offence, the sections of the Criminal Code alleged to have been breached, and the punishment recommended by the prosecutor. The punishments which can be included in the order currently consist of day fines, a suspended prison sentence of up to one year, suspension of a driving licence, forfeiture of the profits of the crime, and sundry other practical sanctions. As yet the Community

[12] Ibid.
[13] K. W. Lidstone, R. Hogg, and F. Sutcliff, *Prosecutions by Private Individuals and Non-police Agencies*, Royal Commission on Criminal Procedure, Research Study No. 10. (London, 1980), 234.

Service Order, which has not been developed as a sanction in itself in the judicial sphere of sentencing, cannot be included as a punishment in a prosecutor's penal order.

As with other forms of dismissal, the judge's consent is required. His signature is required to make the penal order legally binding. It is this which confers on the penal order the legal status of a judicial procedure; with the judge's consent the penal order is binding as a court order and carries a record of a conviction. Indeed, in Table 5.1 above, the statistics for Lower Saxony include penal orders with prosecutions for the purpose of analysing the disposal of cases.[14]

However, it is commonly acknowledged by academics and practitioners alike that a judge's consent is rarely withheld (depending again on the degree of respect between the individual prosecutor and judge). Given the extent to which penal orders are used,[15] judges rarely have time to scrutinize any but the most complex or controversial cases, and a prosecutor will attach to a penal order the degree of punishment he thinks the judge will find acceptable. Practitioners interviewed agreed that a degree of bargaining may occur between judges and prosecutors to modify the tone of a penal order before it is authorized. However, the routine rubber-stamping of penal orders has led to academics such as Johannes Feest, Thomas Weigend, and Christian Pfeiffer to suggest that the *Strafbefehl* is in fact, although not strictly in law, a form of prosecutorial sentencing.[16] Indeed, Lidstone et al. go so far as to say: 'one is bound to say that it seems to be verbal cosmetics to describe the [penal order] process as a prosecution.'[17]

Once judicial authorization has been obtained and the order despatched to the accused, there follows a period of 14 days during which he can lodge an objection either to the facts alleged or to the terms of the order and request a trial in court. Until as recently as 1991, this period was only seven days, but was extended to protect defendants who are ill, or absent from home, or unable to read their mail. Nevertheless, the procedure is still unfair to those who are illiterate, homeless, or unable to understand complex legal appeal procedures, for whom there is no special consideration or assistance. However, the appeal rate remains relatively high and Weigend estimates that about one third of those receiving penal orders appeal against them.

[14] Out of the prosecution figures quoted in Table 5.1 for 1990, around 50,000 were actually penal orders, about 56.5% of all prosecutions and around 34% of all prosecutable offences.

[15] See Note 14 above. Also, Feest estimates that in Bremen 20% of all prosecutable offences are dealt with by means of a penal order. Further, the rate of use of penal orders is increasing due to the pressure of increasing workloads and restricted manpower and resources; see Section 11 below.

[16] Weigend, Feest, and Pfeiffer, interviews, June 1991.

[17] K. W. Lidstone, et al., (1980) op. cit., 234.

Once penal orders are accepted, whether actively or by default, the offender is bound to comply with the conditions contained therein. Under the 'day fine' procedure, the sum to be paid is expressed as the income of the accused over a specified number of days (between one week and 360 days). The automatic punishment on default is the same number of days' imprisonment. It is the duty of the prosecutor to enforce the penalty and, on default, to commit the offender to prison, without referring the case back to court. The prosecutor may therefore be seen as having an extended sentencing role here by indirectly issuing a prison sentence. The civil liberties and accountability problems inherently involved in imposing potentially custodial penalties without trial are immense. These will be discussed below in the context of the German prosecutor's new power to impose suspended prison sentences within a penal order.

In the last few years, however, the use of imprisonment for default of a penal order has been replaced wherever possible by the use of community service, with the term of imprisonment being commuted into a corresponding period of community work. This was a deliberate measure to reduce the use of imprisonment, as part of the general trend in Germany over the last ten years to reduce custodial sentences (see Section 7 below). Figures for Lower Saxony provided by the Ministry of Justice indicate that in 1990, 2,485 offenders accepted a community service order instead of imprisonment for default of a penal order, avoiding an estimated total of 484,000 days of imprisonment. Organizations have developed over the last ten years to arrange such work, although it is still a relatively new idea in Germany which, as stated, is still not imposed as a sanction in itself, except in the juvenile field.

The default procedure involves prosecutors indirectly in custodial sentencing. A new power for prosecutors to impose sentences of imprisonment directly was introduced by Parliament in March 1993: an amendment to the Code now allows suspended custodial sentences to be included in the penal order (*Strafbefehlsverfahren*). This power is, not surprisingly, causing enormous controversy. The general intention was to relieve pressure on prosecutors and judges by avoiding the trial process. The inclusion of suspended prison sentences of up to one year in the list of possible sanctions written into the orders by the prosecutor was intended to widen the application, and thus the use, of the penal order. Suspended custodial sentences can only be imposed where the defendant is legally represented.

Opposition to the new sanction has come from all branches of the legal profession, including bodies of prosecutors and judges' associations. Generally, the criticism has been founded on the principle that allowing the prosecutor to issue custodial sanctions without an open trial is taking his sentencing role too far. Although the power only extends to suspended sentences, it is estimated that on average 40% of suspended prison sentences are eventually served. The risk is that the new prosecutorial power will undermine all the work that has been done in Germany to reduce the size of the prison population. The rate of imprisonment could rise without any obvious candidate taking the responsibility for it (or at least feeling responsible for it). In the view of the professionals, the risk of abuse of the prosecutorial sentencing power is immediate and one senior prosecutor in Braunschweig stated that he would refuse to use this power.

When this new sanction was first proposed in 1991, Christian Pfeiffer joined other academics and practitioners in petitioning against it. They argued that, in the absence of a court hearing, illiterate and foreign defendants and those of sub-normal intelligence who could not understand the implications of a penal order would be in grave danger of losing their liberty without the proper protection of natural justice. In Pfeiffer's view, the resource and manpower problems of the prosecution service should not be solved at the expense of the fundamental civil liberties of the accused. When the proposal was first aired in Parliament it provoked such enormous professional opposition that it was thought unlikely to be passed as law. Unfortunately, this proved wrong. That such a controversial proposal, extending the prosecutor's sentencing power to such an extent, was passed by Parliament in the face of such opposition is indicative both of the general political shift to the right in German criminal justice policy and of the urgent need perceived by policy-makers to save time and money. This is clearly a case of expediency operating at the expense of the fundamental rights of the defendant to a fair hearing. Both of these issues will be discussed further below.

On the practical side, the new proposal is in any event unlikely to save much time or effort on the part of judges and prosecutors. Judges must give more thorough consideration to the details of penal orders which threaten to deprive offenders of their liberty. Also, the sanction within the penal order may only be used where the defendant has a lawyer to protect his interest, and then after the defendant has been offered an informal (but not open) hearing in which the judge can declare his intention to issue the suspended sentence as part of the penal order, and hear the defendant's views. Having exercised especial care in preparing and checking such penal orders, and having held a judicial hearing equivalent in time and effort to a short trial, work will not be substantially reduced either for judge or prosecutor. Indeed, one German lawyer has already experienced this. In most cases, he argues, lawyers refuse to accept the written penal order and demand an informal hearing (at which the accused is not present) and the procedure resembles a full trial in many aspects, apart from the defendant's absence from the proceedings.[18]

For this reason, the procedure may be little used anyway, given that a

---

[18] See M. Bohlander, 'Expediency over due process' *Legal Action*, March 1994, 9.

trial is unlikely to take longer and is less controversial, and given the objections that many practitioners have to the new penal order provisions. Criminal justice practice often proves that the success of policy ultimately depends on practitioners being willing to implement it. Perhaps the best hope of preserving the natural justice rights of the accused is that prosecutors will continue to express their objections to the power by not using it.

To sum up, the penal order places the prosecutor in a very important position, with a 'quasi-judicial' status extending beyond his increased sentencing powers. It has been described by Lidstone et al.[19] as similar to the guilty plea system in magistrates' courts in England and Wales. However, the prosecutor in Germany is effectively in control of the proceedings, especially since the judge's review of any case is (commentators suggest) often cursory or a 'mere formality'.[20] Furthermore, the penal order procedure applies to all *Vergehen*, so that some important and prevalent types of crime, such as fraud and theft, are dealt with by means of a procedure which is essentially a prosecution, but where the prosecutor carries the bulk of the judicial responsibilities. The procedure in itself, never mind the severity of the penalties, raises a number of constitutional and ethical questions.

A principal concern is the extent to which the accused feels pressurized to accept a penal order in a process of plea-bargaining. The Uniform Rules of Criminal Procedure do not state that guilt must be admitted before a penal order is offered. Until recently, they provided that a penal order should not be offered where the offender was likely to object, but since 1989, Rule 175, paragraph 3 has been amended to provide that penal orders should no longer be avoided for that reason alone. This was clearly intended to encourage prosecutors to make more widespread use of the penal order. Its result is that guilt is presumed when a penal order is made. Given the range of penalties now available to the prosecutor, this is a grave cause for concern.

Moreover, the prosecutor is able to use the penal order as a bargain to encourage a guilty plea from the suspect, especially since the penalties written into the orders tend to be lower than expected judicial penalties, to deter defendants from demanding a formal trial. It should be noted, however, that Sessar failed to find a single case where this happened in his research.[21] Nevertheless, the temptation for defendants to accept a penal order as a damage limitation exercise, even if the defendant is not guilty as charged, may be strong, especially since a trial is seen as something of a lottery. Furthermore, Felstiner argues, the name for penal order,

---

[19] Ibid., 234.   [20] J. H. Langbein, (1977) op. cit.
[21] K. Sessar, 'Prosecutorial Discretion in Germany', in F. W. MacDonald, ed., *The Prosecutor* (Beverley Hills, 1979), 259.

'*Strafbefehl*', (*Befehl* means order) does not indicate an offer and this, together with the wording of the actual document, might lead to confusion over the defendant's right to appeal.

Felstiner expressed fear that a defendant may be penalized at a subsequent trial for not accepting a penal order, but this risk can be negated by the fact that the offender may withdraw his appeal or retract his refusal to consent to the order, and is entitled to accept the original offer at any time before or during the actual trial. Besides, since the prosecutor occupies a neutral position in the proceedings between the state and the defence, in theory he will have no interest in using underhand practices to achieve high penalties. This can be contrasted with the situation in England prior to the establishment of the CPS. The police in England used to carry out investigations and conduct prosecutions up until 1986, and they evidently had a vested interest in securing a conviction. The whole point of separating these functions in both Germany and England was to render the prosecutor neutral and independent from both the police and the judiciary, to prevent such conflicts of interests and any consequent unfairness to the suspect. Indeed, the working philosophies of German practitioners discussed in Section 11 below also indicate that the state's belief in the virtue of punishment in itself has diminished; the defendant, who is usually unrepresented, has a real choice in whether to accept a penal order. Thomas Weigend's estimate of one third of all penal orders being refused[22] shows that a reasonably large proportion of recipients are not afraid to voice their disagreement.

4. At Trial

As well as direct sentencing powers which enable them to impose sanctions in a quasi-judicial manner, German prosecutors also have an indirect influence over the sentencing function of the judge through their prosecutorial decision-making, in a similar way to Dutch, Scottish, and English prosecutors.

(a) Choice of Charge

The German prosecutor's influence over judicial sentencing is not particularly strong in this field of choosing the charges with which the suspect is indicted. As in the Netherlands, the charges are not fixed until a conviction upon the facts of the offence is reached. At that point the prosecutor suggests to the judge the offence for which the offender is to be sentenced,

---

[22] Thomas Weigend, interview, Cologne 1991.

specifying which section of the Criminal Code has been breached. However, this suggestion is not binding on the court and it is for the judge to decide for which offences the offender is to be tried. The prosecutor's influence is again affected by his relationship with the judge, and by his level of experience and the esteem in which he is held. There is some scope for pitching the suggested offence either higher or lower, but generally the prosecutor is under a duty to suggest the most serious crime that can be charged on the basis of the proven facts. The prosecutor, according to Pfeiffer, operates at the more punitive end of the criminal justice system, and it is felt that manipulating the choice of charge is not the best way to avoid a prison sentence.

(b) Mode of Trial

The potential for influence over sentence is greater when deciding the level of the court in which to bring charges. Whilst the matter is principally determined by statutory minimum and maximum sentences for each offence, combined with the sentencing jurisdiction of the court, there is still some leeway for the prosecutor to exercise his discretion and thereby manipulate the judge's sentence. In Germany, the magistrates' court (*Amtsgericht*) and the district court (*Landgericht*) both have jurisdiction over offences punishable by imprisonment of four years or less.[23] Thus the prosecutor has a limited possibility to engage in 'forum shopping', that is selecting the court, or even the particular judge whom he feels will be most sympathetic towards his recommendations for sentence.

One senior prosecutor in Bremen, specializing in sexual offences, offered a practical example of such 'forum shopping' in rape cases.[24] In Bremen, the offence of rape is punishable by 2 to 15 years' imprisonment, but does not have to be sent to the district court, even though it is a felony. Hence, a prosecutor has the choice of whether to send relatively low-key cases, which may be sentenced with 2 to 4 years' imprisonment, to either the magistrates' or the district court. However, in practice he tends to send rape cases, of whatever degree of gravity, to the district court, not always as a means of influencing sentence to obtain a higher penalty, but in the interest of the victim, who need only go through one trial ordeal and give evidence once. This avoids the possibility that a prosecution commenced in the lower court could be transferred to the higher court. Strictly speaking, it is not within the rules in the district of Bremen to refer to the district court a case in which the prosecutor expects a sentence of less than four year's imprisonment. Nevertheless, this prosecutor has persisted in her

[23] Until February 1993 magistrates' jurisdiction was limited to offences punishable with three years' imprisonment or less. Recent legislation has increased this limit to four years.
[24] Example given by a prosecutor in Bremen in interview 1991.

attempts to 'upgrade' cases to the district court and gradually her practice is being accepted more willingly by the judges. Hence, although her motive does not always directly concern the offender's sentence, but often simply the victim's interests, this is a good example of the persuasive influence that a German prosecutor can have in the process of deciding the mode of trial. Whatever her motive, her practice of decision-making in this area has had a marginal impact on the behaviour of Bremen's criminal law judges.

(c) Recommending Sentence

The duty of the prosecutor during the trial to recommend a sentence to the judge is, as in the Netherlands, a wide opportunity for him to influence the judge's sentencing decisions, and thereby the extent of the use of imprisonment. However, as with the obtaining of consent for s. 153 orders and penal orders mentioned above, the degree to which judges will allow a prosecutor to modify their sentencing depends very much on the individual personalities involved. Generally, if a prosecutor is experienced or specialized, the judge will be more susceptible and responsive to their suggestions for the type and level of sentence. The reverse is also true, so that those who are less experienced or are reputed to be more radical in their recommendations have less direct influence. Again two prosecutors recounted differing experiences with judges in this part of their work in Bremen. Whilst one, being highly specialized and experienced in her field of sexual offences, is usually successful in convincing judges to follow her suggested pattern of sentences, the other, being much less experienced and confessing that he follows a personal, liberal policy which is vastly different from the policy laid down by the Chief Prosecutors in his office, is often unsuccessful here and his recommendations are less frequently followed.

Similarly, the beliefs and policies of the individual judge affect the extent to which he will allow his decisions to be swayed by the recommendations of the prosecutors. The practice of recommending sentence, carried on in both Germany and the Netherlands, can be a hit and miss affair; unless the two parties have coinciding views on both the individual case and on criminal policy generally, the recommendation is likely to be ignored. It is questionable, therefore, whether there is really any purpose to the recommendation. The prosecutor in theory provides all relevant information to the judge, whether this operates to increase or to reduce the sentence to be passed. Since the recommendation of the prosecutor has no binding effect in law (which would be an unconstitutional fetter on the sentencing discretion of the judge), and since in practice only the recommendations of the most respected and experienced prosecutors are adopted, there seems little point in the general practice of prosecutors recommending a sentence.

It should be stated, however, that the function of recommending sentence to the judge can be useful. Like the pre-sentence report, in England and Wales, a recommendation of sentence provides the judge with guidance about the sentencing legislation and the prosecutor can make an informed suggestion since he or she may know more about the accused than the judge, who will only have seen the offender in court. The prosecutor may have met the offender, and even if not, may know more about that offender's previous criminal record and domestic circumstances.

5. Appeals

One of the essential safeguards against the abuse of the prosecutor's discretionary powers to dismiss or to continue cases is the possibility of various types of appeal by both the offender and the victim. The prosecutor's right of appeal against a judge's sentence also serves as a direct influence on the judge's sentencing behaviour.

(a) The Victim

Only the actual victim of the offence can appeal against a dismissal of a prosecution in Germany. The German definition of 'victim' in this context does not, as in the Netherlands, include parties loosely connected with the crime, such as victim support groups. There are three routes through which the victim can take his appeal.

First, the victim can lodge a formal complaint with a Chief Prosecutor the head of prosecution in the district where the case was dismissed. The matter is then dealt with internally within the prosecution service and the Chief Prosecutor acts as adjudicator in deciding whether to order a prosecution or not. If the Chief Prosecutor decides not to order a prosecution, the victim's appeal may be heard by a judge in an appeal court (*Klageerzwingungsverfahren*), part of the High Court. The judge has the power to review the prosecutor's file and any other evidence which may be available. If he finds that there are sufficient grounds for a prosecution to take place he can order a prosecutor to submit accusatory papers to the appropriate court and begin trial proceedings. This form of judicial review can only be used by the victim where the individual prosecutor and the Chief Prosecutor have both refused a prosecution, and only where the decision not to prosecute was not made on so-called 'policy' grounds (An appeal can be made against non-prosecution on the basis of insufficiency of evidence). Evidently, it is not for a member of the public to make any contribution or comment on the concept of 'public' interest!

The final possibility for the victim is to exercise his right of private prosecution (*Privatklage*) and perform the prosecutorial role himself. The

Code of Criminal Procedure provides that in certain specified offences (usually the sort of very private offences such as slander, or offences committed within the family or within marriage) which may not concern the public interest, an indictment may be brought by a lawyer acting as a prosecutor on behalf of the victim.[25] The public prosecutor can, however, take over the proceedings on behalf of the state if he feels there is public interest in the prosecution.[26] In more severe, but less private, cases there is the possibility of a *Nebenklage*, or a 'side-by-side' prosecution.[27] In these cases the victim or the victim's lawyer may join the prosecutor in conducting the prosecution during the trial. (Strictly, of course, this is not a way of circumventing a diversionary decision by the public prosecutor, since a *Nebenklage* depends on a decision by the public prosecutor to prosecute.)

None of these three possibilities are used frequently by victims. In Lower Saxony, figures compiled by the Ministry of Justice show that in 1990 there were only 2,961 appeals to the High Court by victims out of the 146,876 prosecutable offences; that is only 2% of the total number of cases with sufficient evidence, and only 3.3% of all prosecuted offences. The right of private prosecution is exercised less frequently. Nevertheless, these (almost theoretical) possibilities of appeal by the victim are important as mechanisms to control the prosecutor's use of his wide discretion.

(b) The Accused

The possibilities for the accused to appeal against the manner in which his case is dealt with are built into the structure of the decision-making powers of the prosecutor. All the options for dismissal described above are voluntary and thus the main way in which a defendant can object to the disposal of his case is by objecting to the conditions of a s. 153a order or to the principle of a s. 153 disposal, or by not accepting a penal order, thereby forcing the prosecutor to send his case to court for trial. In this way, the accused can proclaim his innocence and be heard by a judge if he feels he has been aggrieved, and so there are no extra appeal procedures.

However, the problems with the appeal procedure in connection with the penal order have already been outlined and similar procedures apply to s. 153 and s. 153a orders. The time limit may be sufficient now that it has been increased to fourteen days, but it does not solve the problem of illiterate or homeless people, who will encounter difficulties in merely reading or receiving the written order of dismissal, as well as those who simply cannot understand the significance of the order. In respect of the

[25] Code of Criminal Procedure, s. 374.   [26] Ibid., ss. 376–377.
[27] Code of Criminal Procedure, s. 395.

penal order, there has been a proposal to abolish the right of appeal in cases involving a fine of 30 days of income or less, in which cases it is seldom used, but the existence of the right of appeal is significant in itself and its abolition would be a dangerous erosion of the accused's rights. This is another controversial proposal, and it is thought doubtful that Parliament will implement it, especially since the Federal Ministry of Justice is currently under the political control of the Liberal Party.[28]

(c) The Prosecutor

The prosecutor can appeal against a sentence after conviction either if it is considered too lenient or, with his neutral role in the trial, if he thinks it is too severe. Each sentence will be routinely scrutinized by the Chief Prosecutor in each office and the decision to appeal is taken at that level. Therefore, it is possible for the prosecution to appeal against a sentence which the prosecutor concerned had recommended to the judge if the Chief Prosecutor disagreed with the original recommendation. This appeal possibility is not used extensively, probably in less than 5% of all prosecuted cases, in the opinion of academics interviewed.[29] Indeed, in Bremen, the state guidelines on appeal procedure by prosecutors specifically discourage the use of the option except where there is a substantial difference between the sentence given and that recommended. These appeals are apparently seen as a waste of the resources of the prosecution service.

6. REPARATION

The German Code of Criminal Procedure has, since 1975, provided for the use of conciliation and reparation at the pre-trial stage as a means of disposing of cases. s. 153a allows for reparation to be a condition of a policy waiver. However, until recently reparation has not been much used by German prosecutors. Without any organized schemes of reparation it was very much up to the individual prosecutor, often at the instigation of the defendant or his lawyer, to bring the two parties together and chair the negotiations for a settlement. Not surprisingly, given that it took up much more of the prosecutor's time and effort than other conditions of a s. 153a order, reparation was used comparatively sparingly. In recent years, its use

---

[28] Although clearly, despite the Liberal Party's control, other equally controversial and less than liberal reforms have become law in the last few years!

[29] This might be considered a low figure, particularly considering that the German prosecutor may appeal against a sentence in any type of case. In England and Wales, however, the figure of 5% may be considered rather high, but it must be remembered that the Crown Prosecutor may appeal against an unduly lenient sentence in indictable cases only.

has statistically increased somewhat and whilst it is still not a major part of criminal policy, the whole area of restorative justice is now being discussed by policy-makers in Germany much more seriously.

In the juvenile field, reparation has been much more widely developed.[30] In the adult field, a considerable amount of research is currently being conducted, principally by Christian Pfeiffer, director of the research institute, Kriminologisches Forschungs Institut Niedersachsen (KFN), into extending the use of reparation in the adult field, and more particularly to structure the organization of reparation schemes. Pfeiffer set up one such scheme (*Waage Hannover*) in Hanover in the autumn of 1991, similar to scheme in Cologne (*Waage Köln*) set up some years earlier. These schemes employ specialized social workers concentrating solely on reparation and mediation, and acting in co-operation with both the prosecution and the police. The police, being in contact with both the victim and the offender, seem the ideal body to select cases suitable to be handled by this scheme. Once in receipt of a proposal, the prosecutor initiates the reparation procedure and may waive the prosecution after a satisfactory settlement has been reached, or may send a particularly serious case to trial, using the success of the reparation agreement as a strong mitigating factor to influence the sentence. Thus it is envisaged that there is room for reparation, at least as part of the overall sentence, even in more serious cases such as unarmed robbery or serious assault.

Further, a proposal has been made to Parliament to change the emphasis given to reparation agreements by the judge in passing sentence. The suggestion is that the current situation, whereby the judge orders a fine as the foremost sanction and then leaves the victim to retrieve his own compensation in the civil court at a later date, has proved unsatisfactory. Compensation orders are hardly ever used in German criminal procedure and thus the victim's only option is to sue for compensation at a later time. By then the offender is likely to be unable to pay (possibly because of the original fine) or is not motivated to pay because he feels he has already paid for his crime to the state. This proposal aims to change the attitude of the judge by encouraging him to order a fine payable to the Treasury only where he has first ordered compensation or satisfied himself that a voluntary payment to the victim has been made. This mirrors a provision in the Criminal Justice Act 1982 in England and Wales, which provides that a compensation order should have priority over a fine where the offender has insufficient means to pay both, or where ordering both would be inconsistent with the principle of proportionality.[31] Both the German

---

[30] See C. Pelikan, 'Conflict Resolution between victims and offenders in Austria and in the Federal Republic of Germany' in F. Heidensohn, and M. Farrell, eds., *Crime in Europe*, (London, 1991).

[31] See further A. Ashworth, *Sentencing and Criminal Justice* (London, 1992), 249–252.

and the English provisions clearly aim to put the victim's interests as high on the list of priorities as is consistent with the public interest in sentencing.

According to Pfeiffer, this is part of a general shift in criminal policy whereby the offender/victim relationship has become the centre of interest in the resolution of crime, with the punishment aspect of criminal justice falling into second place, part of what he calls the 'disarmament of justice'. A change in the attitude of practitioners at ground level has, according to his surveys and research, produced a general level of scepticism towards the use of prison as a sanction and a growing interest in the practical resolution of the immediate conflicts caused by criminal behaviour: 'I would say that reparation schemes are the fascinating future of a criminal justice system where the conflict and the victim are the central interests, and not the lust for punishment.'[32]

A further example of Pfeiffer's work in this area is the establishment of a 'victim fund' in Hanover. Fines ordered by a prosecutor as a condition of a s. 153a dismissal are sent to a special fund rather than to a charity or to the state. The fund is then used to compensate the victim in cases where the offender cannot pay full compensation himself; instead he will perform a period of community service, or he will make the largest donation to the fund that he can afford in the form of a fine. In this way the victim can be compensated before trial, making the use of reparation available to those less wealthy or unemployed offenders for whom financial reparation would previously have been unaffordable.

Hence, Pfeiffer himself is advancing the causes of the victim in the criminal justice process most successfully from his research post in Hanover, and his influence is likely eventually to spread over much of Germany, particularly if Parliament gives legal effect to the proposals which have been made in this area. However, whether the sentencing role of prosecutors in the context of reparation schemes is yet this widespread is debatable. Pfeiffer, being closely involved with the current reforms, may be unable objectively to predict the success of a national application of this scheme, being perhaps prevented by the detail of his work from forming a realistic view of the situation as a whole. Other academics who commented on the restorative aspect of criminal justice[33] agreed that reparation has a strong future in adult justice in Germany, but would not class it as the 'number one issue' as Pfeiffer does. To them, the penal order is at present more appropriate, as its increased use enables the system to cope with a greater workload, which view is borne out by criminal statistics.

---

[32] Christian Pfeiffer, interview, Hanover 1991.
[33] Weigend and Feest, interviews, June 1991.

7. Current Trends

(a) Remand

The decision to remand a suspect in custody, ultimately taken by the judge, is initiated by the prosecutor. The prosecutor proposes remand custody and the judge will merely sign if he agrees. The prosecutor's initial proposal has a substantial influence on the ultimate sentencing choice between imprisonment and an alternative sanction. On one hand, the evidence of remand custody may encourage the trial judge to view the case with more severity and thus increase the likelihood of a prison sentence. In this way, pre-trial detention effectively pulls down the barriers to custody and makes the judge more inclined to use custodial sentences after conviction. Conversely, if the prosecutor is able to restrict the use of remand, the judicial sentence after conviction may be more constructive. The German prosecutor's influence over remand custody includes the power to order the release of remand prisoners without the consent of the judge. This power, which remains firmly within the judicial realm in England and Wales, is further evidence of the wide and influential discretion of the prosecutor in Germany.

On the other hand, prosecutors may influence the sentencing process through their remand decision in the opposite way. A judge may be inclined to offer a sentence of probation or some other non-custodial sanction when the offender has already served time in prison. In some cases, therefore, the prosecutor may act as a sentencer in using pre-trial custody as a sanction in itself, an immediate punishment with sufficient deterrent value to enable the judge to offer a milder, non-custodial sentence after trial. Indeed, Pfeiffer estimates that in around 50% of trials following remand detention, the defendant did not ultimately receive a custodial sentence. However, the figure is similar in England and Wales. Given the lesser influence of the CPS over the remand decision and also the English judiciary's lack of interest in reducing the remand population, it seems less likely that remand custody is used as a punishment in itself, or as a tactic to reduce the likelihood of a subsequent custodial sentence. Further, previous years' statistics were not available to compare with this figure and therefore it is impossible to tell whether the number of such cases has increased and if so, whether that is due to a change in tactics on the part of the judiciary and the prosecutors, or, more likely, due to a change of circumstances connected with prison capacity and changing attitudes of the German judges towards the use of long-term imprisonment. By contrast, in the Dutch juvenile justice system for example, remand orders are sometimes issued by the judge without any intention to execute the order and imprison the juvenile, who will 'wait' to serve his remand period until a cell becomes available.[34]

The extent to which the prosecutor uses his power to influence the remand decision will nevertheless have a substantial effect on the overall pattern of imprisonment in Germany, which has been wavering in recent years. The dramatic and much discussed fall in the prison population of West Germany from 1983, as reported by Johannes Feest in his lecture to the NACRO Annual General Meeting in 1988,[35] was, according to Feest, due as much to the drop in the use of remand as to a fall in the number of sentenced prisoners. Indeed, Prowse et al.[36] document the historical cause for this reduction, concluding that the main force behind the rejection of remand was a body of vociferous practitioners. A professional association of defence lawyers (*Deutscher Anwaltverein*) launched a press campaign in 1983 arguing an excessively frequent and gratuitous use was made of remand for lengthy periods under a harsh regime, which in their view breached acceptable social standards. This public discussion of the problems with remand custody in Germany caused a general change in attitude amongst both prosecution and judicial practitioners, and heightened awareness of the remand problem amongst the public generally.[37]

However, the decrease in remand leading to the fall in the prison population generally, appears now to have been reversed. Feest noted a slight increase in the use of remand from 1989.[38] Statistics produced by the Federal Ministry of Justice show a rise of nearly 2% in the number of remand prisoners in Germany between 1988 and 1989, despite a continued drop in the number of sentenced prisoners.[39] Figures produced by the Lower Saxony Ministry of Justice[40] confirm this upward trend, with a sharp rise beginning in mid-1989 and continuing throughout 1990 and 1991. The consensus of opinion, though, seems to indicate that there has not been an abandonment of the rationale behind the original decline; that is, there has not been any radical change in the working philosophy of

[34] M. Kommer, 'The Role of the Prosecutor in Pre-Court Decision-Making'. Unpublished paper presented at the one day conference: 'Young Adults in the Criminal Justice System', Nottingham Polytechnic, 5 Dec. 1990, 4.

[35] J. Feest, *Reducing the Prison Population: Lessons from the West German Experience*, lecture given at NACRO AGM, 10 Nov. 1988, London, 2.

[36] R. Prowse, H. Weber, and C. Wilson, 'Reforming Remand Imprisonment: Comparing Britain and Germany (A Working Paper)', unpublished paper presented to the Annual Conference of the European Group for the study of Deviance and Social Control, Haarlem, the Netherlands, 4–7 Sept. 1990, 14–15.

[37] M. Gebauer, quoted in Prowse et al., (1990) op. cit., 14.

[38] J. Feest, 'Reducing the Prison Population: Lessons from the West German experience?' in J. Muncie, and R. Sparks, eds., *Imprisonment: European Perspectives*, (London, 1991).

[39] Ibid., Table 1, 13.

[40] B. Hasenpusch, *Capacity and Population of Correctional Institutions in Lower Saxony* (Hanover, 1991), Table 4, 'Remand Prisoners in Lower Saxony 1975–1991'.

practitioners. Pfeiffer argues that the increase has been caused mainly by new crime problems in Germany connected with foreign offenders, particularly those from the Eastern European countries whose borders with West Germany have recently been opened. One particular problem was caused by a general amnesty in East Germany in 1989. Because of overcrowded prisons and the threat of prison riots, the East German prison authorities released 20,000 prisoners without making any preparation. As a result a large number of people who flocked to the 'bounteous West' after the borders were opened seized the opportunities presented to them for further criminal activities. Additional problems arose when other East Germans committed crime for the first time, after the unsettling reunification with the West which caused job losses, homelessness in Western cities and other problems of social inadequacies from which petty crime often results. Several commentators have suggested that the increase in pre-trial detention may be due to those specific socio-political factors, and that the problem may be a temporary interruption of the progress towards reduction of imprisonment. Only time will tell whether this is the case, or whether these academics, (unlike Feest) are overly optimistic about the future of the German prison population.[41]

On the other hand, there have been positive trends in the remand sector. In the juvenile field there has been a substantial decline in the use of remand custody. In particular, the Minister of Justice in Lower Saxony became interested in the issue after a controversial case in which three youths died in remand custody. He intervened by instructing all prosecutors in that state only to recommend the use of remand where they could provide him with written reasons showing that it was absolutely necessary. The use of pre-trial detention halved within a year of that directive and after two years the rate of remand fell to about ten cases per year. The abolition of remand custody for juveniles was subsequently effected by statute in Lower Saxony, a reform initiated by politics rather than any moral objections from practitioners.

A further reform in the field of juvenile remand, initiated by Christian Pfeiffer from the KFN, has been the foundation of an organization called *Brücke* ('Bridge'). The pilot scheme was founded twelve years ago in Munich, and is now being introduced in many other parts of Germany, and there is pressure on the government to introduce it into all ninety-two jurisdictions of Germany. 'Bridge' is a bail hostel scheme (similar to the experimental schemes in England over the last ten years). It provides rented accommodation for young defendants awaiting trial, where they can obtain counselling, help in finding employment, and other support. The Munich

---

[41] J. Feest, (1991) op. cit., 143–4.

scheme has had some measure of success, with even the most conservative of prosecutors using it, especially for youths who are homeless or whose domestic situation is problematic. It is generally believed that such organizations not only help juveniles avoid pre-trial detention, but also result in a milder punishment upon conviction, as a result of the defendant's participation in the scheme and of pre-trial counselling. The scheme has shown that the offender can be adequately dealt with outside the prison system, without adverse effects.

Given the positive effects of these reforms in the juvenile field, it would be encouraging to see similar reforms taking hold in the adult field. Indeed, Prowse et al.[42] report that the Green Party in Germany (*Die Grünen*) have proposed very similar reforms. As well as the actual abolition of remand for juveniles and the provision of bail hostels like those provided by 'Bridge', they have called for the use of remand in adult cases to be restricted to situations where it is absolutely necessary, using pre-trial custody as a last resort only in very serious cases of criminality. This would certainly prevent the use by prosecutors of remand as a sanction in itself, which in any case may be unconstitutional.

(b) The Prison Population

The reduction in the remand population detailed above was followed in 1985 by a substantial fall in the number of sentenced prisoners. This reduction is also documented by Feest.[43] He attributes this dramatic change in imprisonment rates to the activities of judges and prosecutors at ground level, and dismisses theories that the fall is connected with crime rates, legislation, or demographic factors: 'The reduction of the West German prison population is . . . clearly attributable to changes in the behaviour of prosecutors and/or judges. It is what the Council of Europe likes to call 'de facto' as opposed to 'de jure' decriminalisation.'[44] Jung shares this view, and attributes the fall in the prison population to the activities of prosecutors diverting cases away from the courts.[45]

The foundation on which Feest based his thesis is unclear. Indeed, he himself admits that his proof was rather 'impressionistic' and based on his knowledge of local professionals in Bremen alone. Weigend and Range also have their doubts about the cogency of Feest's argument. They consider it unlikely that the sentencing practice of prosecutors in the use of s. 153 and s. 153a orders and penal orders would make a large statistical difference on the imprisonment rate throughout Germany, not least because

---

[42] R. Prowse, et al., (1990) op. cit., 22.   [43] J. Feest, (1988) op. cit., 2.
[44] Ibid., 3.
[45] H. Jung, 'Criminal Justice—a European Perspective' [1993] *Crim. LR* 243.

those disposals usually cover only minor offences which would at most attract a suspended prison sentence. Under general sentencing patterns in West Germany, only a serious crime will result in a sentence of immediate imprisonment. Hence, whilst the number of prosecutions or judicial fines might decrease, they thought it improbable that prosecutors' activities had any direct impact on the rate of imprisonment.

Nevertheless, the body of opinion amongst practitioners in Germany, and their general disillusionment with the use of imprisonment as an effective sanction, must have had some influence on that substantial decarceration process, especially through their powers to recommend sentence at trial and to decide on mode of trial. Many practitioners, even those who once admired the educational and treatment values of imprisonment, are now becoming more and more disenchanted with it. As Feest said: 'The euphoria has gone about building a modern prison system with lots of treatment.'[46] This change of attitude is not connected with a new academic school of thought of any significance, but rather to do with a new generation of professionals whose attitudes and opinions, formed during their training years in the 1960s, are now being put into practice. The contributions of criminologists and other academics to the general policy-making within the prosecution system is also significant, and is discussed below.

(c) *Prison Capacity*

The influence of the prosecutor over the level of imprisonment may be negated by the prison authorities who, conversely, may affect the decision-making of prosecutors. The available prison capacity will clearly affect such prosecutorial decisions because when prisons are overcrowded, the prosecutor is likely to make more use of his diversionary powers. Range's figures based on institutions for adult prisoners in Lower Saxony show that there has been a considerable decrease in the availability of both remand and sentenced accommodation since 1983. Indeed, the expansive prison building schemes embarked upon by most German states in the 1980s have now slowed down considerably or ceased altogether. At the same time, some older and relatively disused prison places will be closed over the next decade, and most German states are planning to halt the increase of prison capacity or even plan to decrease prison places. With remand custody already increasing and the sentenced prison population set to follow, the prosecutor may, in his choice of disposals, be obliged to avoid overcrowding.

[46] Feest, interview, Bremen 1991.

8. JUDICIAL INDEPENDENCE

The reaction from the judiciary to the widening sentencing powers of the prosecutor has been mixed. Naturally, judges are reluctant to give away a substantial part of their jurisdiction and for this reason judges' associations protested very heavily against the new power which allows prosecutors to issue low-level suspended sentences in connection with the penal order procedure. Certainly many criticisms and anxieties about discretionary decision-making have focused on intrusion by prosecutors into the judge's sentencing province. Weigend goes as far as to say that this is unconstitutional, that criminal sentencing is a role for the judiciary and that s. 153 and s. 153a breach article 92 of the German constitution which gives legislative authority to that proposition:

Even where, as in West Germany, the constitution permits only judges to impose criminal sanctions, many prosecutors assume the function of a magistrate in choosing among the alternatives of filing criminal charges, imposing a non-criminal sanction or simply dismissing the case.[47]

On the other hand, the relationship between the prosecution and judicial branches of the legal profession is not particularly acrimonious. There is an affinity, perhaps stemming from the historical link between them, the office of prosecutor having been created out of the multiple roles of the judge. Certainly, given that transition between professions occurs frequently, since the two bodies receive the same legal training in the initial stages, the separation between them is considerably narrower than, for example, in England and Wales. In policy-making, judges' associations join forces with bodies of prosecutors (as their powerful, joint rejection of the suspended sentences proposal has proved) and prosecutors evidently reserve their neutral, objective stance for the courtroom. The prospect of judges and prosecutors meeting to discuss a joint stand on policy seems distinctly remote, almost laughable, in England and Wales, even in the top echelons of the CPS and the Lord Chancellor's Department, where the neutrality of the prosecutor and the separation of the judiciary from the prosecution are considered far too important to be kept in the confines of the courtroom.[48]

---

[47] T. Weigend, 'Prosecution: Comparative Aspects' in S. H. Kadish, ed., *Encyclopedia of Crime and Justice—Volume 3* (New York, 1983), 1298.

[48] In practice this may indirectly have been remedied through the Criminal Justice Consultative Council, set up following a suggestion by Lord Woolf in his report on the prison disturbances in England in 1991. The Criminal Justice Consultative Council is a committee whose membership comprises of the heads of each branch of the criminal justice process, whose aim is to set a policy agenda for criminal justice based on the mutual agreement of all those involved in the process. The Council also has local branches, local Area Committees, to enhance co-operation and working relationships between branches of the process at the

German judges may also regard the role of prosecutors as useful in regulating the number of cases going to trial. Whilst they are obviously concerned that their caseloads do not exceed the limits of manageability, they are also concerned that their services are not under-used, which may result in their transfer to a civil court. The use of diversionary discretion by the prosecutor certainly affects the judge's caseload. Where a prosecutor increases his use of diversion, a recidivist offender may come before the judge only at a later stage of his criminal career. He will be treated in court as a first-time offender, even though the judge will be made aware of the previous decisions of the prosecutor. In this rather indirect way, the increase of prosecutorial diversion can produce a decrease in the use of prison, since the offender steps slightly higher up the criminal ladder before he appears in court when the question of imprisonment may be addressed. In this way, there is more patience in a more lenient system if prosecutors have a wide discretion which they actually use on a regular basis.

9. SAFEGUARDS AND ACCOUNTABILITY

The anxieties voiced by both academics and professionals about the wide-ranging sentencing powers of the prosecutor, in particular about the new power to include suspended sentences in the penal order system, have been outlined above. The situation has now arisen where, if the penal order is accepted as a prosecutorial dismissal, the prosecutor is disposing of a significant majority of prosecutable offences.[49] The cases are all dealt with in the hidden arena of the prosecutor's office, without the constitutional liberties of the accused being safeguarded as they are by court procedures. There are, however, a number of practical measures aimed at avoiding the abuse of these powers. But it is debatable whether they provide safeguards in proportion to the risk to the accused.

First, as described above, most dismissal powers available to the prosecutor are subject to the defendant's consent, and some require the consent of a judge, although the latter category is diminishing as the prosecutor is becoming more autonomous. Whilst the judge's consent may be too readily forthcoming and inadequately informed, the requirement of the defendant's acceptance of the conditions of a dismissal, and the right to appeal against them, constitute a basic safeguard of civil liberties and are deeply embedded in the structure of these procedures.

---

local level. See further, Howard League, *The Dynamics of Justice* (London, 1993), which welcomed the establishment of the Council but recommended further changes (such as joint training procedures) to make it more effective.

[49] Based on the figures for Lower Saxony contained in Table 5.1, the prosecutor dealt with no less than 73.8% of all cases with sufficient evidence to prosecute in 1990.

Other than the appeal procedures, which are often overlooked or misunderstood by the accused, the only other prosecutorial accountability lies in supervision by the higher ranking members of the prosecution service. The existing guidelines are ineffectual in preventing discriminatory and improper decision-making since they are so generalized and vaguely-worded. Issued on a parochial basis, their primary purpose is to define and disseminate policy. Senior ranking prosecutors, however, in addition to checking all files after trial to see that they have been correctly handled and to assess the need for any appeal against sentence, also routinely check a sample of dismissal cases. The only department in which all cases have to be thoroughly checked and countersigned by a superior is in the economic crime department. These cases are usually very complex, often involving large-scale corporate fraud, but are fewer in number, and the extra work involved in this supervisory procedure is deemed to be justified by the penalties at stake. Generally, it was the opinion of practitioners in Bremen that senior prosecutors do discuss with their juniors the criteria which they apply. However, the purpose of this consultation is apparently to achieve uniformity of policy and to reduce regional discrepancies, rather than to discuss the rationale behind any individual prosecutor's decisions. The example of the Bremen prosecutor mentioned above (Section 2(e)) was certainly more indicative of hierarchical supervision being used to bring a 'maverick' prosecutor into line, rather than a concern that he was using improper criteria or abusing his discretionary powers to dismiss.

Checks on a federal level in Germany are also inadequate. Statistics compiled on a national scale produce national averages which ignore significant regional discrepancies and are of little real use. There are, however, plans to develop a nationwide computer network to collect detailed data on individual prosecutors' behaviour. With more detail and improved technology, Chief Prosecutors will be better equipped to identify any abuse of power, and to assess sentencing trends and their repercussions more accurately. Until then, however, the task of seeking out improprieties and abuses in prosecutorial sentencing behaviour is left to researchers, physically sorting through files to detect such abuses, and analysing the effect of new provisions and laws on prosecutors decision-making.[50]

Another internal check on the prosecutor is his obligation to give written reasons for his disposal of a case. In this way, not only is he forced to give careful consideration to the proper criteria and to rationalize his decision, but, as Herrmann suggests: 'the reasons provide supervisors with

---

[50] Wolfgang Langer's recent study on sentencing cultures in Germany is a good example of such a methodology. See W. Langer, *Organisational and Human Factors in Judges' Sentencing—a Comparative Study of Three 'Local Legal Cultures'* (Hanover, 1991).

means to standardise and structure the exercise of discretion',[51] providing, though, that those supervisors actually check the reasons given.

With such a wide (and increasing) sentencing discretion, combined with relatively few effective checks on its application, the possibility of the prosecutor engaging (whether consciously or not) in the process of net-widening is as great in Germany as it is in the Netherlands and Scotland (see Chapters 4 and 3 respectively). In particular there is a danger that prosecutors may now use s. 153a dismissals, with a considerable range of conditions, to dispose of a case which would otherwise have been uncon-ditionally dismissed under s. 153, and that the new, higher penalties under the penal order procedure may be imposed inappropriately. According to Pfeiffer, however, the 'danger' of net-widening depends very much on the 'sanction' used. In his opinion, the use of victim/offender reparation schemes constitutes a more positive approach, rather than a questionable extension of social control. It means the avoidance of a further civil trial by the victim to gain compensation, rather than a widening of the net. However, in cases where the condition attached to non-prosecution is more punitive, such as community service (in the juvenile area) or a fine, net-widening probably does occur, such conditions being imposed in cases which merit no more than a warning or an unconditional waiver, although it is ex-tremely difficult to prove this process. The careful, statistical analysis of individual prosecutors' behaviour is the only means of detecting and eradic-ating such a problem. Meanwhile, it is considered something of an occu-pational hazard by many practitioners, and whilst Pfeiffer is concerned that net-widening is an abuse of a power (and also a misuse of the funds and resources of the projects in which he is involved), he would not try to deter practitioners from using any form of diversionary schemes.

10. POLICY MAKING

The influence of the prosecutor over sentencing is particularly strong in the context of their law-making activities. A significant majority of new pro-posals and legal provisions in Germany have their foundation in the prac-tice of the professionals of the criminal justice system, and the dissemination of new ideas by academics and criminologists. In Germany there are many research projects in the field of criminal justice, particularly since research centres, such as the KFN in Hanover, are set up within the fragmented structure of the prosecution system, so that many state-based centres are carrying out local research, rather than one national centre, a result of the federal system. There also appears to be more integration between academics

[51] J. Herrmann, 'The German Prosecutor (American comments on American and German Prosecutors)' in K. C. Davis, ed., *Discretionary Justice in Europe and America* (Chicago, 1976), see conclusion, Ch. 2.

and the practitioners themselves—prosecutors, judges, police, and social workers. The discussion of ideas between these groups, and their alliance in expressing their views on current issues and putting forward proposals, represents a major force in achieving reform. Pfeiffer suggested the same during an interview in Hanover, June 1991:

It is fascinating at the moment to study social change—how it arises and who is able to initiate social change and change within the fields of juvenile delinquency and adult justice. In my view that combination of reform-orientated practitioners together with scientists can create a force which changes public opinion and at the end changes the law.[52]

Thus, the development of new schemes, practices, and ideas at grass-root level is the driving force for changes in the law. Usually, new proposals laid before Parliament have already been well-rehearsed in practice to prove their viability. The changes in law come at the end of the process; Parliament follows the development of the 'hands-on' policy of professionals, and legislative action is usually of a confirmatory nature, giving a legal, statutory framework to the current practice.

. Most recent commentators on the German prosecution system, and particularly on the role of the prosecutor in the decarceration process of the last ten years, have arrived at the same conclusion. Rutherford has suggested that:

Both the example from West Germany and recent developments regarding juvenile offenders in England and Wales suggest that a crucial key to penal reform is held by practitioners and that occasions arise when practice is able to lead policy.[53]

Recent changes in the law relating to prosecutions, as well as the overall changes in imprisonment rates, provide an abundance of contemporary examples of this 'grass-roots' reform process. There is a general consensus of opinion, expressed in Feest's lecture to the NACRO Annual General Meeting,[54] that the reduction in imprisonment over the last decade may be the result of a change of attitude amongst those who determine the extent of imprisonment. The disillusionment with the effectiveness of imprisonment and the philosophical rejection of its values and justifications were mentioned repeatedly by practitioners and academics alike in the interviews conducted in Germany. This is partly due to the realization, through the published reports of research and surveys, that public attitudes towards crime are not as punitive as was expected, which led many prosecutors to believe that practitioners should use the criminal law simply to restore peace to society. Some prosecutors interviewed were surprised, for example,

[52] Christian Pfeiffer, KFN, interview, Hanover, June 1991.
[53] A. Rutherford, 'The English Penal Crisis: Paradox and Possibilities' (1988), *Current Legal Problems*, 41: 109.
[54] J. Feest, (1988) op. cit.

at the tone of the recent English White Paper[55] which they considered to be very punishment-orientated, that is aiming to use punishment as a goal in itself, with the criminal practitioner's role being to ensure that punishment is fairly imposed. Graham sums up the effect of this change in attitude in Germany:

The most persuasive explanation appears to be that the decline [in the prison population] stems from a radical change in the practice of public prosecutors and judges, which in turn has been brought about by a shift in their perceptions of the efficacy and legitimacy of incarceration.[56]

Recent examples include the drop in the use of remand imprisonment. It has already been mentioned how a press campaign launched by practitioners, voicing their views on the use of pre-trial detention, gave the initial impetus for the decline in the figures. Feest also mentions a most important conference organized by the German Lawyers' Association in 1982, which was attended by prosecutors, lawyers, judges, and federal and state government representatives, bringing together the widest possible range of viewpoints under one roof. One observer summed up the importance of the conference as a turning point in the professional thinking of workers in the justice system: 'Undoubtedly, these two days were a politically fateful hour for abolitionism in West Germany. Never before have we had a forum as widely noticed.'[57] Pfeiffer's work in setting up reparation schemes and the network of 'Bridge' bail hostels are also good examples of the work of influential academics in informal co-operation with sympathetic and enthusiastic practitioners which has led to proposals for pragmatic and reactive reform on the part of Parliament.

The importance of practice-based policy-making as a momentum for reform is clear. However, the range of the prosecutor's discretion, as well as his pivotal position, give him ample opportunity as a key player in this climate of change to influence not only the pattern, but also the legal limits of sentencing, from the core of the justice system.

11. WORKING PHILOSOPHIES IN GERMAN CRIMINAL JUSTICE

(a) Restorative Justice

General evidence of this new outlook in the criminal justice system is presented in the sections above concerning the current procedure and trends

[55] Home Office White Paper, *Crime, Justice and Protecting the Public* Cm 965, (London, 1990).
[56] J. Graham, 'Decarceration in the Federal Republic of Germany: How practitioners are succeeding where policy-makers have failed' (1990) *British Journal of Criminology*, 30: 150–170.
[57] Detlev Spalt, quoted in J. Feest, (1988) op. cit., 5.

in prosecutorial decision-making. The 'disarmament of justice' (as Pfeiffer calls it), where the punishment aspect of justice is gradually being replaced by a more constructive, restorative approach, is part of the general move away from imprisonment in Germany, and is another result of the widespread rejection by practitioners of its values. New developments, such as reparation schemes, bail hostel schemes, victim funds, and community service orders, have all acted like a Trojan horse in the criminal justice system; they have discreetly imported a new working ideal which has altered the traditional views of the aim of punishment, and focused the attention of decision-makers on the resolution of the conflict that crime produces and the redressing of the social imbalances caused by criminal behaviour. Overall, as prosecutors become rather less inclined to use the prosecution option in favour of the constructive alternatives now available, the punishment levels at the pre-trial stage are decreasing and, further, through the influence of the prosecutor generally over sentencing, the punishment levels at trial are also decreasing. This, as Feest has suggested, is the most probable cause of the decarceration process started in 1983.

Surveys conducted by the KFN have shown that the punitive attitudes of both prosecutors and judges have changed significantly over the last ten years and many more are now willing to use reparative options where possible. The new generation of prosecutors seem to be less interested in the rigidity of the rules and more interested in communication with the offender and the victim to resolve background problems which may have led to the criminality. This new philosophy is still very much in the speculative stages, expounded mainly by a few individuals. However, future trends in German criminal justice are likely to be strongly influenced by the growing leniency and empathy now infiltrating the realm of prosecutorial discretion.

(b) Cultures of Penality

The division of the prosecution system into 92 separate offices is not the only cause of discrepancies in the pattern of disposals. Discrepancies also arise from background guidelines and official, hierarchical supervision in each jurisdiction, usually founded on individual assessments of policy. A set of 92 different 'court cultures' has developed, each producing different rules and practical procedures, so that discrepancies are inevitable. The punitivity of any particular prosecution district is traditional, some regions having a very liberal culture, such as Frankfurt-on-Main, and others with a stricter tradition, such as Bavaria in the traditionally conservative south of Germany. The cultures are ensconced in office policy, many having existed since the 1920s and having been passed down through generations of prosecutors in a process of osmosis, instilling the local culture into the training and practice of probationary prosecutors. New blood entering the prosecutorial office is assimilated into that culture through their training by their experienced colleagues.

The extent to which these office cultures of penality influence prosecution policy and judicial sentencing is considerable. Wolfgang Langer's recent study on the prosecutor's influence on the sentencing behaviour of judges in Hannover found that: 'there are informal conditional programmes in prosecutors' offices and the courts resulting in sentencing disparities.'[58] The three jurisdictions studied there were shown to have vastly differing approaches to punishment, based on different ideologies, with resulting discrepancies in the outcome of cases. The roots of each culture are unclear. They may be related to the local politics of each individual state, which may vary from time to time. Alternatively, the culture-based practices of prosecutors may be determined by their own perception of their role in the criminal justice system. The position of the prosecutor on the leniency/severity scale, and a prosecutor's view of his role as sentencer, social worker or whatever, will determine the informal rules and customs which underpin the practice of each district.

There is little doubt about the powerful influence these traditional cultures can have over both the local exercise of discretion and national trends. On a local scale, a Bremen prosecutor was mentioned above as an example of how a maverick prosecutor, that is one who disagrees with the local philosophy, was promptly brought into line by the use of local rules and guidelines. On a national scale, the discrepancies between the different cultures, producing differing proportions of prosecutions, dismissals, and penal orders, can make the detection of national trends difficult. On the other hand, if the 92 different cultures unite together and coincide on a particular practice, a definite and pronounced change in overall policy could be produced. The recent decarceration process may well be an example of this. The net disillusionment with imprisonment, prevalent in many of the 92 districts, could have produced the momentum needed to effect the radical reduction in imprisonment rates. Prowse et al., comparing the German remand situation with that of Britain, certainly found that the decline in Germany was due to the professional culture of both prosecutors and judges, which seems to be less significant in Britain where a rise in the remand population has recently occurred:

However far an awareness of the remand problem [in Britain] might have arisen amongst the legal profession, it has so far not served as a mechanism for triggering off differentiated sentencing behaviour. We cautiously attribute this to a fundamental difference in the judicial culture of the two countries under investigation.[59]

[58] W. Langer, (1991) op. cit., 7.　　　　[59] R. Prowse, et al., (1990) op. cit., 15.

(c) The Erosion of the Legality Principle

It was stated in the introduction above that the prosecution of crime in Germany is governed by the overriding principle of legality, the compulsory prosecution rule. The principle was incorporated when the Code was first drawn up in 1877, and it replaced the opportunity principle previously practised by the Prussian criminal justice authorities. The aim of the principle, and the reason why that of opportunity was replaced, was to restore the Rule of Law, and to achieve an equal application of the law which was more constitutionally acceptable than the previous situation where prosecutors may have used 'the criminal laws in a one-sided fashion to persecute opponents of the regime in the reaction to the "revolution" of 1848'.[60]

Since 1877, however, a variety of new provisions have been incorporated into the Code which widen the prosecutor's discretion to over-rule the principle of mandatory prosecution. Sections 153 and 153a of the Code provide a major exception to the rule, as does the penal order procedure. Indeed, such is the freedom of the prosecutor to dispose of cases that the legality principle may arguably have been eroded, and seems now only to apply to felonies, and then only in the adult field. Nevertheless, practitioners still talk about those diversionary provisions as *exceptions* to the rule, and the legality principle has certainly not been completely abandoned.

Today, the principle applies mainly to the police in Germany, who, in theory, have no discretion at all in screening investigated cases. All reported cases of crime should, according to the law, be refered to the prosecutor who makes the first discretionary decision whether or not to waive prosecution. The police do not, as in England, have any filtering role. In practice, however, the police evidently do exercise a minimal amount of discretion, albeit unlawfully. As part of a hidden dismissal procedure they probably do settle family conflicts which have resulted in crime, turn a blind eye to certain types of criminality, or simply not record cases which they consider to be unduly trivial. As Weigend points out:

There is strong evidence that [the police] can and do predetermine prosecutorial decision-making by the amount of investigative effort they invest in particular cases or types of offences. As most continental prosecutors are neither able nor willing to counteract such police strategies, the prosecutor's impact on the case-flow from complaint to adjudication is merely negative: he screens out cases previously 'cleared' by the police but he cannot restore cases lost because of insufficient police work.[61]

---

[60] G. Schram, 'The Obligation to Prosecute in West Germany' *American Journal of Comparative Law* (1970), 17: 627.

[61] T. Weigend, (1983) op. cit., 1299.

Some academics interviewed argued that the legality principle should be counteracted even further, and that the growing pressures on the criminal justice system as a whole provided reasons for giving the police even more discretion. The power to give warnings, which they do not possess at the moment, would be an example. Making legal provision for police discretion would, after all, merely bring many hidden practices out into the open and allow for police officers to be properly trained to carry out that discretionary role. The constitutional importance of the legality principle, however, is far too great and too deeply rooted in history to allow the rule to be abolished altogether in favour of the discretionary principle of opportunity. The principle of equal application of the law is regarded as a sacrosanct provision aimed at freeing the prosecutor from political influence by the executive and limiting the power of the government. This is understandably valued in a country which witnessed the breach of all those constitutional principles during the Nazi era and, a century earlier, during the monarchy of the Prussian Empire.

Meanwhile, the discretionary provisions which have seeped into the Code in defiance of the spirit of compulsory prosecution are justified in today's climate by the growing need to save resources to prevent an overload on the system. Even twenty years ago these pressures were reported by Jescheck:

> where the legality principle is applied completely without limits, the activities of the organs of criminal justice would quickly grind to a halt. Police, prosecutors and courts would be inundated with such an abundance of petty suits that soon the work onslaught could no longer be handled. Thus there are dominating practical reasons which compel limitations on the legality principle in certain circumstances ... In these situations one speaks of the principle of expediency.[62]

Those pressures still exist today and, if anything, they have grown. Since the reunification of Germany in 1990, all East German prosecutors have been suspended from their duties and as a result, prosecutors from West German cities are being 'lent' to East German offices to cope with a staggering back-log of cases. Consequently, West German offices are also struggling to keep up with workloads, with shortages of staff, and are not helped by the increase in crime rates. Prosecutors interviewed in Bremen admitted that it was standard practice in their offices to use the dismissal procedure and the penal order increasingly as a compromise to save time. The penal order, after all, involves far less work than preparing for a trial or arranging reparation meetings, and particularly in the field of economic crime, the process offers a simple way of disposing of very complex cases. Bohlander has heavily criticized this trend in Germany to sacrifice important

[62] H-H. Jescheck, 'The Prosecutor in West Germany', *American Journal of Comparative Law* (1970), 18: 512–513.

constitutional principles and fairness for the sake of efficiency. In his view, the legality principle has certainly disappeared in practice, and has almost done so in theory, with unfortunate consequences for the accused:

Politicians and practitioners alike who complain about costs, caseloads, abuse of procedural rights and so on are in danger of losing sight of what the rule of law originally was and still is about: not efficient prosecution or punishing the guilty, but protecting the innocent—at any cost.[63]

Whether this concern for efficiency is sufficient justification for the erosion of such a stalwart element of the constitution is highly debatable, but evidently under the current working pressures in the German criminal system, where crime is increasing and a large number of staff were seconded to the former Eastern states, prosecutors are probably faced with little choice but to try and make savings. Ideally (though perhaps not easily in practice) a simple compromise could be reached by increasing the resources of the judicial and prosecution branches of the criminal justice process. This might be achieved by redirecting resources from the expansion of the prison estate towards more immediate needs at these earlier stages of the process.

12. CONCLUSION

The prosecutor in Germany, like his counterpart in the Netherlands, has become the central player in the criminal justice system. Prosecutors' large (and increasing) array of discretionary powers is a practical necessity for the filtering of cases proceeding to the later stages of the criminal process, to prevent an overload on the courts and the prison authorities:

the criminal process cannot function without a filter that prevents undeserving cases from advancing to trial . . . it is typically the prosecutor who is entrusted with sifting out those cases that do not merit the attention of the court—a task that cannot be carried out adequately without some measures of discretionary power.[64]

The provisions for conditional and unconditional dismissals, contained in s. 153a and s. 153 respectively, and the penal order procedure are discretionary powers which have been granted to the prosecutor by the legislature over the past seventy years, although the unofficial equivalent of these diversionary measures was probably being practised in prosecution agencies even before that. The prosecutor's role as the regulator in the process, controlling and stabilizing the pressure of work on the judges, has become most important. Indeed, in recent years, with criminality having increased to such a large extent, (due to various reasons including the Eastern

[63] M. Bohlander, (1994) op. cit., 9.　　　[64] T. Weigend, (1983) op. cit., 1296.

European influx of crime mentioned above) the prosecutor's filtering role has become even more crucial, for it is that branch of the process which has to absorb such a sudden influx of work, and the diversionary power of the prosecutor assumes prominence as a means of assuring the smooth-running of the rest of the system. Not surprisingly, the number of dismiss-als, conditional waivers, and penal orders have substantially increased in the last few years, while the number of prosecutions has decreased slightly.[65]

Throughout the time that this study was being conducted there was a discernable trend towards the increase of the prosecutor's autonomy in exercising his sentencing discretion. This has included new powers to offer suspended sentences as part of a penal order, removing a large number of offences from the categories which require judicial consent for disposal at the pre-trial stage, and diminishing the extent to which the defendant's protestations of innocence influence a diversionary decision. In official policy circles, the justification for this trend is firmly stated to be a need for increased efficiency in an increasingly overburdened system where crime rates are soaring and staff resources are stretched to the limit. However, aside from these domestic and practical considerations, which are no doubt very pressing, it is submitted that this trend can also be explained by examining the wider political context in which the criminal justice system is operating.

There has been a significant shift to the right in German politics over the last few years, in terms of both the make-up of Parliament and of public opinion. It is therefore less surprising that such controversial measures as the prosecutorial power to issue suspended sentences were passed by Par-liament and entered the statute books. The prosecutor has acquired a wide and powerful sentencing jurisdiction in a series of reforms which have centred on the need to dispense justice with maximum efficiency and in-creasing severity, often at the expense of the accused's fundamental rights and liberties, and without a corresponding increase in the prosecutor's accountability. The conservative tone of this policy of increased crime control has been driven by a general public fear of crime. This fear stemmed from both the re-unification process which, it is claimed, resulted in a crime wave caused by East Germans flocking to the 'bounteous West' and, ironically, from a spate of xenophobic violence by a growing neo-Fascist movement, caused in part by the influx of Eastern Europeans into Ger-many. The expansion of prosecutorial discretion has caused consternation on the part of liberal professionals, not least because further safeguards for the defendant's civil liberties have not been correspondingly extended.

It is interesting to compare the situation in Germany with that in the

---

[65] The total number of prosecutions throughout Germany has decreased from 981,083 in 1982 to 878,305 in 1990. (German Federal Ministry of Justice).

Netherlands, described in Chapter 4. In both systems the prosecutor is recognized as an important filter, diverting trivial and low-key cases away from the courts. Clearly the German prosecutor is being used as the Federal Ministry of Justice's weapon against a social crime problem. In both countries, prosecutorial dismissals are being used principally to cope with the increasing workloads under the pressure of static, even diminishing, resources. The difference is that in the Netherlands the use of the prosecutor as a filter of less important cases has been carefully planned as a proactive measure, the prosecutor playing an instrumental part in implementing the Ministry of Justice's new punishment philosophy for a greater intervention ratio in trivial cases. Whereas the conditions attached to dismissals in Germany are effectively replacing court sentences which would have imposed after conviction if the rule of compulsory prosecution was observed, in the Netherlands the prosecutor is sentencing cases which would have been waived unconditionally and is carrying out a deliberate policy of net-widening. In both systems, however, the development of the prosecutor's role as sentencer with direct sentencing powers affords them a quasi-judicial status which in turn enhances the prosecutor's indirect influence over the sentencing of judges.

6
Models of Prosecutorial Sentencing

1. INTRODUCTION

THE preceding chapters have shown that the extent to which a public prosecutor is regarded as having a significant impact on the sentencing process differs substantially in the four jurisdictions compared. Various haphazard contributory factors have produced an incoherent pattern of degrees of prosecutorial power in the sentencing field. The four European countries have, for circumstantial and historical reasons, pursued reform in this area at different paces and times and consequently have arrived at different stages of evolution. Comments in the previous chapters have also shown how background factors in each jurisdiction, as well as the operational philosophies and self-reflective attitudes of practitioners, have had a substantial influence, whether restrictive or librational, over the evolution of the prosecutor's role. Hence, the present picture of prosecutorial change in Scotland, the Netherlands, Germany, and England and Wales reads rather like a league table of that evolution. In ascending order, the English CPS, being in its infancy in comparative terms, allows only a strictly limited role for the Crown Prosecutor in influencing sentence; that influence is limited to an indirect, consequential exercise of persuasion related to their procedural decision-making, except for their power under s. 36 Criminal Justice Act 1988 to appeal against unduly lenient sentences. This is the only explicit and direct form of influence over sentencing that Crown Prosecutors currently possess. However, there exists in England and Wales an abundance of potential for development and improvement of the prosecution system, by virtue, principally, of that infancy and immaturity.

The Scottish Procurator Fiscal system, having witnessed a sudden spurt of reform in the late 1980s, and being longer established as a service, has proceeded beyond that kindergarten stage. However, progress in Scotland has been limited and came to an abrupt halt upon the retirement of its key instigator, William Chalmers, so that the likelihood of further development seems smaller than in England and Wales although the potential is still significant.

In Germany the basis for prosecutorial influence, both over judicial sentencing and in issuing pre-trial sanctions, has firmer foundations, and enhancement of that sentencing role is continuing at a steady and quite rapid pace.

At the top of the league table, in terms of the pace and direction of reform, is the Dutch system, where progress has been radical and dynamic, even since the 1990 Policy Plan described in Chapter 4, which has halted the advancement of the 'lenient' or informal approach to justice in order to reassess general criminal policy.

In this chapter the operation of decision-making of those prosecution systems will be considered on the basis of three models. What has clearly emerged from the preceding chapters is that the prosecutor is undoubtedly involved, albeit to differing degrees, in the process of sentencing. In some jurisdictions, for example England and Wales, this involvement is principally indirect and takes the form of influencing judicial sentencing through decisions on choice of charge and mode of trial and through appeal procedures and advocacy in the courtroom. In others, mainly the continental European jurisdictions, the involvement is more direct and takes the form of issuing penalties which are, in all but name, sentences. The national studies have thus far indicated that, whether policy-makers in any one system wish to accept it or not, the prosecutor can be termed a 'sentencer'. The cross-national comparison, however, highlights the degree to which those policy-makers have chosen to acknowledge this role of the public prosecutor and the degree to which this is explicitly provided for in procedures and practices.

Having established the prosecutor's involvement in the sentencing process, this chapter will analyse the public prosecutor's sentencing role on the basis of three theoretical models of decision-making expounded below. Then, in Chapter 7, the viability of these models will be tested against the common problems and issues which arise in any system of informal administrative decision-making. The models will be used as tools for discussing and analysing problems such as net-widening, the use of the public interest criteria, and the constitutionality of the sentencing role of the prosecutor, and to illustrate how these problems have been approached in Europe.

2. MODELS OF PROSECUTION DECISION-MAKING

During the course of researching recent developments in prosecution policy in four jurisdictions, a number of rationales for enhancing prosecutors' sentencing powers emerged. The models are ideal foundations for prosecutorial decision-making and are unlikely to exist either in isolation or completely in any one system; they are not a trichotomy of models. They emerged directly from observations of the three mainland European jurisdictions, but each model is not tied directly to any one system; indeed, all three jurisdictions incorporate aspects of at least two of the models in their prosecution policy and practice. Furthermore, the models are dynamic and are constantly changing with the patterns and policy of prosecutorial decision-making. Prosecution policy, and criminal justice policy generally in any system, continually change with the context in which it operates. The models formulated here will evolve with the policy in which they operate. They can be said, however, to have emerged from a snapshot view of these prosecution systems in the early 1990s.

The reasons given by the practitioners and academics interviewed as to why pre-trial diversion was considered necessary in both practical and policy terms tended to be loosely consistent throughout each of the Northern European countries. The governing principles which provide a basic model for all reform ideas generally fall into one of three main categories. Where prosecutorial sentencing had been adopted as an essential practice in fulfilling the main aims and duties of the criminal justice process, its justification was consistently founded upon principles either of efficient management of an expanding justice system, or of restoring the offender and/or the victim to their status before the criminal behaviour concerned had its destructive or violatory effect, or, more generally, of restoring social norms which had became blurred by extensive criminality and restoring the conventionality of approach by criminal justice authorities in dealing with these crime problems. These core models of decision-making have been labelled the Operational Efficiency Model, the Restorative Model and the Credibility Model respectively. These three thematic principles of prosecutorial decision-making appear, when considered in depth, incongruous with the traditional dichotomy of criminal justice decision-making involving notions of due process and crime control proposed by Herbert Packer,[1] although on the surface several initial aspects of the prosecution systems described in the previous chapters may appear to coincide with his models.

Packer developed two models or 'value systems' as a convenient means of representing the fundamental value choices and the competing considerations that underlie decision-making in criminal law. In the first, the Due Process model, Packer describes the criminal justice system as an 'obstacle course' through which any prosecution must overcome a series of impediments designed to protect the defendant's rights and liberties before a

---

[1] H. Packer, *The Limits of the Criminal Sanction* (Stanford, 1968). See also M. King, *The Framework of Criminal Justice* (London, 1981), 15–19, for a briefer summary of Packer's two models of justice.

conviction can satisfactorily be obtained. The possibilities of false accusations or a miscarriage of justice are of paramount importance in a system where cases should be heard by an objective court before which the defendant is given a full opportunity to defend himself and dispute the charges against him. Under this model, the system is designed to err on the side of caution and allow all criminal prosecutions to run their full course before the state is satisfied that an adjudication of guilt is just and fair. With such a heavy emphasis on procedural propriety and the importance of the full fact-finding process, common to all adversarial justice systems, the concept of prosecutorial diversion and the presumption of guilt at an early stage of the criminal justice process are inconsistent with the general characteristics of the Due Process model. Indeed, later sections of this chapter which discuss the dangers of hidden decision-making and the risk of violating the civil liberties of the accused, will show that this form of pre-trial sentencing is almost antithetical to this model.

In contrast the role of the prosecutor discussed here has many more features in common with Packer's second model of justice, the Crime Control model. This focuses on repressing crime and on punishment. Hence, in the name of efficiency or 'speed and finality' a justice system of this model will seek to process suspects and punish them at the earliest possible stage of the criminal justice process, avoiding wherever possible the opportunity for dispute or contention, and maximizing the ability to punish according to the suspect's just deserts. The prosecutor becomes a significant character in the process of justice, making decisions as to the guilt of the accused and issuing his own quasi-judicial penalties. As Packer himself states: 'It follows that extra-judicial processes should be preferred to judicial processes, informal operations to formal ones. But informality is not enough; there must also be uniformity. Routine, stereotyped procedures are essential if large numbers are to be handled.'[2] The standardized systems of prosecutorial sanctioning, such as the transaction in the Netherlands, the penal order in Germany, and particularly the procurator fiscal fine in Scotland where the degree of punishment is fixed and not subject to any form of discretion, are clear examples of crime control systems. Indeed, the third prosecution model explained below, the Credibility model, has few distinguishing factors from Packer's Crime Control model. However, in the particular context of the jurisdictions compared, and the current criminal policy within those jurisdictions, it is argued that the Credibility model, whilst embodying most of the standard characteristics of the Crime Control model, goes further in addressing the public image of the criminal justice system, and is closely related to the key role of that system in society.

---

[2] Ibid., 159.

3. THE OPERATIONAL EFFICIENCY MODEL

This model, governed by principles of administrative efficiency and re-source saving, gives the prosecutor a managerial role in performing his sentencing duties. The primary rationale behind the pre-trial diversion procedure is to control and manage an increasing workload within the constraints of a limited workforce and budget. The prosecutor's central aim in diverting cases at a pre-trial stage is to avoid a costly court case involving many hours of work in the preparation and presentation of evidence.

This model emerged in the Netherlands, Scotland, and Germany as a justification for substantially restricting the number of prosecuted cases. In the Netherlands, for example, operational efficiency and problems of over-loading the criminal justice system have been driving forces affecting the working philosophy of the criminal justice authorities. The adoption dur-ing the 1970s of a positive interpretation of the expediency principle, as described in Chapter 4, arose out of the intolerable burden on prosecutors caused by an increase in reported crime without any corresponding in-crease in resources. Practical necessity drove the Openbaar Ministerie to-wards greater practice of non-prosecution. Whilst the 1990 policy plan produced by the Ministry of Justice aimed to counteract that practice and reduce the number of unconditional disposals, the prosecutor has retained his important sentencing role, again through practical necessity, to avoid a flood of cases streaming to the courtroom. Further, for the first time, the 1990 policy plan explicitly acknowledged the importance of administrat-ive, managerial considerations in this field, by devoting a part of the plan to organizational and bureaucratic matters such as increasing staff num-bers and introducing computerization.[3]

In Germany, the governing principle of efficiency has had equally signifi-cant effects on the formulation of policy. Constraints of a practical nature in stretching limited resources to deal with a burgeoning crime problem (with the added problem in Germany with their reunification with the East German states; see Chapter 5) have led to erosion of the legality principle. This fundamental constitutional principle advocates compulsory prosecu-tion of all reported criminal cases, to protect the offender from the abuse of State power and the other dangers that Packer's Due Process model describes. Overlooking such dangers and informally disposing of cases in the interests of saving time and money is accepted as a necessary, if not desirable, consequence of the concerns about rising crime rates in Ger-many today.

[3] See R. van Swaaningen, J. Blad, and R. van Loon, eds., *A Decade of Criminological Research and Penal Policy in the Netherlands. The 1980s: the era of business-management ideology* (Rotterdam, 1992).

Such reservations about the propriety of allowing efficiency to govern the administration of justice are also apparent in Scotland. Whilst several persons interviewed agreed that the introduction of fiscal fines, for example, arose from the need to reduce workloads of prosecutors and the courts, they were quick to point out the benefits for the accused of diversion: avoiding a court appearance and a criminal record. The procurator fiscal's reticence in accepting a sentencing role is evidently matched by his reluctance to become involved in the management of the criminal process, and unwillingness to allow such considerations to influence justice.

These reservations became open indignation in England and Wales at the idea of allowing these considerations to invade the public interest area of discretion. A newspaper article quoted in Chapter 2 illustrated the distaste of the police at the onset of the practice by Crown Prosecutors.[4] More recently, similar criticisms of the CPS bureaucracy have been made in strong terms: '[the CPS] is a bureaucracy whose sole purpose in life is to process files and churn them out like a machine in Willie Wonka and the Chocolate Factory'.[5] This bureaucratic ethos is consistent with the 'corporate ideology' of the CPS and the desire to achieve optimum efficiency. Indeed, the corporate ideology is likely to increase if the government proceed with plans, currently being considered, effectively to privatize the CPS. The proposal is that the CPS will cease to be a national service, will return to a regional management structure and will contract out services to solicitors and barristers in private practice in order to increase efficiency.[6] Running the CPS according to privatized, commercial principles can only increase the emphasis given to operational efficiency in their decision-making, perhaps to an unacceptable degree.

Nevertheless, that restricted resources and growing crime problems culminate in severe organizational problems for the criminal justice authorities is a basic and inevitable fact of life, so inevitable that even the English prosecutor has not been able to resist the temptation to consider these problems in exercising his limited, diversionary discretion. Indeed, Sanders predicted that the pressure to economize within the English justice system is probably the main, and possibly the only, factor encouraging policymakers to enhance the Crown Prosecutor's sentencing role.[7] His prediction was apparently accurate. The Royal Commission on Criminal Justice, whose report in 1993 was extensively discussed in Chapter 2, provided a prime example of this. In their extensive review of the criminal justice system,

---

[4] J. Weeks, 'Prosecutors drop charges to save time', *Daily Telegraph*, 19 May 1989.
[5] Mike Bennett in an unpublished speech to the Metropolitan Police Federation, 27 Oct. 1993.
[6] F. Gibb, 'Future of CPS divides top law officers', *The Times*, 13 July 1994.
[7] A. Sanders, 'The Limits to Diversion from Prosecution' (1988) *British Journal of Criminology*, 28: 529.

most of their recommendations are clearly aimed at saving resources. The reasoning behind these recommendations is scant, and is dominated by a concern to increase the smooth-running and efficiency of the system, with only a secondary concern about preventing further miscarriages of justice.

An unfortunate aspect of this inevitable result, however, is that (aside from the victim, whose interests will be discussed in the second model below) it is the defendant who will suffer from the adoption of this model of the decision-making process. As the prison system of England and Wales has discovered, problems caused by a lack of manpower and coherent organization of resources, have had their gravest impact on the prisoner who loses rights, privileges, and basic standards of living conditions. Similarly, at the prosecution stage, restrictions on resources, and failure to exploit their maximum potential, has resulted in a system which largely overlooks the due process rights which should be afforded to every defendant. Although those due process rights clearly exist and are not negated by a system of pre-trial administrative justice, economizing resources to this extent should be accompanied by safeguards which preserve those rights. This point of principle may be academic, given that in many cases the relatively informal outcome of a case under the operational efficiency model may be acceptable to the defendant. Offenders may be happy to have their case dealt with at the prosecution stage, thereby avoiding the stigmatization of a full trial and criminal conviction, and may consider themselves better off under such a system. Nevertheless, a fundamental standard of safeguards must be set down within which the informal approach under this model can operate.

Baldwin and McConville's study, concerning the extent of plea-bargaining in Birmingham Crown Court, made just this point. They found that defendants are often heavily pressurized in negotiation with the prosecution into pleading guilty to reduce their charge or to secure a discounted sentence. This prompted the authors to conclude that economizing with justice was severely prejudicing and overriding the due process rights of defendants. The concluding chapter of their study complains repeatedly about the administrators of justice taking short cuts with the criminal process and placing the saving of resources at the top of their agenda, at the great expense of the defendant, who is afforded little protection against the abuse of the discretion of practitioners in a system which they may find bewildering and heavily weighed against them:

The injustices we have encountered are, in our judgement, essentially the product of a system that gives too little protection to the innocent and too often sacrifices the needs of the individual to the requirements of bureaucratic efficiency . . . if we continue to pay scant regard to the rights of suspects and to devote insufficient resources to the administration of justice, we are perpetuating a system of negotiated justice that, with some frequency, produces results of a fundamentally inequitable nature.[8]

Feeley on the other hand has argued that the concern to reduce workloads arises from the misconception that if it were not for diversion, all cases reported would ordinarily be pursued right through the court system in accordance with due process principles.[9] Further, he argues that this myth is often perpetuated by criminal justice authorities as a standard plea in defence of criticisms about their practices and policies: 'Heavy caseloads, understaffing and inadequate funding are all "enemies" which everyone can safely point to as causes for poor performance.'[10] Although growing pressures of time and money are common features in the working life of any civil servant in this country and economies must inevitably be made, it is questionable whether these economies need necessarily be made in connection with compromising the key constitutional ideals of the justice system, and, indeed, in Feeley's study, when greater resources were allocated to a number of lower courts in the USA, there appeared to be no reduction in anxiety about the size of their caseloads:

The common interest in processing defendants rapidly is far more than an attempt on the part of various actors to keep their heads above the rising waters in an overburdened court . . . regardless of caseload there will always be too many cases for many of the participants in the system, since most of them have a strong interest in being some place other than in court.[11]

Whilst Feeley's study relates specifically to the American system of prosecution, it is useful and relevant to consider his point in analysing European systems. The implications of his study are equally applicable to the jurisdictions under consideration here in that, whilst operational efficiency is an understandable policy goal since the criminal justice systems are under economic pressure, the degree to which this should dominate prosecution policy (and in particular the prosecutor's sentencing policy) is questionable, as revealed when those economic pressures are subjected to scrutiny. Where those pressures actually exist, the operational efficiency model can be justified as a matter of practical necessity; on the other hand, where such pressures acquire an exaggerated, mythical status, the compromise between operational efficiency and due process is of questionable propriety.

[8] J. Baldwin, and M. McConville, *Negotiated Justice: Pressures to Plead Guilty* (Oxford, 1977) 115–16.
[9] M. Feeley, *The Process is the Punishment: Handling cases in a lower criminal court* (New York, 1979), ch. 8.
[10] Ibid., 270.   [11] Ibid., 272.

4. THE RESTORATIVE MODEL

The Restorative model describes a system of prosecution decision-making which promotes the restoration of social balance which may have been damaged by an act of criminal behaviour. Social imbalance typically arises in the relationship between the victim and the offender when the offender's behaviour has caused the victim to experience some form of loss, whether material, physical, or emotional. Whilst it may not be possible to 'restore' equality between those two parties, since in today's society that equality is unlikely to have existed in the first place, it can amend any inequality caused by the crime. As Dworkin has stated:

Government must treat those whom it governs with concern, that is, as human beings who are capable of suffering and frustration, and with respect, that is, as human beings who are capable of forming and acting on intelligent conceptions of how their lives should be lived. Government must not only treat people with concern and respect, but with equal concern and respect.[12]

So also must the criminal justice system recognize that the victim is equally entitled to consideration in a process that is ordinarily heavily offender-oriented and this is achieved by the application of this restorative philosophy. Matters such as compensation (in money or kind) and the victim's satisfaction with the outcome of a particular case will be prime objectives in a restorative system.

The aim under this model is clearly not punishment. When the victim's interests are a paramount consideration in the criminal process, the desire to impose negative, punitive sanctions diminishes in favour of resolving the case in a positive, helpful way. In the same way, Braithwaite's theory of criminal justice aims at 'reintegrative shaming' rather than punishment. Braithwaite argues that the aim of criminal justice should be to repair any damage done by the criminal act and to restore the perpetrator into society, rather than merely punishing the perpetrator for retributive purposes:

The crucial distinction is between shaming that is reintegrative and shaming that is disintegrative (stigmatization). Reintegrative shaming means that expressions of community disapproval, which may range from mild rebuke to degradation ceremonies, are followed by gestures of reacceptance into the community of law-abiding citizens. These gestures of reacceptance will vary from a simple smile expressing forgiveness and love to quite formal ceremonies to decertify the offender as deviant. Disintegrative shaming (stigmatization) in contrast, divides the community by creating a class of outcasts.[13]

---

[12] R. Dworkin, *Taking Rights Seriously* (London, 1981), 272–273. See also P. Cooper, *Reparation in the Criminal Justice System: The concept and reflections upon its application*, (Research and Information Unit, Merseyside Probation Service, 1991) for an analysis of the jurisprudential aspects of reparation and restorative justice.

[13] J. Braithwaite, *Crime, Shame and Reintegration* (Cambridge, 1989), 55. See also J. Braithwaite, 'Shame and Modernity' *British Journal of Criminology* (1993), 33: 1–18.

Those punitive sanctions focus on the offender, on deterring or preventing further criminality, whereas the latter, positive sanctions, which may or may not have punishment elements within them,[14] focus on restoring the victim to his position prior to the commission of the crime. Hence, this model heralds a shift in the focus of the criminal justice process away from the interests and rights of the defendant, and towards a more satisfactory service for the victim. Martin Wright has summarized the general philosophy of this model thus: 'The present system of criminal justice has many flaws: it is suggested that many of these could be rectified by the adoption of a different primary aim: to restore the condition of the victim of crime as far as possible (and to improve it if the victim was already suffering hardship).'[15]

For the victim, however, material compensatory benefits may not be necessary in order to accord him concern and respect. Christie has argued that mere participation by the victim in the criminal proceedings and decision-making process may be a sufficient benefit to the victim. Christie views the relationship between the victim and the offender, beginning with the crime itself, as a conflict, and describes this conflict as the 'property' of the victim, so that the denial of his opportunity to participate in the solving of that conflict is as much of a loss to the victim as any material loss caused by the crime:

Material compensation is not what I have in mind with the formulation of 'conflicts as property'. It is the conflict itself that represents the most interesting property taken away, not the goods originally taken away from the victim, or given back to him. In our types of society, conflicts are more scarce than property. And they are immensely more valuable. . . . The victim is a particularly heavy loser in this situation. Not only has he suffered, lost materially or become hurt, physically or otherwise. And not only does the state take the compensation. But above all he has lost participation in his own case. It is the Crown that comes into the spotlight, not the victim.[16]

This is particularly true in the adversarial nature of the English system for example, where the trial is dominated by issues of guilt/innocence or evidential problems, so that wider social issues of public interest, including the victim's point of view, may be overlooked.[17]

---

[14] The shaming process can include punishment or 'reprobation', in the form of community disapproval of the offender's conduct. Reintegrative shaming, however, includes a restorative element in this shaming process. See J. Braithwaite and P. Pettit, *Not Just Deserts: A Republican Theory of Criminal Justice* (Oxford, 1992), particularly Ch. 6.

[15] M. Wright, '*Victim-Offender Mediation as a Step Towards a Restorative System of Justice*' in H. Messmer, and H-U. Otto, eds., *Restorative Justice on Trial: Pitfalls and Potentials of Victim-Offender Mediation—International Research Perspectives* (Dordrecht, 1992), 537.

[16] N. Christie, 'Conflicts as Property' (1977) *British Journal of Criminology*, 17: 7.

[17] M. Wright, *Justice for Victims and Offenders* (Buckingham, 1991), 10–15. See also T. Kirby, 'Families of murder victims find justice system insensitive' *Independent*, 30 Mar. 1989.

Under this model, the prosecutor occupies a place of prime importance in restoring the victim's 'property', including the right to equality of treatment by criminal justice authorities, and in restoring a 'normal' relationship between the victim and the offender. Whilst the prosecutor is emphatically not the representative of the victim in either an adversarial or an inquisitorial system, he can champion the victim's cause by asking for compensation (which is a possibility in all four jurisdictions studied) or by recommending a restitutive sentence to the court (currently possible only in Germany and the Netherlands). At the pre-trial stage, the potential for this restorative role is enormous. Chapter 3 showed how reparation and mediation schemes, specifically designed to restore imbalances and relationships, and to allow the victim a meaningful role in settling the case to his satisfaction, have been successfully operated in Scotland.[18] There have been similar experimental reparation schemes from time to time in England and Wales where victims and offenders are referred to specialist mediators at the pre-trial stage,[19] although, as yet, the Crown Prosecutor's record in promoting the victim's interests is poor. The provision of the public interest criteria which relates to victims (paragraph 6.7 of the Code) is sketchy and ambiguous and the prosecutor's practice in keeping victims informed about the progress of the resolution of their conflict is almost non-existent. This is despite the publication by the Home Office in 1990 of the grandiosely named *Victim's Charter*[20] which sets out the roles of the police, prosecutors, and the court in according fair treatment to victims when dealing with their cases, including the payment of compensation and avoidance wherever possible of submitting victims to the ordeal of giving evidence. How effective this Home Office statement will be remains to be seen, but it is to be hoped that its spirit at least will be fully implemented, not least by the prosecutor under the restorative model, and that it will not simply be another statement of high principles and unrealistic aims on the part of the government.

Provision for victims in the Netherlands is similarly scant, with any attempts at reparation or mediation between victim and offender being dependent upon the enthusiasm and efforts of individual prosecutors. It is interesting to note the anti-restorative and pro-retributive attitude towards victim support of the Dutch Ministry of Justice in their 1990 Policy Plan:

[18] For example, the SACRO Scheme described in Chapter 3.

[19] For example, see J. Dignan, *Repairing the Damage: An Evaluation of an Experimental Adult Reparation Scheme in Kettering, Northants.* (Sheffield, 1990) for an evaluation of one such scheme which operated between 1987 and 1989. See also T. Marshall and S. Merry, *Crime and Accountability: Victim/Offender Mediation in Practice* (London, 1990), and R. I. Mawby and M. L. Gill, *Crime Victims: Needs, Services and the Voluntary Sector* (London, 1987).

[20] Home Office, *Victim's Charter: A Statement of the Rights of Victims of Crime* (London, 1990).

We do not consider it right that the monies required for this new policy on victims should be obtained by siphoning off resources from the budget headings for crime prevention, detection and prosecution. Support for victims should not, in our view, result in a weakening of the measures to tackle crime. This is because the very purpose of such measures is to prevent further victimization.[21]

Dato Steenhuis reflected on this stance of policy-makers with some regret. He argued that under a restorative model of decision-making at the prosecution stage: 'the main target group of the [criminal justice] system might not be the perpetrator of the crime but the law-abiding citizen'. However, 'the theory that I have developed is that the problems of the criminal justice system have a lot to do with the fact that it has more or less neglected the fair interests of the law-abiding citizen.'[22] Since 1990 there have been a number of moves to develop organized forms of victim support in Holland. Prior to the policy plan, in the 1980s, a number of government committees addressed the issue of victim support and compensation, including the Vaillant Committee. Their report, published in 1985,[23] prompted the introduction of guidelines for the police and prosecutors in the treatment of victims, first of sex offences (*Staatscourant* 1986) and later of all types of crime (*Staatscourant* 64 of 1987). Under these guidelines, a prosecutor is required to send a standard letter to those victims who have already told the police that they would like to be kept informed of the progress of their case; also, the victim is to be given the opportunity to ask for compensation and is invited to meet the prosecutor to discuss the case.[24] More recently, the report of van Hecke and Wemmers on the reparation and mediation scheme in Middelburg[25] is an example of how the prosecutor's role in respect to victims is beginning to be put into practice after a number of fundamental policy statements.

The German prosecutor works under a system much closer to the restorative model, particularly in the juvenile field. Chapter 5 described how reparation schemes, as well as individual arrangements for reparation, operate throughout Germany; indeed, the restorative aspect (what Pfeiffer calls the 'disarmament of justice') is becoming a strong feature of criminal

[21] The Netherlands, *Law in Motion: A Policy Plan for Justice in the years ahead* (The Hague, 1990), 44.

[22] Dato Steenhuis—Interview, The Hague, Nov. 1990.

[23] Vaillant Committee, *Eindrepport van de werkgroep Justitieel beleid en slachtoffer* (The Hague, 1985).

[24] See J. M. Wemmers and M. I. Zeilstra, Dutch Penal Law and Policy: Notes on criminological research from the Research and Documentation Centre, Ministry of Justice, The Hague. Number 03—*Victim Services in the Netherlands* (The Hague, 1991) for an explanation of how these guidelines have been put into practice by prosecutors throughout the Netherlands.

[25] T. van Hecke and J. M. Wemmers, *Schadebemiddelingsproject Middelburg* (Arnhem, 1992) (English Summary pp. 71–2).

policy in Germany, currently competing with 'education' as the central aim of the criminal justice process.[26]

The aims and objectives of the restorative model also inform the practice of the American prosecutor, who has a wide discretion to drop sensitive cases if a prosecution is considered harmful to the suspect, to his family, or to the victim. The prosecutor then has the discretion to use informal diversionary or civil sanctions, for example, settling disputes between neighbours, or between husband and wife in non-support cases where a husband has failed financially to support his wife and family (a criminal offence in some states of the USA under the Uniform Desertion and Non Support Act), or using the so-called 'court of no record'. In this procedure, used particularly for juveniles, an informal hearing is held in the prosecutor's office between the juvenile and his/her parents and the prosecutor, who administers a warning, similar to a caution in England or Scotland, which is recorded only locally by the police.[27] This diversionary discretion, aimed at resolving conflicts rather than punishing assailants, is deemed 'necessary to transform broad legislative proscriptions into pragmatically satisfactory social policy.'[28]

More recently, prosecutors in the USA have taken a much more active role in diverting offenders at the pre-trial stage to constructive rehabilitation and reparation schemes, as a form of 'caution plus'. Most notable perhaps was the Manhattan Court Employment Project set up by the Vera Institute in 1967, intended to facilitate conditional waivers of prosecution and to divert offenders (some charged with serious felonies) to a counselling project aimed at avoiding recidivism and helping the offender to find a job. 'It is, in other words, an attempt to convert his arrest from a losing to a winning experience—to build a bridge for the accused between the fractured world of the street and the orderly world of lawfulness and responsibility.'[29] This is a clear illustration of the operation of the restorative model, in attempting to rehabilitate the offender to law-abiding society.

Alper and Nichols also evaluate the merits of a number of diversion schemes with similar aims: '. . . pretrial diversion may be seen as a tempering process, an intervention that tends to deformalize rather than increase

[26] See further, H. Messmer, 'Victim-Offender mediation in Germany' in G. Davis, *Making Amends: Mediation and Reparation in Criminal Justice* (London, 1992), ch. 9.

[27] Ibid., see Chapter 18.

[28] Ibid., 162.

[29] Vera Institute of Criminal Justice *Programs in Criminal Justice Reform: Ten Year Report 1961–71* (New York, 1972), 80. See F. E. Zimring, 'Measuring the Impact of Pretrial Diversion from the Criminal Justice System' (1974) *University of Chicago Law Review*, 41: 224–241, for a full evaluation of this particular pre-trial diversion scheme. Further analysis of the process of mediation in the USA can be found in E. Weitekamp, 'Can Restitution Serve as a Reasonable Alternative to Imprisonment? An Assessment of the Situation in the USA' in H. Messmer and H-U. Otto, eds., (1992) op. cit. 'Pretrial Diversion from the Criminal Process' (1975) *Yale Law Journal*, 83: 827–854.

the importance or severity of the acts and circumstances that brought the offender to book. In this context, diversion may be regarded as a process of decriminalisation that aims to reduce recidivism and the likelihood of extended criminal careers.'[30]

However, many of the schemes currently being operated across the USA incorporate the more traditional aims of restorative justice, that is, the resolution of the conflict between the victim and the offender. Waivers of prosecution, conditional on the successful co-operation of the offender in the diversion scheme, often involve payment of compensation to victims, community service, or mediation. For example, simple restitution agreements, where the offender agrees to pay a compensatory sum to the victim, can be arranged informally by individual prosecutors. However, where restitution is combined with a conciliatory meeting to enable the victim to confront the offender and the offender to confront his guilt, the case is usually referred to a recognized organization where specialist staff complete the negotiations and guide the meetings. Some examples of these schemes analysed by Alper and Nichols include the Ontario Victim-Offender Reconciliation Project and, for juveniles, the Youth Services Restitution Program set up by the Department of Youth Services in Massachusetts in 1979.[31]

The prosecutor's restorative role and his participation in the reparation process are not without critics. Davis, Boucherat, and Watson[32] argue that in many instances reparation meetings and agreements are used purely as diversion for diversion's sake, without any of the benefits of the restorative model of justice. In their cynical view, the prosecutor, possibly for reasons of operational efficiency, may induce the parties to make an agreement primarily to divert cases away from the expensive and time-consuming court process. Also, the accused, aware that he is likely to suffer more from the court process, may be inclined to offer false remorse and promises to the victim simply to avoid a harsher punishment. Davis has argued further that reparation schemes currently in operation, both in England and Wales and in Europe, often place too heavy an emphasis on the needs and interests of the defendant at the expense of the victim: 'Advocates of diversion and, it has to be said, some practitioners within reparation schemes appear to be afraid of victims. Victim involvement, it is assumed, will lead to offenders being punished more severely.'[33] However, it could equally be argued that in negotiating a reparation agreement, practitioners may focus varying degrees of attention on the victim and offender, but in order for

---

[30] B. S. Alper and L. T. Nichols, *Beyond the Courtroom: Programs in Community Justice and Conflict Resolution* (Massachusetts, 1982), 39.
[31] B. S. Alper and L. T. Nichols, (1982) op. cit., at Part II, ch. 5.
[32] G. Davis, J. Boucherat, and D. Watson, 'Reparation in the service of diversion: The subordination of a good idea' (1988) *Howard Journal*, 27: 127–133.
[33] G. Davis, (1992) op. cit., 203.

a fully agreed settlement to be reached, more is learnt about the offender himself, his characteristics, his background, and his motivation for committing the offence. In revealing such characteristics and thereby reaching behind the label of 'offender' and the particular offence charged, practitioners may be able to impose sanctions which are more rational, and more constructive from the victim's point of view. Unfortunately, this may mean that the focus of practitioners' attention tends to be primarily on the defendant rather than on the victim.

Nevertheless, Davis's research on a Mediation Scheme in Coventry revealed that an excessive enthusiasm on the part of practitioners to bring a victim and offender together, in the service of diversion, can result in an awkward and often falsely polite meeting between two people who would not, without the intervention of such as the Coventry Scheme, have any desire to talk with each other. It was the embarrassment and insincerity of such mediation meetings, as observed by Davis, that led him to conclude:

reparation schemes in England and Wales suggest that the term 'reparation' is applied to offender actions in the aftermath of crime that make little, if any, contribution to remedying the harm done to the victim. It is applied to letters written at the virtual dictation of a probation officer; to material reparation that is merely 'symbolic' of an expressed willingness to meet the victim; and to a muttered apology offered in the shadow of a pending (or threatened) court appearance. Thus many schemes, interested primarily in diversion or mitigation, have manipulated the reparation concept to the point where it offers victims little beyond the possibility of serving the interests of 'their' offender.[34]

Such examples might well exist, although as Dignan's study showed,[35] a positive response was received from both victims and offenders to the experimental reparation scheme in Northamptonshire, with around half of all participating offenders being satisfied with their opportunity to apologize and to make amends, and around 62% of victims being similarly satisfied with the arrangements. Whether the offenders' contrition was genuine or not is impossible to tell, but at least the agreements made were more constructive than the punitive sanctions generally imposed by the courts. Certainly, in fulfilling its aims, the criminal justice process should not overlook victims. Whatever model of justice the system operates, the victim plays a significant role. Any legal system relies on victims for much of its evidence about crime; it relies on victims reporting offences to the police or other regulatory authority, and on their co-operation in giving evidence. Far from being harmful to victims or inflicting more trauma on them, the criminal justice process should focus more on the needs of the

---

[34] G. Davis, 'Reparation in the UK: Dominant Themes and Neglected Themes' in H. Messmer and H-U. Otto, eds., (1992), op. cit., 456.

[35] J. Dignan, (1990) op. cit., 32–34.

victim. The process effectively owes them a debt, and therefore should seek, as one of its aims, to repay that debt in an appropriate way. Indeed, Ashworth identifies the interest of the victim as a core 'value' which should, and usually does, underpin the criminal justice system.[36] The movement towards a more restorative approach in judicial sentencing and in policing has been well-documented,[37] but it is submitted here that the victim's interest has just as much importance in prosecutorial sentencing. Systems of prosecution which operate under the restorative model, if only partially, have recognized this and moved that interest further towards centre-stage.

Most research conducted on restorative justice, including all of the work quoted above, has concentrated on the role of the criminal justice process to restore the victim's condition and to provide a satisfactory service to those who have suffered harm as a result of criminal behaviour. However, it is suggested here that the restorative model is not merely restitutive. In addition to the restitution of various property rights to the victim, this model also incorporates the restoration of the offender to his previous law-abiding position and to a pattern of more normal, civilized behaviour. As Durkheim has stated, restorative justice involves: 'a restoration of the *status quo ante*. Suffering proportioned to his [the offender's] offence is not inflicted upon him who has broken the law or failed to realize it. He is merely condemned to submit to it.'[38] This would suggest that sanctions imposed under this model, rather than having a merely punitive and re-tributive aim, aspire more to the goals of rehabilitation and reform of the underlying background problems, of which their criminal behaviour is merely one symptom.

In all the systems compared, except England and Wales, prosecutors are able to issue sanctions such as diversionary schemes involving treatment for drug and alcohol addictions and psychiatric care. At present these options are not available to the prosecutor in England, where offenders with such problems will be judicially sentenced either to similar rehabilita-tion institutions, or to a more punitive form of sanction such as a fine or imprisonment. Whilst many have criticized the somewhat outmoded ideal of the welfare or treatment models of punishment,[39] this form of rehabilita-tion, in the community and outside the prison system, is a much more constructive means of punishing the offender. Nevertheless, in England and Wales the CPS has not adopted this restorative diversion of offenders to such institutions at the pre-trial stage. Whilst some police forces do

---

[36] See A. Ashworth, *The Criminal Process: An Evaluative Study* (Oxford, 1994), particu-larly ch. 2.

[37] See W. Cragg, *The Practice of Punishment: Towards a Restorative Theory of Justice* (London, 1992), chs. 6 and 7.

[38] S. Lukes and A. Scull, eds., *Durkheim and the Law* (Oxford, 1983), 49.

[39] See for example, B. Hudson, *Justice Through Punishment: A Critique of the 'Justice' Model of Corrections* (Basingstoke, 1989), particularly ch. 1.

operate a 'caution plus' scheme,[40] a more constructive and positive form
of the cautioning procedure with diversion to various types of assistance,
including intermediate treatment, reparation or mediation, the CPS at present
have no such scheme, although in their evidence to the Royal Commission
on Criminal Justice they indicated a number of advantages of such a
diversionary role for the prosecutor.[41] The Royal Commission did recommend that the 'caution plus' idea be implemented nationally (although
administered by the police and the probation service, not the CPS) but this
has largely been ignored in the government's agenda for criminal justice
reform.

Further, the compensatory aspect of the restorative model might be
extended to the community at large. Prosecutors who are able to impose
periods of community service as conditions of a pre-trial disposal can
operate a system which restores the imbalance created within society, especially in the case of 'victimless' crimes. Christie justifies the restorative
benefits of community service thus:

Compensatory justice presupposes that compensation can be given. The offender
must be able to give something back. But criminals are most often poor people.
They have nothing to give. . . . We let the poor pay with the only commodity that
is close to being equally distributed in society: time. Time is taken away to create
pain. But time could be used for compensatory purposes if we so wished. It is an
organizational problem, not an impossibility.[42]

The restorative model therefore extends beyond the traditional concern
about the victim-offender relationship. It incorporates the wider notion of
restoration; that is the reparative, mediatory, or compensatory element
which addresses the position of the victim and the rehabilitation of the
offender, as well as the restoration of social imbalances and the consideration of community interests. All three are aims of prosecutorial sentencing
under this model.

5. THE CREDIBILITY MODEL

As stated, this model of prosecutorial decision-making, with its governing
principles of repressing petty criminality at an early stage in the criminal
process and its retributive and deterrent aims, is very similar to Packer's

[40] In 1990, 18 police forces in England and Wales were reported to be operating 'caution
plus' schemes. The majority were for juveniles, but one was for adults. See R. Evans and C.
Wilkinson, 'Variations in Police Cautioning Policy and Practice in England and Wales' (1990)
Howard Journal, 29: 169–171.
[41] Crown Prosecution Service (1991) Evidence to the Royal Commission on Criminal
Justice, p. 97, paras. 6.8.5–6.8.8.
[42] N. Christie, *Limits to Pain* (Oxford, 1982), 95.

Crime Control model of justice. The prosecutor's informal adjudication of guilt and his sanctioning powers, his quasi-judicial role, are of great significance under this model, in which the aim of the prosecutor is to punish offenders, and thereby to deter others from committing similar crimes, as well as maintaining a positive image for the criminal justice system as an institution which is providing a useful service.

The clearest example of the credibility model in operation is the new, 'repressive' policy in the Netherlands. The problems were described in Chapter 4, of the extensive amount of petty crime being overlooked by the criminal justice authorities, leading to a 'blurring of social norms' whereby certain anti-social and unlawful forms of behaviour have become accepted and commonplace. These problems in the Netherlands, which a justice system based on either Packer's Crime Control model or on the credibility model will seek to overcome by a repressive, proactive but informal system of sanctioning, are almost identical to those quoted by Packer:

If the laws go unenforced—which is to say, if it is perceived that there is a high percentage of failure to apprehend and convict in the criminal process—a general disregard for legal control tends to develop. The law-abiding citizen then becomes the victim of all sorts of unjustifiable invasions of his interests. His security of person and property is sharply diminished, and, therefore, so is his liberty to function as a member of society. The claim ultimately is that the criminal process is a positive guarantor of social freedom.[43]

In the Netherlands, attempts to increase the intervention ratio, that is, to increase the number of cases diverted by conditional waiver of prosecution, are in fact attempts to restore the public faith in the criminal justice system, without burdening the courts with an influx of petty cases. Hence, a new policy of repression has placed the emphasis of severity upon the prosecution system rather than the courts. The number of cases proceeding to court for judicial sentencing is expected to remain relatively stable, whilst the prosecutor's sentencing is to increase in severity. The prime responsibility for implementing this new jurisprudence has fallen on the prosecutor, rather than the judiciary, as might have been expected in England and Wales, for example. The penal order in Germany and the fiscal fine in Scotland are similar attempts by justice systems to process and appear to be punishing a large number of petty offenders, without placing extra pressure on the court system. Thus the prosecutor's filtering role and the exercise of his sentencing powers are central to this model. In order to satisfy society's expectations that the criminal justice system will protect their property and personal freedom, the prosecutor is charged with absorbing an increase in crime or a change to a more repressive policy, without compromising operational efficiency by burdening the courts. Duff

[43] H. Packer, (1969) op. cit., 158.

has noted how, in Scotland, one of the main purposes of the introduction of the fiscal fine was to reduce fiscals' 'no pro' rates, that is their rate of unconditional dismissals. Political influence, driven by bad publicity about high and inconsistent 'no pro' rates, gave extra weight to the case for giving fiscals more diversionary powers: '. . . it was important to introduce the prosecutor fine in order to maintain an acceptable level of enforcement within the current resources of the criminal justice system.'[44] Thus, using the fiscal fine, procurators fiscal have been able to increase their intervention ratio, whilst pursuing the goals of the operational efficiency model.

However, the credibility model differs slightly from Packer's Crime Control model, in that it aims for public satisfaction with the criminal justice process, public confidence that it will protect their rights and freedoms. The word 'credibility' reveals that, as well as legal protection, this model requires the justice system to conduct its own PR exercise. As well as providing value for money, the criminal process also has to portray a satisfying image to the public, most notably through the channels of the media. Now that criminal justice is regarded as an important political issue, the media have centred more attention on the criminal justice system and so the credibility model gains more influence in prosecution policy to ensure that this media coverage is positive.

It is useful again to make brief reference to the American criminal justice system where the credibility model is in operation in many States. The public interest criteria are used wherever possible to punish as many offenders as possible informally, outside the courtroom, to achieve crime control. Cole notes that: 'It has been said that the prosecutor should make justice 'be seen publicly as being done'. The public respect for the judicial process will in no small way be affected by prosecutorial behaviour. The prosecutor must decide if the public's regard for the law will be harmed if a man is brought to trial and is not convicted.'[45] It is interesting to note that, in preserving credibility and public confidence in the criminal justice process, the evidential sufficiency criteria rather than the public interest part of the prosecutor's discretion are used to justify a non-prosecution as it is felt that this form of non-prosecution is more acceptable to the public:

Any general newspaper campaign asserting directly or even implying any 'softness' in law enforcement is likely, therefore, to have some effect on the decisions made by . . . officials. It is clear, for example, that prosecutors are less willing to 'bargain' in cases which have received considerable public attention. That the evidence is insufficient is likely to be a more palatable explanation to the public than would an explanation that reflected a conclusion that a probably guilty man should not be prosecuted despite adequate evidence of guilt.[46]

---

[44] P. Duff, 'The Prosecutor Fine and Social Control: The Introduction of the Fiscal Fine to Scotland' *British Journal of Criminology*, 33: 494.

[45] G. F. Cole, *Politics and the Administration of Justice* (Beverley Hills, 1973), 45.

[46] Ibid., 156.

The relationship between the media and the criminal justice authorities is an important element in the credibility model, since public dissatisfaction with the criminal justice process is often voiced in or even created by the reporting of controversial cases and policies in newspapers and on television and radio. Perhaps with the concerns of the credibility model in mind, the United States Attorney's Office in North Carolina has issued a guideline policy which sets out the basic procedures and limits for disclosing information about prosecution and investigation policy to the press.[47] Indeed, the guidelines form part of a *Media Guide*, designed to explain the work and role of US Attorneys in North Carolina, and which gives contact addresses for all key prosecutors and judges in the District. The publication of such factual information will increase public awareness of the prosecution function in the USA, which is a key element in securing an understanding of the diversionary sentencing practice of prosecutors which may otherwise appear to be a lenient policy towards criminality.

The credibility model thus also aims to enhance the public's understanding of the criminal justice system's policies, as well as their satisfaction with them. Statistical data gathered from victim surveys suggests that greater public confidence in the criminal justice system is needed before the public will condone the rehabilitative and community measures used under the restorative model. Studies have been conducted in various countries, including the Netherlands and England and Wales, to show how the public's perception of the crime rate and their degree of victimization affect their expectations of the criminal justice process. In the Netherlands, van Dijk and Steinmetz[48] conducted a victim survey in 1982 which showed that the public's attitude towards criminal justice policy changed with personal experiences of victimization. Those who had been victims of crime tended to demand a higher *quantity* of crime control measures from the government, and were generally less concerned about whether these measures were 'repressive' or 'preventive' in nature;[49] that is, whether they reflected the credibility model with its emphasis on informal punitive measures, or whether they reflected the restorative model using rehabilitative measures. Victims wanted to see a greater response to crime on the part of the criminal justice system, but were not necessarily concerned that the response should be retributive. This suggests general public support for the credibility model, with an increased intervention ratio, but where the intervention is prosecutorial rather than judicial, and may be punitive or repressive depending on which of the other two models is combined with the credibility model.

[47] M. P. Currin, *Media Guide* (US Attorney's Office, Eastern District of North Carolina, 1989). See particularly the Department of Justice Media Policy, 19–22.
[48] J. J. M. van Dijk and C. H. D. Steinmetz, 'Pragmatism, ideology and crime control: three Dutch surveys' in N. Walker and M. Hough, eds., *Public Attitudes to Sentencing: Surveys from Five Countries* (Aldershot, 1988).
[49] Ibid., Table 4.6 and generally pp. 80–81.

In England and Wales, a survey of victims was conducted by Mike Hough and David Moxon, which also indicated that victims did not necessarily form a more punitive view towards offenders: 'policy makers and courts can treat with a degree of scepticism the claims often made by the media that public opinion demands a tougher line with offenders.'[50] However, in that survey the data reflected the view that the increased use of informal sanctions would only gain public support if the public were more aware of current statistics on crime rates and sentencing levels, and were less influenced by the sometimes disproportionate reporting of crime in the media. Reducing people's (often unjustified) fear of crime promotes the acceptance of increased prosecutorial sentencing powers: '. . . effective policies of fear reduction might lessen the pressure for heavier sentences.'[51] Barbara Mills QC has also suggested that the general public in England and Wales might better understand the use of public interest criteria to stop prosecutions if the prosecutor were seen to be reacting positively to crime, rather than merely writing off cases to prevent them going to court.[52]

The results of those surveys indicate the essential role of the credibility model in increasing public confidence in the criminal justice system's ability to deal adequately with rising crime. First, the credibility model ensures that the system penalizes as many offenders as possible, whilst keeping the penalty system as informal and flexible as possible. (The model is consistent with the reality that the victimized public do not demand more severe treatment of offenders, despite the contrary myth.) This will in turn boost public confidence that criminal justice is effective. Secondly, the public will understand the benefits, and therefore accept the greater use, of more constructive sanctions such as reparation and rehabilitation promoted by the restorative model.

The credibility model of prosecutorial sentencing is therefore a response by the criminal justice system to calls from the public (or from the media) for stricter law enforcement and tighter control over petty crime. The prosecutor becomes involved in a pre-trial sentencing system which is justified on the basis of maintaining the credibility of the system without undermining the aims of operational efficiency; that is, managing the criminal justice system with limited resources. 'tHart has commented on this process of legitimizing the informal sanctioning process on the basis of credibility: 'The argument goes that if the state as society's representative controls and governs society, then it has the responsibility of fulfilling the wishes of its citizens and must for this reason also have the opportunity

[50] M. Hough and D. Moxon, 'Dealing with offenders: popular opinion and the views of victims in England and Wales' in N. Walker and M. Hough, eds., (1988), op. cit., 147.

[51] Ibid. 147.

[52] DPP's evidence to the Home Affairs Committee, recorded in *Minutes of Evidence*, HC 193–i, (HMSO, 1994).

to do so.'[53] Peters summed up this management process of petty crime in the interests of preserving credibility thus:

Emphasis has shifted from maintenance of the Criminal Code and other criminal statutes to more general control of volumes of delinquent activity. Criminal policy is no longer occupied primarily with concrete offenders, nor with problems of doing justice, but with the management of aggregate phenomena of social activity, with criteria for selective law enforcement, with quantitative regulation in the organisational processing of offenders.[54]

Whilst both these commentators were noting developments in criminal law policy in the Netherlands where recent policy developments provide the clearest example in this study of the credibility model operating in its pure form, it should be noted that this model does have a wider application in most jurisdictions. A common problem faced by any policy-makers will be to promote an efficacious image of the criminal justice system whilst maintaining optimum efficiency and upholding the principles of justice. Under this model, it has been shown that a prosecutor with a sentencing role can assist in this juggling act.

[53] A. C. 'tHart, 'Criminal Law Policy in the Netherlands' in J. J. M. van Dijk et al., eds., *Criminal Law in Action: An Overview of Current Issues in Western Societies* (Deventer, 1988), 87.

[54] A. A. G. Peters, 'Main Currents in Criminal Law Theory' in J. J. M. van Dijk et al., eds., (1988), op. cit., 32.

7
Using the Models in Practice

1. INTRODUCTION

THE prosecutor is inherently involved in the sentencing process and the three models expounded in the last chapter illustrate theoretical bases upon which this sentencing role can be analysed. The models are theories; they are not descriptive of the prosecution function in any one jurisdiction. They are useful, however, in finding a justification and rationale for the development of this part of a prosecutor's duties. The models also have a practical application, as tools for considering the common problems encountered in any criminal justice system where informal, administrative decision-making becomes a prominent feature. The core tenets of the models are not restricted to an analysis of a prosecution system, but they were constructed from a study of that branch of the criminal justice process. The applicability of any theory of criminal justice is as varied and complex as the system itself. Just as the branches of the system are not discrete but interlinked, so too are the theories that seek to rationalize them.

The particular issues considered here, such as the constitutionality of a prosecutor's sentencing role, 'net-widening', accountability and the concept of the public interest, have been discussed in the light of the three models, in an attempt to explain and rationalize them. The models do not necessarily prescribe solutions to these problems, but they can be used to illustrate how such issues have been approached in various jurisdictions, and the policy choices available to balance the harm caused by problems of 'hidden' decision-making with the benefits of a 'sentencing process' at this early stage.

Unlike Packer's models, these three models of prosecution decision-making are not mutually exclusive, and in each of the four systems studied, some or all of them co-exist and apply to different forms of prosecution sanctioning. None of the systems applies one of the models to the complete exclusion of the other two. Indeed, the models overlap. For example, under the credibility model, although the central aim is to increase intervention in petty criminal cases, the responsibility for this is placed upon the prosecutor who, in the interests of operational efficiency, is able to dispose of cases more quickly and less expensively than the court system. In the Netherlands, the interaction of these two models was clearly illustrated in the 1990 policy plan. In order to prevent a shift towards lawlessness and a 'blurring of norms' in Dutch society, (see Chapter 4) the intervention ratio has been increased. The credibility model demanded a more interventionist approach to petty crime because of the general public concern about rising crime levels: 'There is a sort of conservative climate in public opinion now, perhaps tending to be a little authoritarian again and even left-wing television companies are having talk programmes with conservative talk about crime. It is a sort of neo-realism.'[1] However, in order to implement the primary aims of the credibility model without undermining those of the operational efficiency model, the increased intervention in cases of minor criminality in the Netherlands is being implemented at the pre-trial stage; prosecutors are handling more cases and making increased use of the transaction, without placing an undue burden on the time and resources of the court system. A similar trend can be identified in Scotland with the introduction of the fiscal fine. These examples illustrate the combined application of aspects of two models of prosecutorial decision-making to implement a policy initiative.

On the other hand, the models may be contradictory and may conflict in policy terms. For example, the restorative model, with its emphasis on rehabilitation schemes and reparation and mediation processes, may conflict with the operational efficiency model, because, although court resources are saved, the organization of and participation in the schemes and negotiations often takes more of a prosecutor's time than fining or prosecuting the accused. In Scotland, one of the primary objectives in enhancing the sentencing role of the prosecutor was a concern to reduce the burden on, and cut the costs of, court proceedings. The Stewart Committee certainly had these economies in mind when recommending the introduction of fiscal fines. However, since then the prosecutor's diversionary role has burgeoned with the establishment of various rehabilitative schemes, promoting constructive benefits for the offender, rather than cutting costs. Jacqueline Tombs pointed out that these schemes are not particularly cost-effective, but that this negative aspect is far outweighed by the benefits of the restorative model: 'Experiments with diversion didn't really aim to save money . . . diversion often takes more time and money but it is felt to be the right way of dealing with people.'[2] Rutherford also found that over-emphasis on efficiency and management in the criminal justice process conflicts with and may even destroy the 'decency' or 'humanity' of criminal justice, that is, its capacity to care.[3]

The reverse could also be said: the over-use of operational efficiency as a rationale for pre-trial diversion or disposal could prejudice the interests of victims and their satisfactory compensation under the restorative model.

[1] John Blad, Erasmus University, Rotterdam; interview, Rotterdam, November 1990.
[2] Dr Jacqueline Tombs, Scottish Office Central Research Unit; interview, Edinburgh, March 1990.
[3] A. Rutherford, *Criminal Justice and the Pursuit of Decency* (Oxford, 1994).

Some American scholars have argued that too much diversion at this stage removes the opportunity for the victim to play a meaningful role in the prosecution or settling of their case: '. . . the American criminal justice system currently vests the public attorney with exclusive discretion over the initiation of criminal proceedings and denies the crime victim any formal role in the prosecution of a criminal suspect. Though justified in most cases by values of procedural fairness and administrative efficiency this configuration denies a certain class of victims the protection of the law.'[4] The conflict between the operational efficiency model and the restorative model in prosecutorial decision-making in the USA has prompted Wainstein to suggest a procedure whereby victims can ask a judge to initiate a prosecution where the prosecutor has failed to do so, overruling the prosecutor's decision in a form of judicial review.[5] Kennard also suggests that victims themselves should have an active voice in the decision whether to prosecute, in the form of a veto of alternative dispositions being considered.[6]

In the next section, the constitutional propriety and legality of the sentencing role of the prosecutor will be discussed, as well as the views of the other branches of the criminal justice system, for whom increased diversion at the prosecution stage will have knock-on effects.

2. ISSUES OF CONSTITUTIONALITY

Van de Bunt saw the prosecutor as having three roles: those of magistrate, government employee, and manager.[7] The first of these is the most important in the constitutional context. The magisterial role of a neutral, objective participant in the trial process (whether inquisitorial or adversarial), who presents all relevant evidence without bias, is widely ackowledged and has been documented throughout the previous chapters. This magisterial role is compared to that of a Minister of Justice: 'The vocation of an advocate who is prosecuting a criminal is to be in the strictest sense a minister of justice. His duty is to see that every piece of evidence relevant and admissible is presented in due order, without fear and without favour.'[8] However, a rather more controversial side of this magisterial role, which has been emerging in the jurisdictions studied, more closely resembles

---

[4] K. L. Wainstein, 'Judicially Initiated Prosecution: A means of preventing Continuing Victimization in the Event of Prosecutorial Inaction' (1988) *California Law Review*, 76: 727.
   [5] Ibid.
   [6] K. L. Kennard, 'The Victim's Veto: A way to Increase Victim Impact on Criminal Case Dispositions' (1989) *California Law Review*, 77: 417–453.
   [7] H. G. van de Bunt, *Officieren van Justitie: Verslag van een Participerend observatieonderzoek* (Zwolle, 1985). See English summary, 398–405.
   [8] Sir John Simon addressing the Canadian Bar Association in 1922, quoted in B. A. Grosman, *The Prosecutor: An inquiry into the exercise of discretion* (Toronto, 1969).

the role of the judicial magistrate. As well as impartially weighing the strength of the evidence in a case, the prosecutor goes a step further and makes an adjudication of guilt and often prescribes a punishment or sanction. How far, within the current bounds of constitutional principles, can the prosecutor's discretion extend? The constitutional principle of judicial independence and its freedom from executive influence could be breached if the demarcation between the prosecution and the judiciary is allowed to be blurred. If the prosecutor's role is seen to infringe upon the decision-making jurisdiction of the judge, the boundaries between these two branches of the criminal justice process will be blurred, so as to prejudice fairness and objectivity in the administration of justice.

However, the above view assumes clear, precise boundaries between the respective roles of prosecutor and judge in a justice system which is regarded as a series of separate and independent organizations. Instead, perhaps the justice system should be viewed more as a single process, whose branches are interdependent with flexible boundaries of influence. MacDonald,[9] for example, prefers to view the prosecutor and the judge as having a domain which is shared and constantly changing according to the demands made of the system and the goals it is trying to achieve. MacDonald's thesis is that the role of the prosecutor has historically evolved from a virtually non-existent role in the criminal process to one where the prosecutor has a substantial domain, although as stated in the previous chapter, the extent and pace of this evolution has varied substantially in different countries. In a system where the prosecutor, whether through necessity or otherwise, takes a more dominant role in disposing of cases at the pre-trial stage, it is inevitable that the prosecutor will enter the judge's domain. Indeed, in some jurisdictions, such as the Netherlands, the increased caseload of the prosecutor has significantly diminished that of the judge, the prosecutor handling and settling a large majority of cases outside the courtroom. Under each of the models of prosecutorial decision-making proposed above, there has been a natural progression of the prosecutor's sentencing role into the realms of judicial sentencing with the cogent and rational justifications outlined there.

In an overburdened criminal justice system, the prosecutor's increased caseload will ease the pressure on the judiciary, and for that reason is often welcomed and even necessary under the operational efficiency model. As less serious crimes are dealt with in the prosecutor's office, only more serious, complicated, or controversial cases will come before the judge; that is, those cases which have some special public interest reason for being prosecuted (under the positive interpretation of the expediency principle). This has two important constitutional implications.

[9] W. F. MacDonald, ed., *The Prosecutor* (Beverley Hills, 1979). See Chapter 1.

First, where even in the lower courts only the more serious cases are tried, and the less serious bulk of cases are being dealt with by the prosecutor, the prosecutor's office itself effectively becomes a lower 'court' of justice, below the first tier of the judicial court system which rises to the second step in the general structure of the justice system. However, this lower 'court' lacks the constitutional safeguards, such as evidential requirements, public accountability, and in some cases the possibility of appeal, which are central features of the judicial court system. Lack of openness and official scrutiny of prosecutorial sentencing will be discussed in the next section. The second implication is the indirect effect of the prosecutor's sentencing practice on that of the judge. Few statistics are available with which to gauge any change in judicial sentencing patterns as a result of the development of the prosecutor's sentencing function. Quantitative research is lacking in this important area, and any such impact needs to be assessed and analysed. In this more qualitative study, such information was not obtained. However, it seems likely that, if the judge perceives himself as dealing only with more serious criminality, his sentencing practice might become more severe to reflect the gravity of his caseload. It is interesting to note, though, that this trend did not occur in comparable changes to the juvenile justice system of England and Wales in the 1980s. The number of juvenile offenders cautioned between 1980 and 1990 rose substantially (by 18 per cent for males and 33 per cent for females[10]) resulting in far fewer cases being prosecuted in the juvenile court. On this basis, and considering the deliberate policy of police officers, and later Crown Prosecutors, to use prosecution only as a last resort in respect of young offenders, the juvenile courts were likely to be sentencing only the minority of hard-core offenders. Despite this fact, the number of custodial sentences imposed, as a proportion of total sentences, also fell by 5 per cent. Evidently, magistrates during this period did not increase the gravity of their sentencing policy as a result of meeting only the deep end of juvenile criminality. Conversely, if the judge does not recognize that his caseload has been filtered in this way, he may continue to sentence according to a lower tariff which does not take into account the many minor cases of criminal behaviour which are not reaching this level of the process.

As mentioned above, it is difficult without comprehensive statistics to quantify or even substantiate the existence of such an influence, and any such influence will be dependent on the level of prosecutorial diversion practised in a particular jurisdiction. However, it can be surmised that where the level of prosecutorial disposal of cases is high, as in the Netherlands and increasingly in Germany, the prosecutor's sentencing decisions are more likely to affect judicial sentencing levels than, for example, in

[10] A. Rutherford, *Growing Out of Crime: The New Era* (Winchester, 1992), Table 2B at p. 14.

Scotland where prosecutors' diversionary powers are more limited and the judge retains a more dominant role. Again, there is very little empirical data available either to support or to negate this view, but the consequences of prosecutorial sentencing on judicial sentencing can be predicted or estimated as procedural repercussions. Further, where the prosecutor has a variety of dispositional options, there is the possibility that a persistent offender who has been dealt with in various ways by the prosecutor, may be treated as a first-time offender in his first appearance at court, and therefore sentenced according to a lower tariff, especially where prosecutorial disposals are not treated as previous convictions for the purpose of the court.

The influence of the prosecutor's decision-making extends, however, far beyond his own domain and that of the judge, and has wider-ranging effects on all branches of the criminal justice process, including the police, the prison system, and the probation service. Any discretion exercised at the 'front door' of the process by the police might be tempered by the way in which prosecutors dispose of cases at the next stage. For example, if the prosecutor continually decides not to prosecute a particular crime or offender (or, as in the English system, continually returns such cases to the police with a request for a caution) then the police might change their referral procedure so that such cases are not referred to the prosecutor at all.[11] Similarly, the demands on the prison system, at the other end of the process, concern criminal justice practitioners in any country, and criminal justice policy is often determined by a need to reduce overcrowding in prisons. The prosecutor shares this concern and is in the best position to divert away from court cases which might attract short-term (and often unnecessary) terms of imprisonment, although it is clear that serious cases which may attract long custodial sentences are less suitable for diversion at the prosecution stage. Finally, prosecution decision-making under the restorative model, where extensive use is made of rehabilitation measures, will incur a greater workload for such as probation officers and social workers, whose responsibility in carrying out the restorative diversion options at the pre-trial stage will increase.

The central position of the prosecutor in the justice system means that an increase in his power has a knock-on effect on other criminal justice agencies. This flexible, pivotal role is well illustrated by the use of the prosecutor, particularly in the Netherlands, to implement a number of very different criminal law policies, ranging from the reductionist approach of the 1970s to the current, relatively severe, interventionist or repressive policy. Whichever policy is in force, the prosecutor has consistently been used as a tool for implementing policy, with consequences for the other criminal justice authorities.

[11] See further Ashworth, *The Criminal Process* (Oxford, 1994), 182.

It is the prosecutor's filtering role which has the most widespread influence on the caseload and working practices of the other agencies. It was this filtering role which prompted Jan van Dijk to label the prosecutor as 'the spider in the web of criminal justice' and inspired an American academic to describe him as 'the sentry at the gate of the criminal court system.'[12] The prosecutor acts like a sluice gate, regulating the flow of cases both to the courts (and, possibly beyond that, to the prison system) and to probation services, by dealing with defendants at the pre-trial stage. The prosecutor's influence also extends back to the police investigation stage, both directly, in those jurisdictions where the prosecutor's remit includes active involvement in investigations, and indirectly through their prosecution decisions. As Tarling has suggested,[13] a consistent policy of non-prosecution of minor offences could have an influence on police clear-up rates where offences are not prosecuted. For example, where only one offence is prosecuted while several others are taken into consideration on public policy grounds, their clear-up rates will be diminished in one fell swoop. Anxieties have certainly been voiced that the prosecutor in England and Wales, where cases can be handed back to the police with a request for a caution, has made excessive use of expediency and that this may have had an adverse effect on the morale and working practices of police officers. This may be the result of the situation in England and Wales, unique among the jurisdictions studied whereby the police have a higher influence on prosecution. The inter-relationship between the CPS and the police is more subtle than in some other European systems, in that the police in England retain the initial discretion to prosecute and therefore practice diversion perhaps on a wider scale than the public prosecutor. (Scottish commentators noted that the English police had been rather more 'sophisticated'[14] than the Scottish police in retaining at least some decision-making discretion, whereas the Scottish police, in theory if not in reality, operate under a form of the legality principle whereby reference of all cases to the prosecutor is mandatory.) The sharing between the police and the CPS of this aspect of the prosecution process can cause antagonism when they fail agree; that is, when their working ideologies conflict and their individual practices appear at odds. In this case the shared filtering process may be a source of friction.

Influence extends in the other direction, as discussed above, to the extent that the prosecutor's activities at the pre-trial stage determines the boundaries of the judge's sentencing jurisdictions, by restricting the flow of certain

[12] P. J. Utz, 'Two models of prosecutorial professionalism' in W. F. MacDonald, ed., (1979) op. cit., 100.
[13] R. Tarling, 'Interdependence and the Crown Prosecution Service' in T. E. Hall Williams, ed., *The Role of the Prosecutor* (Aldershot, 1988).
[14] Dr Jacqueline Tombs, interview, Edinburgh, March 1990.

cases to the courtroom. Whilst the constitutional implications of this situation are problematic, in a positive sense the prosecutor's influence can be employed to effect a measure of judicial sentencing reform in jurisdictions such as England and Wales where judges tend to be opposed to radical change. The prosecution system, being more malleable, can achieve limited reform from a distance by controlling the nature of a judge's caseload. It is for this reason that Andrew Rutherford chose to view the CPS as the 'Trojan Horse of the criminal justice process'[15]—with the potential for achieving sentencing reform from within the prosecutor's office.

More indirectly, the prosecutor can influence the prison population.[16] Whilst the majority of cases in which a prison sentence is likely to be imposed are more likely to be prosecuted in the public interest, the prosecutor can prevent shorter custodial sentences being imposed in less serious cases where alternative sanctions are more appropriate. Sir Clive Whitmore, Permanent Secretary in the Home Office, suggested the same in an address to a Criminal Justice Conference in London in 1991. In his view, with regard to regulating the input into the prison system, we in England should be considering: '. . . fundamental questions about our capacity to continue to process what seems likely to be an increasing volume of crime through our existing, apparently increasingly expensive, procedures and structures, or whether we should adopt simpler and less expensive procedures, perhaps operated by the Crown Prosecution Service, for certain types of offences,'[17] a clear example of extending the prosecutor's diversionary role in the interests of operational efficiency in the criminal justice process. Similarly, in the Netherlands and Germany, where prosecutors are under a duty to recommend a sentence to the judge in the course of a trial, the prosecutor can moderate the use of imprisonment by consistently recommending alternative sanctions where appropriate. This form of influence is, however, limited by the extent to which such recommendations are followed by the judiciary, which, in turn, is largely dependent on the constitutional relationship between judges and prosecutors in any particular jurisdiction. Constitutionally, judges in the Netherlands and Germany are not bound by the prosecutor's recommendation and in practice it often appeared that less experienced prosecutors had little influence here. However, in those jurisdictions the careers of the judge and the prosecutor are interchangeable and both are trained together, so that their

---

[15] A. Rutherford, 'The English Penal Crisis: Paradox and Possibilities' (1988) *Current Legal Problems*, 41: 93–113.

[16] For an analysis of the prosecutor's influence over the use of imprisonment in Scotland see J. Tombs, 'Prosecution Approaches and Imprisonment' in S. Backett, J. McNeill, and A. Yellowlees, eds., *Imprisonment Today: Current Issues in the Prison Debate* (Basingstoke, 1988).

[17] Sir Clive Whitmore, 'Management of Change: Whitehall Experience', notes for his address to the Criminal Justice Conference, London, 13–18 Jan. 1991.

relationship is closer and mutual respect may extend the prosecutor's influence further than in Scotland and England, where the judiciary remain superior in the constitutional hierarchy.

The prosecutor's role as a 'sluice gate' or gatekeeper of the criminal process is centrally important to both the operational efficiency and credibility models of justice. In the former, the filtering of trivial cases away from the court will save time and money for both judge and prosecutor. In the credibility model, the prosecutor is the safety valve which absorbs trivial cases and prevents an overload on the court which would be damaging to the public image of the criminal justice system. Under this model, however, the prosecutor is required to do more than simply divert cases away from the courts. He must also direct those diverted cases to another, equally effective if less informal and cost-efficient, sanction. Public confidence in the system's ability to process the required quantity of offenders may, however, be countered to a corresponding loss of faith in the quality of justice administered, as informal procedures and hidden, administrative decision-making increase at the expense of accountability and constitutional principles and rights. These criticisms will be discussed in Section 5 below.

One further relevant constitutional issue is whether the prosecutor's sentencing role is inconsistent with the adversary system of justice in England and Wales. For the prosecutor to be an effective sentencer, it is imperative that he is objective and fair, fulfilling the role of a minister of justice as described above. This neutrality conflicts with the prosecutor's role in the English trial where counsel for the prosecution acts on behalf of the state, in a contest with the defence, particularly in a jury trial. This is certainly the public view of practitioners in England and Wales, and perhaps even the view which prosecutors have of themselves. However, one senior civil servant working for the CPS, quoted by Rutherford, highlighted a shift in opinion of English practitioners towards the perhaps more favourable view of the European systems:

There is a very real concern that a prosecutor in the sense of someone standing up in court, should be a minister of justice rather than an avenging angel; and there is a very strong resistance to the prosecutor actually asking for a particular sentence, as in some other jurisdictions, or seeking to give broad advice on appropriate sentences, which happens even in some jurisdictions with a more Anglo-Saxon tradition. There is still a lot of concern in some quarters that the CPS should not go in that direction. There are others who take the different view that the tradition is not particularly well-founded.[18]

In the inquisitorial systems of Germany and the Netherlands, the prosecutor is seen as a neutral party, distanced from both the judge and the

---

[18] A. Rutherford (1993) op. cit., 148.

defence. The prosecutor merely reads the charge, puts forward all relevant mitigating or aggravating evidence, and then recommends a sentence. The examination and cross-examination is conducted between the defence and the judge. Whilst English prosecutors maintain that they have no interest in securing the maximum sentence on behalf of the state, their participation in a contest between the state and the defendant is apparent in both trial procedures and rules of evidence. Unless prosecutors in England display greater neutrality, it will be difficult to satisfy critics that they are sufficiently objective and independent from the state to be entrusted with a 'hidden' sentencing role. It is interesting to note that in Scotland, where the prosecutor's role has been more fully developed than in England, the trial process has come to resemble the inquisitorial trials of Northern Europe, in that the prosecutor regards himself less as the adversary of the defendant, and more like the neutral prosecutor in inquisitorial systems in Europe (although the Scottish system still has as its foundation the adversary structure). It is common to see prosecutors in Scotland introduce evidence favourable to the defence as well as to the prosecution, and the procurator fiscal's objective position is actually carried out in practice; it is not merely a theoretical statement of principle.

Whether this development is coincidental with the development of the prosecutor's role is arguable, but it may be that the enhanced powers of the prosecutor (in particular, the introduction of a duty to recommend a sentence) will be very difficult to achieve in, if not wholly inconsistent with, an adversarial system. Jacqueline Tombs in Scotland argued that many of the reforms that could be made to the prosecution systems of both Scotland and England would not be so easily achieved in an adversarial system, and she suggested that this was why the European systems studied here had been able to push the role of the prosecutor so much further.[19] In particular she was of the opinion that the biggest mistake made upon the introduction of the CPS was to leave so much power in the hands of the police, rather than having a much less sophisticated police role as is the case in Scotland. Nevertheless, Scotland is a fine example of how progress can be made in an adversarial system, as also is the United States of America. Whilst the American system did not form part of the study conducted here, it provides a useful example of a widely developed sentencing role for a prosecutor in a criminal justice system firmly rooted in adversarial principles. The American materials reviewed here indicate how far this sentencing function can be adopted within the realms of an adversarial system, and to some extent refute the argument that such a function is inconsistent with the prosecutor's role in an adversarial system.

William Rhodes, an American academic, has argued that the adversary

[19] Dr Jacqueline Tombs, interview, Edinburgh, March 1990.

justice process is more aimed at the due process model of justice, the participants in the system being rather more concerned with issues of guilt and innocence and conviction or acquittal than with the more utilitarian aims of crime control.[20] Whilst the choice of an adversary system may be admirably justified in protecting the liberty of individuals from the abuse of state power, it is clear that adversary principles of due process must, inevitably, be compromised: 'The adversary mode of delivering justice is frequently compromised in practice. In part, this compromise arises because criminal courts are similar to other organizations in which informal organizational goals sometimes replace official public-endorsed goals.'[21] In particular, under the three models of justice described above, the due process goals of the system must necessarily be compromised, to achieve the 'informal goals' inherent in those models, namely saving resources, preserving the credibility of the system through rigorous crime control mechanisms, and resolving conflicts. This may explain why the extension of prosecutorial sentencing discretion is regarded with such distaste and anxiety in adversarial systems where such reform requires a compromise of the principles which form the very foundation of the criminal justice system, whereas in the inquisitorial systems of Europe the extension of a prosecutor's discretion is a more natural, and hence palatable, progression.

In the USA, the adversary approach and the principles of due process have undoubtedly been compromised by the extension of the discretionary powers of the prosecutor. Perhaps the most overt example of such discretionary power is in the process of plea-bargaining where the prosecutor will negotiate with the defendant to plead guilty to a less serious charge to avoid a lengthy trial process and to avoid a more severe punishment. The operational efficiency model is clearly seen in operation in this process even though it may overlook some due process concerns,[22] and the problems of 'net-widening' and of unfair coercion on defendants to plead guilty to the lesser charge have been well researched.[23] These due process concerns are perhaps heightened in the event of a particular plea-bargain being breached by a prosecutor. Indeed, the prosecutor did just that in the case of *People* v. *Navarroli*;[24] he agreed to reduce the charges against the

    [20] W. Rhodes, 'Plea-bargaining, crime control and due process: A Quantitative Analysis' in W. F. MacDonald, and J. A. Cramer, eds., *Plea-Bargaining* (Massachusetts, 1980), 115.

    [21] Ibid., 115.

    [22] This issue is discussed by Church in 'In Defense of "Bargain Justice"' in M. J. Gorr and S. Harwood, eds., *Controversies in Criminal Law: Philosophical Essays on Responsibility and Procedure* (Colorado, 1992).

    [23] See for example S. S. Nagel and M. G. Neef, *Decision Theory and the Legal Process* (Massachusetts, 1979), particularly Chapters 4 and 5. Also J. Hagan and I. Nagel Bernstein, 'Sentence Bargaining in Federal District Courts', and W. F. MacDonald, J. A. Cramer and H. H. Rossman, 'Prosecutorial Bluffing and the Case against Plea-Bargaining' both in W. F. MacDonald, and J. A. Cramer, eds., (1980), op. cit.

    [24] (1988) 121 Ill. 2d 516.

defendant if the latter assisted with the arrest of other members of a drug distribution network, but later refused to reduce the charges. The court in this case awarded no redress for the grievance of the defendant, finding that he had not in fact been induced to plead guilty, and therefore that there had been no abuse of due process (although a dissenting judge argued that this decision laid down a grave precedent for future cases in which a prosecutor could renege on his word without accountability). Nevertheless, other cases[25] have suggested that where a defendant has been induced to enter a guilty plea, some redress can be sought against breach of the bargain by a prosecutor, either on contractual or constitutional grounds.[26]

The American prosecutor also has a wide discretion as to whether to prosecute an offender or not, similar in many respects to the powers of European prosecutors in inquisitorial systems to drop cases with a conditional or unconditional waiver. The American prosecutor may waive cases for evidential insufficiency reasons, or under a list of public interest criteria, where the offence was particularly trivial, where the victim does not wish to proceed with a prosecution, where the cost of a trial cannot be justified, where the effects of a prosecution may be considered to cause 'undue harm to the suspect', or where there are adequate informal procedures for dealing with the defendant.[27] According to Miller's description of the use of these discretionary powers, the justification for policy waivers tends generally to fall into one or more of the three models of justice. Indeed, pre-trial diversion has been justified on the basis of both the operational efficiency and restorative models: 'The goals of pretrial diversion include: (1) unburdening court dockets and conserving judicial resources for more serious cases; (2) reducing the incidence of offender recidivism by providing an alternative to incarceration—community-based rehabilitation—which would be more effective and less costly than incarceration; and (3) benefitting society by the training and placement of previously unemployed persons.'[28]

The importance of the prosecutor's influence over sentencing in some systems of the USA was also substantially increased by the use of sentencing grids. A grid is drawn up with offence type along one index and characteristics of offenders along the other, with guideline sentences or a

---

[25] E.g. *Santobello* v. *New York* (1971) 404 US 257.

[26] W. M. Ejzak, 'Plea bargains and non-prosecution agreements: What Interests should be Protected when Prosecutors Renege?' [1991] *University of Illinois Law Review*, 107–136, gives a full analysis of these cases. A further discussion of the protection afforded to the defendant in these circumstances can be found in P. Yin Sit, 'Double Jeopardy, Due Process and the Breach of Plea Agreements' *Colombia Law Review*, 87: 142–160.

[27] See F. W. Miller, *Prosecution: The decision to charge a suspect with a crime* (Boston, 1969), Part IV. See also J. Vennard, 'Decisions to Prosecute: Screening Policies and Practices in the United States' [1985] *Crim. LR* 20–28.

[28] 'Pre-trial Diversion from the Criminal Process' (1975) *Yale Law Journal*, 83: 827.

range of sentences within which a judge can reasonably and lawfully sentence in any case.[29]

Thus in a system where a grid is used the judge's discretion is substantially reduced, the sentence being determined by the offender's characteristics and the offence charged. The charge is the only real variable in the equation and it is within the prosecutor's discretion to choose the charge. The prosecutor's choice of charge at an early stage in the proceedings is, thus, seen to be of more direct importance to the sentencing decision, and a policy by the prosecutor of charging severely or lightly can have a significant impact on sentencing levels where the judge's discretion is so heavily reliant on the particular charge on the indictment. Although it could be said that the prosecutor came by this form of influence over sentencing rather accidentally, in the sense that the sentencing guidelines were drawn up to maintain a firmer control over the sentencing discretion of judges, and not deliberately to increase that of the prosecutor, the rationale behind the development of such grids (whether expansionist or reductionist) could be significantly furthered or hampered by the choice of charge and by the policy-making aims of the individual prosecutor. Alschuler has quantified the effect of sentencing guidelines on the discretion of the prosecutor thus:

a system of sentencing guidelines that on its face prescribes severe sentences but leaves plea bargaining unconstrained is a prosecutor's paradise. Sentencing guidelines masquerade as the sentencing commission's determination of appropriate penalties. In reality, the guidelines are bargaining weapons—armaments that enable prosecutors, not the sentencing commission, to determine sentences in most cases. In operation, the guidelines do not set sentences; they simply augment the power of prosecutors to do so.[30]

Thus, the prosecutor can implement a policy to increase or decrease average sentences in court either in compliance with the spirit of the guidelines or in contradiction to them. In the process of plea-bargaining, the prosecutor wields the power to determine the sentencing structure of the judge.

Hence the prosecutor in the adversarial system of the USA has just as important a role in the sentencing process as the prosecutor in Europe. The considerable amount of research into the prosecutor's role in the United States[31] has shown that, in order to operate a smooth-running and efficient

---

[29] See A. Rutherford, *Prisons and the Process of Justice* (Oxford, 1986), Table 7.3, p. 166 for an example of one such sentencing grid drawn up by the Minnesota Sentencing Guidelines Commission.

[30] A. W. Alschuler, 'The Failure of Sentencing Guidelines: A Plea for Less Aggregation' (1991) *University of Chicago Law Review*, 58: 926. See also, K. S. Kelley, 'Substantial Assistance under the Guidelines: How Smitherman transfers sentencing discretion from judges to prosecutors' (1990) *Iowa Law Review*, 76: 187–207.

[31] See for example, J. Kaplan, 'The Prosecutorial Discretion—A Comment' (1965) *New Utah Law Review* 60: 174 and Cates 'Can we Ignore Laws?—Discretion not to Prosecute' (1962) *Alabama Law Review* 14: 1, and more recently, G. F. Cole, *Politics and the Administration*

criminal justice system, compromises have to be made to the adversarial principles of due process. The goals of the three models of justice have been used to justify a high degree of prosecutorial sentencing without overriding the fundamental principles of the justice system. Rehabilitative schemes for example are undoubtedly used, in the USA, as a form of pre-trial sentencing. Indeed, one American academic described pre-trial diversion as: 'both . . . an exchange and a sentencing process. It is a sentencing activity by nonjudicial personnel. Upon the initiative of program staff and with the consent of the prosecutor, the accused is sentenced to a term of probation before trial without effective intervention of defense counsel or judge.'[32]

The American example illustrates how wide the sentencing powers, both direct and indirect, can be within the context of an adversarial system. This, to some extent, reduces the effectiveness of arguments, sometimes put forward in England and Wales, that the notion of the prosecutor as a sentencer is a particularly European concept; that is, that the sentencing role of a public prosecutor fits rather more neatly into an inquisitorial system of justice, but would have grave constitutional and due process consequences if implanted into an adversarial system. The analysis will now return to the European jurisdictions under consideration.

3. ACCOUNTABILITY

Despite the perceived benefits of the three models of justice mentioned above, the increased use of diversion at the pre-trial stage is not without its problems and difficulties. In serving the interests of those three models, that is, in preserving the credibility of the criminal justice system, managing an efficient and cost-effective system, and satisfying the aims of the restorative model, it has been argued above that a lower 'court' of justice is effectively created in the prosecutor's office. The presumption of guilt is implicit in diversionary decision-making followed by the imposition of any kind of penalty. This lower 'court', however, is not subject to the same rules of procedure and evidence as the judicial courts, whose rules are designed to ensure that sentencing decisions are procedurally fair, non-discriminatory and proportionate to the offence committed. It is argued that the enhanced sentencing powers of the prosecutor should be counter-balanced with appropriate standards of accountability and supervision so

of Justice (Beverley Hills, 1973), Chapter IV—'Prosecuting Attorney', A. P. Worden, 'Policy-making by Prosecutors: the uses of discretion in regulating plea-bargaining' (1990) *Judicature*, 73: 335–340. V. Langer, 'Public Interest in Civil Law, Socialist Law and Common Law Systems: the Role of the Public Prosecutor' (1988) *The American Journal of Comparative Law*, 36: 279–305—a study comparing the role of the American prosecutor with some of his European counterparts.

[32] 'Pre-trial Diversion from the Criminal Process' (1975) *Yale Law Journal*, 83: 827–854.

that the fundamental rights of natural justice are not overlooked in a covert system of discretionary sentencing, especially in jurisdictions such as the Netherlands where the prosecutor's domain has become wider than that of the judge.

Allowing administrative justice to progress to such an extent, no matter how necessary or desirable it may be under the three models of justice, risks abuse of power by the prosecutor. Rights of defendants to a fair hearing, the opportunity to defend the charges made against them and appeals against the justice of the 'conviction' or the severity of the sentence may be overlooked, and the temptation for the prosecutor to enter into a bargain with the defence to avoid a trial in a case where the guilt of the accused is in doubt may be overwhelming. (The problem of 'net-widening' will be discussed in more detail below). The dangers are not confined to the defendant, though. On the wider social scale, without proper regulation the individual sentencing practices of prosecutors could produce disparity in the use of particular sanctions and an unequal application of the law; indeed, similar criticisms have been made of judicial sentencing in England and Wales which is also relatively unregulated.[33] Where practices rely on the enthusiasm and working philosophies of individual practitioners to apply them, an effective system of regulation is essential to rectify unjustifiable variations in sentencing statistics which are not related to geographical or demographic factors. In Germany, where prosecutorial decision-making is regulated, but only on an office-by-office basis, wide variations occur in the use of certain disposals not only between states, but also between neighbouring districts of the same region (see Chapter 5).

An obvious solution to these accountability problems is explicitly to acknowledge the prosecutor's sentencing role and to open it up to public scrutiny. As Utz has argued: 'The problem of invisibility lies in the persisting illegitimacy of the policy-making role of the prosecutor.'[34] In the Netherlands, the prosecutor is openly acknowledged as a sentencer. Indeed, prosecutors are referred to as the 'standing magistracy' (by contrast with the 'sitting magistracy' which is their term for the judiciary). However, as long as there is a reluctance on the part of English and Scottish prosecutors to admit to their role in the sentencing process, and as long as commentators continue to deny prosecutors' interest in sentencing, in comments such as those made by witnesses to the Stewart Committee (see Chapter 3), and those made by the likes of Sir Clive Whitmore in England quoted

---

[33] See generally Ashworth, *Sentencing and Criminal Justice* (London, 1992), particularly ch. 12.

[34] P. J. Utz, (1979) op. cit., 101. See also F. W. Miller, (1969) op. cit., who argues that since the prosecutor is best qualified to make certain sentencing decisions, being often more in tune with community problems and social values than the judiciary, it is inevitable that accountability problems will arise unless suitable legal and informal controls are placed on his discretion.

below (in Section 7), open accountability for the actual sentencing role is unlikely to develop in the near future. At the moment when prosecutors themselves realize that they are making sentencing decisions, as well as decisions on the issue of whether to prosecute or not, then they will be more conscious of the need for accountability.

In the United States, prosecutorial sentencing and policy-making is much more widely acknowledged and accepted. For example, the practice of plea-bargaining is a recognized and open practice in American criminal procedure[35] and a number of controls exist to limit the exercise of the prosecutor's charging decisions, which openly recognize that the prosecutor has an important policy-making role at the pre-trial stage in applying the public interest criteria. The problems with hidden decision-making by the police are more evident. Calls for more police accountability in recent years have been directed at their initial filtering role, rather than at the prosecutor whose sifting out of cases not meriting the full enforcement of the criminal law is now fully recognized. The low visibility of police discretion has come under criticism similar to that of the prosecutor in Europe: 'A regularized system of review is a requisite for insuring substantial compliance by the administrators of criminal justice with these rule-of-law principles. Implicit in the word "review" and obviously essential to the operation of any review procedure is the visibility of the decisions and conduct to be scrutinized.'[36] To secure the acceptance of discretionary decision-making at very early stages of the criminal process, and to formulate appeal and review procedures for them, it is essential to bring that whole decision-making practice out into the open and to recognize that this discretion is necessary for the smooth running of an efficient system of justice.

When considering the accountability of prosecutors, whether to Parliament or to the general public, it is necessary to determine which of their functions require which type of accountability. Generally, those functions which can be described as judicial in nature and which are exercised on a case-by-case basis do not require accountability to Parliament. When the prosecutor fulfils a sentencing role, case by case accountability is more suitable. Under the three models of justice the prosecutor steps into judicial shoes for one reason or another. Under the restorative model, the prosecutor imposes quasi-judicial sanctions in the interests of restoring the conflict between the victim and the accused; under the operational efficiency model the prosecutor takes over the judicial role in order to save the time and resources of the court; and under the credibility model the

---

[35] See for example, D. W. Maynard, *Inside Plea-Bargaining: the Language of Negotiation* (New York, 1984).
[36] J. Goldstein, 'Police Discretion not to invoke the Criminal Process: Low Visibility Decisions in the Administration of Justice' (1984) *Yale Law Journal*, 69: 543–594.

prosecutor 'sentences' defendants who otherwise would have been unconditionally diverted from the system in order to preserve the credibility of the criminal justice system. Therefore the same case by case accountability which applies to judicial sentencing should also apply here. The separation between the executive and the judiciary should be maintained, whether those judicial functions are performed by prosecutors or judges; the constitutional principle should not be compromised merely because such functions are performed by a body of civil servants who are, in a wider sense, answerable to Parliament through their political head of service. On a case by case basis, however, accountability is more suitably effected through supervision by either the judiciary or a superior level of the prosecution service itself, although general accountability to Parliament is still important for policy-making.

Secondly, the basic standards of objectivity and fairness should be clearly defined, especially where an adjudication of guilt is concerned. In all four of the jurisdictions compared here, the starting point of any prosecutorial decision is sufficiency of evidence, to prevent weak cases being prosecuted in circumstances where they should be dropped for lack of evidence. This evidential sufficiency criterion, which is the first and paramount consideration before public interest matters are considered, is a key element in maintaining fairness and equality of treatment in prosecutorial sentencing. However, further standards and limits should be applied to prevent any form of discriminatory or wayward decision-making.

These standards may be administered and controlled within the prosecution service itself, by a superior level of prosecutors, or they may be monitored through review of decisions by the courts. One form of review of individual decisions practised in some of the jurisdictions is where a prosecutor states the reason for his decision on the cover of the file. These reasons can then be checked by higher level prosecutors and collated as a statistic which can be used by policy-makers to identify inconsistencies and develop guidelines. Further, under the quasi-judicial role that is demanded of the prosecutor under the three models of justice, it would be anomalous to allow a discretionary sentencing decision to be made without some form of justification or explicit reasoning, in the same way that a judge is required to give his legal reasoning. In the Netherlands, the prosecutor will briefly state his reasoning by quoting on the file the reference number of the public interest criterion relevant to that decision. Similarly, in Germany, reasons are briefly quoted on the file cover. Not only does this practice serve as a useful justification for a decision in the event of an appeal, but it also provides, in Germany, a means for higher ranking members of the prosecution service to check that their more junior staff are complying with practice rules. In the Netherlands, where no such supervisory checks are made, one can only assume that the purpose of the practice is to make the prosecutors themselves consciously aware of how they are making decisions, in an effort to correct for themselves any discriminatory or stereotyped decision-making, as well as providing information for any possible appeal against the decision.

In Scotland, prosecutors are not required to give reasons, and claim that to do so would take up too much of their time, although Feeley's 'myth of the heavy caseload'[37] may be appropriate here since all that is needed is the quick noting of a reference number on the file. Indeed, the Scottish system illustrates a problem created within the restorative model of justice where accountability, even on this low level, is lacking. Where procurator fiscals make decisions concerning the mental or physical health of a defendant for the purposes of referral to a rehabilitation unit, although they often have the benefit of social inquiry reports, no checks are made by the Crown Office of the use of this quasi-medical discretion, for which no formal training has been received. Only detailed empirical research would reveal any abuses of this discretionary power. In the absence of any requirement to justify (if only briefly) his decisions, a fiscal could continue to make stereo-typed judgements regarding the extent of a defendant's alcohol addiction or drug problem, for example.

This form of accountability is also lacking from the Crown Prosecutor's exercise of his limited discretion. However, there appears to be little justification for distinguishing the CPS from any administrative body in other government departments which exercises a discretion affecting individual members of the public, such as the planning authorities, the parole board or the immigration department. Indeed, JUSTICE recently called for a more open form of government, where civil servants or officials should be required to give reasons for their decisions: 'Those who exercise administrative authority should be ready to give an account of what they do. When they make decisions which affect individuals they should justify and explain their actions. The attainment in practice of these desirable aims is impeded by the fact that there is no general rule of law that reasons must be given for administrative decisions.'[38] Such reforms should include the Crown Prosecutor, especially since, as experience in Germany and the Netherlands has shown, it is possible to formulate a system of giving reasons for sentencing and prosecutorial decisions without prejudicing the course of justice. The task simply is to ensure that their discretionary decisions fulfil the criteria of rationality set forth by Galligan; that is, 'a)

---

[37] M. Feeley, *The Process is the Punishment: Handling Cases in a Lower Criminal Court* (New York, 1979), ch. 8, 'The Myth of Heavy Caseloads: A Explanation and Rejection of an Alternative Explanation'.

[38] JUSTICE, *Administrative Justice: Some Necessary Reforms*. Report of the Committee of JUSTICE, All Souls Review of Administrative Law in the United Kingdom, (Oxford, 1988), 24.

that there be findings of primary facts based on good evidence and b) that decisions about facts be made for reasons which serve the purposes of the statute in an intelligible and reasonable manner.'[39] The High Court and the Court of Appeal have certainly approved of the process of giving reasons when considering the sentencing discretion of judges. In *R. v. Harrow Crown Court, ex parte Dave*[40] the High Court decided that the Crown Court Rules 1982 'pointed towards an obligation to give reasons' when the judge was sitting in his appellate capacity. The Court of Appeal went further in *R. v. Skinner*[41] in holding that judges should be obliged to give reasons when passing sentence, in order to encourage them to 'consider the likely effect and public reception' of that sentence. It would be highly illogical if a prosecutor, acting in a quasi-judicial capacity, were not to subject to similar obligations, particularly as their sentencing discretion is exercised at a less public and more covert stage of the criminal process.[42] This practice would also facilitate any appeal or judicial review process; if improper reasons were given, the appellant would have a clear foundation upon which to base their claim.

Another method of accountability, also practised in Germany, the Netherlands, England, and Scotland involves the more precautionary step of issuing guidelines to prosecutors with advice on how to exercise their discretion. The guidelines are not, in any of the jurisdictions, mandatory and therefore do not significantly fetter that discretion, but provide general 'rules of thumb' to regulate and inject consistency into decision-making. Formulated by a group of high-ranking prosecutors, these guidelines serve as a means by which those superiors can exercise limited control over decision-making, especially in Holland where such guidelines are drafted on a national basis and are generally followed by prosecutors on the ground level, who have some input into their formulation. By contrast, in Germany, guidelines are highly generalized and vague and tend to be drafted on a local, regional basis, so that policy and practice in two neighbouring regions may be highly disparate. The position is similar in Scotland and England and Wales. There are few written guidelines in Scotland, most of the prosecutor's discretion being exercised on the basis of 'rules of thumb' acquired through training and practical experience. In England and Wales, the written guidelines take two forms; the published Code for Crown Prosecutors and the unpublished Policy Manuals. After the recent review

---

[39] D. Galligan, *Discretionary Powers* (Oxford, 1986), 266.
[40] [1994] *Crim. LR* 346.   [41] (1993) 14 Cr. App. R (S) 759.
[42] Indeed, the obligation to give reasons is a rapidly developing doctrine in other areas of administrative or quasi-judicial decision-making, although it has not yet developed into a legal duty to do so. See *R v. Civil Service Appeal Board, ex parte Cunningham* [1991] 4 All ER 310, and *R v. Secretary of State for the Home Department*, ex parte *Doody* [1993] 3 WLR 154; c.f. *R v. Higher Education Funding Council*, ex parte *Institute of Dental Surgery* [1994] 1 WLR 242.

and redrafting of the Code, the published guidelines are now much more vague and ambiguous and it appears that the real, structured guidance for Crown Prosecutors has shifted into the confidential Policy Manuals.

A more formalized control on the prosecutor's discretion, practised mainly in Germany and the Netherlands, and to a much lesser extent in Scotland and England and Wales, is the opportunity for an aggrieved defendant or victim to appeal to the courts or to a superior prosecutor against a decision on non-prosecution. Indeed, in the Netherlands this possibility extends to any sufficiently 'interested party'. Whilst cases of judicial review of prosecution decisions are comparatively rare in those jurisdictions, and often unsuccessful, it is an important matter of principle that a citizen is able to seek redress from the courts in respect of a decision by a government department which affects them. With growing powers of the prosecutor in both England and Wales and Scotland, where appeal to a senior prosecutor is the only redress for both victim and accused, there seems to be a conspicuous gap in the law here where judicial review is concerned. In England and Wales, Spencer[43] has reported the growing use of judicial review of criminal proceedings and judges' sentencing practices, but only recently has there been consideration of applying the *Wednesbury* principle[44] to the sentencing or other discretionary powers of the prosecutor.[45] Whether one views the prosecutor in a quasi-judicial role, or as a civil servant making decisions on behalf of the governing Secretary of State, judicial review under the *Wednesbury* principle would still be an appropriate means of preventing a misuse of prosecutors' discretionary powers. Judicial review may result in a finding that their decisions are 'illegal', 'irrational', or unreasonable and of 'procedural impropriety' (as per Lord Diplock in *Council of Civil Servants' Union* v. *Minister for the Civil Service*[46]). Any intention to increase the discretionary powers either of the Crown Prosecutor in England or of the procurator fiscal in Scotland would be wholly inappropriate without a suitable system of meaningful and formal accountability on a case-by-case basis. For the victim there are obvious retributive benefits in persuading a court to reverse a non-prosecution decision. Similarly, the accused should not be denied access to court to defend his case, under the principles of natural justice, and it is not altogether

---

[43] J. N. Spencer, 'Judicial Review of Criminal Proceedings' [1991] *Crim. LR* 259–263.

[44] This principle was laid down in *Associated Provincial Picture Houses Ltd.* v. *Wednesbury Corporation* [1948] 1 KB 223, and states that the court has the authority to review decisions of government departments and ministers where it is claimed that they have not acted 'fairly' in making their decision and where such a decision was so unreasonable that no reasonable body could have arrived at the same conclusion. See de Smith, *Constitutional and Administrative Law* 6th Edition eds. Harry Street and Rodney Brazier, (Harmondsworth, 1989), at ch. 29.

[45] These cases are discussed in Chapter 2. See also Ashworth (1994) op. cit., 187–190.

[46] [1984] 3 All ER 935.

unknown in the Netherlands and Germany for defendants to pursue an appeal against non-prosecution so that a trial might be ordered in which the prosecutor's presumption of guilt could be questioned or even reversed.

In addition, the accused should have an opportunity to appeal against the sentence of the prosecutor, either by judicial review of the decision, or more simply by refusing to accept the offer of a prosecutorial sanction, which, in all jurisdictions, are usually voluntary. The English Crown Prosecutor, for example, cannot consider a referral for caution in a case where there is no lawfully obtained admission. Similarly, in those jurisdictions considered here in which the prosecutor can refer the defendant to a rehabilitation scheme, the willingness of the defendant to take part in the scheme is necessary as both an evidential requirement and a prerequisite for the success of the rehabilitation.

Similar appeal procedures exist in the USA in the form of mandamus actions, where the court can overturn a decision by the prosecutor not to prosecute if that decision has been made under the public interest criteria. However, such appeal procedures are rarely used and the discretion of the judge to reverse such a decision is regarded as a residual discretion to be used only in cases where the prosecutor's decision has been made under inappropriate or illegal criteria: '. . . the body of law which has developed is nearly exclusively concerned with the corrupt or the inefficient and not with the problems of the honest man who is seeking guidance.'[47] For example, the Supreme Court has ruled that race and religion are illegal criteria for prosecution decision-making.[48] Prosecutors may themselves be prosecuted for a breach of public trust or malfeasance in office, in common with all US public officials, although it is likely that this severe form of judicial review in the criminal courts is used extremely rarely, and reserved for the most serious abuses of discretion.

Further guidance is given to American prosecutors in the form of legislation which prohibits the non-prosecution of some crimes, particularly those which involve a victim or which are not considered 'morally colourless', or in offences where public opinion requires greater law enforcement, such as prostitution or gambling; a clear example of the credibility model operating from the level of the legislature.[49] Policy reasons for prosecuting such crimes are incorporated in statute imposing an absolute prohibition on non-prosecution. In this aspect, the American prosecutor's generally wide discretion is strictly controlled by the legislature. The existence of such controls may be a reason why the prosecutor's role has been allowed to progress so far in an adversary system, compared with England where such controls over the prosecution decision do not currently exist and

---

[47] F. W. Miller, (1969) op. cit., 158.
[48] See for example *Oyler* v. *Boles* (1962) 82 Sup. Crt. 501.
[49] See Baker and Delong, 'The Prosecuting Attorney' (1934) *Journal of Criminal Law*, 24: 1025.

where the legislature may be hesitant about defining, and thereby limiting, prosecution policy.

4. 'NET-WIDENING'

The appeal processes described above, as well as providing a system of accountability in a process of hidden decision-making, also act as what the Stewart Committee in Scotland called the 'essential safeguard'[50], a means of ensuring that the accused is never denied access to a court to prove his innocence. However, this safeguard, whilst protecting the civil liberties of the accused, may not be sufficient to guard against the process of 'net-widening', where defendants are drawn into the criminal justice process and dealt with informally, in circumstances where they would previously not have been prosecuted and their cases would have been dropped unconditionally. This process, which Cohen describes as both 'thinning the mesh' and 'widening the net'[51] occurs where alternatives to prosecution and diversion schemes are practised so widely, and adopted so enthusiastically, that intervention by the criminal justice system actually increases rather than decreases; as Cohen stated, community-based diversion schemes will be under 'great pressure to work with parts of the population not previously "reached".'[52]

This process has been widely discussed in England and Wales in the context of the proliferation of community penalties and the increased use of cautions and 'caution plus'.[53] Effectively, by extending the range of possible community or diversionary punishment schemes, the state extends its capacity to observe, control, and manipulate a wider section of that community, thus creating what Cohen called the 'Punitive City'. An extension of the prosecutor's role as part of a trend away from imprisonment, with an increase in disposal options, fits within these theories and raises questions about the efficacy and possible dangers of a prosecution policy which discourages imprisonment.

The 'net-widening' process has also been recognized and much debated in the juvenile area of criminal justice in England an Wales[54] where diversion

---

[50] Scottish Home and Health Department, 2nd Report of the Stewart Committee *Keeping Offenders Out of Court: Further Alternatives to Prosecution* (Edinburgh, 1983), para. 5.23.
[51] S. Cohen, 'The Punitive City: Notes on the Dispersal of Social Control' (1979) *Contemporary Crises*, 3: 347. See also generally S. Cohen, *Visions of Social Control* (Cambridge, 1985).
[52] Ibid., 348.
[53] For an analysis and literature review on this subject, see M. Cavadino and J. Dignan, *The Penal System: An Introduction* (London, 1992), ch. 7.
[54] See for example L. Gelsthorpe and H. Giller, 'More Justice for Juveniles: Does more mean better?' [1990] *Crim. LR* 153–164. D. P. Farrington and T. Bennett, 'Police Cautioning of Juveniles in London' (1981) *British Journal of Criminology*, 21: 123–135. J. Pratt, 'Diversion from the Juvenile Court' (1986) *British Journal of Criminology*, 26: 212–231. J. Mott, 'Police Decisions for dealing with Juvenile Offenders' (1983) *British Journal of Criminology*, 23: 249–263.

programmes developed much earlier than that in the adult sphere, especially with the greater use of formal cautioning. Nevertheless, with the
growing use of alternative sanctions for both juvenile and adult crime in
other jurisdictions particularly at the informal pre-trial stage under the
restorative model, the process is becoming more of a problem. By its very
nature, the restorative model involves an individualization of justice, with
an emphasis on curing the behavioural problems of an individual offender.
With this emphasis, the pressure to intervene in a 'problem' case for the
sake of rehabilitation may overtake the criminal justice policy aims to
decrease the number of offenders processed. Hence 'net-widening' may
result from rehabilitative aims, in sending offenders to schemes which
alleviate behavioural problems, rather than from a policy of disapplying
the criminal process in cases where prosecution is not justified under the
public interest criteria. Although the power to divert offenders to such
schemes would be preferable to the previous practice of the police in
England of prosecuting 'problem' cases to alert the attention of the social
services to the personal problems of the accused (as described in Chapter
2), the Good Samaritan motives of the prosecutor should not become the
cause of a process of 'net-widening' and official involvement of criminal
justice authorities in cases where the public interest criteria deem it unnecessary. It could be argued that the prosecutor's pre-trial sentencing
discretion may remove some of the 'obstacles' that Packer described in his
due process model which impede miscarriages of justice and inappropriate
intervention, and 'net-widening' could be considered the price that the
justice system pays for extending the diversionary role of the prosecutor.

It became clear from the interviews conducted in the Netherlands,
reported in Chapter 4, that 'net-widening' was not only seen as a natural
consequence of increasing diversion at the prosecution stage, but was a
deliberate part of the policy to increase intervention. Under the credibility
model, Dutch prosecutors are now positively encouraged to 'widen the net'
by adding conditions to waivers which previously would have been unconditional, thereby intervening punitively in cases which, under the more
lenient policy of the 1970s and early 1980s, would have gone unpunished.
Some Dutch commentators, such as Dato Steenhuis, preferred to see the
process, not in the negative sense as 'net-widening', but rather as a positive
step towards decriminalization in society.

This, however, is not the overall view and another faction of commentators have criticized the new policy for its emphasis on crime control and
its lack of attention to due process in the punishment of individual defendants. Peters[55] has outlined the move in the Netherlands away from a 'moral'

[55] A. A. G. Peters, 'Main Currents in Criminal Law Theory' in J. J. M. van Dijk et al.,
eds., *Criminal Law in Action: An Overview of current issues in Western Societies* (Deventer,
1988).

and individualistic approach and towards an approach more based on social control, even before the publication of the 1990 policy plan and the emergence of the credibility model. According to Peters the rationale behind modern criminal justice policy is the management of a large bulk of criminal cases with optimum efficiency (reflected now in the operational efficiency model of prosecutorial decision-making): '. . . the emerging model is one that in many ways parallels the rational organization of an industrial enterprise in which the various departments work together in a well coordinated fashion towards the same goal.'[56] This approach was criticized by Peters for extending the discretion of decision-makers far beyond rational limit: 'Discretion thus generalized is beyond the reach of law and governs it. The constitutional framework of codified law no longer furnishes the main determinants of official action, but rather the non-legal, wise or unwise, policy considerations of social control.'[57] Hence, he argues, many criminal cases have been removed from the remit of the court, and, under all three prosecutorial models, have been placed in the hands of welfare agencies. Bureaucratizing the criminal process in this way, and removing notions of retribution in the punishment system, have taken the morality out of the criminal law and the determination of criminal liability. The definition of criminal offences, as well as the way in which suspects are dealt with, has become dominated by organizational considerations, rather than those based on morality: 'The criminal law is seen as only one of several legal and non-legal, formal and informal, alternative forms of social control from among which one has to choose in a rational way, without being hampered by moral considerations.'[58] Indeed, the sanitization of decision-making is, in Weberian terms, an inherent product of a system administered by a bureaucratic organization.[59] The basis upon which such organizations make decisions is an ideology founded upon routine, efficiency, and uniformity rather than on moral or emotional concerns.

The loss of morality in the criminal justice system means that the natural limits on intervention by the system, imposed by the consciences of those working within it, are lost. Indeed, Christie has argued that criminal justice systems which are increasingly modelled on a corporate ideology seek deliberately to expand; expansion means increased profits and mass production produces efficiency.[60] Adoption of the operational efficiency model therefore paves the way for 'net-widening' on a large scale, as prosecutors are provided with a wide discretion at a less open stage of the process.

[56] Ibid., 32.   [57] Ibid., 33.   [58] Ibid., 32.
[59] M. Weber, *The Theory of Social and Economic Organization*, ed. T. Parsons, (London, 1947). See also D. Garland, *Punishment and Modern Society: A Study in Social Theory*, (Oxford, 1993), 180–9.
[60] N. Christie, *Crime Control as Industry: Towards GULAGS, Western Style?* (London, 1993).

Expansion can be justified under the broad aims of each model. For example, in Germany the decision to expand the prosecutor's discretion to include the power to impose a suspended sentence as part of the penal order is a form of widening the prosecutor's net of control, justified by the operational efficiency and credibility models. The moral issues concerning civil liberties did not prevent the passing of this provision through the legislature.

The Dutch approach to this issue is, however, divided into several camps. Steenhuis and others justify the expansion of discretion on the basis of restoring credibility to the criminal justice system, and condone the 'net-widening' effects of that discretion as a 'corporate' strategy to combat social delinquency. Peters, on the other hand, argues that the criminal policy in the Netherlands has gone too far down the road of expediency, with 'net-widening' in terms of diversion to the welfare state being a negative consequence and a cause for moral concern.

Perhaps a third camp is represented by Louk Hulsman's work in 1981–2. In considering the expansion of diversionary alternatives in the criminal justice system, Hulsman warned against the risk that 'net-widening' would prejudice the satisfactory participation of the victims involved. Hulsman adopted the stance of the restorative model in criticizing what was, in the early 1980s, a plan to increase non-custodial sentencing options for judges, but what has more recently, under the credibility and operational efficiency models, been a shift towards even more informal diversion. In his view, the victim stands to lose participation in his own 'conflict' as well as any compensatory benefits under this deliberate policy of 'net-widening':

within the context of the c.j.s. there is a much greater chance that 'internal interests' of the system itself (the regulations and particular needs of the organisation) determine the way the conflict is dealt with, instead of the interests of those directly involved. Thus the involvement of the c.j.s. creates the danger of undesired consequences for those directly involved in the conflict and which only causes them harm.[61]

In the other jurisdictions, however, the process of 'net-widening' is viewed more as an inevitable hazard arising from the adoption of community alternatives to prosecution and imprisonment. Indeed, in England and the United States, many academics have criticized the failure of community alternatives to reduce the use of imprisonment and other formal sanctions.[62] The potential for 'net-widening' in both Germany and Scotland,

---

[61] L. Hulsman, 'Penal Reform in the Netherlands: Part I—Bringing the Criminal Justice System under Control' (1981) *Howard Journal*, 20: 157. See also L. Hulsman, 'Penal Reform in the Netherlands: Part II—Criteria for Deciding on Alternatives to Imprisonment' (1982) *Howard Journal*, 21: 35–47.

[62] See M. McMahon, 'Net-widening': Vagaries in the Use of a Concept' (1990) *British Journal of Criminology*, 30: 121–149, for a critical analysis of recent literature on 'net-widening' in England and Wales and the United States.

where diversion in the form of cautions, fines, and community rehabilitation schemes has reached unprecedented levels, is high. Indeed, in Scotland, the introduction of the fiscal fine was intended to achieve 'net-widening', being used by fiscals for cases where a prosecution could not be justified on the grounds of triviality, yet an unconditional non-prosecution would not be severe enough. Duff's research produced evidence that fiscals found the fines useful in such borderline cases where the decision not to prosecute was not clear-cut, and noted that over half of his sample of fiscals affirmed that they used the fines in cases where a prosecution may not have been justified under the public interest.[63] Even in England, where diversion is confined to cautioning, the prosecutor and the police are in danger of drawing inappropriate cases into the net, whether consciously or unconsciously.

On a practical level, it is very difficult to find a ready solution to what appears to be an inherent hazard of prosecutorial sentencing. Those interviewed in Holland, Scotland, and Germany all pointed to the positive benefits of diverting cases away from the courts and of allowing a prosecutor to sanction offenders, which, according to them, outweighed the comparatively smaller danger of 'net-widening'. (Indeed, the extent of 'net-widening' is very difficult to prove without a detailed set of statistics and empirical data). McMahon[64] was also of the opinion that those who had strongly criticized 'net-widening' problems in the current literature had a tendency to be unduly pessimistic about it and tended to over-dramatize the extent and effects of the problem.

A system of detailed and close monitoring of prosecutorial decision-making may help to eradicate 'net-widening', but even under such a system, the process would be difficult to detect. Policy-makers have little option in practice but to balance the advantages of prosecutorial sentencing in achieving the aims of the three models of justice described above, with the less obvious dangers of 'net-widening'. Whether the benefits or dangers tip the balance may depend on which of the three models of justice are adopted and emphasized and it is likely that in the interests of saving resources, maintaining the credibility of the system, and rehabilitation, 'net-widening' may be an unavoidable negative consequence of an otherwise acceptable process of reform.

5. NATURAL JUSTICE AND ACCESS TO THE COURTS

Each model of prosecutorial sentencing discretion has its own rationale, and each merits inclusion in the policy and practice of European prosecutors. The diversion options available to prosecutors also have benefits,

[63] P. Duff, op. cit., 493–4.   [64] Ibid.

such as the avoidance of stigma, effective rehabilitation, economy with resources, and enhancing confidence in the system, which the models reflect. However, all three models, inevitably conflict with fundamental civil liberties of the accused. Indeed, it has already been acknowledged that the models are almost antithetical to Packer's due process model, which is, in essence, an extreme libertarian model of justice. Civil libertarians who support Packer's due process model may well be anxious about the very concept of pre-trial diversion which my three models attempt to explain. This section examines the nature of that conflict.

(a) The European Perspective

All the jurisdictions under consideration here are signatories to the European Convention of Human rights and Fundamental Freedoms, which is a good starting point for an analysis of the civil liberties which may be infringed by pre-trial diversion. Article 6 of the Convention reads as follows:

1. In the determination of his civil rights and obligations or of any criminal charge against him, everyone is entitled to a fair and public hearing within a reasonable time by an independent and impartial tribunal established by law . . .
2. Everyone charged with a criminal offence shall be presumed innocent until proved guilty according to law.
3. Everyone charged with a criminal offence has the following minimum rights:
    (a) to be informed promptly, in a language he understands and in detail, of the nature and cause of the accusation against him;
    (b) to have adequate time and facilities for the preparation of his defence;
    (c) to defend himself in person or through legal assistance of his own choosing . . .
    (d) to examine or have examined witnesses against him and to obtain the attendance and examination of witnesses on his behalf under the same conditions as witness against him . . .

Under Article 6, therefore, any system of law requires, *inter alia*, that the defendant be given a chance to be heard in a public tribunal, that the trial be open and impartial, and that he be presumed innocent until proven guilty.[65] Procedures whereby a suspect is adjudicated upon and dealt with, without reference to an open court, appear to conflict with this Article. Indeed, the purpose behind prosecutorial sentencing seems, from the evidence adduced in previous chapters, to be to avoid the hindrances and inconvenience that compliance with this Article involves. So, can the present sentencing practices of European prosecutors be justified with reference to

---

[65] For a further, general, discussion of this Article, see H. Fenwick, *Civil Liberties* (London, 1994), 46–51.

this Article of the European Convention, or are these procedures inherently illegitimate in human rights terms? The sentencing options of prosecutors in each jurisdiction will be briefly discussed in turn.

In Scotland, the procurator fiscal's sentencing options are warnings, fines, and diversion to rehabilitative schemes. It was noted in Chapter 3 that fiscal warnings are treacherous in civil libertarian terms. Whilst sufficient evidence for a prosecution is required before a warning can be issued, there is no requirement that the offender admits his guilt. Therefore, not only is the presumption of innocence lost when the procurator fiscal issues a warning, but a recipient of a warning who wishes to prove his innocence is given no opportunity to do so. Access to a court is denied, because once a warning has been issued the case is closed, and whilst petitioning to a senior prosecutor may or may not satisfy a grievance, the case is unlikely to proceed to court for an open adjudication of the guilt or innocence of the aggrieved. Furthermore, given that there are few written or published criteria upon which fiscals judge the suitability of a case for a warning, the fiscal's office can hardly be considered an 'open' or 'public' tribunal.

Other sentencing options for the fiscal are different in that they require agreement by the defendant. Diversion to rehabilitative schemes or counselling must be voluntary to be effective and such diversion is offered as a condition of non-prosecution. Similarly, fines can be imposed only where the defendant agrees to pay. The refusal of consent to these options, in theory, provides the accused with access to an open tribunal. If a condition of non-prosecution is refused or not met, the case will be prosecuted and heard in court. The same is true of the transaction in the Netherlands. As its name suggests, it is a negotiation between the prosecutor and the defendant and the latter can refuse to consent to its terms. In Germany, the penal order can also be appealed where the recipient refuses its terms and opts instead for a trial. Hence, (except for the fiscal warning) these diversionary sentences by prosecutors are all subject to an appeal mechanism, which leaves the recipient with the choice of a judicial forum. Guilt is not irreversibly presumed because the accused has the right to challenge a prosecutorial decision.

In practice, however, the issue is more problematic. A full trial may not be the automatic consequence of the defendant's refusal to accept the prosecutor's offer; it may be decided that an unconditional waiver of the case is the most suitable course of action. Given that the prosecutor must have decided at an earlier stage that prosecution was inappropriate or not in the public interest, and given that the purpose of these alternative out-of-court settlements is to avoid a full trial, the momentum is likely to be towards dropping the case rather than prosecuting it.

In the Netherlands, some prosecutors preferred to prosecute in these circumstances for credibility reasons, to maintain the authority of, and respect for, their threat to prosecute. However, there is no obligation to do so, and in all the jurisdictions prosecutors retain a discretion to drop a case where their offer of conditions has been refused. In these situations, the due process principles are muddied. A quasi-judicial adjudication of guilt has been made, a punishment offered but abandoned, and although the accused is not formally convicted, he has no access to the courts to challenge the way in which he has been treated or the informal presumption of guilt made against him. A guilty defendant may count himself lucky in this situation; but we are concerned here with matters of principle, and the fact remains that suspects, whether guilty or not, are charged with offences which are 'tried' only in a private forum which operates with, at best, unpublished rules of evidence and procedure.

It is here that the conflict between the models proposed and the principles of due process conflict most starkly. Faced with a second decision of whether to prosecute or not, after an offer of settlement terms has been refused, the prosecutor may find that the models of justice under which he or she works point him towards a negative conclusion. Operational efficiency would demand that the case be dropped in the interests of preserving resources. The restorative model is rather more ambiguous, depending on the outcome of a possible trial. The victim may benefit from a trial, but only if compensation (whether moral or material) is gained which outweighs any trauma and inconvenience caused by the proceedings. On the other hand, from a rehabilitative point of view, the trial may be unduly stigmatizing to the defendant and, particularly if a custodial or financial penalty is imposed following a conviction, may be less effective in modifying his behaviour than doing nothing at all.

The credibility model may appear most strongly in favour of prosecution here. Confidence in the criminal justice system is likely to be boosted where the due process rights of the defendant are upheld. However, confidence may conversely be damaged if the system is seen as prosecuting weak or trivial cases, or where such cases are seen to overload the court system and create delays and backlogs. Whilst this model may not be as persuasive as the others in swaying a decision towards non-prosecution, it should be noted that its operation in the jurisdictions under consideration here has been linked with operational efficiency; that is, maintaining confidence in the least expensive and least time-consuming way possible. Therefore, its conflict with the due process model is no less problematic than that of the other models, and combined with the operational efficiency model, it will cast a strongly negative influence over the decision on whether to prosecute.

Hence the sentencing role of the prosecutor raises important questions of principle regarding the protection of civil liberties. Policy-makers considering an expansion of this facet of the prosecution function undertake a difficult balancing exercise in trying to justify procedures which tend to overlook such liberties. The benefits inherent in the identified models of prosecutorial sentencing are utilitarian in nature, in that they offer advantages for the general public or the criminal justice system as a whole, often at the expense of the individuals directly concerned in the decision-making process. The further prosecutorial sentencing is extended, the more the defendant stands to lose. Germany provides us with a stark example of this. The expansion of the German prosecutor's discretion to allow a suspended prison sentence to be included in a penal order has led to a greater concern for the protection of civil liberties in this area. The procedural safeguards are greater when a suspended prison sentence is involved, and rightly so. However, whatever safeguards over prosecutors' powers exist are minor compared with those which govern court procedure, and policy-makers in Germany have been severely criticized for taking the prosecutor's role too far. It is submitted that where loss of liberty is at stake, pre-trial decision-making, which has the concern of operational efficiency at its heart, can never provide the fairness and openness to which the defendant is entitled.

All this is not to deny any benefits for the accused and the victim, but these have to be weighed against the dangers. The question whether due process rights can or should be ignored in order to satisfy practical demands on the criminal justice system leads to an academic debate that cannot be fully expanded here. Rather, the intention is that the models described above should be used to inform and clarify the debate on the merits and demerits of quasi-judicial prosecutorial discretion. The models set the disadvantages of such discretion alongside the advantages which seemed to be emphasized by the practitioners and academics interviewed. Certainly, if English policy-makers were minded to increase the diversionary powers of the Crown Prosecutor, the dilemma would be no less. Their choice is ultimately between effective management and a principled stand in upholding fundamental liberties. The ethos of both the report of the Royal Commission on Criminal Justice and the Criminal Justice and Public Order Bill 1994 does not bode well for the latter option. A brief excursus into the developing doctrine of natural justice in English law, and its relationship with the existing cautioning procedure, illustrates this moral dilemma.

(b) Natural Justice in England and Wales

The concept of natural justice in the law of England and Wales is nebulous. Academic debate over its meanings and pre-requisites has persisted for some time.[66] Recent case law, however, has sought to clarify the issue. First, it has been established that the principle only applies to decision-making which can be termed 'judicial', as opposed to 'administrative'.[67] This distinction is unlikely to exclude the prosecutor's decision-making from the application of the principle because the definition of 'judicial' decision-making has subsequently been greatly extended.[68] *Glynn* v. *Keele University*[69] provides the most relevant example of these cases, in assessing whether the prosecutor's decision-making is quasi-judicial. That case involved the Vice-Chancellor of Keele University who fined a student and expelled him from the university, failing to give him adequate notice or opportunity to appeal against the decision. In deciding whether the student had been denied natural justice, Pennycuick V-C held that such a decision, involving the issue of a penalty which was 'fundamental to the position of the student in the university'[70] was judicial in nature. The gravity of a decision's consequences for those affected by it seems to be a determining factor in assessing whether the decision was administrative or judicial. Natural justice is more important where those consequences are serious. This principle, or more particularly its converse, may favour progressive prosecution policy-makers in England, countering undue concern for civil liberties where the penalties to be issued by prosecutors are low. One would hope, however, that this principle would preclude English policy-makers from taking the Crown Prosecutor's role as far as that of the German prosecutor, and that it would preclude penalties which involve either actual or potential loss of liberty from the prosecutor's sentencing powers.

Once the prosecutor is found to be subject to the laws of natural justice, it is necessary to define those laws. Rawls has defined natural justice in broad terms, regarding it as 'fairness', which includes the right to fair and open trials, before an impartial judge.[71] Maher and others have refined this definition and identified a number of specific requirements. To summarize, these requirements are that the trial is public (except where this would be impracticable or injurious to the parties),[72] that there be no undue delay in hearing the case, that the defendant be given adequate notice to prepare a response to the charges against him, that there be an opportunity for appeal, that judges be impartial, and that the outcome of the trial is accurate

---

[66] See G. Maher, 'Natural Justice as Fairness' in N. MacCormick and P. Birks, *The Legal Mind: Essays for Tony Honore* (Oxford, 1986), for a full discussion of this debate.

[67] See C. Harlow and R. Rawlings, *Law and Administration* (London, 1984), 25.

[68] See, for example, *Cooper* v. *Wilson* [1937] 2 KB 309; *R* v. *Commission for Racial Equality*, ex parte *Cottrell and Rothon* [1980] 1 WLR 1580.

[69] [1971] 2 All ER 89.

[70] Ibid., 96.   [71] J. Rawls, *A Theory of Justice* (Oxford, 1972).

[72] *Scott* v. *Scott* [1913] AC 417.

in terms of deciding guilt or innocence.[73] Maher and Flick[74] have gone further in adding the requirement for adjudicators to give reasons for their decisions and to be open in their application of the law, so that, in the words of Lord Widgery, 'justice [is] not only done but [is] manifestly seen to be done'.[75]

These requirements apply to the Crown Prosecutor's existing discretion to request a caution from the police. The cautioning system has been widely discussed as a beneficial and generally effective means of dealing with petty crime, especially where young offenders are concerned. Criticisms of the procedure have tended, though, to concentrate on the concept of 'net-widening' and the degree to which discrimination has affected decisions in this field. Civil liberty concerns are also topical, at a time when criminal justice is becoming more 'Europeanized' and therefore more concerned with human rights.[76] More importantly, these natural justice principles will apply to any extension in prosecutors' sentencing powers. For example, if the Royal Commission on Criminal Justice's recommendation that they be allowed to impose fines instead of prosecuting were to become law, legislators would need to consider carefully whether to compromise on these natural justice principles. If not, safeguards need to be securely built into the procedure for imposing such fines.

The cautioning system in England and Wales is similar to the transaction in the Netherlands or the diversion to rehabilitative schemes in Scotland in that the consent of the offender is a prerequisite, and therefore there is no presumption of guilt. Police officers and prosecutors cannot even consider the possibility of a caution unless the offender has admitted the offence and consented to the caution being given. There is also, therefore, a *prima facie* avenue of appeal for an offender who opts for the more traditional form of trial in a courtroom. It is acknowledged that, as in Europe, if the caution is not administered because the police refuse to comply with the prosecutor's request, then it is most unlikely that a prosecution will automatically ensue. The requirement of an admission of guilt, however, acts as a safeguard, preventing an unfair adjudication of guilt and imposition of punishment in these situations where, even though there is no formal conviction, the defendant may have a grievance with the pre-trial procedures.

[73] See M. D. Bayles, *Procedural Justice: Allocating to Individuals* (Dordrecht, 1990) and P. Jackson, *Natural Justice* 2nd Edition (London, 1979).
[74] G. Maher, (1986) op. cit., and G. A. Flick, *Natural Justice: Principles and Practical Application* 2nd Edition (London, 1984).
[75] *R v. Thames Magistrates' Court*, ex parte *Polemis* [1974] 1 WLR 1371, per Lord Widgery, 1375.
[76] See Jung's discussion of this phenomenon in 'Criminal Justice—A European Perspective' [1993] *Crim. LR* 237, 240–2.

What is more problematic in England and Wales, however, is the requirement that adjudicatory procedures and 'judicial' decision-making should be carried out with open application of publicly declared rules, and that reasons be given. The criteria that Crown Prosecutors apply when deciding whether to refer a case to the police for a caution are, to a large extent, contained in their confidential Policy Manuals, and the recent re-draft of the Code for Crown Prosecutors appears to have pushed more of the previously published guidelines into this more secret form of guidance. This may have adverse consequences for natural justice in current decision-making, and any extension of the prosecutor's powers may well prove prejudicial unless the Policy Manuals are made more public. A defendant who is not aware of the criteria applied in the cautioning decision, or who is not given reasons for the particular disposal of his case, cannot make a properly informed decision as to whether to plead guilty, and will have more difficulties in challenging a decision to caution by way of judicial review. The more numerous the prosecutor's diversionary options or influences over sentencing (including plea-bargaining), the greater will be the incentive and pressure to plead guilty at this very early stage. If the accused is to be given a fair opportunity to weigh up the advantages of an early guilty plea, then the prosecutor's adjudicatory criteria should be more open. As Maher has pointed out: '. . . the person against whom the decision has been made has suffered in that his status as a morally autonomous being has been denied and the reason why this is so is that it has not been shown why the particular decision should be proceeded with against *him*'[77] (original emphasis).

Therefore, the Crown Prosecutor's advance along the sentencing road is a hazardous journey, which should not be made without full consideration of the safeguards necessary to protect these natural justice principles. The moral dilemma is again between the essentially (though not entirely) utilitarian aims of pre-trial diversion in what Dworkin has described as the 'cost-efficient' society,[78] and the more moral policy of safeguarding civil liberties, despite their costs to the system. According to Dworkin, it is difficult to find a middle ground and a system which aims to be cost-efficient, but at the same time pays lip service to the safeguard of natural justice, is guilty of 'moral inconsistency'.[79] To some extent he is right; extending the role of the prosecutor as a pre-trial sentencer will inevitably involve making decisions at a hidden stage and in as speedy and informal

[77] G. Maher (1986) op. cit., 115. Street also expressed concern about decision-makers deciding 'citizens' claims according to rules which they conceal from citizens', in *Justice in the Welfare State* (London, 1975).
[78] R. Dworkin, 'Principle, Policy, Procedure' in Tapper, ed., *Crime, Proof and Punishment: Essays in Memory of Sir Rupert Cross* (London, 1981).
[79] Ibid., 203.

a way possible, otherwise nothing is achieved by avoiding the courtroom. These characteristics of prosecutorial sentencing do seem to prejudice natural justice principles by their very nature. However, where the aims of prosecutorial sentencing are less utilitarian and have real benefits that a courtroom trial cannot always offer (under the restorative model for example), it is conceivable that policy-makers could establish a set of procedures which, as far as possible, safeguard due process rights by providing at every stage an exit for the accused which leads directly to court. Furthermore, where the utilitarian aims of prosecutorial sentencing are concerned, safeguards need to be found which suitably match the inherent dangers and the seriousness of their consequences.

6. PUBLIC INTEREST

The diversionary decision-making of the prosecutor in his sentencing role is governed by considerations of public interest. Although the primary consideration requires sufficiency of evidence as a safeguard against 'net-widening', thereafter public interest determines, to a large degree, the extent of diversion practised in any jurisdiction. The concept of public interest is particularly difficult to define satisfactorily; it is perhaps easier to state what it is not, rather than what it is. For example, matters of public interest in all four jurisdictions studied here have very little to do with public opinion; the public interest criteria are paternalistically formulated by policy-makers with minimal reference to the views and needs of members of the public, although widespread public concerns voiced through the media may influence their formulation. Thus, policy-makers, through the criteria, unilaterally impose the minimum standards required to protect citizens from victimization and to ensure at least a minimum level of retribution and deterrence.

Ashworth discusses the concept of the public interest and considers a number of general policy areas which, in his opinion, the prosecutor should consider in deciding whether or not to prosecute. These revolve around the interests of the defendant, the victim, and the public as taxpayers who pay for the criminal process and require efficiency and value for money from it.[80] The three models of justice help to illustrate which considerations may be dominant in any list of public interest criteria, and how widely or narrowly they should be defined. Both the defendant's and the victim's interests are dominant considerations in a narrow definition of public interest under the restorative model, which aims constructively to reform

---

[80] A. Ashworth, 'The "Public Interest" Element in Prosecutions' [1987] *Crim. LR* 595–607.

the circumstances and emotions of both offender and victim after the commission of an offence. However, a wider view of public interest is taken under the credibility and operational efficiency models. Under the former, the interest of the public, both as potential victims and as taxpayers who fund the criminal justice system, and who require value for money and effective performance from the system, will be important considerations. Under the operational efficiency model, again the interests of the public as taxpayers should be positively considered in the decision-making process; it is reasonable for them to expect their taxes to be well-spent, and not wasted in an inefficient system. The use of informal sanctions, under the operational efficiency model, reserves the precious resources of court time and funds for only the most serious or complex cases. Hence the model adopted in any prosecution system may help, to a limited extent, to define the public interest as either a narrow or a wide concept. In terms of collating a substantive, average set of public interest criteria in everyday use, the models may also be useful. Within the wide or narrow concept of public interest, the individual criteria may also be governed or determined by the model of justice operated in a system.

The concept of public interest is, however, very difficult to define as a substantive list of considerations, and the considerations will differ from jurisdiction to jurisdiction. The actual criteria listed in each of the jurisdictions differ slightly in content and more radically in number. The Attorney-General's public interest criteria listed in the Code for Crown Prosecutors in England and Wales covers the main considerations also provided in Scotland, Germany, and the Netherlands. With varying emphasis and wording, prosecutors in four jurisdictions have regard to the age, and mental and physical health of the defendant and the victim, the gravity of the offence, the degree of damage caused, reparation or compensation voluntarily offered by the defendant, and aggravating factors such as the nature of any fiduciary relationship between victim and defendant. An important consideration in prosecutorial sentencing is that of cost and resources and the operational efficiency model of justice has an increasing influence with the pressures of an increasingly criminalized society. These operational efficiency considerations, which involve waiving cases to save time and money, are, however, more openly accepted as a public interest criteria in the Netherlands, Scotland, and Germany than in England and Wales. In the former jurisdictions it is acknowledged that restricting the flow of cases to court to prevent overburdening the criminal justice system with unreasonable delays and backlogs is as much in the interests of the public as any other criterion, since financial savings benefit the public as taxpayers. It is also recognized in the USA that a relatively high degree of disposals at the prosecution stage is necessary to operate a system with limited resources, and this is a deemed valid consideration for prosecutors weighing up the public interest elements of a case. This has received acknowledgement and support from the American judiciary: 'Still other factors are the relative importance of the offense compared with the competing demands of other cases on the time and resources of investigation, prosecution and trial. All of these and numerous other intangible and imponderable factors must be carefully weighed . . . in deciding whether or not to prosecute.'[81] In England and Wales, on the other hand, such considerations are still regarded with a certain distaste and cause jurisprudential anguish at what are seen as unjustifiable reasons for compromising the course of justice, and for informalizing the legal process. Crown Prosecutors were instructed by their old Code to weigh the cost of proceedings against the seriousness of the offence,[82] but even this brief consideration of cost has been removed from the new draft of the Code.

A difference also emerged between the four jurisdictions in the way that the public interest is interpreted and in the emphasis given to it in the course of decision-making. It was discussed in Chapter 2, for example, how English prosecutors operate under a general presumption for prosecution, and that public interest criteria apply negatively to justify non-prosecution, whereas the Dutch prosecutor, since the adoption of the expediency principle disfavouring prosecution, uses the criteria to justify a prosecution counter to that presumption. This positive interpretation is also practised in Scotland[83] and Germany. The presumption in favour of non-prosecution, and the use of the public interest criteria to justify a deviation from that presumption, suggest a more utilitarian definition of public interest itself. For various reasons, and particularly for operational efficiency, it appears that prosecutors in each case use the least possible penalty required to preserve public safety while still maintaining the credibility of the system. Public interest in those jurisdictions which practise the positive interpretation of expediency places the good of the general public, that is their safety, satisfaction, and value for money, above the interests of the individual victim and thus eschews a punitive, retributive application of criminal justice.

Whatever the interpretation of public interest, it is part of the prosecutor's sentencing discretion to have regard to non-legal policy matters, especially where public interest criteria are vaguely stated or even, as in Germany, where they are not formally recorded at all. This part of the prosecutor's sentencing role overlaps with his role as policy-maker, and, as

---

[81] *Pugach* v. *Klein* (1961) (Supreme Court of New York) 193 F. Supp. 630, 635.
[82] Code for Crown Prosecutors (1992), para. 8(i).
[83] See S. Moody and J. Tombs, 'Alternatives to Prosecution: The Public Interest Redefined' [1993] *Crim. LR* 357, who argue that as the procurator fiscal's discretion has increased and the number of disposal options has burgeoned, their interpretation of the public interest criteria has become more expedient.

Greenawalt has also suggested, the influence he exercises in setting the boundaries of his own sentencing jurisdiction through his interpretation of public interest criteria is substantial: 'Many decisions in favour of amelioration require delicate judgements about complex considerations. To some extent, the guides to these judgements may be found within the law as a whole, but often the decision-maker must reach outside the law and make an independent determination of the legitimate purposes of the criminal law and of the proper basis for social interference with individual action.'[84]

The time has come for all four of the jurisdictions under consideration to reassess the public interest criteria so that they properly reflect the justifications for increased diversion described in the three proposed models of justice. With a growing need to save resources, the notion of cautious spending of public funds and the practice of compromising due process ideals in pursuit of this aim should be re-emphasized in the light of the wider interpretation of the public interest under the operational efficiency model. The current lists of public interest criteria give these considerations at best secondary importance, and in England and Wales do not allude to them at all. The growing role of the prosecutor as a manager of resources, in a criminal justice process more often viewed as a commercial institution pursuing business-like strategies,[85] should be explicitly and adequately provided for in the criteria which govern their decision-making.

The credibility and restorative models could also provide insight into the concept of the public interest. For example, the credibility model might require that the protection of the image of the criminal justice system as an efficient and constructively effective body be added to the list of criteria, since this model includes in the interests of the public, 'consumer satisfaction', and public order. Similarly, the restorative model would require the rehabilitation of offenders with behavioral problems, and the underlying goal of restoring conflicts created by criminal behaviour, to be reflected in the public interest considerations. To some extent, attention to the needs of victims is provided for in the public interest criteria of all the jurisdictions, albeit to a limited extent in England (see Chapter 2). However, the underlying personal characteristics of the defendant, which may be causative factors in the commission of the offence in question (such as drug addiction and alcoholism) could be considered in addition to his age and mental or physical health. In general terms, the philosophy behind the concept of public interest in any jurisdiction, and the extent to which that

---

[84] K. Greenawalt, *Conflicts of Law and Morality* (Oxford, 1989), 373. See also generally ch. 8 'Techniques of Amelioration in the Criminal Process: Non-prosecution, Nullification, Sentencing and Pardon'.

[85] See D. Steenhuis, 'Coherence and Coordination in the Administration of Criminal Justice' in J. J. van Dijk et al., eds., (1988) op. cit., for a general exposition of the organization of the criminal justice process under corporate principles.

concept reflects the rationale behind diversionary prosecution decision-making, should be addressed with a view to giving these models of justice explicit recognition in official policy documents.

7 POLICY-MAKING

The final part of the prosecutor's multi-faceted role, which merges with and complements his magisterial role and his influence over sentencing, and is equally reflected in the three models of justice, is that of the policy-maker. Van de Bunt has referred to 'the prosecutor as a government employee . . . expected to engage in mutual consultation in order to develop directives as a framework for their decision-making in individual cases'.[86] In this way, prosecutors in some of the jurisdictions studied become directly involved in formulating the guidelines and rules which limit their own sentencing field and, in some instances, affect the direction of general criminal policy from their own practice. Not only does the prosecutor influence the perimeters of his own sentencing jurisdiction in this way, but he may also influence that of the judge. In Scotland, the Netherlands, and Germany examples were cited of the power of the prosecution service to determine criminal policy.

In the Netherlands, as explained in Chapter 4, individual prosecutors can be highly involved in the process of formulating guidelines and future policy. A high level of consultation preceded the publication of the 1990 policy plan, which prosecutors played a large part in implementing. Indeed, the importance of the Openbaar Ministerie as a body of independent policy-makers was marked in 1990 when they published their own prosecution policy plan for the first time.[87] Similarly, in Germany, examples were cited of prosecutors instituting new laws and procedures directly by their progressive practices at grass roots level, as well as indirectly controlling the level of imprisonment.

Perhaps the clearest example of a prosecutor (albeit a very senior one) with an enormous influence on criminal policy is William Chalmers. Chapter 3 explained how the rush of reform measures in the procurator fiscal service in Scotland was consistently attributed to the enthusiasm, enlightenment, and charisma of the Crown Agent of the day, whose research and experiences inspired the reforms proposed by the Stewart Committee, of which he was a member. However, the Scottish experience also illustrates the other side of the coin, how reluctance on the part of individual prosecutors to become involved in policy-making can have a widespread

---

[86] H. van de Bunt, (1985) op. cit., 399.
[87] The Netherlands, *Strafrecht met beleid: Beleidsplan openbaar ministerie 1990–1995* (The Hague, 1990).

hindering effect on the progress of reform. The marked and abrupt cessation of reform after the retirement of Chalmers serves only to confirm that the reluctance of individual fiscals to recognize their own important function and role in sentencing offences has handicapped changes in the direction that their continental European counterparts have taken.

There is a similar reluctance to accept the role of sentencer on the part of Crown Prosecutors in England, where involvement in policy-making by the Home Office is virtually non-existent[88] apart from the opinions and views offered to relevant committees of enquiry with those of other departments and pressure groups. Links between the Home Office and the Attorney-General's Department have traditionally been tenuous. Until the establishment of the Crown Prosecution Service in 1986, the Attorney-General's Department was a small and less significant department than its distant cousin, the Home Office. Consequently, involving practising prosecutors in policy formulation, and giving them a meaningful role in deciding the future direction of reform of their service, is likely to be difficult since communications and professional partnerships between these two departments are so insubstantial. This is not helped by the firm view of Home Office officials that the practitioner's role is merely to implement the law and carry out dictated policy. Sir Clive Whitmore voiced this debatable proposition during an address to a London conference in 1991: 'It is not for judges, or policemen, or probation officers, or civil servants to use their positions to promote particular social or moral causes. Their job, to use some rather well-worn metaphors, is to make sure that the pitch is level and the goal posts are kept in place—it is not to score goals, win victories or take sides.'[89]

However, recent experience in England and Wales, particularly in the juvenile justice field, has shown that this can easily be refuted in practice. In the late 1980s practitioners have clearly 'scored goals' and won many 'victories' over policy-makers in implementing their own policy, contrary to the aims and spirit of the legislative framework within which they were working at the time. Between 1985 and 1990 a substantial fall in the use of custody for young offenders and young adult offenders, both in absolute numbers and in the proportion of the total sentenced,[90] has been

---

[88] Although the CPS Headquarters does have its own body of policy-makers, collectively working in their Policy Group. This is a relatively influential group, who formulate the response of the Service to various Home Office documents and the evidence that the CPS give to various Committees. The importance of this group in the whole criminal justice policy agenda is reflected by the fact that it is actively involved with the Criminal Justice Consultative Council, set up after the recommendations of the *Woolf Report* (1991, Cm 1456—paras. 10.157–10.180) to promote inter-agency collaboration in the formulation and implementation of criminal justice policy.

[89] Sir Clive Whitmore (1991) op. cit., 4.

[90] The figures for 14- to 17-year-olds fell from 5,900 custody orders (12% of total sentenced) in 1985 to 1,400 (7%). Similarly, for the 17–21 age group, the figures fell from 24,500 (21%) to 11,900 (14%). See A. Rutherford, (1992) op. cit., at 15, Table 3.

attributed mainly to the impact of practitioners' working ideologies and the use of their discretion. Social workers and probation officers, with their commitment to the developmental approach to juvenile offending and their belief in allowing juveniles the time and opportunity to grow out of their offending phase, formed the driving force for a change in national policy by consistently campaigning for the use of alternative community sanctions in place of custody. In creating a united front (aided by the establishment, in 1986, of the practitioners' pressure group, the Association for Juvenile Justice) probation officers and social workers were able to influence the sentencing practice of magistrates and instill an anti-custody ethos at the foundation of the juvenile justice system. Andrew Rutherford summed the process up thus: 'The primary thrust for change has been made by social workers working within the statutory and voluntary agencies. In a very real sense, basic grade workers have dictated both the pace and direction of reform ... without doubt, practitioners have made the running, generated the enthusiasm and sustained the change process.'[91] These developments have shown how powerful practitioners' influence can be on the formulation of national policy, and the German experience has also proved how the prosecutor, as well as probation officers and social workers, can be influential to this extent in directing national policy from ground level.

It seems inconsistent to develop a prosecutorial role with a high level of discretion in prosecution and sentencing decisions, but with a subordinate position in policy-making. With this lack of involvement, as well as the lack of self-reflection by the prosecutor on his own role in the criminal justice system, the sentencing role of the Crown Prosecutor in England and Wales is unlikely to proceed much further. It is not suggested here that the English prosecutor should champion social and moral issues within the course of their decision-making, nor should they become in any way politically involved with the Home Office or the public, in the way that local (though not federal) American prosecutors might do, for example. The latter are often voted into and out of office in some States, and may have more careful regard to public feeling about certain sensitive political issues.[92] The establishment of the Criminal Justice Consultative Council in

---

[91] A. Rutherford, 'The Mood and Temper of Penal Policy: Curious Happenings in England during the 1980s', paper given at a conference organised by the Coornhertliga on Penal Climate and Prison Systems in a Caring Society, University of Utrecht, 3 June 1988. See also A. Rutherford, (1992) op. cit., ch. 1 and R. Allen, 'Out of Jail: The Reduction in the Use of Penal Custody for Male Juveniles 1981–8' (1991) *Howard Journal* 30: 30–52, for a general commentary on these developments in juvenile justice in England and Wales during the 1980s.

[92] The highest ranking Federal Prosecutor is a political appointee but not elected, whereas at county level individual prosecuting attorneys are expected to run for office. See G. F. Cole, (1973) op. cit., 150–3, for an analysis of the political role of the prosecuting attorney in the USA.

England and Wales, with members drawn from the senior levels of all of the branches of the criminal justice process, and its local Area Committees, should improve the extent to which practitioners are involved in policy-making and communication with other branches of the criminal process. This may encourage self-reflection and consideration of change amongst the CPS as a whole, as well as by individual prosecutors. The Howard League has also recently recommended the establishment of a Criminal Justice Institute which would serve as a forum in which criminal justice practitioners could collaborate across the system and disseminate and discuss policy ideas, research findings, international developments in their fields, and the like.[93] The experience in Germany, Holland, and Scotland has shown that, where practitioners are involved in the criminal justice debate, real progress can be achieved at a policy level. The German experience and the widespread influence of the Utrecht School in the Netherlands are both examples of this phenomenon. Prosecutors can successfully be integrated into the policy-making process and often become more informed, enlightened and contented decision-makers as a result.

On the other hand, the CPS is experiencing problems of staff shortages, due in part to financial restrictions, but which could largely be solved by a policy to attract high-calibre, enthusiastic lawyers to the service. Until the prosecutor's discretion is enhanced to a sufficient degree to make the prosecutor's role more attractive and better respected within the criminal justice system, this situation is unlikely to change. A service with prosecutors who exercise their own initiative and discretion in a sentencing jurisdiction, with importance tantamount to that of a judge in minor cases, is more likely to attract lawyers with a positive enthusiasm for the job. Indeed, Greenawalt suggested the same in respect of American prosecutors:

Not only is the prosecutor less constrained by legal standards than judges who apply the law, he is also politically more responsible, subject to dismissal or being voted out of office. Moreover, like most administrative officials, prosecutors will generally do a better job and better people will be attracted to the job of prosecutor, if they conceive of their role as involving some scope for individual judgement about desirable policy rather than transmitting as accurately as possible the uncertain sentiments of the legislature or the community.[94]

8. Conclusion

The discussion of each national prosecution system in the preceding chapters has produced the central, underlying theme of this analysis; that the

---

[93] Howard League, *The Dynamics of Justice* (London, 1993), 22–3.
[94] K. Greenawalt, (1989) op. cit., 353.

public prosecutor is inherently involved in the process of sentencing defendants in the criminal justice system. This involvement may simply take the form of an indirect influence over judicial sentencing through pre-trial decision-making. The mainland European systems considered here have shown how the prosecutor's involvement in sentencing can be more proactive, actually penalizing offenders at this early stage. Leading on from that conclusion, this chapter has illustrated the central position of the prosecutor's sentencing role in both determining and implementing criminal justice policy across the three mainland European jurisdictions considered.

There followed cross-national comparisons on the degrees to which this sentencing role has been acknowledged in each jurisdiction as a key element in criminal justice policy. From the substantive question of how the prosecutor's sentencing role is represented in the procedures and practices of practitioners in the individual systems, the analysis turned, in the previous chapter, to a consideration of the theoretical basis upon which this role can be explained and justified. Three models of justice have emerged, the operational efficiency model, the restorative model, and the credibility model, which offer alternative sets of principles as reference points for consideration of this informal process of administrative pre-trial sentencing. Whilst these models may, like Packer's dichotomy of models, explain and justify criminal justice principles in a particular system as a whole, their particular significance lies in illustrating the rationale for elevating the prosecutor to the role of sentencer. In this chapter, this theoretical justification for prosecutorial sentencing has been tested by considering a number of general anxieties caused by this pre-trial sentencing power. The models have been used to illustrate new ways of addressing such problems, based on the experience of policy-makers in the European jurisdictions which formed the basis of this study. The models provide a vantage point from which to view the policy choices open to criminal justice practitioners in implementing the prosecutor's sentencing role with minimum damage to fundamental principles of due process, natural justice, and judicial independence.

The problems expounded above are inherent in prosecutorial sentencing in any system. They are not insignificant, especially when considering potential reform for the English Crown Prosecutor along this path. Reflection upon the overuse of the operational efficiency model as a justification for increased informal disposal at an early stage exposes the dangers of 'net-widening' and of lack of prosecutorial accountability, for example, and the models serve, to some extent, to warn of such dangers as well as to pinpoint directions for successful reform. These problems, together with the constitutional and civil liberties issues arising under the credibility and the restorative models, are equally present in the European jurisdictions considered as well as the American system, to which brief reference has been made in this chapter. However, the illustration of the applicability of the models in the USA serve to dispel the myth that prosecutorial sentencing is inappropriate, perhaps even unconstitutional, in an adversarial system such as that of England and Wales.

Finally, the interaction of the models amongst themselves in prosecution policy across Europe has been explored and enables comparisons within jurisdictions as well as between them. The tensions arising in the, sometimes conflicting, aims of the models in any one jurisdiction are as interesting as the differing policies in the cross-national comparison. In each jurisdiction there are a number of schools of thought, as well as different social, economic, and crime problems, which require the implementation of the principles of one particular model of prosecutorial justice, often complementing the operation of other models and providing a coherent objective for policy, but at other times producing contrasting, even incoherent aims for criminal justice.

In drawing together the threads of both the European experience of pre-trial sentencing and this theoretical analysis of it, cross-national comparisons can be made to assess how far each jurisdiction has acknowledged and developed the prosecutor's sentencing role within the structure of these three models. Chapter 8 will consider the attitudes of policy-makers in each system towards the concept of prosecutorial sentencing and the efforts made to utilize this centrally important and flexible mechanism for disposing of minor criminal cases at an early stage.

8
Conclusion: Recognition and Reform of the Prosecutor's Sentencing Role

THE prosecutor's direct and indirect roles in the sentencing process are undoubtedly expanding in each of the three mainland European jurisdictions studied. However, the pace and direction in which these roles are developing in each country varies quite considerably, and is in proportion with the acknowledgement given to this role of the prosecutor. The degree to which the prosecutor's sentencing role has progressed requires comparison with each of those other jurisdictions, as well as with England and Wales. The rate at which these changes are occurring depends on the momentum for reform within each prosecution service and on the willingness of other branches of each criminal justice system to respond to change. A highway analogy can usefully be employed to illustrate the speed and direction of developments in these jurisdictions.

If the prosecution system of each country is viewed in terms of a car setting off on a journey, the route taken by the car in Scotland, the Netherlands, Germany, and England and Wales differs substantially, with some cars travelling further distances, while others have not got very far. None of them, however, has yet determined its destination, since the prosecutors' sentencing roles are limited only by vague standards of constitutionality, and by the extent to which each prosecution system has clearly determined its objective. On this journey, any number of wrong turnings or U-turns may be made before that final destination is identified, and before criminal justice policy allows for that destination to be reached.

In Scotland, the procurator fiscal system set off on a slow but steady journey in the direction of explicit prosecutorial sentencing. Under the inspiration of William Chalmers, the Crown Agent in Scotland during the early 1980s, fiscals acquired the power to fine defendants without reference to the court and the Stewart Committee re-emphasized the importance of prosecutors' warnings as a diversionary tactic to dispose of cases without a full prosecution. However, when Chalmers retired in 1986 and when the legislation proposed by the Stewart Committee was fully implemented by 1987, the procurator fiscal system reached a crossroad and the direction in which to proceed was far from clear. The Scottish prosecution system still stands at that crossroad and the question of whether it will continue in the same direction, with further reform to increase the prosecutor's sentencing influence, or whether it will change direction or even turn back, remains to be answered, and to some extent depends on the current Crown Agent, Duncan Lowe, and his enthusiasm for reform. The future progress of the system also depends on the attitudes of individual prosecutors working in the system, and the present abrupt halt has been caused in part by their reluctance to accept any sentencing role at all, let alone a wider one. Their unwillingness to relinquish the traditional idea of a fully neutral prosecutor with no interest in the sentencing process, and their somewhat bureaucratic approach to their work, will block further reform in this area and unless the fiscals develop a working philosophy which recognizes the prosecutor as an active and appropriate sentencer, changes requiring a prosecutor to recommend a sentence to a court, or even a prosecution right of appeal against unduly lenient sentences, will be difficult to implement.

Notwithstanding this reluctance, one indication of the road which the fiscal service might take has come from the government, rather than from the service itself. Legislation is planned which would increase the procurator fiscal's sentencing role and would accelerate his journey in the same direction as was taken in the 1980s. The recent White Paper, *Firm and Fair*,[1] proposes, *inter alia*, to extend the scope of fiscal fines to a wider range of offences, thus widening the sentencing jurisdiction of the fiscal, with the specific purpose of saving resources and making more productive use of court time in more serious cases. It is surprising to see the inspiration for further reform along mainland European lines coming from government circles, rather than from the ground level. However, the heavy influence of the operational efficiency model in this White Paper explains why these reforms of the public prosecution system in Scotland merit such priority in the legislative agenda.

The Dutch prosecutor started his journey much earlier than the procurator fiscal in Scotland. In the 1970s, when the policy of expediency was emphasized and the public interest criteria were re-interpreted as obstacles to prosecution rather than justifications for non-prosecution, the Dutch prosecutor embarked on a high-speed journey down the pre-trial sentencing road, and has continued this path in the fast lane of the motorway throughout the 1980s and the early 1990s. This expedient policy was reconfirmed in the Ministry of Justice policy plan of 1985 and prosecutors gained fuel in the form of increased powers to offer transactions to more serious offenders in 1983 under the Property Sanctions Act, in addition to

[1] (1994) Cm 2600, (Edinburgh: HMSO).

their existing powers to drop cases unconditionally, to warn suspects, and to arrange reparation. By 1990, although the Ministry of Justice appeared to be reversing its tolerant policy of the 1980s regarding petty crime, the prosecutor's high-speed journey continued in the same direction, since the new policy of expanding intervention by criminal justice authorities in relation to prevalent petty offences has revolved around the increased use by prosecutors of their informal sentencing powers, rather than putting the burden on judges to use their sentencing powers in court. Hence the prosecutor in the Netherlands emerged as the key player in the implementation of the new and more severe policy laid down by the Ministry of Justice. Although criminal policy in Holland has, in the opinion of some commentators, made a U-turn, the sentencing role of prosecutors has most certainly not; in fact that sentencing role is becoming more important with each step in policy development.

The Dutch prosecutor has been recognized as a sentencer for many years, as witness the prosecutors' title of 'standing magistracy' as compared with the 'sitting magistracy' which is the term given to the judiciary. It has been argued here that the rapid developments in the prosecutor's sentencing role and this long-standing recognition of the prosecutor's impact on the sentencing process are not unconnected. Indeed, it is likely that the latter phenomenon precipitated the former.

The German prosecutor's journey has been almost as rapid and just as steady. Setting off along an A-road, progress in Germany has been continuous and steady, and is rapidly catching up with the Dutch prosecutor. Since the 1970s, a consistent trend has emerged towards the increase of the prosecutor's sentencing powers. This trend began in 1975 with the inclusion of section 153a in the Code for Criminal Procedure which allowed prosecutors to attach sentencing conditions to the waiver of a case, such as the payment of a fine or of a sum to the victim in compensation for damaged caused by the criminal offence. The trend has continued in practice with the increasing use of penal orders, a form of pre-trial sentencing in the opinion of the majority, and has gathered much momentum and pace with the introduction of a new penalty, the suspended prison sentence, into the penal order procedure. The recent reunification of West Germany with the Eastern states has amplified the importance of the prosecutor, since a greater volume of crime has had to be dealt with by a decreasing number of criminal justice professionals as Western prosecutors, judges, and lawyers have been seconded to Eastern cities to take over the administration of justice. The prosecutor has had to increase the effectiveness of the pre-trial sifting stage by diverting more offenders away from the courts to prevent serious delays and has had to make greater use of his sentencing powers to divert offenders in a constructive way. These sentencing powers have increased in strength in order to maximize the potential for diversion. Reforms in Germany have reached the stage where many regard the prosecutor's sentencing powers as excessive and inappropriate. Further, the growing emphasis on the idea of restorative justice in the working philosophy of many prosecutors has highlighted the use of constructive, diversionary pre-trial measures so that trials and the higher judicial sentences can be avoided wherever possible. This gives practical effect to the general disillusionment with imprisonment in Germany that has been voiced in academic circles since the early 1980s. Hence, reparation schemes and compensation orders for victims have become prime concerns in prosecutorial sentencing in Germany over the last few years.

However, whilst the direction of German prosecutorial reform has been consistent and the road clear and straight, the speed of reform was originally hampered by the continued application of the legality principle in pre-trial decision-making. This principle is gradually being eroded, removing restraint on the speed of the German prosecutor's journey; the new powers mentioned above illustrate how the legality principle is less of an impediment to change than it might once have been. Nevertheless, its retention in theory, as an important constitutional safeguard against state interference in the administration of justice, has acted like a tachometer, monitoring the momentum of change and setting limits on the constitutionally acceptable extent of prosecutorial sentencing. The developments mentioned above have all taken their toll on the operation of the principle in practice and as further reforms are suggested and implemented, that continuing erosion will enable the prosecutor's speed to accelerate. Nevertheless, all commentators in Germany were confident that the principle will not disappear altogether, and therefore the German prosecutor is likely to continue on the A-road rather than joining the Dutch prosecutor in a high-speed motorway chase.

Finally, in England, where the Crown Prosecution Service was established in 1986, the prosecutor has only just begun to make a hesitant start on his own journey towards sentencing. Some progress has already been made; the introduction of the appeal against unduly lenient sentences in 1988 was the first step in recognizing the prosecutor's interest in the sentencing process. In addition, under the Attorney-General's public interest criteria listed in the Code for Crown Prosecutors, cases can be dropped unconditionally according to the discretion of the prosecutor. However, further sentencing powers, such as attaching conditions to those waivers, recommending a sentence at court, and diverting cases to rehabilitation schemes have not yet emerged, although suggestions for some movement in that direction have been made by the Royal Commission on Criminal Justice. Indeed, the publication of the Royal Commission's report in the summer of 1993 may have provided the requisite navigational assistance to enable the Crown Prosecution Service to embark upon a more purposeful journey of reform. They recommended that English Crown Prosecutors be given powers to fine defendants without reference to the court (along the lines of the Scottish fiscal fine system), and also recommended an extension of the 'caution plus' system, although this would not involve the prosecutor directly. Policy in England and Wales could, with this positive assistance from the Royal Commission, reflect the organized and directed process of reform that has occurred in the Netherlands, for example. However, it can hardly be said that the Royal Commissions's report was a well thought out and considered suggestion of development for the CPS (by contrast to the highly organized policy plans produced by the Dutch Ministry of Justice). There was little discussion of the general role of the prosecutor in the criminal justice system; their recommendations were less forward-looking. The proposed introduction of prosecutor fines was justified on the basis that it would save resources and that it appeared to work well in Scotland. It was not part of a wider agenda to offer the prosecutor a more active, potent role in the ciminal justice process. Rather they suggested piecemeal changes to the prosecution system in England and Wales, not unlike the changes which have occurred over the six years since the establishment of the CPS, without a coherent policy objective.

There has been a long-standing reluctance on the part of English policy-makers and practitioners to accept that the prosecutor may usefully be engaged in the sentencing process, as reflected in the judicial comments quoted in Chapter 2. However, these views are not unanimous and there is a move amongst some practitioners to recognize the potential of the prosecutor's sentencing role and to acknowledge that their existing powers and duties at the pre-trial stage do have an inherent influence on sentencing at trial: 'The strong belief in the English legal system that the prosecutor should not be concerned with sentence is an utterly simplistic view because the way that the prosecution process deals with the defendant inevitably postulates a view about sentence, right down to the policeman who does not report the offence because he knows it will be a £2 fine. Provided it is done within a proper ambit, the prosecutor has scope for going for a charge that may carry a lesser penalty, or asking for summary trial rather than trial on indictment.'[2] This view has been shared by academics. For example, Ashworth has acknowledged that: '. . . the prosecutor's choice of charge may itself affect sentence; prosecutors' representations on mode of trial are closely linked with magistrates' decisions to commit cases for trial; and the enormous increase in committals for trial in the 1980s has been reflected by a steep rise in the remand population in prison.'[3] However, the reluctance of policy-makers in the Home Office or in Parliament similarly

[2] A senior official with the Crown Prosecution Service quoted in A Rutherford, *Criminal Justice and the Pursuit of Decency*, (Oxford, 1993), 147.
[3] A. Ashworth, *Sentencing and Criminal Justice* (London, 1992), 21.

to acknowledge this part of the prosecutor's role may account for the fact that it remains relatively indirect and implicit, except for the only explicit influence over sentencing, the power to appeal against unduly lenient sentences under s. 36 Criminal Justice Act 1988. It may be that the utility of a diversionary sentencing role for the prosecutor is now being recognized, on whichever model of justice this is based, and the proposals of the Royal Commission on Criminal Justice regarding 'caution plus', albeit leaving the primary responsibility with the police, were a step in this direction.

The net result of the progress of reform in Europe, at whatever speed or direction, has been a general widening of the role of the prosecutor in the sentencing field, with the prosecutor in Scotland, the Netherlands, and Germany wielding varying degrees of influence over the process of sentencing both indirectly, in pre-determining judicial sentences passed at court, and directly in exercising their own sentencing powers. The net result of this study is that, whether policy-makers are reluctant to acknowledge it or not, the prosecutor does have a function to perform in the sentencing process which may be of practical use to policy-makers who manage the criminal justice process. It is, therefore, not particularly useful to analyse the sentencing process as a solely judicial function, performed in the courtroom by magistrates or judges. The European jurisdictions considered here show that the prosecutor can, and often does, take over a substantial part of that sentencing function and performs it at the pre-trial stage. Sentencing, in other words, is not merely for judges. The prosecutor, in common with other practitioners in the criminal justice system who have decision-making power which affects the ultimate penalty given to an offender, does perform a sentencing function. This, then, includes the police, who in England and Wales as well as in Scotland, the Netherlands, and Germany, are entitled to issue fixed penalty tickets for minor traffic offences, and who in England and Wales carry the responsibility for cautioning and the initial responsibility for charging a suspect. Similarly, the parole board, who have the power to reduce the prison sentence served by an offender, have an impact on the sentencing process. This study concerns the public prosecutor; a similar study, however, could also be conducted on the sentencing role of any of these other branches of the criminal justice process.

This study sought a rationale for this increased importance of the prosecutor and in considering the central position of the prosecutor in the criminal justice system, three models of justice emerged from the interviews with practitioners and academics as they attempted to explain why the prosecutor, rather than any other branch of the system, had risen to such importance.

First, it has been shown that Herbert Packer's two models of justice do not adequately explain recent developments. Packer's due process model simply does not fit into the theoretical consideration of pre-trial sentencing;

this is in fact exactly the sort of criminal justice activity that the due process model seeks to avoid and is the antithesis of that model, since the sentencing process takes place at such an early stage of the system, in an atmosphere which is informal compared to that of a court trial. The three models which rationalize prosecutorial sentencing are founded on reasons for avoiding the trial paraphernalia altogether. If one tries to justify widespread prosecutorial disposals under the due process model, the problems of accountability of prosecutors, 'net-widening', and constitutionality raise insurmountable barriers to change in this direction (see below).

Nevertheless, the justification for prosecutorial sentencing does not fit wholly within Packer's crime control model either, although Packer's second model to some extent falls within the three models of justice suggested here. The operational efficiency model, the restorative model, and the credibility model go further in justifying this level of sentencing at an early stage in criminal procedure. The operational efficiency model is based upon considerations of saving resources, a necessary consideration in any criminal justice system where resources rarely keep up with the steep rises in crime levels. This model shows how prosecutors have been utilized to dispose of many cases at a very early stage to prevent a drain on court time and manpower and to balance the increasing burden of crime control with the need to operate an efficient, well ordered, and relatively inexpensive criminal justice system. The rationale here is simply to make economies wherever possible in the administration of justice without compromising the aims of justice too far, and the prosecutor is in the flexible position to make such economies and to soak up any sudden pressures on the system without knock-on effects for other parts of the system.

The restorative model is founded upon the need to deal with offenders and victims in a constructive way, instead of using certain traditional criminal sanctions such as fines and imprisonment which have been termed the 'blunt instruments of the criminal law' because of their punitive and often destructive nature. The core of this model is to resolve the conflict between victim and offender in a way that satisfies both parties, and to prevent, as far as possible, the future commission of criminal offences by removing the problems underlying the original offence, in as efficient a way as possible to uphold the aims of the operational efficiency model. Hence the prosecutor in mainland European jurisdictions is able to divert offenders to pre-trial rehabilitation, reparation, and mediation schemes, so that the cost of a full trial is avoided, and to avoid destructive and stigmatizing effects of a court appearance on either party.

Finally, the credibility model is aimed at maximizing crime control to maintain the confidence of the public in the effectiveness of the criminal justice system, while also upholding the aims of the operational efficiency model. Prosecutors are given wider powers to fine, caution, or order compensation payments so that sanctions are seen to be imposed on offenders, again with reduced recourse to the courts.

In all the European jurisdictions studied attempts have been made to maximize the accountability of the prosecutor, who has effectively become a lower court of justice. All diversionary options under the restorative model, and most sanctions under the credibility model, are voluntary on the part of the offender and the interests of natural justice are preserved as far as possible by allowing the defendant to refuse to accept a sanction and to proceed to the open forum of the courtroom. Further, efforts are made to control the prosecutors' activities and the often powerful discretion they now have. These controls may take the form of guidelines (whether advisory or mandatory), legislative limits (such as the limit of the amount of a fiscal fine in Scotland), or the monitoring of their decisions by checking files and compiling statistics.

The problem of 'net-widening', however, is an ever-present danger in decision-making at this level. Indeed, the credibility model inevitably involves 'net-widening' in that defendants are dealt with more severely by prosecutors who would previously have dropped their cases unconditionally. In fact, in the Netherlands some commentators have suggested that 'net-widening' is a deliberate policy of the Ministry of Justice, implemented by prosecutors. Without an adequate degree of accountability for prosecutors' decisions under the restorative model, 'net-widening' could be even more of a danger. It is very difficult for policy-makers to detect the extent or even the existence of 'net-widening', especially where the prosecutor is empowered under his policy-making role to set the limits on his own sentencing jurisdiction and to interpret the public interest criteria under which he is working, when the problem could increase without detection. 'Net-widening' may be tolerable under a system of low-key sentencing as the price to be paid for other, more positive benefits. Nevertheless it is a problem, and it is not suggested here that the European systems of prosecution studied are operating without any defects.

Indeed, whether the journey of each jurisdiction on the prosecutorial sentencing road constitutes positive progress or not depends on which of Packer's crime control and due process models one prefers. If one takes the crime control approach and adheres to arguments which rationalize prosecutorial sentencing on the basis of the three models proposed in Chapter 6, then this journey might be described as forward-moving. The sentencing powers of the prosecutor offer positive, principally utilitarian, benefits for the criminal justice system, as well as some benefits for the defendant and the victim. If, on the other hand, one takes the due process side, these journeys can be seen as dangerous steps into uncharted territory, at the increasing expense of civil liberties.

The extent to which prosecutorial sentencing conflicts with the accused's due process rights is discussed in Chapter 7. The inherent presumption of guilt and the removal of the sentencing process to a hidden and less accountable arena are clear dangers inherent in this policy trend. The justifications for this trend, put forward in the three models, should not obfuscate these dangers or attempt to justify a breach of such fundamental rights. The choice for policy-makers is a balancing exercise between the degree of power vested in the prosecutor and the severity of the sanctions they are empowered to impose on the one hand, and the ethical considerations of the natural justice rights of the defendant on the other. Criminal justice systems which use the expediency principle, yet at the same time wish to safeguard the due process rights of the defendant, may well be self-contradictory. The models of justice proposed in this study clarify the relevant issues, to facilitate consideration of whether there is a compromise which resolves this dilemma.

Ultimately, the principles underlying the models and the benefits (utilitarian or not) of implementing them must be set against the dangers involved. It might well be that the benefits of, say, the restorative model, implemented in respect of minor cases, can exceed the prejudice caused by the loss of natural justice rights such as access to a court. On the other hand, where the penalties become more severe, such as the suspended sentence in Germany or transactions in the Netherlands with fines amounting to millions of guilders, the balance is not so easy to strike. Policy-makers in these cases need to be more careful in securing safeguards. There is evidence of this in the German prosecution system, where the legislation which provided for the issue of suspended sentences in a penal order required that the defendant be legally represented and able to demand a hearing before a judge to negotiate the terms of the order. Here at least, attempts were made to make the compromise between informal and formal justice as fair as possible. It appears that, providing the prosecutor's powers are kept within reasonable limits and are only applied to a range of relatively minor offences, a compromise can be struck. The demarcation between what is reasonable and what is not, however, is difficult to define. It is suggested here that any power invested in the prosecutor which may result in a loss of liberty crosses the boundary of unreasonableness. However, providing the prosecutor is sufficiently accountable and providing that appeal procedures are secure, some forms of diversion and prosecutorial fines or compensation orders may be reasonable, especially where their use can be justified according to the principles outlined in the models of justice.

This study has not necessarily sought to suggest wide-ranging reforms for the English prosecution system on the basis of the European experience. None of the European systems can be directly transplanted into the English system, and it is likely that, as the recognition of the prosecutor's sentencing role increases and as views such as that of a senior civil servant working for the CPS (quoted above) become more widespread, the English prosecutor's sentencing influence will increase. This direction of change could include diversionary options, providing they can be justified on the grounds of reasonableness, as discussed above. However, a more active role of the prosecutor at trial, with the power/duty to recommend sentences as a form of assistance to, as well as influence over, judicial sentencing is advocated here. This appears to have been achieved relatively smoothly in Scotland (after the vision of William Chalmers that the fiscal service should be more explicit about its sentencing influence) and similarly in the Netherlands and Germany.

The purpose of this study has been rather to reflect on the operation of prosecution systems and to understand the rationale behind the prosecutor's sentencing function in several jurisdictions. As mentioned above, the development of the prosecutor's sentencing influence in England and Wales is more likely to come from an evolution in attitudes towards his or her function than from any technical overhaul of criminal justice procedures; the process of change in this area in Europe is rather more attitudinal than technical or legal. If there is a fundamental shift in the attitudes of policy-makers towards each branch of the process, as well as in the attitudes of each branch towards each other and towards the politics of criminal justice policy, then it is possible that the English Crown Prosecutor might join the league table of his European counterparts in terms of his sentencing role. Moreover, both the European and the American experience considered here have shown that it is possible to fit the notion of the prosecutor as a sentencer into the constitutional, legal, and political context of the English criminal justice process.

Bibliography

Allen, M. J., (1989) 'The Sentencing of Offenders', *Independent*, 17 Oct. 1989.

Allen, R., (1991) 'Out of Jail: The Reduction in the Use of Penal Custody for Male Juveniles 1981–88', *Howard Journal*, 30: 30–52.

Alper, B. S. and Nichols, L. T., (1982) *Beyond the Courtroom: Programs in Community Justice and Conflict Resolution*, Massachusetts: Lexington Books.

Alschuler, A. W., (1991) 'The Failure of Sentencing Guidelines: A Plea for less Aggregation', *University of Chicago Law Review*, 58: 901–951.

American Bar Association, (1970) *Standards Relating to the Prosecution Function and the Defense Function*, Chicago: American Bar Association.

Andel, H. van, (1989) 'Crime Prevention that works: The Care of Public Transport in the Netherlands', *British Journal of Criminology*, 29: 47–56.

Anon, 'Pretrial Diversion from the Criminal Process' (1974) *Yale Law Journal*, 83: 827–854.

Ashworth, A., (1979) 'Prosecution and Procedure in Criminal Justice' [1979] *Criminal Law Review*, 480–492.

—— (1984) 'Prosecution, Police and the Public—A Guide to Good Gatekeeping?', *Howard Journal*, 23: 72–85.

—— (1985) 'From Policing to Prosecutions' [1985] *Criminal Law Review*, 1–3.

—— (1987) 'The "Public Interest" Element in Prosecutions' [1987] *Criminal Law Review*, 595–607.

—— (1992) *Sentencing and Criminal Justice*, London: Weidenfeld and Nicolson.

—— (1993) 'The Royal Commission on Criminal Justice: (3) Plea, Venue and Discontinuance' [1993] *Criminal Law Review*, 830–840.

—— (1994) *The Criminal Process: An Evaluative Study*, Oxford: Oxford University Press.

—— and Fionda, J., (1994) 'Prosecution, Accountability and the Public Interest: the New CPS Code' [1994] *Criminal Law Review*, 894–903.

Backett, S., McNeill, S., and Yellowlees, A., (1988) *Imprisonment Today: Current Issues in the Prison Debate*, Basingstoke: Macmillan.

Baker and Delong, (1934) 'The Prosecuting Attorney', *Journal of Criminal Law*, 24: 1025–1065.

Baldwin, J. and McConville, M., (1977) *Negotiated Justice: Pressures to Plead Guilty*, Oxford: Martin Robertson.

Bayles, M. D., (1990) *Procedural Justice: Allocating to Individuals*, Dordrecht: Kluwer.

Beerling, H. W. R., (1976) 'An Outline of Dutch Criminal Procedure', *Anglo-American Law Review*, 5: 50–63.

Bennett, M., (1993) Unpublished Speech to the Metropolitan Police Federation, delivered 27 Oct. 1993.

Bennion, F., (1986) 'The New Prosecution Arrangements: (1) The Crown Prosecution Service' [1986] *Criminal Law Review*, 3–15.

Blankenburg, E., Sessar, K. and Steffan, W., (1978) *Die Staatsanwaltschaft im Prozess strafrechtlicher Sozialkontrolle*, Berlin: Duncker und Humblot. (Summary translated into English).
—— and Treiber, H., (1985) *The Establishment of the Public Prosecutor's Office in Germany*, Amsterdam: Free University Press.
Bohlander, M., (1994) 'Expediency over Due Process', *Legal Action*, March 1994, 9.
Bottomley, A. K., (1986) 'Blue-prints for Criminal Justice: Reflections on a Policy Plan for the Netherlands', *Howard Journal*, 25: 199–215.
—— and Pease, K., (1986) *Crime and Punishment: Interpreting the Data*, Milton Keynes: Open University Press.
Braithwaite, J., (1989) *Crime, Shame and Reintegration*, Cambridge: Cambridge University Press.
—— 'Shame and Modernity' (1993) *British Journal of Criminology*, 33: 1–18.
—— and Pettit, P., (1992) *Not Just Deserts: A Republican Theory of Criminal Justice*, Oxford: Oxford University Press.
Brantingham, P. L. and Blomberg, T. G., (1979) *The Courts and Diversion: Policy and Operations Studies*, London: Sage Publications.
Brazier, R., (1991) *Constitutional Reform: Re-Shaping the British Political System*, Oxford: Oxford University Press.
Breitel, C. D., (1960) 'Controls in Criminal Law Enforcement', *University of Chicago Law Review*, 27: 427–435.
Brown, C., (1989) '"Failure" of CPS blamed on staff shortages', *Independent*, 12 May 1989.
Bunt, H. van de, (1985) *Officieren van Justitie—verslag van een participerend observatieonderzoek*, Zwolle: Tjeenk Willink.
Burrows, John, (1986) 'Prosecution Decisions in respect of repeat offenders', *Home Office Research Bulletin*, London: HMSO, 20: 52–56.
Campbell, I. G., (1985) 'The Role of the Crown Prosecutor on Sentence', *Criminal Law Journal*, 9: 202–231.
Carter, N., (1990) 'Crown Prosecutors make convenient scapegoats', *Independent*, 2 Mar. 1990.
Cates, A. M., (1962) 'Can We Ignore Laws?—Discretion not to Prosecute', *Alabama Law Review*, 14: 1–10.
Cavadino, M. and Dignan, J., (1992) *The Penal System: An Introduction*, London: Sage.
Choo, A., (1993) *Abuse of Process and Judicial Stays of Criminal Proceedings*, Oxford: Oxford University Press.
Christie, N., (1977) 'Conflicts as Property', *British Journal of Ciminology*, 17: 1–15.
—— (1982) *Limits to Pain*, Oxford: Martin Robertson.
—— (1992) *Crime Control as Industry: Towards GULAGS Western Style?*, London: Routledge.
Church, T. W., (1992) 'In Defense of "Bargain Justice"' in Gorr, M. J. and Harwood, S., eds., (1992) *Controversies in Criminal Law: Philosophical Essays on Responsibility and Procedure*, Colorado: Westview Press.
Clarke, M., (1994) 'They Don't Understand', *Police Review*, 4 Feb. 1994, 24.

Cohen, S., (1979) 'The Punitive City: Notes on the Dispersal of Social Control', *Contemporary Crises*, 3: 339–363.

—— (1985) *Visions of Social Control*, Cambridge: Polity Press.

Cole, G. F., (1973) *Politics and the Administration of Justice*, Beverley Hills: Sage.

Collins, H., (1991) 'Methods and Aims of Comparative Contract Law', *Oxford Journal of Legal Studies*, 11: 396–406.

Committee on the Penalty for Homicide, (1993) *The report of an independent inquiry into the mandatory life sentence for murder*, London: Prison Reform Trust.

Cooke, D., (1991) 'Psychological Treatment as an Alternative to Prosecution: A Form of Primary Diversion', *Howard Journal*, 30: 53–65.

Cooper, P., (1991) *Reparation in the Criminal Justice System: The Concept and Reflections upon its Application*, St. Helens: Research and Information Unit, Merseyside Probation Service.

Corstens, G. J. M. and Tak, P. J. P., (1982) *Het Openbaar Ministerie*, Zwolle: Tjeenk Willink.

Cragg, W., (1992) *The Practice of Punishment: Towards a Theory of Restorative Justice*, London: Routledge.

Crequer, N., (1993) 'Businesses urged to join city crime fight', *Independent*, 8 Jan. 1993.

Crown Office, (1992) *The Prosecution of Crime in Scotland*, Edinburgh: Crown Office.

—— (1993) *Annual Report of the Crown Office and the Procurator Fiscal Service 1992/93*, Edinburgh: Crown Office.

Crown Office and Procurator Fiscal Service (1994) *Annual Report 1993/4*, Edinburgh: Crown Office.

Crown Prosecution Service, (1986) *Code for Crown Prosecutors*, London: CPS.

—— (1989) *Annual Report 1988/89*, London: CPS.

—— (1992) *Code for Crown Prosecutors*, London: CPS.

—— (1994) *Code for Crown Prosecutors*, London: CPS.

—— (1994) *An Explanatory Memorandum for use in connection with the Code for Crown Prosecutors*, London: CPS.

Currin, M. P., (1989) *Media Guide*, United States Attorney's Office, Eastern District, North Carolina.

Daugherty, D. A., (1988) 'The Separation of Powers and Prosecutorial Discretion —' *Morrison* v. *Olson*, 180 S. Ct. 2597', *Journal of Criminal Law and Criminology*, 79: 953–996.

Davis, G., (1992) *Making Amends: Mediation and Reparation in Criminal Justice*, London: Routledge.

—— (1992) 'Reparation in the UK: Dominant Themes and Neglected Themes' in Messmer, H. and Otto, H-U., eds. (1992) *Restorative Justice on Trial: Pitfalls and Potentials of Victim-Offender Mediation—International Research Perspectives*, Dordrecht: Kluwer.

—— Boucherat, J. and Watson, D., (1988) 'Reparation in the Service of Diversion: The Subordination of a good idea', *Howard Journal*, 27: 127–133.

——Boucherat, J., and Watson, D., (1989) 'Pre-Court Decision-making in Juvenile Justice', *British Journal of Criminology*, 29: 219–235.

Davis, K. C., ed. (1976) *Discretionary Justice in Europe and America*, Chicago: University of Illinois Press.

Devlin, J. D., (1966) *Police Procedure, Administration and Organisation*, London: Butterworths.

Devlin, P., (1960) *The Criminal Prosecution in England*, Oxford: Oxford University Press.

Dhondt, J., (1988) 'Holland—Is the penal honeymoon over?', *Prison Report*, 6–7.

Dick-Erikson, T., (1990) 'Europe needs British justice', *Independent*, 21 Sept. 1990.

Dignan, J., (1990) *Repairing the Damage: An Evaluation of an Experimental Adult Reparation Scheme in Kettering, Northants*, Sheffield: Centre for Criminological and Legal Research, University of Sheffield.

Dijk, J. J. M. van, (1983) *The Use of Guidelines by Prosecutors in the Netherlands*, The Hague: Ministry of Justice.

—— et al., eds. (1988) *Criminal Law in Action: An Overview of current issues in Western Societies*, Deventer: Kluwer.

—— and Steinmetz, C. H. D., (1988) 'Pragmatism, ideology and crime control: three Dutch surveys' in Walker, N. and Hough, M., eds., *Public Attitudes to Sentencing: Surveys from Five Countries*, Aldershot: Gower.

Dobash, R. E. and Dobash, R. P., (1979) *Violence against Wives*, New York: Free Press.

Donovan Committee, (1965) *Report of Interdepartmental Committee on the Court of Criminal Appeal*, Cmnd 2755, London: HMSO.

Downes, D., (1988) *Contrasts in Tolerance: Post-war Penal Policy in the Netherlands and England and Wales*, Oxford: Oxford University Press.

—— (1990) 'Response to Herman Franke', *British Journal of Criminology*, 30: 94–96.

Duff, P., (1993) 'The Prosecutor Fine and Social Control: The Introduction of the Fiscal Fine in Scotland', *British Journal of Criminology*, 33: 481–503.

—— and Meechan, K., (1992) '*The Prosecutor Fine*' [1992] *Criminal Law Review*, 22–29.

Duyne, P. van, (1987) 'Simple Decision Making' in Pennington, D. and Lloyd-Bostock, S., eds., (1987) *The Psychology of Sentencing: Approaches to Consistency and Disparity*, Oxford: Centre for Socio-Legal Studies.

Dworkin, R., (1981) *Taking Rights Seriously*, London: Duckworth.

——(1981) 'Principle, Policy, Procedure' in Tapper, C. F. H., ed., *Crime, Proof and Punishment: Essays in Memory of Sir Rupert Cross*, London: Butterworths.

Edwards, S., (1985) 'Compelling a Reluctant Spouse: Protection and the Prosecution Process', *New Law Journal*, [1985] 1076–1078.

Ejzak, W. M., (1991) 'Plea Bargains and Nonprosecution agreements: What interests should be protected when prosecutors renege?' [1991] *University of Illinois Law Review*, [1991] 107–136.

Elliman, S., (1990) 'Inadequate Guidance' [1990] *New Law Journal*, 14–16.

Evans, R., (1990) 'Cautioning: Counting the Cost of Retrenchment' [1994] *Criminal Law Review*, 566–575.

—— and Wilkinson, C., (1990) 'Variations in Police Cautioning Policy and Practice in England and Wales', *Howard Journal*, 29: 155–176.

Farrar, J. H. and Dugdale, A. M., (1990) *Introduction to Legal Method*, 3rd Edition, London: Sweet & Maxwell.

Farrington, D. P. and Bennett, T., (1981) 'Police Cautioning of Juveniles in London', *British Journal of Criminology*, 21: 123–135.

Feeley, M., (1979) *The Process is the Punishment: Handling Cases in a Lower Criminal Court*, New York: Russell Sage Foundation.

Feest, J., (1988) *Reducing the Prison Population: Lessons from the West German Experience*, London: NACRO.

—— (1990) *New Social Strategies and the Criminal Justice System: Courses of action designed to avoid entry in the criminal justice process or to interrupt the process*, Report on 19th Criminological Research Conference, Strabourg, 24th Sept. 1990, Strasbourg: Council of Europe.

—— (1991) 'Reducing the Prison Population: Lessons from the West German Experience?' in Muncie, J. and Sparks, R., eds., (1991) *Imprisonment: European Perspectives*, London: Harvester Wheatsheaf.

Felstiner, W. L. F., (1979) 'Plea-contracts in West Germany', *Law and Society*, 13: 309–325.

Fenwick, H., (1994) *Civil Liberties*, London: Cavendish Press.

Finlayson, A., (1989) 'The Police, the Prosecutor and pre-trial procedure', LL. B dissertation, (Edinburgh, 1989).

Fionda, J., (1993) 'Prosecuting Counsel and the Sentencing Process: A Changing Debate', *Criminal Lawyer*, March 1993, 1–2.

—— (1994) 'The Crown Prosecution Service and the Police: A Loveless Marriage?', *Law Quarterly Review*, 110: 376–379.

Fisher, H., (1977) *Report of an Enquiry by the Hon. Sir Henry Fisher into the circumstances leading to the trial of three persons on charges arising out of the death of Maxwell Confait and the fire at 27 Doggett Road, London SE6*, London: HMSO.

Flick, G. A., (1984) *Natural Justice: Principles and Practical Application*, Sydney: Butterworths.

Fokkema, D. C., Chorus, J. M. J., Hondus, E. H. and Lisser, E. C., (1978) *Introduction to Dutch Law for Foreign Lawyers*, Deventer: Kluwer.

Foucault, M., (1977) *Discipline and Punish: The Birth of the Prison*, Harmondsworth: Penguin Books Ltd.

Franke, H., (1990) 'Dutch Tolerance: Facts and Fables', *British Journal of Criminology*, 30: 81–93.

Galligan, D. J., (1986) *Discretionary Powers*, Oxford: Clarendon Press.

Garland, D., (1993) *Punishment in Modern Society: A Study in Social Theory* Oxford: Oxford University Press.

Gelsthorpe, L. and Giller, H., (1990) 'More Justice for Juveniles: Does More Mean Better?' [1990] *Criminal Law Review*, 153–164.

Gibb, F., (1990) 'Policemen accused of hindering the prosecution service', *Times*, 1 Feb. 1990.

—— (1990) 'DPP urges Crown Court Rights for prosecutors', *Times*, 7 Feb. 1990.

—— (1991) 'Tougher sentences in death drivers appeal', *Times*, 17 Oct. 1991.

—— (1993) 'DPP says defendant's right to jury trial should be scrapped', *Times* 21 Apr. 1993.

Giller, H. J. and Covington, C., (1985) *Hampshire Constabulary Youth Help Scheme*, unpublished summary report of research findings.
—— and Gelsthorpe, L., (1990) 'Prosecuting Juveniles: CPS and the Decision-making process', AJJUST, February 1990, 11–14.
Gilvarry, E., (1992) 'CPS advocacy rights bid', *Law Society Gazette*, No. 40, 4 Nov. 1992, 4.
Goldsmith, P., 'Rights of Audience', *Counsel*, July 1993, 13.
Goldstein, J., (1984) 'Police Discretion not to invoke the Criminal Process: Low Visibility Decisions in the Administration of Justice', *Yale Law Journal*, 69: 543–594.
Goodwin, S., (1990) 'Mayhew says CPS crisis claims are alarmist nonsense', *Independent*, 13 Feb. 1990.
Gorr, M. J. and Harwood, S., eds., (1992) *Controversies in Criminal Law; Philosophical Essays on Responsibility and Procedure*, Colorado: Westview Press.
Graham, J., (1990) 'Decarceration in the Federal Republic of Germany: How Practitioners are succeeding where Policy-makers have failed', *British Journal of Criminology*, 30: 150–170.
Green, A., (1990) 'Asking for More? References of Unduly Lenient Sentences', *Current Legal Problems*, 50: 55–75.
Greenawalt, K., (1989) *Conflicts of Law and Morality*, Oxford: Oxford University Press.
Grosman, B. A., (1969) *The Prosecutor: An Inquiry into the exercise of discretion*, Toronto: University of Toronto Press.
Haan, W. de, (1990) *The Politics of Redress: Crime, Punishment and Penal Abolition*, London: Unwin Hyman.
Hagan, J. and Nagel Bernstein, I., (1980) 'Sentence Bargaining in Federal District Courts' in MacDonald, W. F. and Cramer, J. A., (1980) *Plea-Bargaining*, Massachusetts: Lexington Books.
Hall Williams, J. E., ed., (1988) *The Role of the Prosecutor*, Aldershot: Gower.
Harlow, C. and Rawlings, R., (1984) *Law and Administration*, London: Weidenfeld & Nicolson.
Harris, B., (1986) *The Criminal Jurisdiction of Magistrates*, 10th Edition, Chichester: Barry Rose Publishing.
'tHart, A. C., (1988) 'Criminal Law Policy in the Netherlands' in Dijk, J. J. M. van, et al. eds., (1988) *Criminal Law in Action: An Overview of current issues in Western Societies*, Deventer: Kluwer.
Hasenpusch, B., (1989) *Capacity and Population of Correctional Institutions in Lower Saxony*, Hanover: Lower Saxony Department of Justice.
Hawkins, K., (1984) *Environment and Enforcement: Regulation and the Social Definition of Pollution*, Oxford: Clarendon Press.
Hecke, T. van, and Wemmers, J. M., (1992) *Schadebemiddelingsproject Middelburg* Arnhem: Gouda Quint.
Heidensohn, F. and Farrell, M., eds., (1991) *Crime in Europe*, London: Routledge
Helm, S., (1989) 'Police and Prisons targeted', *Independent*, 16 Nov. 1989.
Henham, R., (1994) 'Attorney-General's References and Sentencing Policy' [1994 *Criminal Law Review*, 499–512.
Herrman, J., (1976) 'The German Prosecutor' in Davis, K. C. ed. (1976) *Discretionary Justice in Europe and America*, Chicago: University of Illinois Press.

Hetherington, T., (1989) *Prosecution and the Public Interest*, London: Waterlow Publishers.

Heuni (1986) *Non-prosecution in Europe: Proceedings of the European Seminar*, Helsinki: Heuni.

Hilson, C., (1993) 'Discretion to Prosecute and Judicial Review' [1993] *Criminal Law Review*, 739–747.

Holthuis, H., (1993) 'The Role of the Public Prosecutor in the Netherlands' in NACRO, (1993) *International Comparisons in Criminal Justice: The London Seminars*, London: NACRO.

Home Office, (1983a) *Prosecution Policy*, Home Office Circular No. 26 of 1983. London: Home Office.

—— (1983b) *An Independent Prosecution Service for England and Wales*, Cmnd 9074. London: HMSO.

—— (1986) *Criminal Justice: Plans for Legislation*, Cmnd. 9658. London: HMSO.

—— (1990a) *The Sentence of the Court: A Handbook for Courts on the Treatment of Offenders*, 5th Edition, London: HMSO.

—— (1990b) *Crime, Justice and Protecting the Public: The Government's Proposals for Legislation*, Cm 965. London: HMSO.

—— (1990c) *Victim's Charter: A Statement of the Rights of Victims of Crime*, London: HMSO.

—— (1994) *The Cautioning of Offenders*, Home Office Circular No. 18/1994, London: HMSO.

Hough, M. and Moxon, D., (1988) 'Dealing with offenders: popular opinion and the views of victims in England and Wales' in Walker, N. and Hough, M., eds., (1988) *Public Attitudes to Sentencing: Surveys from Five Countries*, Aldershot: Gower.

House of Commons, (1990a) *Crown Prosecution Service: Home Affairs Committee Memoranda of Evidence*, HC 118–i, London: HMSO.

—— (1990b) *Crown Prosecution Service: Fourth Report of the Home Affairs Committee*, HC 118–1. London: HMSO.

—— (1990c) *Crown Prosecution Service: Government Reply to Fourth Report of Home Affairs Committee*, Cm 1145. London: HMSO.

—— (1990d) *Review of Crown Prosecution Service: Second Report of Committee of Public Accounts*, London: HMSO.

—— (1994) *Home Affairs Committee—Minutes of Evidence*, HC 193–i, London: HMSO.

Howard League, (1993) *Dynamics of Justice*, London: Howard League.

Hudson, B., (1987) *Justice through Punishment: A Critique of the 'Justice Model' of Corrections*, Basingstoke: MacMillan Education.

Hulsman, L. H. C., (1979) 'An Abolitionist Perspective on Criminal Justice Systems', paper presented at the School of Criminology, Louvain-la-Neuve, May 1979.

—— (1981) 'Penal Reform in the Netherlands—Part 1—Bringing the Criminal Justice System under Control', *Howard Journal*, 20: 150–159.

—— (1982) 'Penal Reform in the Netherlands—Part 2—Criteria for Deciding on Alternatives to Imprisonment', *Howard Journal*, 20: 35–47.

Illingworth, G., (1985) 'Judicial Review and the Attorney-General' [1985] *New Zealand Law Journal*, 176–183.

Independent, The, (1990) 'Green wants CPS Lawyers to appear in crown courts', *Independent*, 7 Feb. 1990.

Jackson, P., (1979) *Natural Justice*, London: Sweet & Maxwell.

Jescheck, H-H., (1970) 'The Prosecutor in West Germany', *American Journal of Comparative Law*, 18: 508–517.

Jones, T. H., (1990) 'Common Law and Criminal Law: The Scottish Example' [1990] *Criminal Law Review*, 292.

Joutsen, M., (1988) 'The Role of the Prosecutor: the United Nations and the European Perspective' in Hall Williams, J. E., ed., (1988) *The Role of the Prosecutor*, Aldershot: Gower.

Jung, H., (1993) 'Criminal Justice—a European Perspective' [1993] *Criminal Law Review*, 237–245.

JUSTICE, (1970) *A Report: The Prosecution Process in England and Wales*, London: Justice.

—— (1988) *Administrative Justice: Some Necessary Reforms*, Report of the Committee of JUSTICE, All Souls Review of the Administrative Law in the UK, Oxford: Clarendon Press.

Kadish, S. H., ed., (1983) *Encyclopedia of Crime and Justice: Volume 3*, New York: The Free Press.

Kaplan, D. F., (1985) 'Where Promises End: Prosecutorial Adherence to Sentence Recommendation Commitments in Plea Bargains', *University of Chicago Law Review*, 52: 751–772.

Kaplan, J., (1965) 'The Prosecutorial Discretion—A Comment', *North Western University Law Review*, 60: 174.

Kalmanoff, A., (1976) *Criminal Justice*, Boston: Little Brown.

Kelly, K. S., (1990) 'Substantial Assistance under the Guidelines: How Smitherman transfers Sentencing Discretion from Judges to Prosecutors', *Iowa Law Review*, 76: 187–207.

Kennard, K. L., (1989) 'The Victim's Veto: A Way to Increase Victim Impact on Criminal Case Dispositions', *California Law Review*, 77: 417–453.

King, M., (1981) *The Framework of Criminal Justice*, London: Croom Helm.

Kirby, T., (1989) 'Families of murder victims find justice system insensitive', *Independent*, 30 Mar. 1989.

—— (1989) 'Police say CPS ignores victims', *Independent*, 19 May 1989.

—— (1991) 'Fight against crime obscured by statistics used out of context', *Independent*, 27 Mar. 1991.

—— (1991) 'Justice in a User-Friendly Court', *Independent*, 1 March 1991.

Kommer, M. M., (1988) 'The Problems of Imprisonment, including strategies that might be employed to minimize the use of custody' (Unpublished paper delivered to European Colloquium on Research on Crime and Criminal Policy in Europe—Oxford, 3–7 July 1988).

—— (1990) 'The Role of the Prosecutor in Pre-court Decision-making', paper presented at the one-day conference: 'Young Adults in the Criminal Justice System', Nottingham Polytechnic, 5 Dec. 1990.

Kommers, D. P., (1976) *Judicial Politics in West Germany: A Study of the Federal Constitutional Court*, Beverley Hills: Sage Publications.

Langbein, J. H., (1977) *Comparative Criminal Procedure: GERMANY*, Minnesota: West Publishing Co.

Langer, V., (1988) 'Public Interest in Civil Law, Socialist Law and Common Law Systems: the Role of the Public Prosecutor', *American Journal of Comparative Law*, 36: 279–305.

Langer, W., (1991) *Organizational and human factors in judges' sentencing: A comparative study of three local legal cultures*, Hanover: KFN.

Law Society Gazette, (1992) 'Williams: "no" CPS audience rights', *Law Society Gazette*, No. 40, 4 Nov. 1992, 6.

Leigh, L. H. and Hall Williams, J. E., (1981) *The Management of the Prosecution Process in Denmark, Sweden and the Netherlands*, Leamington Spa: James Hall.

—— and Zedner, L., (1992) *A Report on the Administration of Criminal Justice in the Pre-Trial Phase in France and Germany*, Royal Commission on Criminal Justice Research Study No. 1, London: HMSO.

Lidstone, K. W., Hogg, R. and Sutcliffe, F., (1980) *Prosecutions by Private Individuals and non-police agencies*, Royal Commission on Criminal Procedure: Research Study No. 10, London: HMSO.

Linton, M., (1990) 'Police "obstruct" work of CPS', *Guardian*, 1 Feb. 1990.

Lord Chancellor's Department, (1988) *The Work and Organisation of the Legal Profession*, Cm 570, London: HMSO.

—— (1989) *Committal Proceedings: A Consultation Paper*, London: HMSO.

Lucas, J. R., (1980) *On Justice*, Oxford: Clarendon Press.

Lukes, S., and Scull, A., eds., (1983) *Durkheim and the Law*, Oxford: Martin Robertson.

Maguire, M. and Corbett, C., (1986) *Victim Support Schemes*, Home Office Research Bulletin, 22: 21–23, London: Home Office.

Maguire, M., Morgan, R., and Reiner, R., (1994) *The Oxford Handbook of Criminology*, Oxford: Oxford University Press.

Maher, G., (1986) 'Natural Justice as Fairness' in MacCormick, N. and Birks, P., eds., *The Legal Mind: Essays for Tony Honore*, Oxford: Oxford University Press.

Mansfield, G., and Peay, J., (1987) *The Director of Public Prosecutions: Principles and Practices for the Crown Prosecutor*, London: Tavistock Publications.

Marshall, T. F., and Merry, S., (1990) *Crime and Accountability: Victim/Offender Mediation in Practice*, London: HMSO.

Mawby, R. I. and Gill, M. L., (1987) *Crime Victims: Needs, Services and the Voluntary Sector*, London: Tavistock Publications.

Maynard, D. W., (1984) *Inside Plea-Bargaining: The Language of Negotiation*, New York: Plenum Press.

McCluskey, Rt. Hon. Lord, (1980) 'The Prosecutor's Discretion', *International Journal of Medical Law*, 1: 5–9.

McConville, M. and Baldwin, J., (1981) *Courts, Prosecutions and Conviction*, Oxford: Clarendon Press.

—— and Mirsky, C., 'The Skeleton of Plea-Bargaining', (1992) *New Law Journal*, 142: 1373–1381.

—— Sanders, A., and Leng, R., (1991) *The Case for the Prosecution: Police Suspects and the Construction of Criminality*, London: Routledge.

MacCormick, N. and Birks, P., eds., (1986) *The Legal Mind: Essays for Tony Honore*, Oxford: Oxford University Press.

MacDonald, W. F., ed., (1979) *The Prosecutor*, Beverley Hills: Sage.

—— and Cramer, J. A., eds., (1980) *Plea–Bargaining*, Massachusetts: Lexington Books.

—— Cramer, J. A. and Rossman, H. H., (1980) 'Prosecutorial Bluffing and the case against Plea-Bargaining' in MacDonald, W. F., and Cramer J. A., (eds.) (1980) *Plea-Bargaining*.

MacKinnon, I., (1993) 'Police to seek review of boy's rape sentence', *Independent*, 8 Feb. 1993.

McLeod, J., (1992) 'CPS pushes for new trial powers', *Law Society Gazette*, No. 40, 4 Nov. 1992, 5.

McMahon, M., (1990) ' "Net-widening": Vagaries in the use of a concept', *British Journal of Criminology*, 30: 121–149.

Messmer, H., (1992) 'Victim-Offender Mediation in Germany' in Davis, G., *Making Amends: Mediation and Reparation in Criminal Justice*, London: Routledge.

—— and Otto, H-U., eds., (1992) *Restorative Justice on Trial: Pitfalls and Potentials of Victim-Offender Mediation—International Research Perspectives*, Dordrecht: Kluwer.

Miller, F. W., (1969) *Prosecution: The Decision to Charge a Suspect with a Crime*, Boston: Little, Brown and Co.

—— (1979) ed., *The Prosecutor*, Beverley Hills: Sage Publications.

Mills, H., 'Justice threads a way through court's chaos', *Independent*, 2 Feb. 1990.

Moedikdo, P., (1976) 'de Utrechtse school van Pompe, Baan en Kempe' in Kelk, C. et al., eds., *Recht, Macht en Manipulatie*, Utrecht: Uitgeverig het Spectrum.

Moody, S. R. and Tombs, J., (1982) *Prosecution in the Public Interest*, Edinburgh: Scottish Academic Press.

—— (1993) 'Alternatives to Prosecution: The Public Interest Redefined' [1993] *Criminal Law Review*, 357–367.

Morris, A. and Giller, H., (1987) *Understanding Juvenile Justice*, London: Croom Helm.

Mott, J., (1983) 'Police Decisions for Dealing with Juvenile Offenders' *British Journal of Criminology*, 23: 249–263.

Moxon, D., ed., (1985) *Managing Criminal Justice: A Collection of Papers*, London: HMSO.

—— and Hedderman, C., (1994) 'Mode of Trial Decisions and Sentencing Differences Between Courts', *Howard Journal*, 33: 97–108.

Muncie, J., and Sparks, R., eds., (1991) *Imprisonment: European Perspectives*, London: Harvester Wheatsheaf.

Munday, R., (1985) 'The Crown Prosecution Service: A Developing Discretion' *Justice of the Peace*, 564–567.

Nagel, S. S. and Neef, M. G., (1979) *Decision Theory and the Legal Process*, Massachusetts: Lexington Books.

National Audit Office, (1989) *Prosecution of Crime in Scotland: Review of the Procurator Fiscal Service*, report by the Comptroller and Auditor General, HC 187, London: HMSO.

National Audit Office, (1989) *Review of the Crown Prosecution Service*, report by the Comptroller and Auditor General, HC 345, London: HMSO.

Netherlands, Ministry of Justice, (1985a) *Samenleving en Criminaliteit: Een beleidsplan voor de kommende jaren*, (English translation—Society and Crime: a Policy Plan For The Netherlands). The Hague: Ministry of Justice.

—— (1985b) *Committee Vaillant: Eindrapport van de werkgroep Justitieel beleid en slachtoffer*, The Hague: Ministry of Justice.

—— (1986) *Eindrapport Commissie kleine criminaliteit*, (Report of the Roethof Committee on Petty Crime), The Hague: Ministry of Justice.

—— (1987) *The Dutch Court System*, The Hague: Ministry of Justice.

—— (1990a) *Crime Control Policy in the Netherlands—Five years of policy efforts*, The Hague: Ministry of Justice.

—— (1990b) *Recht in beweging: een beleidsplan voor Justitie in de kommende jaren*, The Hague: Ministry of Justice.

—— (1990c) *Recht in beweging: een beleidsplan voor Justitie in de kommende jaren—SAMENVATTING*, The Hague: Ministry of Justice.

—— (1990d) *Law in Motion: a policy plan for Justice in the years ahead*, The Hague: Ministry of Justice.

—— (1990e) *Jaarverslag openbaar ministerie 1989: Het openbaar ministerie in de handhaving van de milieuwetgeving*, The Hague: Ministry of Justice.

—— (1990f) *Tekstenbundel Kantongerechtsovertredingen*, The Hague: Ministry of Justice.

—— (1993) *Effective Detention: Summary and Implementation Plan* (English Translation of Werkzame Detentie), The Hague: Ministry of Justice.

Netherlands, Openbaar Ministerie, (1990) *Strafrecht met beleid: Beleidsplan openbaar ministerie 1990–1995*, The Hague: Openbaar Ministerie.

Nicholson, C. G. B., (1981) *The Law and Practice of Sentencing in Scotland*, Edinburgh: W. Green & Son Ltd.

Packer, H., (1969) *The Limits of the Criminal Sanction*, Stanford, California: Stanford University Press.

Pelikan, C., (1991) 'Conflict Resolution between victims and offenders in Austria and in the Federal Republic of Germany', in Heidensohn, F., and Farrell, M., eds., (1991) *Crime in Europe*, London: Routledge.

Pennington, D., and Lloyd-Bostock, S., eds., (1987) *The Psychology of Sentencing: Approaches to Consistency and Disparity*, Oxford: Centre for Socio-Legal Studies.

Peters, A. A. G., (1988) 'Main Currents in Criminal Law Theory' in Dijk, J. J. M. van, et al., eds., *Criminal Law in Action: An overview of current issues in Western Societies*, Deventer: Kluwer.

Petzold, F., and Netzig, L., (1992) 'Waage Hanover E. V.—A Reconciliation and Restitution Program for Adult Offenders and Victims: The Concept for Practice and Research' in Messmer, H., and Otto, H-U., eds., *Restorative Justice on Trial: Pitfalls and Potentials of Victim-Offender Mediation—International Research Perspectives*, Dordrecht: Kluwer.

Pienaar, J., (1989) 'CPS Lawyers "obstructed by hostility of police"', *Independent*, 26 Oct. 1989.

—— (1990a) 'DPP accuses police of obstructing CPS', *Independent*, 1 Feb. 1990.

—— (1990b) 'Green warns police against attempts to override CPS decisions', *Independent*, 1 Feb. 1990.

—— (1990c) 'National Inspectorate to monitor CPS decisions', *Independent*, 18 July 1990.

—— (1990d) 'Feuding between police and CPS increases', *Independent*, 31 Jan. 1990.

258 Public Prosecutors and Discretion

Pienaar, J., (1990e) 'Peers criticise plan for CPS lawyers', *Independent*, 30 Jan. 1990.
—— (1990f) 'Criminal Justice System at crisis point, senior police tell MP's', *Independent*, 8 Feb. 1990.
—— (1990g) 'Pressure grows for pay rises to combat CPS staff shortages', *Independent*, 12 Feb. 1990.
—— (1990h) 'Call to caution for minor offences', *Independent*, 15 Feb. 1990.
—— (1990j) 'Prosecution Service gives poor value, MPs report', *Independent*, 16 Feb. 1990.
Platt, A. M., (1969) *The Child Savers: The Invention of Delinquency*, Chicago: University of Chicago Press.
Pratt, J., (1986) 'Diversion from the Juvenile Court', *British Journal of Criminology*, 26: 212–231.
—— (1989) 'Corporatism: The Third Model of Juvenile Justice', *British Journal of Criminology*, 29: 236–254.
Prowse, R., Hartmut, W., and Wilson, C., (1990) 'Reforming Remand Imprisonment: Comparing Britain and Germany (A Working Paper)', paper presented to the Annual Conference of the European Group for the Study of Deviance and Social Control, Haarlem, the Netherlands, 4–7 Sept. 1990.
Rawls, J., (1972) *A Theory of Justice*, Oxford: Oxford University Press.
Renton, R. W. and Brown, H. H., (1983) *Criminal Procedure according to the Law of Scotland*, Edinburgh: W. Green & Son Ltd.
Rhodes, W., (1980) 'Plea-bargaining, crime control and due process: A Quantitative Analysis' in MacDonald, W. F., and Cramer, J. A., eds., *Plea-Bargaining*, Massachusetts: Lexington Books.
Rideout, R., and Jowell, J., (1988) *Current Legal Problems*, Vol. 41, London: Stevens and Sons.
Rijksen, R., (1958) *Meningen van Gedetineerden over de Strafrechts-pleging*, Assen: van Gorcum.
Rinaldi, (1984) 'Crown Appeals against Sentence in Australia', *Criminal Law Journal*, 8: 1.
Robb, L. J., (1988) 'Note: A Scottish Contribution' in Hall Williams, J. E., ed., *The Role of the Prosecutor*, Aldershot: Gower.
Rock, P., (1990) *Helping Victims of Crime*, Oxford: Clarendon Press.
Royal Commission on Criminal Procedure, (1978a) *The Prosecution Process*, Memorandum No. VIII, Evidence No. 92, Evidence from the Home Office, Part III-*Criteria for a Prosecution System*, London: HMSO.
—— (1978b) *Written Evidence of the Prosecuting Solicitor's Society of England and Wales*, Evidence No. 136, Part II—*Policy*, London: HMSO.
—— (1980a) *Prosecution by private individuals and non-police agencies*, Research Study No. 10, London: HMSO.
—— (1980b) *The Prosecution System—Survey of Prosecuting Solicitor's Departments (1) and Organisational Implications of Change (2)*, Research Study Nos. 11 and 12, London: HMSO.
—— (1981a) *The Investigation and Prosecution of Criminal Offences in England and Wales: The Law and Procedure*, Cmnd 8092–1, London: HMSO.
—— (1981b) *Report*, Cmnd 8092, London: HMSO.
Royal Commission on Criminal Justice, (1993) *Report* Cm 2263, London: HMSO.

Rozenberg, J., (1987) *The Case for the Crown: The Inside Story of the Director of Public Prosecutions*, Wellingborough: Equation.

Rutherford, A., (1986) *Prisons and the Process of Justice*, Oxford University Press.

—— (1988a) 'The English Penal Crisis: Paradox and Possibilities' in Rideout, R., and Jowell, J., (1988) *Current Legal Problems*, 41: 93–113.

—— (1988b) 'The Mood and Temper of Penal Policy: Curious Happenings in England during the 1980s', paper given at a conference organized by the Coornhertliga on Penal Climate and Prison Systems in a Caring Society, University of Utrecht, 3 June 1988.

—— (1989) 'The Spider in the Criminal Justice Web', paper given to a conference of Crown Prosecutors in Southampton, 1989.

—— (1992) *Growing out of Crime: The New Era*, Winchester: Waterside Press.

—— (1993) *Criminal Justice and the Pursuit of Decency*, Oxford: Oxford University Press.

SACRO, (1990) *Reparation and Mediation Project—Annual Report 1989–90*, Edinburgh: SACRO.

Sage, A., (1991) 'Law Society calls for reform in criminal courts', *Independent*, 19 Nov. 1991.

Sanders, A., (1985a) 'The Prosecution Process' in Moxon, D., ed., *Managing Criminal Justice: A Collection of Papers*, London: HMSO.

—— (1985b) 'Prosecution Decisions and the Attorney-General's Guidelines' [1985] *Criminal Law Review*, 4–19.

—— (1986) 'The New Prosecution Arrangements—(2): An Independent Crown Prosecution Service?' [1986] *Criminal Law Review*, 16–27.

—— (1988a) 'The Limits to Diversion from Prosecution', *British Journal of Criminology*, 28: 513–532.

——(1988b) 'Incorporating the "public interest" in the decision to prosecute' in Hall Williams, J. E., ed., *The Role of the Prosecutor*, Aldershot: Gower.

——(1994) 'From Suspect to Trial' in Maguire, M., Morgan, R., and Reiner, R., eds., *The Oxford Handbook of Criminology*, Oxford: Oxford University Press.

Schramm, G., (1970) 'The Obligation to Prosecute in West Germany', *American Journal of Comparative Law*, 18: 627–632.

Scottish Home and Health Department, (1990) *Criminal Proceedings in Scottish Courts*, Statistical Bulletin, No. 1 1990, Edinburgh: Scottish Home and Health Department.

Scottish Office, (1994) *Firm and Fair*, Cm 2600, Edinburgh: HMSO.

Sessar, K., (1979) 'Prosecutorial Discretion in Germany' in MacDonald, W. F., *The Prosecutor*, Beverley Hills: Sage Publications.

Shea, M., (1974) 'A Study of the Effect of the Prosecutor's Choice of Charge on Magistrates' Sentencing Behaviour' (1974) *British Journal of Criminology*, 14: 269–272.

Sheehan, A. V., (1975) *Criminal Procedure in Scotland and France: A comparative study with particular emphasis on the role of the public prosecutor*, Edinburgh: HMSO.

—— (1990) *Criminal Procedure*, Edinburgh: Butterworths.

Shiels, R., (1991) 'Focus on the Fiscals', *CPS Journal*, May/June 1991, 2–3.

Shute, S., (1994) 'Prosecution Appeals Against Sentence: The First Five Years', *Modern Law Review*, 57: 745–72.

Sieghart, P., (1988) 'A View from JUSTICE' in Hall Williams, J. E., ed., *The Role of the Prosecutor*, Aldershot: Gower.

de Smith, (1990) *Constitutional and Administrative Law*, 6th Edition, eds. Street, H., and Brazier, R., Harmondsworth: Penguin.

Smith, L. J. F., (1989) *Domestic Violence*, Home Office Research Study Report No. 107, London: HMSO.

Social Work Services Group, (1990) *Alternatives to Prosecution—National Guidelines on Diversion to Social Work Agencies*, Edinburgh: Social Work Services Group.

Spencer, J. (1987) 'Do we need a prosecution appeal against sentence?' [1987] *Criminal Law Review*, 724–736.

—— (1991) 'Judicial Review of Criminal Proceedings' [1991] *Criminal Law Review*, 259–262.

Stalk, J., (1993) 'Dutch Prisons Get Overcrowded, Guests May Get Roommates', *International Tribune Herald*, 9 June 1993.

Stedward, G., and Millar, A., (1989) *Diversion from Prosecution: Volume 1—Diversion to Social Work*, Central Research Unit Paper, Edinburgh: Scottish Office.

Steenhuis, D. W., (1988a) 'Coherence and Co-ordination in the Administration of Criminal Justice' in Dijk, J. J. M. van, et al., eds., (1988) *Criminal Law in Action: An overview of current issues in Western Societies*, Deventer: Kluwer.

—— (1988b) 'Criminal Prosecution in the Netherlands' in Hall Williams, J. E., ed., (1988) *The Role of the Prosecutor*, Aldershot: Gower.

——Tigges, L. C. M., and Essers, J. J. A., (1983) 'The Penal Climate in the Netherlands: Sunny or Cloudy?' *British Journal of Criminology*, 23: 1.

Stewart Committee, (1980) *The Motorist and Fixed Penalties*, Cmnd 8027, Edinburgh: HMSO.

—— (1983) *Keeping offenders out of Court: Further Alternatives to Prosecution*, Cmnd 8958, Edinburgh: HMSO.

Stolwijk, S. A. M., (1988) 'Alternatives to Custodial Sentences' in Dijk, J. J. M. van, et al., eds., (1988) *Criminal Law in Action: An overview of current issues in Western Societies*, Deventer: Kluwer.

Stone, C., (1990) *Public Interest Case Assessment*, Volume Two of the Final Report on the Probation Initiative 'Diversion from Custody and Prosecution', New York: VERA Institute of Criminal Justice.

Straelen, F. W. H. van, and Dijk, J. J. M. van, (1981) *Equality before the Law and Decisions not to prosecute: The practice of public prosecutors in the Hague appeal court jurisdiction*, Research Bulletin of the Ministry of Justice, The Hague: WODC.

Street, H., (1975) *Justice in the Welfare State*, London: Stevens.

Swaaningen, R. van, Blad, J. and Loon, R. van, (1992) *A Decade of Criminological research and Penal Policy in the Netherlands. The 1980s: the era of business-management ideology*, Rotterdam: Erasmus University, Centre for Integrated Penal Sciences.

Tak, P. J. P., (1986) *The Legal Scope of Non-prosecution in Europe*, Helsinki: HEUNI.

—— and Kalmhout, A. M. van, (1988) *Sanctions Systems in the member states of the Council of Europe. Part I—Deprivation of Liberty, Community Service and other substitutes*, Arnhem: Gouda Quint.

Tapper, C. F. H., ed., (1981) *Crime, Proof and Punishment: Essays in Memory of Sir Rupert Cross*, London: Butterworths.

Tarling, R., (1988) 'Interdependence and the CPS' in Hall Williams, J. E., ed., (1988) *The role of the Prosecutor*, Aldershot: Gower.

Temby, I., (1986) 'The Role of the Prosecutor in the Sentencing Process', *Criminal Law Journal*, 10: 199–215.

Thomas, D. A., (1989) 'The Criminal Justice Act 1988—(4) The Sentencing Provisions' [1989] *Criminal Law Review*, 43–55.

Thompson, A., (1993) 'A Say in Sentencing', *Times*, 23 Feb. 1993.

Times, The, (1991) 'Lenient sentences increased by court', *Times*, 5 Feb. 1991.

Timmons, J., (1986) 'The New Prosecution Arrangements (3)—The Crown Prosecution Service in Practice' [1986] *Criminal Law Review*, 28–32.

Tombs, J., (1988) 'Prosecution Approaches and Imprisonment' in Backett, S., McNeill, J., and Yellowlees, A., eds., (1988) *Imprisonment Today: Current Issues in the Prison Debate*, Basingstoke: MacMillan.

Utz, P. J., (1979) 'Two Models of Prosecutorial Professionalism' in MacDonald, W. F., ed., (1979) *The Prosecutor*, Beverley Hills: Sage.

Vennard, J., (1985) 'Decisions to Prosecute: Screening Policies and Practices in the United States' [1985] *Criminal Law Review*, 20–28.

VERA Institute of Criminal Justice, (1972) *Programs in Criminal Justice Reform: Ten-Year Report 1961–71*, New York: VERA Institute.

von Hirsch, A., and Ashworth, A., eds., (1992) *Principled Sentencing*, Edinburgh: Edinburgh University Press.

Wainstein, K. L., (1988) 'Judicially Initiated Prosecution: A Means of Preventing Continuing Victimization in the Event of Prosecutorial Inaction', *California Law Review*, 76: 727–767.

Walker, N., and Hough, M., eds., (1988) *Public Attitudes to Sentencing: Surveys from Five Countries*, Aldershot: Gower.

Warner, S., (1990) *Evaluation of the SACRO Reparation and Mediation Project— Summary of Final Report*, Stirling: University of Stirling.

—— (1991) 'Reparation and Mediation in the Scottish Criminal Justice System', unpublished paper given at the NATO Advanced Research Workshop 'Conflict, Crime and Reconciliation—The Organisation of Welfare Intervention in the field of Restorative Justice', II Ciocco, Italy, 8–12 Apr. 1991.

Weber, M., (1947) *The Theory of Social and Economic Organization*, ed. T. Parsons, London: MacMillan.

Webster, S., 'Change is a matter of trial and error', *Independent*, 15 Oct. 1993.

Wechsler, (1962) 'The Challenge of a Model Penal Code', *Harvard Law Review*, 65: 1097.

Weeks, J., (1989) 'Prosecutors "drop charges to save time"', *Daily Telegraph*, 19 May 1989.

Wemmers, J. M., and Zeilstra, M. I., (1991) *Victim Services in the Netherlands*, Dutch Penal Law and Policy: Notes on criminological research from the Research and Documentation Centre, Ministry of Justice, No. 03, The Hague: Ministry of Justice.

Weigend, T., (1983) 'Prosecution: Comparative Aspects' in Kadish, S. H., ed., *Encyclopedia of Crime and Justice*, Volume 3, New York: The Free Press.

Weitekamp, E., (1992) 'Can Restitution Serve as a Reasonable Alternative to Imprisonment? An Assessment of the situation in the USA' in Messmer, H., and Otto, H-U., eds., (1992) *Restorative Justice on Trial: Pitfalls and Potentials of Victim-Offender Mediation—International Research Perspectives*, Dordrecht: Kluwer.

Whitmore, C., (1991) 'Management of Change: Whitehall Experience', address to the Criminal Justice Conference 13–18 Jan. 1991.

Wilcox, A. F., (1972) *The Decision to Prosecute*, London: Butterworths.

Windlesham, Lord, (1987) *Responses to Crime*, Oxford: Clarendon Press.

Wood, J., (1988) 'Relations with the Police and the Public, and with Overseas Police and Judicial Authorities' in Hall Williams, J., ed., (1988) *The Role of the Prosecutor*, Aldershot: Avebury.

Woolf, Lord Justice, and Tumim, Judge Stephen, (1991) *Prison Disturbances April 1990—Report of an Inquiry by Lord Justice Woolf and Judge Stephen Tumim*, Cm 1456, London: HMSO.

Wordern, A. P., (1990) 'Policy-Making by Prosecutors: the uses of discretion in regulating plea-bargaining', *Judicature*, 73: 335–340.

Wright, M., (1991) *Justice for Victims and Offenders*, Milton Keynes: Open University Press.

—— (1992) 'Victim-Offender Mediation as a Step Towards a Restorative System of Justice' in Messmer, H., and Otto, H-U., eds., (1992) *Restorative Justice on Trial: Pitfalls and Potentials of Victim-Offender Mediation—International Research Perspectives*, Dordrecht: Kluwer.

Wynn Davies, P., (1989) 'Drivers' Penalties Were "too Lenient"', *Independent*, 17 Oct. 1989.

—— (1990) 'Green's revolution aimed to improve chain of command', *Independent*, 2 Feb. 1990.

——(1991) 'Law Reformers urge switch to Scottish System', *Independent*, 16 Mar. 1991.

Yin Sit, P., (1987) 'Double Jeopardy, Due Process and the Breach of Plea Agreements', *Colombia Law Review*, 87: 142–160.

Zellick, G., (1979) 'The Role of Prosecuting Counsel in Sentencing' [1979] *Criminal Law Review*, 493–503.

Zimring, F. E., (1974) 'Measuring the Impact of Pretrial Diversion from the Criminal Justice System', *University of Chicago Law Review*, 41: 224–241.

Index

Access to courts, 219–27
  credibility model, 222
  European perspective, 220–3
  Netherlands, 222
  Scotland, 221
Accountability, 207–15
  administrative justice, and, 208
  appeal, 213–14
  Crown Prosecution Service, 211
  fairness, and, 210
  functions requiring, 209–10
  Germany, 210
  guidelines, 212–13
  legislation prohibiting non-prosecution,
    214
  Netherlands, 210
  objectivity, and, 210
  presumption of guilt, and, 207
  public scrutiny, 208
  Scotland, 211
  statement of reasons, 210–12
  United States, 209
Adversarial system
  nature of, 6–7
Association of Chief Police Officers
  proposal as to secondary discretion to
    prosecute, 34
Attorney-General
  accountability, 60
Australia
  sentencing role of prosecutor, 44–5

Bail
  opposition to, 57
Barristers
  rights of audience, 20–1

Cautioning, 38–41
  'caution plus' system, 39
  condition of non-prosecution, as, 40
  juveniles, 24–5
  natural justice, and, 225
  non-discretionary approach, 41
  practice, 38–9
  removal from police, 40
Charging, 54–6
  plea-bargaining, 55–6
  selection, 54
Civil liberties
  protection of, 62

Conservative Party, 10
Constitutionality, 196–207
  adversary system, and, 202–4
  filtering role of prosecutor, and, 200
  implementation of policy, and, 199
  influence of prosecutor, and, 198–9
  influence on prison populaton, and
    201–2
  inquisitorial system, and, 202–3
  interrelationship between CPS and
    police, 200
  justice system as single process, 197
  operational efficiency model, and, 204
  overburdened criminal justice system,
    and, 197
  police, and, 199
  powers of American prosecutor, 205
  prosecutor as 'sluice gate', 202
  prosecutor's sentencing function, and
    198
  role of prosecutor, and, 196–7
  sentencing grids, 205–6
Credibility model, 188–93
  aim, 191
  England and Wales, 189
  Germany, 189
  Netherlands, 189
  public confidence, and, 191
  Scotland, 189
  United States, 190–1
  victims, and, 192
Crime control model
  pre-trial sentencing, and, 242–3
Crime prevention
  Netherlands, 131–2
Crown Prosecution Service, 14–64
  accountability, 60–2
  Attorney-General, and, 60
  background, 16–22
  bureaucratic culture, 64
  cautioning. See Cautioning
  civil liberties, and, 62
  Committee of Public Accounts Report
    1990, 20
  creation, 14
  criticisms of, 19
  easing workload of court, 28
  evidential sufficiency criterion, 22–3
  factors in favour of prosecution, 26–7
  Home Affairs Committee 1990, 21–2

independence, 58–60
indirect influences on sentencing, 51
involvement in sentencing, 35–46
Joint Performance Management
    Machinery Group, 31
judicial review, and, 61–2
juveniles, 24–6
    cautioning, 24–5
    presumption in favour of cautioning,
      24–5
lack of alternative sanctions, 35–7
mental illness, 26
minor cause, 24
'minor guilt', 28
National Audit Office report, 20
neutrality, 57–8
policy considerations, 22
policy-making, 234
Policy Manuals, 26, 27
Pre-Trial Issues, 31
'problem' cases, 36
public interest, 22–30
    reluctance to use, 29
recommending sentence, 41–6. *See also*
    Recommending sentence
reform, 240–1
relationship with police, 30–5
review of, 19–20
rights of audience, 20–1
role in English criminal justice process,
    57–60
saving resources, 28
secondary discretion, 59
setting up of, 19
stress, 26
'trivia', 28
'unduly lenient' appeals, 46–51. *See also*
    'Unduly lenient' appeals
victim, and, 36–7
'youth of the offender', 25

Director of Public Prosecutions, 14
Discretion of the prosecutor, 1–13
Due process model
    pre-trial sentencing, and, 242–3

England and Wales
    reluctance to accept sentencing role of
      prosecutor, 241–2
    role of prosecutor, 5
European Convention of Human Rights
    and Fundamental Freedoms, 220
Expendiency principle, 9–10

Fines
    procurator fiscal, 73–8
Fixed penalty system, 37

German prosecution system, 133–71
accountability, 160–2
academic influence, 162–3
    checks on federal level, 161
    supervision, 161
    written reasons for disposal of case,
      161–2
appeals, 149–51
    accused, 150–1
    prosecutor, 151
    victim, 149–50
choice of charge, 146–7
combining offences, 137–9
conditional dismissals, 136–7
consent of defendant, 160
cultures of penality, 165–6
    traditional, 166
current trends, 145–8
'day fine' procedure, 143
disposals in Lower Saxony 1985–1990,
    155–6
emphasis on neutrality and
    independence, 134
erosion of legality principle, 167–9
    discretion, and, 168
    police, and, 167
federal system, 134
guidelines, 140–1
judicial independence, 159–60
juveniles, 130–40
local discrepancies, 134
mode of trial, 147–8
office of Staatsanwaltschaft, 133
options for dismissal, 135–41
penal orders, 141–6
    civil liberties, and, 144
    consent of judge, 142
    default procedure, 143–4
    informal hearing, 144
    objection, 142
    plea-bargaining, and, 145–6
    quasi-judicial status, 145
policy making, 162–4
    influence of practitioners, 163–4
political changes, and, 170–1
prison capacity, 158
prison population, 157–8
recommending sentence, 148–9
remand, 154–7
    East Germany, 156
    juveniles, 156–7
    statistics, 155–6
    ultimate custodial sentence, and, 154–5
reparation, 151–3
    juveniles, 152
    sentencing, and, 152
    victim fund, 153

restorative justice, 164–5
role of prosecutor, 169–70
safeguards, 160–2
trial, 146–9
unconditional dismissals, 135–6
working philosophies, 164–9
Germany
reform, 239–40
role of police, 32–3
role of prosecutor, 3
Glasgow District Court
workload, 4

Historical factors, 11
Home Office
policy making, and, 232

Inland Revenue
out-of-court financial settlements, 15
Inquisitorial system
nature of, 6–7
Inter-Departmental Working Party on
Prosecution Arrangements 1982, 18

Jersey
recommending sentence, 45
Judicial review
public interest, and, 61–2
Justice
Report 1970, 16
Juveniles
Crown Prosecution Service, and, 24–6
German prosecution system, 139–40
policy-making, and, 232–3

Legality principle, 9–10

Miscarriages of justice, 8
Mode of trial, 51–4
child witnesses or victims, 52
decision as to, 51–2
right to elect trial, 53
role of magistrates, 52
savings in time and money, 53–4
significance, 51
Models of prosecution decision-making,
173–5
access to courts, 219–77. *See also* Access
to courts
accountability, 207–15. *See also*
Accountability
benefits, 245
conflicts in policy terms, 195
constitutionality, 196–207. *See also*
Constitutionality
Crime Control, 175
dangers, 245

natural justice, 219–27. *See also* Natural
justice
net-widening, 215–19. *See also* Net-
widening
overlap, 194–5
policy-making, 231–4. *See also* Policy-
making
pre-trial diversion, 174
public interest, 227–231. *See also* Public
interest
use in practice, 194–236
'value' system, 174–5
Models of prosecutorial sentencing,
172–193

Natural justice, 219–27
cautioning, and, 225
credibility model, 222
England and Wales, 223–7
European perspective, 220–3
meaning, 224–5
Netherlands, 222
scope, 223–7
Scotland, 221
Net-widening, 215–19
cautioning, 215
community penalties, 215
danger of, 244
juveniles, 215–16
monitoring, and, 219
morality, and, 217–18
Netherlands, 216–17, 218
policy, and, 216
Scotland, 219
victim, and, 218
Netherlands
credibility model, 189
crime prevention, 131–2
expediency principle, 28–9
Openbaar Ministerie. *See* Openbaar
Ministerie
prosecutors. *See* Openbaar Ministerie
public interest criteria, 23, 24
recognition of sentencing role of
prosecutor, 238–9
role of prosecutor, 3–4

Openbaar Ministerie, 96–132
academic influence, 121–2
accontability, 124–8
adequacy of public accountability, 129
administrative concerns, 123–4
approach of prosecutors, 113
'blurring of norms', 119–120
changes in sentencing policy, 104
changing nature of prison regimes, 115
charges, 106

constitutional issues, 124–8
control by Ministry of Justice, 126–7
core functions of Ministry of Justice, 111
credibility of criminal justice system, 119
criminal statistics, 109–110
direction of change, 116–19
direction of future policy, 128
evolution of role of prosecutor, 128–9
features of new policy, 109–15
fiscal fraud less than 50,000 guilders, 126
forum shopping, 106
guidelines, 125
high use of transactions, 117, 118
increased power of prosecutor, 124–5
increased use of imprisonment, 114
independence of prosecutor, 125–6
Law in Motion 1990, 110–12
management ideology, 123
mechanisms for policy-making, 105
mode of trial, 106
modernisation, 112
'neo-conservatism', 118
net-widening, 124
networking between directorates, 112
partnership in sentencing, 105
petty criminality, 113
police clear-up rates, 120
policy, 112–13
Policy Plan 1985, 109–10
policy waivers, 98–100
    expediency principle, 99–100
    reasons for, 98–9
    statement of reason for, 99
political accountability, 127
political expediency, and, 111
political reaction, and, 122
prison expansion, 114
prosecutorial powers, 97–103
prosecutorial influence over judicial sentencing, 103–7
public interest, and, 98
rationales for change, 119–24
recommending sentence, 103–6
reductionist aims of policy makers, 118
rising crime figures, and, 109–10
safeguards for suspects, and, 127–8
technical waivers, 97–8
'tolerance', 116–17
transactions, 100–2
    community service, 102
    compensation, 100–1
    discretionary amount, 101
    fine, 100–1
    guidelines, 101–2
    nature of, 100–1

trend of more severe sentences, 113–14
Utrecht School, and, 121–2
variety of powers, 96–7
victims, 107–9
    financial settlement, 107
    guidelines, 108
    reparation, 107–8
warnings, 102–3
    oral, 103
    written, 103
Operational efficiency model, 176–9
    defendant, and, 178
    England and Wales, 177
    Germany, 176
    justification for, 179
    managerial role, 176
    Netherlands, 176
    plea bargaining, and, 178–9
    Scotland, 177
    size of caseloads, and, 179
Opportunity principle, 9–10

Philips Report. *See* Royal Commission on Criminal Procedure 1977
Plea-bargaining, 55–6
    'deals', 55
    German prosecution system, 145–6
    legality, 56
    operational efficiency model, and, 178–9
    pressure to plead guilty, 56
Police, 30–5
    cautioning plus system, 5–6
    constitutional position, 31–2
    Germany, 32–3
    procurator fiscal, and, 66
    prosecution of 'undesirable' groups, 33
    relationship with CPS, 30–5
    undertaking not to prosecute, 34–5
Policy-making, 231–4
    Chalmers, William, 231–2
    Criminal Justice Consultative Council, 233–4
    Crown Prosecution Service, 234
    Home Office, 232
    juveniles, and, 232–3
    Netherlands, 231
    Scotland, 231–2
Political factors, 10–11
Pollution control, 15–16
'Problem' cases
    social services, and, 36
Procurator fiscal, 65–95
    accountability, 89–90
        Lord Advocate, and, 89
        reasons for decisions, 90
    balance of proof, and, 71
    'criteria model', 72

criticisms in National Audit Office
report, 92
diversion, 80–7
bail information schemes, and, 82
Glasgow, 84
mediation, 84
procedures, 80–1
domestic violence, 83–4
European influence, 66–7
fines, 73–78
discretion, and, 74–5
effect, 74
flexible system, 75
'net-widening', and, 77
operation of system, 76
refusal to accept, 73
resistance to idea, 75
restriction on system, 76
fixed penalty, 73
impact on sentencing policy, 93
independence, 66
local attitudes, and, 83
minor offences, meaning, 72
offenders with alcohol problems, 84
origin, 65
police, and, 66
police reports, and, 81–2
policy making, 91–2
quasi-judicial decisions, 94–5
quasi-medical decisions, 82
reasons for decisions, 90
recommending sentence, 87–9
sheriffs, and, 87–8
unduly lenient sentences, and, 88
referrals to social work departments, 81
'reluctant sentencers', 70–1
SACRO Reparation and Mediation
Project, 85–7
social work department guidelines, 83
Stewart Committee, 67–70
personalities, 68–9
proposed reforms, 68
remit, 67
supervision, 65
underlying operational philosophy, 95
warnings, 78–80
disagreement by defendant, 79–80
extension of system, 79
lack of appeal procedure, 79–80
oral, 78
recording, 78
written, 78
Prosecutor fines, 37–8
advantages, 38
Public interest, 227–31
considerations, 228
credibility model, and, 230

Crown Prosecution Service, and,
22–30
interpretation, 229
meaning, 227–8
operational efficiency, 228
policy, and, 227
reassessment of criteria, 230–1
restorative model, 230
Public opinion
unduly lenient sentence, and, 49

Recognition of sentencing role of
prosecutor, 237–46
Recommending sentence, 41–6
Australia, 44–5
constitutionality, 41–2
guidance to trial judge, 42
Jersey, 45
judicial independence, and, 45–6
mainland Europe, 43
role of prosecutor, 42
Reform of sentencing role of prosecutor,
237–46
Remand, 57
Reparation
German prosecution system, 151–3
Restorative model, 180–8
adversarial system, and, 181
aim under, 180
compensatory aspect, 188
criticism of, 185
diversionary schemes, and, 187–8
Germany, 183
material compensatory benefits, 181
Mediation Scheme in Coventry, 186
nature of, 180
Netherlands, 182–3
'reintegrative shaming', 180
research, and, 187
'stigmatization', 180
United States, 184
Royal Commission on Criminal Procedure
1977, 16–18
options, 17–18
research programme, 17–18

SACRO Reparation and Mediation
Project
schema for decision-making process, 85
Scotland
procurator fiscal. *See* Procurator fiscal
reform, 237–8
role of prosecutor, 3
Sentencing
involvement of English prosecutor,
35–46
meaning, 1

Sentencing grids
    constitutionality, and, 205–6
Sentencing role of prosecutor, 1–2
Sociological factors, 11

Trial judge
    role of, 2

'Unduly lenient' appeals, 46–51
    Attorney-General, and, 47
    influence of prosecutor, and, 50

judicial independence, and, 47
new power, 46–7
presumption against increasing, 48
procedure, 49–50
public opinion, and, 49
selection of potential cases, 50
statistics, 48
success rate, 48

Victim
    powers of CPS, and, 36–7